Archival Insights into the Evolution of Economics

Series Editor

Robert Leeson
Stanford University
Department of Economics
California, USA

Aim of the Series

This series provides unique insights into economics by providing archival evidence into the evolution of the subject. Each volume provides biographical information about key economists associated with the development of a key school, an overview of key controversies and gives unique insights provided by archival sources.

More information about this series at
http://www.springer.com/series/14777

Jennifer Hole

Economic Ethics in Late Medieval England, 1300–1500

palgrave
macmillan

Jennifer Hole
University of Western Australia
Crawley, West Australia, Australia

Archival Insights into the Evolution of Economics
ISBN 978-3-319-38859-5 ISBN 978-3-319-38860-1 (eBook)
DOI 10.1007/978-3-319-38860-1

Library of Congress Control Number: 2016947994

Printed on acid-free paper

This Palgrave Macmillan imprint is published by Springer Nature
The registered company is Springer International Publishing AG
The registered company address is: Gewerbestrasse 11, 6330 Cham, Switzerland

Acknowledgements

It is owing to the support and encouragement of the late Professor Philippa Maddern that my thesis was written, first sparking my interest in economic ethics in late medieval England. Philippa was my principal supervisor until her illness prevented her from further participation. Her place was taken by Dr Stephanie Tarbin, who made a tremendous contribution of her time and energy despite her increased workload. Professor Andrew Lynch (English and Cultural Studies) stepped in to offer guidance for the chapter on literary sources and to comment on my revised manuscript as a whole. I must also thank Dr Spencer Young for all of his help as a co-supervisor, both while he was here at the University of Western Australia and since his return to North America.

In the course of my research in the United Kingdom, I received assistance from many people who were kind enough to let me view archives, manuscripts and early printed books or provide me with photographs or microfilm copies. These are the following: the staff of the Western Manuscripts Collection and other departments of the Bodleian Library, Oxford; Mr Stewart Tiley, Librarian, St John's College, Oxford; Dr Anna Sander, Lonsdale Curator of Archives and Manuscripts, Balliol College, Oxford; Dr Julia Walworth and Dr Julian Read, Library, Merton College, Oxford; the staff of the Manuscripts Department and Early Printed Book Collections at the British Library, London; the library staff, Institute of Historical Research, University of London; the staff of the Senate House

Library, University of London; Dr Mark Statham, Librarian, Gonville and Caius College, Cambridge; the staff of the Cambridge University Library; Naomi Van Loo, Librarian, New College, Oxford; Dr Robin Darwall-Smith, Archivist, Magdalen College, Oxford; and Karen Robson, Senior Archivist, University of Southampton Library.

I would also like to thank the members of the palaeography group at the University of Western Australia for their help with interpreting some of the more difficult material.

Contents

Abbreviations and Editorial Notes

Aquinas, *ST*	Thomas Aquinas, *Summa Theologiae: Latin Text with English Translation*, 61 vols., London, The Blackfriars with Eyre and Spottiswoode, 1963.
Armburgh Papers	*The Armburgh Papers*, ed. C. Carpenter, Woodbridge, Boydell, 1998.
Ayenbite of Inwyt	*Dan Michel's Ayenbite of Inwyt*, ed. P. Gradon, 2 vols., London, Oxford University Press for the Early English Text Society, 1979.
Bromyard, *SP(1)*	John Bromyard, *Summa Praedicantium*, Prima Pars, Venice, 1586.
Bromyard, *SP(2)*	John Bromyard, *Summa Praedicantium*, Secunda Pars, Venice, 1586.
CCR	*Calendar of Close Rolls*, 61 vols., London, HMSO, 1900–1963, accessed via British History Online http://www.british-history.ac.uk.
Cely Letters	*The Cely Letters, 1472–1488*, ed. A. Hanham, London, Oxford University Press for the Early English Text Society, 1975.
Confessio Amantis	John Gower, *Confessio Amantis*, ed. R.A. Peck, 3 vols., Kalamazoo, MI, Medieval Institute Publications, 2003–06.

Corpus Iuris Canonici (1)	*Corpus Iuris Canonici, Pars Prior, Decretum Magistri Gratiani*, Union, NJ, Lawbook Exchange Ltd, 2000.
Corpus Iuris Canonici (2)	*Corpus Iuris Canonici, Pars Secunda, Decretalium Collectiones*, Union, NJ, Lawbook Exchange Ltd, 2000.
CPR	*Calendar of Patent Rolls*, 49 vols., London, HMSO, 1900–16, online via Calendar of Patent Rolls Project, G.R. Boynton, University of Iowa Libraries, 2003 http://www.uiowa.edu/~acadtech/patentrolls.
CUP	Cambridge University Press
Cursor Mundi	*Cursor Mundi*, ed. R. Morris, 3 vols., London, Kegan Paul, Trench, Trubner & Co for the Early English Text Society, 1893.
Davis, *MMM*	James Davis, *Medieval Market Morality: Life, Law and Ethics in the English Marketplace, 1200–1500*, Cambridge, Cambridge University Press, 2012.
Dives and Pauper	*Dives and Pauper*, ed. P.H. Barnum, 3 vols., London, Oxford University Press for the Early English Text Society, 1976.
EETS	Early English Text Society
Fasciculus Morum	*Fasciculus Morum: A Fourteenth-Century Preacher's Handbook*, ed. S. Wenzel, University Park, Pennsylvania State University Press, 1989.
Handlyng Synne	*Robert of Brunne's 'Handlyng Synne', A.D. 1303*, ed. F.J. Furnivall, London, Kegan Paul, Trench, Trubner & Co. for the Early English Text Society, 1901.
Hoccleve, *Regiment*	Thomas Hoccleve, *The Regiment of Princes*, ed. Charles R. Blyth, Kalamazoo, MI, TEAMS/Medieval Institute Publications, 1999, accessed online via http://www.d.lib.rochester.edu/teams/text/blyth-hoccleve-regiment-of-princes

Jacob's Well (Brandeis)	*Jacob's Well: An English Treatise on the Cleansing of Man's Conscience, Part I*, ed. A. Brandeis, London, Kegan Paul, Trench, Trubner & Co. for the Early English Text Society, 1900.
Jacob's Well (Salisbury)	*Fons Jacobi*, in Southampton University Library, Salisbury Cathedral MS 103, fol. 1-230r.
Middle English Sermons	*Middle English Sermons*, ed. W.O. Ross, London, Oxford University Press for the Early English Text Society, 1940.
Mirour de l'Omme	John Gower, *Mirour de L'Omme*, in *The Complete Works of John Gower, Vol. 1: The French Works*, ed. G.C. Macaulay, Oxford, Clarendon Press, 1899, pp. 1–334.
ODNB	*Oxford Dictionary of National Biography*, Oxford University Press, 2004; online edn., Jan 2008 http://www.oxforddnb.com.
OUP	Oxford University Press
Parliament Rolls	*The Parliament Rolls of Medieval England, 1275–1504*, ed. C. Given-Wilson, 16 vols., Woodbridge, Boydell, 2005, accessed via British History Online https://www.british-history.ac.uk.
Paston Letters	*Paston Letters and Papers of the Fifteenth Century*, ed. Norman Davis, Richard Beadle and Colin Richmond, 3 vols., Oxford, Oxford University Press for the Early English Text Society, 2005.
Riverside Chaucer	*The Riverside Chaucer*, ed. Larry D. Benson, Oxford, Oxford University Press, 3rd edn., 2008.
SR	*Statutes of the Realm: Printed by Command of His Majesty King George the Third*, 11 vols., 1810–25, accessed online via Hein Online, William S. Hein & Co., 2015 http://heinonline.org.

Testamenta Ebor. I	*Testamenta Eboracensia or Wills Registered at York, Part I: Year MCCC Downwards,* ed. J. Raine, London, J.B. Nichols for the Surtees Society, 1836.
Testamenta Ebor. II	*Testamenta Eboracensia: A Selection of Wills from the Registry at York, Part II*, ed. J. Raine, Durham, George Andrews for the Surtees Society, 1855.
Testamenta Ebor. III	*Testamenta Eboracensia: A Selection of Wills from the Registry at York, Part III*, ed. J. Raine, Durham, Andrews & Co for the Surtees Society, 1865.
Vision of Piers Plowman	William Langland, *The Vision of Piers Plowman: A Critical Edition of the B-Text Based on Trinity College Cambridge MS B.15.17*, ed. A.V.C. Schmidt, London, J.M. Dent, 1995.
Vices and Virtues	*The Book of Vices and Virtues*, ed. W.N. Francis, London, Oxford University Press for the Early English Text Society, 1942.
Wood, *MET*	Diana Wood, *Medieval Economic Thought*, Cambridge, Cambridge University Press, 2002.
Wynnere and Wastoure	*Wynnere and Wastoure*, ed. Stephanie Trigg, London, Oxford University Press for the Early English Text Society, 1990.
YAS	Yorkshire Archaeological Society

Editorial Notes

In transcriptions of Middle English passages, the letters 'yogh' and 'thorn' have been silently modernised.

Bible quotations are taken from the Authorised King James Version, 1611.

1

Introduction

What has ethics to do with economics? Today, corporations and entrepreneurs regard their role as profit-making, but in the medieval period such a consideration was meant to be governed by ethical principles such as the common good, and although economic inequality was accepted, individuals were instructed to moderate their greed and share some of their wealth. I have used the term "economic ethics" as they related to the medieval world in accordance with the definition used by Odd Langholm. Langholm explains that although the word *economica* was known to scholastic philosophers through the works of Aristotle, they did not, initially, have a sense that economics was "a set of separable social phenomena and relationships".[1] Yet theologians and scholastic philosophers were aware of the material needs of humankind and of the various temptations to which these could give rise, and therefore "the economic analysis of the scholastics was subjected to their economic

[1] Odd Langholm, *Economics in the Medieval Schools: Wealth, Exchange, Value, Money and Usury according to the Paris Theological Tradition 1220–1350* (Leiden: Brill, 1992), 1.

J. Hole, *Economic Ethics in Late Medieval England, 1300–1500*,
Archival Insights into the Evolution of Economics,
DOI 10.1007/978-3-319-38860-1_1

ethics … If they studied economic phenomena and relationships, it was in order to advise about proper economic conduct".[2]

Thus, Langholm uses "economic ethics" as a descriptive term for the moral principles applicable to economic practice. As the late Diana Wood has pointed out, the Church dominated medieval life, and therefore its morality governed economic relations. Economic ethics were embedded in commentaries on the Bible and the thought of Aristotle.[3] According to Wood, from the biblical commentaries emerged the Church's doctrine of avarice and expositions of the Commandment against theft, whereas from Aristotle came ideas about moderation, justice, equity and balance.[4] His model of the "just price" was particularly important to medieval theologians and philosophers.[5] Although avarice and theft represented selfish gain and harm to the community, the principles of economic ethics also contained positive ideals. As the work of Richard Newhauser shows, medieval theologians and philosophers promoted the virtues of charity and liberality as antidotes to avarice and theft.[6] To those virtues can be added the ideal of the common good, which was appealed to frequently, and in a wide range of sources, regarding economic practice. It had an ethical as well as a political usage, as Matthew Kempshall's study demonstrates.[7] The common good tended to be applied, however, in the context of either a national or a city government rather than used to describe good or ideal relations between a landowner and his tenants. In the rural setting, the common good was replaced by the ideal of good lordship, which again had an ethical dimension.[8]

---

[2] Langholm, *Economics in the Medieval Schools*, 6.

[3] Wood, *MET*, 2, 6.

[4] Wood, *MET*, 14, 16.

[5] Wood, *MET*, 132, 133.

[6] Richard G. Newhauser, "Justice and Liberality: Opposition to Avarice in the Twelfth Century", in *Virtue and Ethics in the Twelfth Century*, ed. Istvan P. Bejczy and Richard G. Newhauser , (Leiden: Brill, 2005), 295–315; Richard G. Newhauser, "Preaching the 'Contrary Virtues'", *Medieval Studies* 70 (2008): 135–162.

[7] Matthew S. Kempshall, *The Common Good in Late Medieval Political Thought: Moral Goodness and Material Benefit.* Oxford: Clarendon Press, 1999.

[8] Thomas N. Bisson, "Medieval Lordship", *Speculum.* 70 (1995): 752; R.R. Davies, *Lords and Lordship in the British Isles in the Late Middle Ages* (Oxford: OUP, 2009), 15–17.

This book is a socio-cultural study, rather than a purely theoretical one, because I will be examining not only the ideas and beliefs of theologians and philosophers but how these influenced the attitudes, assumptions and preoccupations about material concerns in late medieval English society. Wood has already written an excellent study of medieval economic thought, and James Davis has used an extensive variety of sources to examine the ethics of urban trade and to evaluate their influence on regulation.[9] I aim to complement both of these works by broadening the coverage of ethical thought to other sections of society.

Later medieval England provides a fruitful site of investigation for a number of reasons. Although it had seen growth in urban trade, it still possessed a mostly rural economy: it has been estimated that 80 % of economic activity at this time occurred in the rural sector.[10] Society depended on the successful exploitation of land in order to provide its basic needs. Furthermore, in England, much of the wealth that derived from mercantile activity was invested in estates: as Maurice Keen declared, “Land was the most important source of wealth and power”.[11] This notion, that land was used to gain not just wealth but also power, further underlines the question about ethical standards for landowners. Additionally, studies of economic thought have tended to discuss the thought of theologians who were prominent across western Christendom, whereas the writings of some English theologians have received less attention.

I have chosen the period 1300–1500 because it featured many criticisms of social and economic changes and of economic immorality, which can be found across a wide range of genres: pastoral manuals and sermons, literature, statutes, petitions and letters. Broadly, these sources can be divided into two kinds: those which were didactic and those which describe how people reacted. The pastoral manuals, sermons and literature allow me to investigate whether the ethical thought of earlier theologians and canonists was influential in fourteenth- and fifteenth-century England, and also the kinds of economic practices that were scrutinised in sources at that time.

---

[9] Davis, *MMM*.

[10] James Masschaele, “The Renaissance Depression Debate: The View from England”, *History Teacher* 27 (1994): 409.

[11] Maurice Keen, *England in the Later Middle Ages: A Political History*, 2nd edn. (London: Routledge, 2003), 264.

The statutes, petitions and letters permit an investigation of how government and individuals responded to moral issues arising from economic activity. Against the moralising language of petitions, I also examine a selection of manorial court records to see whether judgements reflected fair and reasonable behaviour on the part of landowners or whether court processes were being used purely as a revenue-raising exercise. Studies of records of land ownership are consulted as well because these provide a broader picture of the manorial system and its sources of revenue.

Late medieval England saw an increase in commerce. Historians quote different figures for the number of royal licences given for markets (J.L. Bolton quotes 2,800 between 1198 and 1483, whereas Keen uses a figure of over 3,000) but agree that most were granted in the thirteenth century.[12] The growth in the number of markets, both within towns and in the countryside, raised concerns within the Church about unethical practices and prompted regulation by secular authorities. What I would like to highlight, however, is the fact that there was also a growth in bureaucracy: the numbers of royal officials associated with the Exchequer and Wardrobe and purveyors grew after the outbreak of war with Scotland in the 1290s.[13] At the same time, there was an increase in crime and disorder, possibly due to the effects of the war, and this led to the appointment of more judges and keepers of the peace.[14] So was there a rise in ethical concerns expressed about the economic roles of the greater numbers of shrieval officials, lawyers, tax collectors and purveyors, as well as the activities of merchants and traders?

In difficult times, there were criticisms of the king. In late medieval England, economic hardship was visited upon many subjects because of the high financial costs of the wars waged with Scotland and France. Not only was taxation heavier and more frequent, and purveying for those wars increased, but exactions continued afterwards in order to meet the burgeoning costs of the royal household. At various times, kings were criticised for over-spending, favouritism and economic mismanagement, and those criticisms are fruitful sources of ethical language. The heavier taxation

[12] J.L. Bolton, *The Medieval English Economy 1150–1500* (London: Dent, 1980), 119; Keen, *England in the Later Middle Ages*, 140.

[13] G.L. Harriss, *King, Parliament and Public Finance in Medieval England to 1369*. Oxford: Clarendon Press, 1975.

[14] Keen, *England in the Later Middle Ages*, 3.

and purveying, which had begun in the 1290s with Edward I's wars in Scotland and Gascony, lasted until the reign of Edward II in 1314. In the 1330s, heavy taxation and purveying were again imposed to fund the Scottish campaigns by Edward III and the Hundred Years' War beginning in 1337. Edward II was seen as profligate and was accused of being unduly influenced, firstly by Piers Gaveston and later by the Despensers. Edward III was accused of listening to poor advice and of wasting resources by the Good Parliament of 1376, and in the reign of Richard II, the attempt to collect a more extensive poll tax in 1381 brought rebellion and the breakdown of law and order.[15]

The reigns of Henry IV and VI saw more criticisms of government, much of them relating to economic mismanagement. Henry IV's financial resources were very limited and he needed to bolster his support from various factions, but his usurpation of Richard II had been on the basis of the latter's tyranny and dissipation of resources, which made his own need for financial aid an extremely sensitive issue. An example of this sensitivity can be seen in the remark made by Arnold Savage, the Speaker of the Commons, in 1404, when he accused Henry IV of making "outrageous" grants and described the advice of the king's counsellors as "malicious".[16] In the reign of Henry VI, there were substantial royal deficits and over-spending in the 1430s and 1440s. Many of the complaints made by Parliament concerned the controlling influence of Henry VI's counsellors and the behaviour of royal purveyors.[17] These were the contexts for much criticism which either placed the blame on the king's advisors or warned him directly of the consequences of his own actions. Clearly Edward IV was aware, not only of the political problems caused by the instability of the Wars of the Roses but also of the problems caused by a shortage of royal finances and poor household governance. He made concentrated efforts to address, and to be seen to address, these matters.

---

[15] Christopher Given-Wilson, "Purveyance for the Royal Household, 1362–1413", *Bulletin of the Institute of Historical Research* 56 (1983): 145–163; Keen, *England in the Later Middle Ages*, 5–6, 32, 41–42, 46, 88, 90, 209–212, 217; J.R. Maddicott, "The English Peasantry and the Demands of the Crown, 1294–1341", in *Landlords, Peasants and Politics in Medieval England*, ed. T.H. Ashton (Cambridge: CUP, 1987), 285–359.

[16] Keen, *England in the Later Middle Ages*, 253.

[17] Ralph Alan Griffiths, *The Reign of King Henry VI: The Exercise of Royal Authority 1422–61* (London: Benn, 1981), 310–322.

Criticisms of lords and gentry landowners featured less in the proceedings of Parliament owing to the nature of its membership, but the economic changes resulting from the population decline that had been caused by the Black Death brought significant changes for landowners and some suffered financially. While labourers were able to bargain for higher wages, many landowners suffered falling rents.[18] Landowners needed to take measures to prevent their incomes from declining.[19] This situation, a depression for many landowners, continued into the fifteenth century as recurrent visitations of the plague prevented a recovery in population growth.[20] While labourers and craftsmen were censured for their greed, not only by the Church but in the Ordinance and Statute of Labourers [of 1349 and 1351], what moral strictures were placed upon landowners? How did landowners themselves understand their obligations to act in an ethical manner in regard to their financial activities?

Economic historians have not always considered medieval ideas of equity and fairness and their possible influence on how economic activity was regulated in the Middle Ages. More recently, there have been critiques which argue that economic activities are shaped by a system of values and that those values, whether or not they can be described as ethical, affect how those activities are regulated.[21] The separation of ethics from economics can be traced back to Adam Smith, for whom the only value which should affect economic activity was "rational" self-interest. Smith's *The Wealth of Nations* was first published in 1776 and was founded on the principles of self-interest and "natural liberty". Smith was inspired by the ideas of Jean-Jacques Rousseau on liberty and was also reacting against a perceived excessive interference of government

[18] Christopher Dyer, *Standards of Living in the Later Middle Ages: Social Change in England c. 1200–1520*, rev. edn. Cambridge: CUP, 1998.

[19] E.B. Fryde, "Economic Depression in England in the Second and Third Quarters of the Fifteenth Century: Effective Resistances of Tenants to Landlords as One of Its Consequences, Defiances and Rent Strikes", in *Violence in Medieval Society*, ed. Richard W. Kaeuper (Woodbridge: Boydell, 2000), 215–226; John Hatcher and Mark Bailey, *Modelling the Middle Ages: The History and Theory of England's Economic Development* (Oxford: OUP, 2001), 115–116.

[20] John Hatcher, *Plague, Population and the English Economy 1348–1530* London: Macmillan, 1977.

[21] Raj Patel, *The Value of Nothing: How to Reshape Market Society and Redefine Democracy.* London: Portobello Books, 2009; Michael Sandel, *What Money Cannot Buy: The Moral Limits of Markets.* London: Allen Lane, 2012; Joseph E. Stiglitz, *The Price of Inequality.* London: Penguin, 2013.

in economic affairs, which was claimed to be detrimental to national prosperity.[22] In 1759, Smith published his *Theory of Moral Sentiments*, in which he proposed that sympathy for others was the basis for a harmonious society. It might be supposed that self-interest and sympathy are fundamentally incompatible, but Smith dealt with the inconsistency by insisting that self-interest was the motivation in the economic sphere but that sympathy belonged in the ethical sphere. Thus, the two realms were separated.[23] Rather than performing acts of charity, the rich provided for the poor by their own consumption, which required the employment of thousands. In this way, the rich "are led by an invisible hand".[24] Attempts have been made to reconcile Smith's notion of sympathy with his declaration of underlying self-interest but the result is a kind of unintentional benevolence, without any sense of obligation, a concept that would have been quite alien to medieval proponents of the cardinal virtues or their belief that giving to the poor was obeying God's will.[25]

Economic thought became further separated from ethical thought with the influence of the free-trade view that markets should be unregulated, allowing an unfettered interplay between supply and demand. In the eighteenth century, Sir William Blackstone described the medieval regulation of prices and trade and the prohibition of usury as "monkish superstition and civil tyranny". According to Smith, opposition to regrating and engrossing (or cornering the market) was akin to the fear of witchcraft.[26] Both of these statements clearly show the emphasis on

[22] Peter Harrison, "Adam Smith and the History of the Invisible Hand", *Journal of the History of Ideas* 72 (2011): 29–49; Robert L. Heilbroner, *The Worldly Philosophers*: *The Lives, Times and Ideas of the Great Economic Thinkers*, 6th edn. (Harmondsworth: Penguin, 1991), 42–74; , *Rousseau and Freedom*, ed. Christie McDonald and Stanley Hoffman. Cambridge: CUP, 2010; Patricia H. Werhane, "The Role of Self-Interest in Adam Smith's *Wealth of Nations*", *Journal of Philosophy* 86 (1989): 669–680.

[23] Edwin R.A. Seligman, Introduction to Adam Smith, *The Wealth of Nations* (London: Dent, 1910), vol. 1, vii; Introduction to Adam Smith, *The Theory of Moral Sentiments*, ed. D.D. Raphael and A.L. MacFie (Oxford: Clarendon Press, 1976) 6, 8, 9.

[24] Smith, *Theory*, 184.

[25] *Propriety and Prosperity*: *New Studies on the Philosophy of Adam Smith*, ed. David F. Hardwick and Leslie Marsh. Basingstoke: Palgrave Macmillan, 2014.

[26] *The Commentaries of the Laws of England of Sir William Blackstone, Knt, Vol. II*: *Of the Rights of Things*, ed. Robert Malcolm Kerr, 4th edn. (London: John Murray, 1876) 408; Smith, *Wealth of Nations*, vol. 2, 34.

"rationality", to the extent that medieval attempts to regulate economic activity were reduced to absurdity.

Economic histories of the late nineteenth century looked at the influence of ethical principles on economic regulation more sympathetically, but the influence of these particular historians gradually waned following the establishment of economics as a discipline based on scientific principles. William Cunningham's *Growth of English Industry and Commerce*, a survey covering the medieval period until the end of the eighteenth century, was first published in 1882. In the fifth edition of his work, published in 1910, Cunningham argued: "Modern theory ... merely attempts to give an explanation of actual practice. The medieval doctrine of price was not a theory intended to explain the phenomena of society, but it was laid down as the basis of rules which should control the conduct of society and of individuals".[27] W.J. Ashley was also interested in moral aspects. In 1888, he published the first edition of the first part of his *An Introduction to English Economic History and Theory*. A substantial portion (a third) of his study was devoted to moral theories and their link with legislation, with several examples from statute law and local court cases. He cited a fourteenth-century guide to conscience, the *Ayenbyte of Inwyt*, and in the second part of his study he quoted the writings of Wyclif and Chaucer.

Significantly, both Ashley and Cunningham were leading figures in a debate over the extent to which economics could be explained and interpreted by universal laws, such as the relationship between prices, wages, rents and profits, or whether historical factors such as legislation, attitudes and beliefs should have primacy. This dispute at the end of the nineteenth century between the adherents of Arnold Toynbee, such as Ashley and Cunningham, and those who espoused a "scientific" approach, such as Alfred Marshall and later on, John Maynard Keynes, has been well documented. (Arnold Toynbee died in 1883 and was the uncle of the perhaps better known Arnold J. Toynbee, author of the multi-volume *A Study of History*, which was published between 1934 and 1961.)[28] Studies of

[27] William Cunningham, *The Growth of English Industry and Commerce during the Early and Middle Ages*, 5th edn., 1910; (repr. New York: Augustus M. Kelley, 1968), 251–260.

[28] T.C. Barker, "The Beginnings of the Economic History Society", *Economic History Review*, New Series 30 (1977): 1–19; D.C. Coleman, *History and the Economic Past: An Account of the Rise and*

this period give the impression that what is now known as economic history but what was then promoted as a study of economics in a historical context failed to gain enough adherents and so it was the "scientific" or universal laws approach to economics which came to dominate. The influence of Ashley and Cunningham had faded away by the end of the Second World War. Some of the economic histories published in the early twentieth century made a brief mention of economic ethics but with little or no exploration of Christian theology or morality. These include H. de B. Gibbins's *Industry in England* (first published in 1897), L.L. Price's *A Short History of English Commerce and Industry* (1900), Edward Lipson's *The Economic History of England* (1915), L.F. Salzman's *English Industries of the Middle Ages* (1913) and *English Trade in the Middle Ages* (1931).

Perhaps because of the economic disruptions of the Great Depression, ethical theory was of much more interest to Frederic Milner, H.O. Meredith, Arthur Birnie and Max Beer. In his *Economic Evolution in England* (1931), Milner wrote that "Economic history, far from being merely materialistic, is essentially a psychological study, and economic ideals are as fascinating as any religious or political ideals".[29] Meredith, in his outline of economic history, published in 1933, stated: "One of the chief interests of economic history is to watch the twists and turns of society in its efforts to establish an environment favourable to commercial morality".[30] Birnie's approach, in his one-volume economic history of Britain, first published in 1935, was that "Economic activities have always been social".[31] In 1938, Beer, a historian of socialism, provided

Decline of Economic History in Britain. Oxford: Clarendon Press, 1987; W. Cunningham, "The Relativity of Economic Doctrine", *Economic Journal* 7 (1892): 1–16; W. Cunningham, "The Perversion of Economic History", *Economic Journal* 7 (1892): 491–506; Alfred Marshall, "[The Perversion of Economic History]: A Reply", *Economic Journal* 7 (1892): 507–519; W. Cunningham, "Dr. Cunningham and his Critics", *Economic Journal* 4 (1894): 508–516; Alon Kadish, *Historians, Economists and Economic History.* London: Routledge, 1989; Gerard M. Koot, *English Historical Economics, 1870–1926.* Cambridge: CUP, 1987; John Maloney, "Marshall, Cunningham and the Emerging Economics Profession", *Economic History Review*, New Series 29 (1976): 440–451.

[29] Frederic Milner, *Economic Evolution in England* (London: Macmillan, 1931) vii.

[30] H.O. Meredith, *Outlines of the Economic History of England: A Study of Social Development* (London: Pitman, 1933), 19.

[31] Arthur Birnie, *An Economic History of the British Isles*, 8th edn. (London: Methuen, 1955), 1.

a broad survey dealing with a selection of medieval philosophers and theologians.[32]

It seems that more post-World War II economic histories, whether they were general histories or of the medieval period, have either ignored ethical ideals or given them only a limited discussion. This may be because economics as a discipline involving analysis of data and the application of universal laws and theories was by then long established. Alfred Marshall, a proponent of the latter, was awarded the professorship of Political Economy at Cambridge in 1884, ahead of his rival Cunningham, and was probably responsible for introducing the Economics Tripos in 1903.[33] As an illustration of this change to a "scientific" approach, by the time *Living Economic and Social History* was published in 2001, the ideas of Ashley and Cunningham had almost disappeared. This is a volume of essays by 103 economic or social historians, who are members of the Economic History Society, on the subject of the meaning of their discipline. The names and works of Cunningham and Ashley, but not their discussion of legislation and moral theory, are mentioned in just three of these essays.[34]

In his *Medieval Economy and Society* (1972), M.M. Postan is, perhaps, the most rigidly "rational" of economic historians. He described the just price as a "church doctrine ... propounded by canonist writers" and stated that its main purpose was to ensure that sellers could maintain themselves according to their social ranks.[35] Postan argued that in the medieval period "all things had their 'natural' values", which were presumed to be those "which had commonly attached to them in the past".[36] Therefore, the concept of the just price could be understood in terms of long-term price behaviour. In the Middle Ages, prices were seen as "customary", so it followed that any price increases were seen as unjust. In another of his works, Postan's focus was on the mechanisms of the

[32] Max Beer, *Early British Economics: From the 13th to the Middle of the 18th Century*. London: Allen & Unwin, 1938.

[33] Maloney, "Marshall, Cunningham and the Emerging Economics Profession", 440–451.

[34] See the essays by Negley Harte, Edward Royle and John Saville, in *Living Economic and Social History*, ed. Pat Hudson. (Glasgow: Economic History Society, 2001), 3, 313, 330.

[35] M.M. Postan, *The Medieval Economy and Society: An Economic History of Britain in the Middle Ages* (London: Weidenfeld and Nicolson, 1972), 225–226.

[36] Postan, *The Medieval Economy and Society*, 226.

attempt to avoid accusations of usury—that is, the *chevisance* or false bargain—rather than its moral prohibition.[37] Other economic histories which focus on quantitative questions such as the use and distribution of resources, the number of operators, prices and profitability are a volume of essays, *Before the Black Death*, edited by Bruce Campbell (1991), economic histories of late medieval England by A.R. Bridbury (1975 and 2008), Richard Britnell's 1993 study of the development of commerce, and a rural economic history and an urban economic history by Edward Miller and John Hatcher (1978 and 1995, respectively).

With their focus firmly on "rational" economic processes, it is not surprising that attempts to enforce moral standards in medieval economic regulation have appeared irrelevant to some modern historians. J.L. Rosenthal and A.R. Bridbury have taken the view that the moral standards enforced on traders were unrealistic and impractical and thus were not taken seriously by contemporaries. They base their argument on the primacy of material gain and the evidence of a large number of offenders. Rosenthal concludes that the assizes of bread and ale and of weights and measures "were simply unenforceable" and that there "was little moral stigma attached to violation of the assizes".[38] According to Britnell, this was "confirming evidence that the law was not regarded as having any moral force".[39] Bridbury places less emphasis on self-interest as such but suggests that the Church was wholly anti-commerce and its demands impractical and unreasonable. Bridbury declares that commerce survived despite these impediments. He posits the existence of a covert support network which gave traders encouragement to continue in the face of the criticisms of the Church.[40]

Yet some historians have begun to recognise that attention to medieval economic ethics is essential for understanding the formation of eco-

---

[37] Postan, *The Medieval Economy and Society*, 225–226. M.M. Postan, *Medieval Trade and Finance.* Cambridge: CUP, 1973.

[38] Joel T. Rosenthal, "Weights and Measures in Medieval England", *Western Political Quarterly* 17 (1994): 422.

[39] R.H. Britnell, "Morals, Law and Ale in Medieval England", in U. Mueller, F. Hundsnurcher and C. Sommer (eds), *Le Droit et sa Perception dans la Litterature et les Mentalites Medievales*, Göppingen, Kümmerle, 1993, p. 29.

[40] A.R. Bridbury, "Markets and Freedom in the Middle Ages", in *The English Economy from Bede to the Reformation*, ed. A.R. Bridbury. (Woodbridge: Boydell, 1992), 242.

nomic policies and legislation. These include essays by Edward Miller and Gabriel le Bras in the third volume of the *Cambridge Economic History of Europe* (1963) and a chapter on economic ideas, by J. L. Bolton in his *Medieval English Economy, 1150–1500* (1980). Although Britnell paid little attention to the role of ethical thought in his 1993 monograph, *The Commercialization of English Society*, he nonetheless recognised its significance in a number of journal articles, "Forestall, Forestalling and the Statute of Forestallers" (1987), "Price-Setting in English Borough Markets"(1992), and "Urban Economic Regulation and Economic Morality in Medieval England" (2009).

Britnell's evidence was drawn largely from urban settings, although his article on the assize of ale was based partly on evidence from manorial court records.[41] In contrast, Christopher Dyer's work clearly shows the significance of ethical thought in a rural setting in his study of John Heritage, a Gloucestershire merchant. Here, Dyer cites Thomas More's views of the selfishness of the rich, and the notions of the just price and usury pursued by theologians and canonists and found evidence of Heritage's own response to morality in some anonymous words of wisdom that he had copied into his account book. Dyer describes these as unoriginal, and although the words copied do not especially relate to economic ethics, he concludes that Heritage was "one of many who derived comfort and satisfaction from conventional wisdom".[42]

A recent study which has more fully acknowledged the connection between moral theory and medieval economic legislation is by James Davis. Concerning the assize of bread, he writes: "An understanding of contemporary cultural mores provides an important context in which to place the aims of commercial legislators of the assize of bread". Markets should be places where trade was in public and in the hands of those who were honest and "the medieval ideal was for an open market, free from fraud, and populated by buyers and sellers who were morally self-aware".[43] Like Ashley over a century before, Davis quotes from contemporary sources such as *The Vision*

[41] Britnell, "Morals, Law and Ale", 21–29.

[42] Christopher Dyer, *A Country Merchant, 1495–1520: Trading and Farming at the End of the Middle Ages* (Oxford:, OUP, 2014), 202, 220, 221.

[43] James Davis, "Baking for the Common Good: A Reassessment of the Assize of Bread in Medieval England", *Economic History Review* 57 (2004): 480, 482, 484–485.

of Piers Plowman, Thomas Wimbledon's sermon of 1388 and the Holkham Bible picture book as well as the just price theories of Aquinas and Albertus Magnus. Davis's *Medieval Market Morality* (2012) is a comprehensive study of the relationship between morality and the regulation of economic activity in late medieval England. Thus far, Davis's approach is similar to my own, but it is confined to urban trade. I intend to complement his work by showing that moral codes were applied to a broader range of economic activity, which includes the behaviour of rulers and landowners. In addition, his conclusion raises questions about the relationship between ecclesiastical writings and secular legislation which I will explore in Chapter 5. Although Davis suggests that legislators were indeed influenced by religious principles, saying "the enactment of medieval law was intimately connected to the predominant moral assumptions of the age, and notions of social justice and the common good figure prominently", he qualifies this by reasoning that they had to consider other factors such as the needs of the consumer and the effects of natural catastrophes or wars.[44]

Davis, like most of the other economic historians surveyed in this chapter, has not considered the rural sector or the role of powerful agents such as lords and kings in economic ethics. The reason for the greater focus on urban trade might be the survival of many city books of customs and records of court decisions and writs, some of which were edited and published as modern editions in the late nineteenth and early twentieth centuries. These regulations, their language and how they were applied were thus more accessible to historians. Good examples are the series of *London Letter Books* edited by Reginald Sharpe between 1899 and 1912, the *Calendars of the Plea & Memoranda Rolls of the Corporation of London*, which were published between 1926 and 1961, and the *Liber Albus* of the City of London edited by Henry Thomas Riley in 1861. For provincial towns, there are, for example, the volumes of the *Records of the Borough of Leicester* edited by Mary Bateson in 1899 and 1901, the *Records of the City of Norwich* edited by William Hudson and J.C. Tingney (which were published in 1906 and 1910, respectively) and similar volumes for York and Northampton.

---

[44] Davis, *MMM*, 136.

The social historians K.B. McFarlane, E.B. Fryde and J.R. Maddicott have investigated economic relations in the rural sector, but their explorations of the moral concepts underlying the criticisms of the unjust behaviour of lords are limited. These works will be discussed more fully in Chapter 6.[45] Maddicott aimed to find evidence of the effects of taxation, purveying and military service on the poor rather than make an extensive inquiry into moral objections against these practices. Apart from William of Pagula's *Mirror of Edward III*, he confined his investigation of literary complaints to two poems: *The Song of the Husbandman* and *A Poem on the Times of Edward II*. However, in his article on the authorship and circulation of poems of complaint, Maddicott made a further investigation of moral criticism where he looked at parallels between condemnations of the rich and of corruption in the poems and similar denunciations in John Bromyard's *Summa Praedicantium*.[46] I intend both to examine a wider range of sources of moral criticism than these other scholars and to investigate the theological and philosophical origins of such criticism in order to show the extent of its influence and acceptance in late medieval England.

Whereas Rodney Hilton was more interested in power relations in medieval England, social historians are more likely than economic historians to comment on underlying moral values or their presence in regulation.[47] For example, Stephen Rigby adopts a Marxist approach in his examination of moral theories governing economic activity, describing theodicy, or the justification of the ways of God, as "the dominant ideology", which was used to legitimate social and economic inequality. Contemporary sources are cited on this topic.[48] Nevertheless, the focus of Rigby's study is on class

---

[45] K.B. McFarlane, *The Nobility of Later Medieval England*. Oxford: Clarendon Press, 1973; E.B. Fryde, *Peasants and Landlords in Later Medieval England*. Stroud: Sutton, 1996; J.R. Maddicott, "The English Peasantry and the Demands of the Crown, 1294–1341", in *Landlords, Peasants and Politics in Medieval England*, ed. T.H. Ashton. Cambridge: CUP, 1987.

[46] J.R. Maddicott, "Poems of Social Protest in Early Fourteenth-Century England", in *England in the Fourteenth Century: Proceedings of the 1985 Harlaxton Symposium*, ed. W. Mark Ormrod. (Woodbridge: Boydell, 1986), 130–144.

[47] R.H. Hilton, *Decline of Serfdom in Medieval England*. London: Macmillan for the Economic History Society, 1969; *The English Peasantry in the Later Middle Ages: the Ford Lectures for 1973 and Related Studies*. Oxford: Clarendon Press, 1975; *Class Conflict and the Crisis of Feudalism: Essays in Medieval Social History*, 2nd ed. London: Verso, 1990.

[48] S.H. Rigby, *English Society in the Later Middle Ages: Class, Status and Gender* (Basingstoke: Macmillan, 1995), 306–316.

structure, status and gender and how conflicts between the classes arose. It is not concerned with economic ethics as such, even though the estates theory was used in the medieval period to justify discrepancies in wealth as well as the class hierarchy. Jeremy Goldberg's social history mentions the use of "biblical language" and the influence of "religious ideas and ideals" on guild ordinances but not elsewhere in society.[49] The volume of social history essays edited by Rosemary Horrox contains a discussion by Gerald Harriss of the ideal that a king should rule for the good of all and that if he ruled for his own gain he was a tyrant; Edward Powell comments on the medieval belief that law and justice reflected God's rule and reinforced the order of society; and Kate Mertes notes the expectation that the nobility would behave with moral rectitude and practise the virtue of liberality.[50] Miri Rubin devoted a chapter of her study of charity in medieval Cambridge to the views of scholastic philosophers on charity, poverty and wealth and how these ideas were transmitted via pastoral manuals and sermons.[51] Rubin also stresses the importance of the theological virtue of charity in the treatment of the poor in her chapter in the volume of social history essays cited previously.[52] Thus, it would appear that on the whole, social historians have been more likely than economic historians to explore and evaluate the importance of moral instruction in their explanations of how society operated. However, social studies, except those by Dyer, tend to address other aspects of late medieval English society, the economic sphere remaining separate.

The commercialisation of English society after 1200 might have generated new legislation and prompted theologians and preachers to give merchants and traders greater attention. However, there remains the question of whether economic ethics also applied to kings, lords and landowners. Some legal historians have revealed the moral foundations of law and justice but at the conceptual level. Where legislation has been investigated, it is in relation to trade and usury and laws or petitions

[49] P.J.P. Goldberg, *Medieval England: A Social History 1250–1550* (London: Arnold, 2004), 62.

[50] G.L. Harriss, "The King and His Subjects"; Edward Powell, "Law and Justice"; Kate Mertes, "Aristocracy" in *Fifteenth-Century Attitudes: Perceptions of Society in Late Medieval England*, ed. Rosemary Horrox. (Cambridge: CUP, 1994), 13–28, 29–41, 42–60.

[51] Miri Rubin, *Charity and Community in Medieval Cambridge*, Cambridge, CUP, 1987, pp. 54–98.

[52] Rubin, "The Poor" in Horrox (ed.), *Fifteenth-Century Attitudes*, pp. 169–182.

concerning activities in the rural economy, and economic responsibilities have received less attention.

Medieval economic and social histories have focused more on the impersonal operations of an economy than contemporary attitudes towards it or any ethical dimension. Studies of medieval economic thought have followed medieval scholastic debates and consequently tend to focus on urban market morality. Legal histories of economic regulation, although they consider ethical implications, also direct their attention towards commerce. Yet the medieval economy was primarily rural, and landowning the main source of wealth. There were many other members of society engaged in transactions for financial or material gain. Given the all-encompassing influence of the medieval Church, what did it have to say about ethical standards for landowners, their officials and officials of the crown? Were the financial demands made by a king upon his people subjected to its moral scrutiny? What particular concepts were employed for those contexts? What was the extent of the influence of those concepts on society?

This study is divided into eight chapters. Chapter 2 introduces late medieval English writings on economic ethics and its origins, covering the doctrines of avarice and usury, notions of justice, theories of the just price and the common weal, notions of lordship and what they implied and how economic inequality was justified. In order to gain some understanding of how ethical concepts were embedded in late medieval English society, it is necessary first of all to examine their origins and longevity. The objective of the next chapter is, also, to provide an underpinning of medieval ethical thought regarding economic activity. It will discuss both Christian and classical sources of the major concepts underlying economic ethics and how they were used by medieval theologians.

Chapter 3 surveys pastoral manuals (both those written for the priesthood and those for lay perusal), sermons, guides for the conduct of rulers and others in authority, and general books of wisdom. Chapter 4 focuses on a selection of literary works by Chaucer, Gower, Langland, Hoccleve and Lydgate for discourses on lords and rulers as ethical role models and for reactions to economic and social change. It also examines evidence of book circulation and commissioning of moralising literary works to assess the extent of possible influence amongst lay readers. Chapter 5 examines the language of relevant legislation and of a selection of petitions and examines through case studies the abuse of purveying, extortion and oppression by lords and gentry, unreasonable tolls and fines, and land enclosures. Chapter 6 investigates the question of whether landowners were rapacious, adhering to their rights and powers over their tenants, or whether they were reasonable and flexible in a period of economic change. Manorial records provide some individual cases, and studies of medieval inquisitions and taxation surveys reveal information about differing levels of wealth among landowners and the composition of their revenues. Wills show that some landowners were concerned to correct any wrongdoings regarding their tenants and their land acquisitions. Chapter 7 discusses the extent to which economic ethics were understood by individuals from the evidence of letters. Throughout, I aim to show that economic ethics had a broader application than urban trade and usury in late medieval England.

2

Economic Ethics

"Economic ethics", as discussed in the Introduction, is a term useful to describe the moral evaluation, judgement and prosecution of offences detrimental to what was thought to be a fair economy in late medieval England. Economic ethics, however, were a means by which not only to criticise dishonesty or greed but also to instil the positive virtues needed to overcome those vices. They could be described as practical ethics in the same way as present-day "business ethics", but the term "economic ethics" gives the sense of a wider application than commerce, including the distribution of wealth, the treatment of the poor, and the livelihoods of all. As shown in the Introduction, this wider view is in contrast to most modern studies of medieval economic ethics, which tend to focus on usury and commerce or on transactions which occurred largely within urban marketplaces.

This chapter surveys the concepts, whether vices, virtues or social ideals, which were cited when economic ethics were discussed by philosophers and theologians. Medieval philosophers and theologians are not easily separable since both were informed by and expounded upon the Scriptures: philosophy was in large part theology. The modern distinction

J. Hole, *Economic Ethics in Late Medieval England, 1300–1500*,
Archival Insights into the Evolution of Economics,
DOI 10.1007/978-3-319-38860-1_2

is owing to the fact that many philosophers wrote about language and logic, metaphysics or natural philosophy, as well as the nature of God, and their work has been considered part of the history and development of philosophical ideas. On the other hand, there are some authorities who are regarded primarily as theologians, because they were writing before the revival of philosophy in the twelfth century. This chapter also explores the relationships between some of these ethical concepts and their role in maintaining an ordered society, since, as will be discussed in Chapter 5, they were appealed to in petitions and legislation. For example, it was considered that the vice of avarice created discord in society because it was a selfish appetite, the opposite of the harmony and balance necessary for social order. Avarice led to crimes such as theft and usury and, in the case of rulers and lords, extortion and oppression of their subjects. On the other hand, the virtue of justice, ideally maintained by good lords, restored harmony and balance and upheld social order.

This chapter firstly examines the sources and traditions of the concepts which comprised medieval economic ethics: excess or artificial wealth, avarice, justice, the just price, the common good and good lordship. It then turns to a discussion of late medieval English theologians and philosophers and their application of economic ethics to practical matters, such as the morality of buying, selling and lending and their views of good lordship, extortion and oppression. The thought of English theologians and philosophers on practical economic ethics was in some respects similar to that of their counterparts in mainland Europe, but their views have received little attention, even though they were an influential part of medieval European thought in other respects. Of particular interest to this study are these thinkers' criticisms of economic exploitation by lords. Finally, this chapter discusses the interconnectedness of the concepts of avarice, justice, the just price, the common good and good lordship and draws conclusions about the importance and influence of these ideals to economic ethics.

Most studies of medieval economic ethics focus on the concept of the just price. These include those by Bernard W. Dempsey (1935), T.P. McLaughlin (1939 and 1940), Raymond de Roover, John T. Noonan and John Baldwin. In "The Just Price in a Functional Economy", Dempsey argued that Albertus Magnus and Thomas Aquinas saw the just price as a principle which should benefit not just the buyer and seller but the whole of society, and it was society or the community which determined the just price. In "The Concept of the Just Price Theory and Economic Policy" (1958), Raymond de Roover argued that there were varying definitions of the just price: the cost of production, including labour, transport and risk; a price that is charged without fraud and coercion; a price fixed by public authorities for the common good; and a price estimated by the market. Studies on the prohibition of usury were made by McLaughlin (1939 and 1940) and Noonan (1957). More recent studies are by Odd Langholm (1979, 1983, 1992, 1998, 2006). His *Merchants in the Confessional* (2003) is the most extensive survey to date of the subjects of avarice and usury in confessional manuals, covering some hundreds of manuals from all over Europe. Just pricing is also covered in two works by Joel Kaye (1998), John R. Owen (2007), Adrian Walsh (2004) and Daniel A. Wren (2000).

Baldwin's *Masters, Princes and Merchants* (1970) differs. It is a study of the thought of Peter the Chanter (d. 1197) and his former English student Thomas Chobham and Chobham's contemporary Robert Courson but moved further away from the just price and usury in those thinkers' coverage of such topics as the ethical application of tolls and tallage as well as the just price and usury.[1] Jacob Viner's unfinished "Religious Thought, Economy and Society" (1978) similarly takes a broader view of economic thought. His chapter on medieval thought leans heavily upon Aquinas but encompasses his ideas of the common good, excess wealth, charity, and treatment of the poor, along with the just price and usury, and this suggests how the concepts of medieval economic ethics were interrelated. Diana Wood's *Medieval Economic Thought* (2002) includes chapters on property rights and attitudes to wealth and poverty, along with the theories of usury, the just wage and the just price. Wood saw medieval economic thought as embracing "material matters" and thus her survey covered rather more than just activities in the marketplace. However, her discussion of avarice is in general terms and does not extend to the consideration of its various manifestations, such as extortion and oppression by landowners. David Harris Sacks's "The Greed of

[1] John W. Baldwin, *Masters, Princes and Merchants: The Social Views of Peter the Chanter and His Circle*, 2 vols. Princeton: Princeton University Press, 1970.

Judas: Avarice, Monopoly and the Moral Economy in England ca. 1300–ca. 1600" (1998) noticed that the fourteenth-century preacher Thomas Wimbledon and some of the writings of John Wyclif also described the behaviour of those in authority, such as kings, lords and mayors, as potentially avaricious, but overall only a few historians of medieval economic thought have extended the range of their enquiry to members of society other than merchants and traders, and there has not been a detailed consideration of how the economic pursuits of landowners might have been subject to moral censure.

The Origins of Ethical Concepts and Some Major Exponents

The concepts of economic ethics need to be considered, first of all, in the context of attitudes to wealth. From the very beginnings of Christianity, there was awareness amongst its principal authorities of the contradiction between acquiring wealth and the ideals of poverty as practised by Christ. He warned of the dangers of attachment to material things: "you cannot serve God and mammon" and "take no thought for the morrow".[2] There was similar contempt in the thought of Plato and Aristotle for wealth-getting, for although poverty or a total lack of materialism was not embraced by them as an ideal, they criticised excessive wealth. Aristotle's views on the difference between excessive and justifiable wealth might have been influenced by Plato, whose prejudice against wealth-getting can be found in the *Republic*. Throughout this work, there are comments from Socrates which clearly show that he viewed money-making as an unworthy occupation, incompatible with being a person of wisdom and understanding. For example, he agreed with Adeimantus's opinion that oligarchs only encourage each other "further into money-making, and the more they value it, the less they value virtue".[3] Socrates divided the soul into three parts: the intellectual, the emotional and the appetitive;

[2] Matthew 6:24, 34 [Authorised King James Version].

[3] Plato, *Republic*, trans. G.M.A. Grube, and rev. C.D.C. Reeve (Indianapolis: Hackett, 1992), 221.

money-loving belonged to this appetitive part.[4] This division of the soul was hierarchical, with reason or the intellectual part of the soul governing the other two parts. The appetitive part was characterised by "worldly lusts and desires".[5] Although there was no Latin translation of the *Republic* until the early fifteenth century, the same ideas, expressed in a more compressed form, were available in translations of Plato's *Phaedo*, which states "we are compelled to acquire wealth on account of the body" (a Latin translation by Henry Aristippus of the *Phaedo* appeared in the mid-twelfth century).[6]

It is a reasonable possibility that Aristotle, as a former student of Plato, might have been influenced to make his distinction between "natural" wealth-getting, which was acquiring those things necessary for life, and artificial wealth-getting, which was simply to acquire money. Thus, natural wealth-getting was the obtaining of goods to maintain a household; the rest was excess. Aristotle believed that natural wealth-getting had a natural limit because once those requirements had been fulfilled, there was no need to obtain more goods. With artificial wealth, however, there was no such limit. The worst instance of this endless acquisition was usury, or making money out of money by charging interest on loans. Aristotle regarded money as purely artificial, a medium of exchange, and therefore making money out of money was quite unnatural: it was breeding from something essentially sterile.[7] Aquinas adopted Aristotle's distinction between natural and artificial wealth in the *Summa Theologiae*, reasoning that because material goods are made for the support of humankind, they must be beneath it, and therefore the gaining of them is not a worthy end in life. Furthermore, spiritual values cannot be bought. Aquinas declared that the desire for material goods or possessions, in contrast to the desire for the supreme or sovereign good, leads to dissatisfaction, "for when they are possessed they are despised and other things craved instead".[8]

---

[4] Plato, *Republic*, 251.

[5] A.H. Armstrong, *An Introduction to Ancient Philosophy* (London, Methuen, 1965), 42.

[6] Plato, *Five Dialogues*, ed. A.D. Lindsay (London: Dent, 1910, repr. 1938), 145; Robert Posnau (ed.), *The Cambridge History of Medieval Philosophy*, ed. Robert Posnau, (Cambridge: CUP, 2010), vol. 2, p. 798.

[7] Aristotle, "The Politics, Book I", in *The Politics and the Constitution of Athens*, ed. Stephen Iverson (Cambridge: CUP, 1996), 22–25.

[8] Aquinas, *ST*, vol. 16, 33, 35.

Thus, medieval theologians' focus was on the desire for wealth as a corrupting influence. At the same time, they were greatly concerned by some of the methods employed to obtain it, not only the malpractices of merchants but also the deeds of landowners. As discussed in the previous chapter, the great majority of studies by modern historians of medieval economic ideas have focused on deceitful trade and usury. They have noted the frequency with which medieval theologians cite the Bible and the Church Fathers to condemn deceitful trade and usury, but the fact that oppression and extortion were also condemned in the Bible has been overlooked.

In Deuteronomy, the use of false weights and measures is specifically forbidden and the practice is also condemned by the prophet Micah.[9] False weights and measures are associated with merchants and traders; usury, on the other hand, could be practised by many others in medieval society. Usury, expecting a repayment greater than the loan, was forbidden in the Book of Exodus: "If thou lend money to any of my people that is poor by thee, thou shalt not be to him as a usurer, neither shalt thou lay upon him usury".[10] The prohibition of usury also appears in the New Testament in Christ's words in the Gospel of Luke: "lend, hoping for nothing again".[11] The biblical condemnations were reiterated by the Church Fathers: Ambrose of Milan rebuked usurers for exploiting the poverty of others, condemning it as being against Christian love; John Chrysostom, Jerome and Augustine all strongly condemned usury.[12]

Because of usury's prohibition in the Bible and the growth of commerce in the medieval period, theologians and canon lawyers devoted much of their attention to it and expounded upon some of its finer points. In canon law, usury included selling as well as lending: selling at an unusually high price was a means of determining usury, as was selling at an unusually low price.[13] The gains involved could consist of goods as well as

[9] Deuteronomy 25:1–16; Micah 6:10–11.

[10] Exodus 22:25.

[11] Luke 6:35.

[12] Robert P. Maloney, "The Teaching of the Fathers on Usury: An Historical Study on the Development of Christian Thinking", *Vigiliae Christianae* 27 (1973): 241–265.

[13] John W. Baldwin, "Medieval Theories of the Just Price; Romanists, Canonists and Theologians in the Twelfth and Thirteenth Centuries", *Transactions of the American Philosophical Society* 49 (1959): 50, 51.

money.[14] Cases in which a higher price was charged for a delayed payment or a discount offered for an advance payment were also regarded by Aquinas and by other theologians as usury.[15] Aquinas, following Aristotle, regarded usury as unnatural because it resembled breeding from something which was essentially sterile or inanimate: money was intended to be only a medium of exchange.[16] Usury was also regarded as unjust by Aquinas because the borrower was forced to pay on a take–it-or-leave-it basis, and William of Auxerre called it theft because the borrower's will was not absolutely free but partially involuntary. Furthermore, the "borrower sinned as well, though not mortally, by agreeing to pay usury".[17] Other theologians accused usurers of selling time itself, which belonged not to them but to God: Peter the Chanter wrote that the usurer profited while he or she slept "et ita vendit tempora dei".[18] This criticism also applied to sales on credit, but a decretal of Pope Gregory IX (1230) allowed a higher price for a credit sale if there was genuine doubt about the future value or quality of the goods. Such a sale was not lawful if the value or quality was known and the intention was only to make excess profit.[19]

Oppression and extortion are also condemned in the Bible. The prophet Ezekiel saw usury as just one way of mistreating the poor. He that

> hath oppressed the poor and needy, hath spoiled by violence, hath not restored the pledge … hath given forth on usury, and hath taken increase: shall he then live? He shall not live: he hath done all these abominations: he shall surely die.[20]

---

[14] "Decreti Secunda Pars", Causa XIV, Questio III, c. I, in *Corpus Iuris Canonici* (*1*), 735.

[15] Aquinas, *ST*, vol. 38, 247; Wood, *MET*, 175–176.

[16] Wood, *MET*, 84; Odd Langholm, "The Medieval Schoolmen (1200–1400)", in *Ancient and Medieval Economic Ideas and Concepts of Social Justice*, ed. S. Todd Lowry and Barry Gordon (Leiden: Brill, 1998), 476–481.

[17] Wood, *MET*, 166.

[18] Jacques Le Goff, "The Usurer and Purgatory", in (ed.), *The Dawn of Modern Banking*, ed. Center for Medieval and Renaissance Studies, University of California, Los Angeles (New Haven: Yale University Press, 1979), 33.

[19] "Decretal. Gregor. IX", Lib. V, Titulus XIX *De Usuris*, cap. VI, cap. XIX in *Corpus Iuris Canonici* (*2*), 813, 816.

[20] Ezekiel 18:12–13.

The need to restore things taken by extortion, theft or deceit is in God's words to Moses: "he shall restore that which he took violently away, or the thing which he hath deceitfully gotten".[21] Those who exploit or deceive are decried: "Woe unto him that buildeth his house by unrighteousness, and his chambers by wrong; that useth his neighbour's service without wages, and giveth him not for his work".[22] And God speaks of the wrongs committed by rulers of a certain land: "Her princes … are like wolves ravening the prey, to shed blood, and to destroy souls, to get dishonest gain", and "the people of the land have used oppression, and exercised robbery, and have vexed the poor and needy".[23] As will be seen later in this chapter, the English theologians Robert of Courson and Robert of Flamborough criticised excessive tolls and tallage charged by lords, and John Wyclif condemned their extortion and oppression, but the condemnations in biblical terms were left to preachers and satirists. The analogy of wolves and other ravening beasts to portray the economic injustice of lords and princes was used by John Bromyard in his *Summa Praedicantium* and in some sermons, which will be discussed in the following chapter. It became commonplace in literary references to extortion, such as the tyrant goshawk in Chaucer's *Parlement of Foules*: "the foules of ravyne/Weere hyest set ... Ther was the tiraunt with his fetheres donne/And grey – I mene the goshauk that doth pyne/To bryddes for his outrageous ravyne". "Ravyne" (sometimes spelt "raveyn" or "ravine") here means taking goods or property by force rather than rape.[24]

To carry out any of the offences described above—that is, to use false weights and measures or to practise usury or extortion—was considered by the Church to not only breach the Commandment against theft but also to commit avarice, the fifth of the seven deadly sins. The love of wealth was considered not so much a temptation which could lead to much evil, as all evil, as expressed in Paul's dictum "For the love of money is the root of all evil" ("Radix omnium malorum est. cupiditas").[25]

[21] Leviticus 6:4.

[22] Jeremiah 22:13.

[23] Ezekiel 22:27, 29.

[24] Chaucer, *Parlement of Foules*, in *Riverside Chaucer*, 389–390.

[25] I Timothy 6:10.

In the tradition of the seven deadly sins, both *cupiditas* and *avaritia* had the same definition of excessive desire for worldly goods or riches, but avarice seems to be the more usual name for the fifth sin and was looked upon as both a desire to acquire ever more wealth and the desire to retain it.[26] Within the Church, differing positions concerning wealth acquisition were taken, ranging from total rejection, because it was a source of temptation, to an acceptance that wealth could be acquired in moderation. For example, Irenaeus of Lyon (d. 202) thought that the very act of acquiring wealth must involve avarice, but his contemporary, Clement of Alexandria (*c.* 150–215), believed that acquiring moderate wealth was acceptable.[27] Augustine (354–430) was concerned not so much with the possession of wealth but with an immoderate desire for it: wealth should not be regarded as an end in itself, and if it was acquired, it should be used to achieve good ends.[28] On the other hand, Augustine's contemporary John Chrysostom (*c.* 347–407) condemned merchants for the ease with which they could acquire wealth simply for its own sake and because of the ease with which dishonest practices could develop.[29] In the twelfth century, John of Salisbury saw wealth as deeply immoral. In a chapter of the *Policraticus* (written *c.* 1159) condemning money in favour of wisdom, he wrote: "The road to salvation is safest for whoever is free of riches and other material possessions".[30] On the other hand, the Franciscan theologian Alexander of Hales (*c.* 1180–1245) took care to distinguish between what could be classified as necessary for survival and what was indeed superfluous wealth. He asserted that it was possible for a person to hold an excess of possessions that were actually for the use of another, but if this was not so, then restitution must be made. Giving to

[26] Richard G. Newhauser, "Justice and Liberality: Opposition to Avarice in the Twelfth Century", in *Virtue and Ethics in the Twelfth Century*, ed. Istvan P. Bejczy and Richard G. Newhauser (Leiden: Brill, 2005), 295.

[27] Richard G. Newhauser, *The Early History of Greed: The Sin of Avarice in Early Medieval Thought and Literature* (Cambridge: CUP, 2000), 8–9, 10.

[28] R.W. Dyson, *Normative Theories of Society and Government in Five Medieval Thinkers: St Augustine, John of Salisbury, Giles of Rome, St Thomas Aquinas, and Marsilius of Padua* (Lewiston, NY: Edwin Mellen, 2003), 50.

[29] Langholm, "The Medieval Schoolmen", 454; and see an epistle of Pope Leo in Gratian's *Decretum*, Secunda Pars, Causa XXXIII, Questio III, C. II, in *Corpus Iuris Canonici* (*1*), 1240.

[30] John of Salisbury, *Policraticus*, ed. Cary J. Nederman (Cambridge: CUP, 1990), 101.

the poor was the recommended way of achieving this. He also put forward the argument that a prelate (perhaps here meaning "leader" rather than a high official in the Church) could wear precious clothing so as to be feared and honoured by his subjects. Such clothing, however, should be worn with humility, not pride.[31] In another of his works, Alexander of Hales argued that a king might have excess wealth in order to defend his country against enemies, to build places of worship and to relieve the poor and that the married laity need a surplus with which to provide for their children.[32] Thus, the ground was laid for claims by others that excess wealth was "needful" or "worshipful" for certain orders in society, a topic which appears in some of the pastoral manuals to be discussed in the next chapter.[33]

The need to restore things taken by extortion, theft or deceit was dictated to Moses by God, as in the passage from Leviticus 6:4 cited earlier. Ideas of justice also had roots in New Testament doctrine and classical thought. Apart from restitution, another corrective to acts of economic injustice was the performance of charity. The first three of the "corporal works of mercy" are core instances: feeding the hungry, giving drink to the thirsty and clothing the naked. Matthew 25:34–46 makes the performance of the corporal works crucial to salvation. Their basis is in the words of Jesus that to "love thy neighbour as thyself" is the second most important Commandment.[34] Justice was one of the works of mercy, along with charity. Charity and justice can also be found in the seven Virtues; these included the four "cardinal" or "moral" virtues of Greek philosophy—prudence, justice, temperance and fortitude—to which Ambrose of Milan (*c.* 339–97) added the three Christian theological virtues of faith, hope and charity, a move adopted by Augustine.[35] The real origin

---

[31] Disputatio 1, point 5 and disputatio 2 point 46 of "Quaestio XVII: De superfluo", in Alexander of Hales, *Quaestiones disputate "Antequam esset frater"*, vol. 1, ed. Collegii S. Bonaventurae (Florence: Quaracchi, 1960), 276, 291.

[32] Hermenegildus Lio, *Determinatio "superflui" in doctrina Alexandri Halensis eiusque scholae* (Rome: Pontificium Athenaeum Antonianum, 1953), 98, 107.

[33] For a more extensive discussion of need and how the wealthy were meant to address poverty, see Andrew Galloway, "The Economy of Need in Late Medieval English Literature", *Viator* 40 (2009): 309–331.

[34] Matthew 22:39.

[35] Gareth B. Matthews, "Augustinianism", in *Cambridge History of Medieval Philosophy*, ed. Posnau, vol. 1, 96.

of the four cardinal virtues might lie in the time before Plato, since in the *Protagoras* Socrates discussed the interrelationship and nature of the five virtues of wisdom, justice, courage, temperance and piety as though his listeners were already aware of them.[36] The three theological virtues originated in Paul's declaration: "And now abideth faith, hope and charity, these three; but the greatest of these is charity".[37] Both justice and charity are also mentioned in the Old Testament:

> But if a man be just, and do that which is lawful and right … And hath not oppressed any, but hath restored to the debtor his pledge, hath spoiled none by violence, hath given his bread to the hungry, and hath covered the naked with a garment; He that hath not given forth upon usury; neither hath taken any increase, that hath withdrawn his hand from iniquity, hath executed true judgement between man and man, Hath walked in my statutes, and hath kept my judgements, to deal truly; he is just, he shall surely live, saith the Lord God.[38]

Apart from the influence of their education, the virtues of classical thought might have appealed to Ambrose and Augustine because "virtue ethics" has a developmental goal similar to that of Christian teaching. "Virtue ethics" is a term given by modern philosophers to the application of the four cardinal virtues and is based on the notion that a person's character is the foundation for ethical behaviour rather than following rules or social norms. An important feature of virtue ethics is that they encouraged the development of certain attributes of character that were meant to improve the way individuals thought and behaved. Virtue ethics is thus distinct from the consequential view of ethics. In a way, this is similar to the Christian Church's urging of the individual to carry out certain moral practices in order to save his or her soul. The practice of virtue depends on the human will, so the medieval Christian Church made appeals to the human conscience, which will become more apparent in the succeeding chapters on pastoral manuals and literary works. It has been argued that in the medieval period, conscience was regarded as

---

[36] Plato, *Protagoras*, ed. Benjamin Jowett (Oxford: Clarendon Press, 1892), 116.

[37] I Corinthians 13:13.

[38] Ezekiel 18:5–9.

knowledge of or being in conformity with the moral order or divine law rather than our modern sense of conscience being subjective, with our sense of morality resembling individual opinion.[39]

The virtue of justice had been important to medieval theologians before the appearance of the full Latin translation of Aristotle's *Nicomachean Ethics* by Robert Grosseteste in the first half of the thirteenth century. In *De officiis*, Cicero defined justice as both the highest virtue and the underlying principle of an ordered society. The Cistercian Bernard of Clairvaux (1090–1153) saw in justice the means of reinforcing obedience as part of monastic reform, whereas his contemporary Peter Lombard (*c.* 1100–60) saw justice as helping the unfortunate.[40] For a number of early medieval and twelfth-century theologians, taking more than was needed was unjust.[41] After the full translations of Aristotle became available, it was apparent that he gave justice a much fuller expression than had previously been recognised. He too regarded it as the principal virtue, the practice of it implying social order or a good society:

> Now this justice is in fact perfect Virtue … because it is the practice of perfect Virtue. And perfect because he that has it is able to practise his virtue towards his neighbour and not merely on himself.[42]

Aristotle was a major influence on Thomas Aquinas: he adopted Aristotle's notion of justice because to him it "implie[d] a certain balance of equality".[43] Aristotle's distinction between commutative justice, or giving one person what was due to him or her, and distributive justice, or giving to the many, was taken up by Aquinas, who added that neither kind of justice should result in harm to the common good.[44] For Aquinas,

---

[39] Dennis R. Klinck, *Conscience, Equity and the Court of Chancery in Early Modern England* (Farnham: Ashgate, 2010), 2.

[40] Newhauser, "Justice and Liberality", 297–299.

[41] Newhauser, "Justice and Liberality", 296.

[42] Aristotle, "Book V" in *The Nicomachean Ethics*, ed. D.P. Chase (London: Dent, 1911), 103.

[43] Aquinas, *ST*, vol. 37, 5.

[44] Aquinas, *ST*, vol. 37, 87, 89.

making restitution was an act of justice since it was returning ill-gotten gains and any recompense should be an amount that was properly due.[45]

There was also the notion of retributive justice, that wrongdoing must be punished as it was breaking the laws of God. The Bible has many references to justice as divine punishment or revenge for sinful behaviour, most notably the Day of Judgement as described in Revelation.[46] Yet the Bible also has passages which ask rulers, and perhaps all people, to carry out justice for the vulnerable members of society. For example, "Learn to do well; seek judgment, relieve the oppressed, judge the fatherless, plead for the widow"[47] and "Judge in favor of the fatherless and oppressed, that man upon earth may lord it over them no further".[48] Therefore, the Bible presents justice both as divine retribution or punishment and as social justice, acting for the good of others in aiding the oppressed against the powerful.

The ideal of the common good from classical thought also implies acting for the good of others. Prior to the widespread distribution of full translations of Aristotle's *Nicomachean Ethics* and *Politics*, Cicero's *De officiis* and extracts from his *De republica* were the main influence on medieval writers. By *res publica*, Cicero meant public affairs or activity, the public interest, the community or country.[49] Cicero knew the works of Aristotle but it has been suggested that his knowledge might have been limited as comparatively few of Aristotle's works were in circulation in Cicero's lifetime.[50] The "common good" has some similarities to *res publica*. Although Aristotle did not employ the terms "common good" or "common weal" as such, his *eudaimonia* or "the good life" meant not the emotions of the individual but living a good life, having one's needs supplied and practising the virtues.[51] Thus, the virtue of justice can be

---

[45] Aquinas, *ST*, vol. 37, 105.

[46] Revelation 14:6–11; 20:1–5.

[47] Isaiah 1:17.

[48] Psalm 10:18.

[49] Malcolm Schofield, "Cicero's Definition of *Res Publica*", in J.G.F. Powell (ed.), *Cicero the Philosopher: Twelve Papers*, Oxford, Clarendon Press, 1995, p. 66.

[50] Powell, "Introduction" and A.A. Long, "Cicero's Plato and Aristotle" in *Cicero the Philosopher*, ed. Powell 18, 42.

[51] D.P. Chase, "Introduction", in Aristotle, *The Nicomachean Ethics*, xiii–xv; Stephen Iverson, "Introduction", in Aristotle, *The Politics and The Constitution of Athens*, xxiv–xxvi, xxix.

practised for the good of others and this, perhaps, is the closest Aristotle gets to the "common good".

Aquinas, in his attempt to synthesise classical thought with Church doctrine, used "common good" in the *Summa Theologiae*, in which he connects acting for the common good with religious principles:

> man is bound in charity to love God, who is the common good of all things [*bonum commune omnium*], more than himself; for eternal happiness is to be found in God as the common principle and source of all things which are capable of sharing such happiness.[52]

Yet "common good" can be either an ethical ideal or goal for individual moral behaviour, such as thinking and acting for the good of others rather than oneself, or a political ideal. In the latter sense, acting for the "common good" might mean for the needs of the majority or a group of interests rather than particular individuals and becomes a way of maintaining peace and order.[53]

The metaphor of the body politic, or, at times, the idea of the three estates or orders of society, was used by both theologians and secular writers to explain the necessity of the common weal or common good. The body politic was also used to explain the need for the division of society into social ranks, with these ranks being represented by the parts of the body. The needs of each part were subordinated to the good of the whole. As expounded by John of Salisbury in his *Policraticus* (completed 1159), all members, from the peasant "feet" upwards, have to function properly: "A badly arranged body politic, in which some or all of the parts seek their own good in separation from the common welfare, is impious, unnatural and ultimately miserable".[54] Weavers and other artisans are classed with the peasants, who represent the feet of the body politic, and they are "to concentrate on the public utility in all matters". In turn, they should be

[52] Aquinas, *ST*, vol. 34, 127.

[53] M.S. Kempshall, *The Common Good in Late Medieval Political Thought* (Oxford: Clarendon Press, 1999), 360.

[54] Nederman and Forhan, "Introduction to *Metalogicon* and *Policraticus*: John of Salisbury", in (eds), *Medieval Political Theory: A Reader: The Quest for the Body Politic 1100–1400*, ed. Cary J. Nederman and Kate Langdon Forhan (London and New York: Routledge, 1993), 27.

cared for because "the health of the whole republic will only be secure if the superior members devote themselves to the inferiors and if the inferiors respond likewise to the legal rights of their superiors".[55] To John of Salisbury, although the common good is distinct from the Christian goal of salvation, it is conducive to it, since the promotion of the common good is "the realization of a just society on earth".[56]

The various definitions of the just price can be linked to the ideal of the common good by virtue of its being a price that is fair to others, or which could be for the common good, rather than its benefitting only the seller. The ideal of the just price became a way for commerce to be acceptable to theologians, a way to provide goods for people and to provide a reasonable standard of living for the seller, rather than commerce being merely profit-taking. Discussion of the just price is relevant to this study because conceptions of it and how it was to be effected were also implicit in a ruler's economic obligations towards his subjects. It was certainly used as a measure by which to judge the behaviour of royal purveyors. Medieval theologians may have taken their cue from the canonist Gratian, who quotes Pope Julius: "For he who buys for less and then sells for more, shameful profits will follow".[57] But how were shameful profits to be detected? The various works comprising the *Corpus iuris canonici* did not provide an indication and the task of formulating a just price was taken on by theologians. Theologians had differing conceptions of the just price but they all fell within the same framework, which was the virtue of justice. According to Peter the Chanter, William of Auxerre (d. 1231) and the canonist Hostiensis (d. 1271), a good or wise man could determine the just price.[58] This tradition that the just price could be determined by a third party was continued by Henry of Hesse (mid-fourteenth century) and San Bernadino of Siena (1380–1444), who both endorsed price-fixing by public authorities as the just price since this was

[55] John of Salisbury, *Policraticus*, Book 6, Chap. 20, *Medieval Political Theory*, 43.

[56] Cary J. Nederman, "Editor's Introduction", to *John of Salisbury's Policraticus* (Cambridge: CUP, 1990), xxiii.

[57] Decreti Secunda Pars Causa XIV, Questio IV, Gratianus, c. IX, in *Corpus Iuris Canonici* (*1*), 737.

[58] Baldwin, "Medieval Theories of the Just Price", 49, 71.

done for the public rather than the individual good.[59] These definitions of the just price belong to the virtue of justice since they assume that the good or wise man or the public authorities will always act for the common good.

The Aristotelian definition of the just price was adopted by Aquinas. For justice was an exercise of moral virtue, that moral virtue being a life of moderation or the mean state. Therefore, Aristotle's conception of the just price was a balance of the needs of the seller and the needs of the buyer.[60] Aristotle used, as an example illustrating the idea of justice as the balance of needs, the exchange of a house for shoes, where money is used as a measure of their relative value.[61] Aquinas's definition of the just price reflected Aristotle's; that is, the just price is reached when an exchange is to the advantage of the buyer as well as the seller. Thus, the seller suffers no loss by no longer possessing the thing and the buyer might pay more than it is worth because of his or her need for it.[62] The principle presumes that a thing has an intrinsic worth but Aquinas left it open as to what this was, saying "we have to make the best estimate we can, with the result that giving or taking a little here or there does not upset the balance of justice".[63] Aquinas's second definition of the just price was that of reasonable costs, which could also be related to Aristotle's notion that obtaining goods for a household was "natural" wealth-getting.[64] Thus, Aquinas allowed the seller to include the costs of providing for his household or family in the selling price. He could also include the costs of producing the good concerned, such as labour and transport, and should include an amount to give to the poor in the selling price. It was not right for the seller to make profits for their own sake. These profits were allowed for a merchant who "conducts his business for the public good in order to ensure that the country does not run short of essential supplies".[65] Thus, for Aquinas, the just price allowed sellers to defray costs and make some

---

[59] Wood, *MET*, 143; de Roover, "The Concept of the Just Price Theory and Economic Policy", *Journal of Economic History* 18 (1958): 423.

[60] Aristotle, *The Nicomachean Ethics*, Book II, 35–36; Book V, 101–104 and 111–114.

[61] Aristotle, *The Nicomachean Ethics*, Book V, 112.

[62] Aquinas, *ST*, vol. 38, 215.

[63] Aquinas, *ST*, vol. 38, 217.

[64] Wood, *MET*, 72.

[65] Aquinas, *ST*, vol. 38, 229.

profits provided that those profits were within moderation and included a consideration for the poor.

Thus far, there were three different ways of determining whether prices were just: the judgement of a good or wise man or a public authority; a balance of the needs of the buyer and seller; and whether profits were reasonable. There evolved a fourth concept, which was that the just price or right value of a thing is the common estimate. The theologians Peter of La Palu (1275–1342), Peter Olivi (1248–98) and John Buridan (1295–1358) all held that prices can be increased because of a common need, though not because of the need of one individual.[66] Henry of Ghent (*c.* 1217–1293) suggested that the common estimate might be the result of haggling or bargaining between the buyer and the seller but, according to Odd Langholm, this was "unusual" and "a different interpretation won through", which was that the just price or right value was the selling price in the common or public market.[67] This theory could well have been a validation of existing practice, as theologians such as Albertus Magnus observed the growth of towns and markets and how trade was being governed.[68] Albertus Magnus defined the just price as "that at which the good sold can be valued according to the estimation of the market at that time". However, this is John of Freiburg's quotation of Albertus Magnus in his *Summa confessorum.*[69] Indeed, John of Freiburg amended it to the price being not the market price at the time of sale but the common or usual market price.[70] Yet this definition that the just price was the customary or public market price was linked to the notion that the price fixed by public authority was the just price. The price of the common market was also related to the notion in justice of a fair and open exchange. Officials believed that this could take place only in the

[66] Langholm, "The Medieval Schoolmen", 467.

[67] Langholm, "The Medieval Schoolmen", 468.

[68] Joel Kaye, *Economy and Nature in the Fourteenth Century: Money, Market Exchange and the Emergence of Scientific Thought* (Cambridge: CUP, 1998), 62–63.

[69] Odd Langholm, *The Merchant in the Confessional: Trade and Price in the Pre-Reformation Penitential Handbooks* (Leiden: Brill, 2003), 52.

[70] Langholm, *The Merchant in the Confessional*, 57.

official marketplace, not elsewhere, as evidenced by numerous local ordinances forbidding secret buying and selling.[71]

Hitherto, all of the discussion has concerned just prices and how they might have been applied in the marketplace of a town, yet the economy of late medieval England was mostly rural. Could the same ideals of a fair exchange or a just price be applied to land rents or the performance of services? Or could they be applied to taxes and tolls? In his *Summa de sacramentis*, Peter the Chanter relied on both John the Baptist's commandment to tax collectors that they should ask "for no more than that which is appointed to you", and the Roman law that unreasonable customs should not be permitted, to argue that knights in the confessional should be asked to abandon tallage unless the circumstances were dire. He also argued that tallage could be imposed by lords in order to raise money from the wealthy to help the poor.[72] The early thirteenth-century English theologians, Robert of Flamborough and Robert of Courson, were influenced by Peter the Chanter. Courson studied at the University of Paris and compiled his *Summa*, a work emphasising penance, in *circa* 1208. Robert of Flamborough was in Paris as a canon and confessor at the Abbey of St Victor and wrote his *Liber poenitentialis* between 1208 and 1213. They were likewise critical of the practice of tallage, arguing that demands for this tax by lords needed to be justified. Tallage was a source of revenue for a lord both from peasants on his estates and from burghers in towns which were part of his domain. It was not right for a lord to demand such payments in order to enrich himself beyond what was necessary or appropriate for his status, but they could be justified, say, for the cost of town fortifications.[73] Similarly, tolls for the use of bridges, roads or rivers should be charged only if the lord was providing actual protection for merchants from attack by brigands or thieves.[74] Robert of Courson proposed that fixed rents (at reasonable rates) be imposed on towns rather than the more arbitrary tallage, and if lords had no other source of income than tallage, then they should use the revenue to build

[71] For examples of such regulations, see Davis, *MMM*.

[72] Baldwin, *Masters, Princes and Merchants: The Social View of Peter the Chanter and His Circle*, vol. 1 (Princeton: Princeton University Press, 1970) 236, 237.

[73] Baldwin, *Masters, Princes and Merchants*, vol. 1, 239.

[74] Baldwin, *Masters, Princes and Merchants*, vol. 1, 240.

houses for the poor or spend it on public infrastructure.[75] No doubt it was ignored, but canon 22 of the Second Lateran Council of 1179 forbade the creation of new tolls, their renewal or increase unless the lord had royal authority.[76]

Aquinas argued that a ruler should not take more from his subjects than was needed for defence in time of war, or for some purpose that was for the common good, or to maintain his status. Rulers had been given lands to make it possible for them to support themselves, and therefore any additional burdens imposed on subjects should only be in an emergency. Nothing should be taken for the ruler's own pleasure or for spending on immoderate living.[77] Although this argument was in relation to taxation, it can also be applied to the morally problematic area of purveying, where both kings and lords purchased or took on credit food, livestock and various goods from their subjects. Peter the Chanter had noticed that princes tended to employ an official estimator who determined what prices should be paid to acquire goods for their households. He argued that the estimator was committing theft if he paid less than the market price.[78] Purveying became a very controversial issue in late medieval England, where it became apparent that estimators not only did not pay the just price but often did not pay at all. The cause of those who had suffered such losses was taken up by the theologian and canonist William of Pagula, who pleaded with Edward III to do justice, and by the House of Commons on several occasions after that. Purveying was also discussed in the early fifteenth-century moral treatise *Dives and Pauper*. William of Pagula's epistle and *Dives and Pauper* will be discussed in the next chapter and the records from the Parliament rolls in Chapter 5.

Such behaviour of lords or princes seems to be against notions of both the common good and justice, yet medieval society was hierarchical, not egalitarian. Rule by princes or lords was regarded as a necessity. Augustine's argument in the *City of God*—that government was a

75 Baldwin, *Masters, Princes and Merchants*, vol. 1, 239–240.

76 J. Gilchrist, *The Church and Economic Activity in the Middle Ages* (London: Macmillan, 1969), 17–72.

77 Elizabeth R. Brown, "Taxation and Morality in the Thirteenth and Fourteenth Centuries: Conscience and Political Power and the Kings of France", *French Historical Studies* 8 (1973), 5.

78 Baldwin, *Masters, Princes and Merchants*, vol. 1, 241.

necessary evil, a consequence of the Fall and humankind's sinful nature—continued to be influential in the late Middle Ages.[79] According to John Rist, Augustine's writings "set the Western theological tone for more than a thousand years".[80] Aristotle argued in the *Politics* that it is necessary to live in society: one person cannot provide for all of his or her requirements by themselves.[81] This argument was used by medieval theologians and philosophers to justify a governing order or hierarchy. Aquinas believed that "the body of a human being or any other animal would disintegrate unless there was some general regulating force within the body which would extend to the common good of all the members".[82] Thus, the common good was best served by some kind of governing order.

Giles of Rome (*c.* 1247–1316), at one time the Archbishop of Bourges, composed his *De regimine principum* for Philip III of France between 1277 and 1280. This work must have been highly influential as over 350 manuscript copies survive, as do a number of early printed editions.[83] He also accepted a governing hierarchy and inequality in wealth and status, stating that it was not expedient for a ruler to formulate laws that would establish equality amongst citizens. Possessions themselves are not the cause of malice, but cupidity, and therefore a ruler should suppress covetousness.[84] It is difficult to see how covetousness could be suppressed by legislation, but Giles's purpose was, rather, to proclaim an ideal to which a ruler should aspire and by doing so justify his position as a moral leader of society. Thomas Aquinas and Ptolemy of Lucca took the view that lordship was permitted by God to the Romans because they pursued justice and maintained social order. Giving examples from the Old

---

[79] Annabel S. Brett, "Political Philosophy", in *Cambridge Companion to Medieval Philosophy*, ed. McGrade, 278.

[80] John Rist, "Augustine of Hippo", in *The Medieval Theologians*, ed. G. R. Evans (Oxford: Blackwell, 2001), 3.

[81] Aristotle, *The Politics and the Constitution of Athens*, Book I, 14.

[82] Aquinas *On Kingship* or *De regimine principum* in *Medieval Political Theory*, 100. See also Anthony Black, *Political Thought in Europe*, 1250–1450 (Cambridge: CUP, 1992), 23; Chase, "Introduction" to Aristotle, *The Nichomachean Ethics*, viii–ix.

[83] *The Governance of Kings and Princes: John Trevisa's Middle English Translation of the "De Regimine Principum of Aeegidius Romanus"*, ed. David C. Fowler, Charles F. Briggs and Paul G. Remley (New York: Garland, 1997), xii.

[84] Aegidius Romanus, *De regimine principum*, Venice, Bernadino Guerralda, 1502, Book III, Part I, Chap. xviii.

Testament, they maintained that tyrants were given lordship by God as punishment for evildoings by their subjects.[85] A good lord or king, however, was expected to rule for the common good of his people, not for his own profit.[86]

Medieval theologians and canonists relied on biblical and patristic authorities, along with classical philosophers such as Aristotle, Plato and Cicero to support their arguments. Writers of the high medieval period were concerned with economic ethics as they applied to society as a whole, rural as well as urban, even if commercial situations and issues such as usury and the just price do seem to dominate. Indeed, they follow those authorities' pronouncements on economic ethics and applied them to a particular view of society in which all are mutually dependent and striving for harmony.

Theologians and Moral Philosophers in Late Medieval England

The thought of English philosophers and theologians concerning practical economic ethics to a large extent mirrored that of their counterparts in mainland Europe, but there are some who made criticisms of lordship and exploitation by landowners which justifies their consideration here. There were extensive connections between English thought and the thought of Latin Christendom. Oxford theologians taught at universities in Europe, notably Paris and Cologne. Examples include Robert of Courson towards the end of the twelfth century, later John Duns Scotus and Walter Burley and several others in the fourteenth century, while scholars from mainland Europe studied at Oxford.[87] Furthermore, copies

[85] *On the Government of Rulers: De Regimine Principum* [*by*] *Ptolemy of Lucca with portions attributed to Thomas Aquinas*, trans. James M. Blythe (Philadelphia: University of Pennsylvania Press, 1997) 160–163. Ptolemy of Lucca completed the work in 1301–1302, but the parts attributed to Aquinas date from the 1260s to 1270s. See Blythe's introduction, 1–2.

[86] *On the Government of Rulers*, 63–65.

[87] J.I. Catto, "Theology and Theologians 1220–1320", in *The Early Oxford Schools*, ed. J.I. Catto and Ralph Evans (Oxford: Clarendon Press, 1984), 471; J.I. Catto, "Wycliff and Wycliffism at Oxford 1356–1430", in *Late Medieval Oxford*, ed. J.I. Catto and Ralph Evans (Oxford: Clarendon Press, 1992), 177; T.H. Ashton , "Oxford's Medieval Alumni", *Past & Present* 74 (1977): 21;

of works by English theologians and philosophers were made, and some eventually printed, in continental Europe. Another common connection between mainland European and English thought is the key influence of Aristotle. Indeed, the first full translation into Latin of Aristotle's *Nicomachean Ethics* was made by an Englishman, Robert Grosseteste, Bishop of Lincoln (d. 1253), and a large number of commentaries by both mainland European and English theologians and philosophers subsequently appeared. Relatively few by English authors survive, for many were lost after the dissolution of the monasteries. Many works on Aristotle's ethics, but without detail as to their content, were recorded by John Bale in his *Illustrium majoris Britanniae scriptorum* in 1548. Of the surviving commentaries on the *Nicomachean Ethics*, only one, by Walter Burley, covers Book V on justice.[88] Book V is the most relevant to practical economic ethics since it has the exchange of goods as an example of justice and a discussion of fair or equivalent value. Among fourteenth-century English writers considered here, John Duns Scotus and William of Ockham were both influenced by Aristotle, even though they did not always make specific reference to him, and Robert Holcot and Walter Burley commented on Aristotle's theories of justice and fair exchange. John Wyclif, however, did not rely on Aristotle but on other sources.

Robert of Courson and Robert of Flamborough, both students of Peter the Chanter, were dealing with matters of economic ethics in the early thirteenth century. Peter the Chanter's *Verbum abbreviatum* is subtitled *opus morale* and was offered as useful for all theologians, priests, confessors, preachers, lawyers and whatever kinds of men. Its chapters include such topics as accepting bribes from a party in a legal dispute, giving money to those deemed to be in morally dubious occupations, warnings about greedy lawyers and usurers, expenditure on sumptuous food, clothes and fine buildings.[89] This interest in practical economic

---

Damian Riehl Leader , "Philosophy at Oxford and Cambridge in the Fifteenth Century", *History of Universities* 4 (1984–1985): 35.

[88] Charles Lohr, "Medieval Latin Aristotle Commentaries", *Traditio* 23 (1967), 313–413; 24 (1968): 149–245; 26 (1970) 135–216; 27 (1971) 251–351; 19 (1973): 93–197; 30 (1974): 119–144.

[89] Chapters 23, 49, 50, 51, 82 and 84 in Petrus Cantor [Peter the Chanter], *Verbum abbreviatum*, ed. J.P. Migne, *Patrologia Latina*, vol. 205.

ethics (Peter the Chanter was a preacher as well as a theologian) probably inspired his student Robert of Courson's own *Summa*, which has chapters on these same topics.[90] Thomas of Chobham, another student of Peter the Chanter, followed by producing two popular handbooks for the clergy rather than repeating the Chanter's ideas in an academic work. Chobham's *Summa confessorum* (*c.* 1216) and the *Summa de arte praedicandi* (c. 1227–1228) were still in use in the late medieval period. The *Summa confessorum* was very popular and still being printed in the fifteenth century. Robert of Flamborough's *Liber poenitentialis*, on the other hand, seems to have been superseded by later works. Although it set out several questions relating to economic ethics, its inclusion of papal decretals and commentary might have led to very few copies being made after the thirteenth century.[91]

The majority of works of English theologians and philosophers dealing with practical economic ethics were written in the fourteenth century. Works by Richard Kilvington and John Dedecus attend to ethical theory rather than practical economic ethics.[92] The Franciscan John Duns Scotus (*c.* 1265–1308) was born in Scotland but was ordained in Lincoln. He studied at Oxford and later taught at the Universities of Paris and Cologne. Duns Scotus is renowned for his writings on logic and metaphysics, and most studies of his work focus on those subjects. His pronouncements on practical economic ethics—wealth and property ownership, fair exchange, the just price, profits from buying and selling, forestalling, regrating and usury—can be found in his commentaries on the *Sentences* of Peter Lombard. Lombard's *Sentences* were the foundation of much theological education and philosophical discussion in universities, and it seems that Duns Scotus's commentary on economic ethics was based on Lombard's discussion of original sin and an extension of his

[90] Baldwin, *Masters, Princes and Merchants*, vol. 1, 23, 57, 58, 193–194, 202, 228–229, 236, 238–240, 240–41, 265–266, 269, 272–274, 301–311.

[91] *Robert of Flamborough*: *Liber poenitentialis*, ed. J.J. Francis Firth (Toronto: Pontifical Institute of Mediaeval Studies, 1971), 20–32.

[92] Elzbieta Jung and Robert Podonski, "The Transmission of English Ideas in the Fourteenth Century: The Case of Richard Kilvington", *Mediaevalia Philosophica Polonorum* 37 (2008): 60, 61; Monika Michalowska, "Kilvington's Concept of Prudence from *Questions on Ethics*", *Mediaevalia Philosophica Polonorum* 37 (2008): 86–87; J.P.H. Clark, "John Dedecus: was he a Cambridge Franciscan?", *Archivum Franciscanum Historicum* 80 (1987) 3–38.

statements about avarice.[93] Citing Augustine, Duns Scotus affirms that private ownership and the division between rich and poor are a result of the Fall. Prior to the Fall, all goods were held in common but owing to humankind's corrupt and evil nature this was no longer possible and property had to be divided. Duns Scotus goes on to state that the resulting violent acts by greedy oppressors led to the need for laws and refers to Aristotle's *Politics*.[94] Duns Scotus's pronouncements on the exchange of goods and property, lack of fraud and just pricing are very similar to those of Aquinas: exchanges of goods or property are just by being free of deception, freely entered into and where the values of the exchange are equivalent. Merchants are allowed to make profits to cover their household and living costs and the risks of transport because of their usefulness to society in supplying needed goods.[95] However, he goes further than Aquinas in stating that those who buy simply to resell, who do not transport goods, store them or improve them in any way are not entitled to such profits: they are termed *regratiers* and should be immediately banished from the community and exiled.[96] Aquinas did not explicitly condemn those who buy goods simply in order to re-sell at a profit, without having improved the goods in any way or incurred any storage or transport costs, but Duns Scotus's attitude to *regratiers* was severe. His attitude could have arisen from the passage in I Corinthians which declares "every man shall receive his own reward according to his own labour"; in other words, a living made from simply passing on goods and charging a higher price was unacceptable.[97] However, Duns Scotus's views revert to orthodoxy when he considers usury: what has been borrowed must be the amount that is returned.[98] He cites Aristotle's argument that money is unnatural, a medium of exchange only, and because it is sterile and inanimate it cannot be used as a medium of increase. Interest is permitted

---

[93] Peter Lombard, *Libri IV Sententiarum: Liber I et II*, 2nd ed., Florence, Collegii S. Bonaventurae, 1916, pp. 531–532.

[94] *Quaestiones in Quartum Librum Sententiarum, Distinctio XV, Quaestio II*, in Joannis Duns Scoti, *Opera Omnia*, vol. XVIII (Paris: Vives, 1894), 258.

[95] *Quaestiones*, 317, 321.

[96] *Quaestiones*, 318.

[97] I Corinthians 3:8.

[98] *Quaestiones*, 292.

only if the lender can prove in a court of law or swear upon his conscience that he did not ask for an additional payment, and this interest can be awarded only if the lender can prove that he suffered loss or damage as a result of making the loan; otherwise, charging interest is sinful. In support, Duns Scotus refers to a passage in the *Extravagantes*, the collection of papal canons added to the corpus of canon law after Gratian's *Decretals*.[99] Therefore, it seems that apart from his more extreme view of regraters, Duns Scotus relies on well-established authorities for his opinions concerning economic ethics: Augustine, Aristotle and papal canons.

The Franciscan William of Ockham (*c.* 1288–*c.* 1348) taught at Oxford and at some Franciscan schools. His writings concerning economic ethics are more pertinent to this study than those of Duns Scotus. Like Duns Scotus, he is renowned for his writings on logic and metaphysics. His writings on practical economic ethics did not address the morality of buying, selling and lending. Instead, he was concerned with the subject of justifiable lordship, for amongst Ockham's controversial tracts on papal power are discussions about the origins and nature of lordship in general.[100] In the third part of his *Dialogue* on the power of the Pope, he explored and agreed with Aristotle's argument in the *Politics* that a secular ruler should be more virtuous, and hence more just, than others, and if the ruler was not the best of men, whether he had concern for the common good.[101] He argued that there could be no such thing as lordship permitted by God since, before the Fall, everything was owned by God: there was no property or ownership. Private property and ownership came about after the Fall; therefore, there was no divine sanction for lordship or ownership.[102] Lordship or ownership was introduced through human law in the first instance and subsequently by the law of kings. Ockham interprets Augustine's assertion that all things belong to the just

[99] See *Quaestiones*, 293.

[100] Takashi Shogimen, *Ockham and Political Discourse in the Late Middle Ages* (Cambridge: CUP, 2007), 61–62; William of Ockham, *A Short Discourse on Tyrannical Government*, ed. Arthur Stephen McGrade (Cambridge: CUP, 1992), xvi–xxix; William of Ockham, "The Work of Ninety Days", Chaps. 26–28, in *William of Ockham: A Letter to the Friars Minor and Other Writings*, ed. Arthur Stephen McGrade and John Kilcullen (Cambridge: CUP, 1995) 34–35.

[101] "Dialogue, Part III, Tract II On the Rights of the Roman Empire", Chap. 17, in *William of Ockham: A Letter to the Friars Minor*, 158–164.

[102] William of Ockham, "The Work of Ninety Days", Chap. 26, 36–37.

to mean that the just are worthy to own things but that the unjust are not.[103] Ockham's challenge to the pope on the matter of property ownership by the Church brought him excommunication and exile.[104] His view on lordship was also controversial, and its implication about the right of ownership was taken up Wyclif.

Walter Burley (*c.* 1275–1344/45), a theologian, logician, mathematician and natural philosopher, was a fellow of Merton College and one of the group known as the Oxford or Merton Calculators. He also taught at the University of Paris. His commentary on the *Nicomachean Ethics*, *Expositio per decem libros ethicorum Aristotelis*, was written sometime between 1333 and 1345 while in the service of Richard de Bury, Bishop of Durham. Burley's discussion of commutative justice between persons or the exchange between individuals continues with Aristotle's example of free or voluntary exchange in commerce, in which the price and the goods are of equal value and there is no deception or force. To buying and selling, Burley adds lending, making a deposit or a pledge, and renting. He gives much attention to involuntary acts which he classifies as being the result of force or deception and among which he includes murder, robbery, rape, poisoning and taking away someone else's servant. Economic crimes such as usury, forestalling, deceptive selling, extortion or oppression are not considered.[105] Some of Burley's examples—such as renting and making a pledge for a loan—extend economic ethics a little further from urban trade because they were clearly relevant to owners of estates, but they are simply part of a list without practical examples or a discussion.

The Dominican Robert Holcot (*c.* 1290–1349) was a theologian and philosopher and another who was in the service of Richard de Bury. Aside from writing a number of theoretical works on the nature of God and commentaries on the *Sentences* of Peter Lombard, he was the author of two commentaries on morality, *Heptalogus* and *Moralitates*, both of which belong to the category of advice literature rather than academic philosophy or theology. These works consist largely of quotations from

---

[103] William of Ockham, "The Work of Ninety Days", Chap. 88, 71–72.

[104] William J. Courtenay, "William of Ockham", *ODNB* (accessed 24 February 2015).

[105] Burley, *Expositiones, super decem libros Ethicorum Aristotelis* (Venice: 1521), fol. 87v.

biblical and patristic sources and appear to have been aimed at a lay readership. Evidently, these works were popular for there are printed editions dating from the late fifteenth and early sixteenth centuries. *Heptalogus* quotes Augustine's definition of avarice as an inordinate desire both to acquire money or other things and to retain them; it is a destructive vice stemming from the desire of Adam and Eve to know good and evil.[106] Holcot cites Augustine on God's intention that the rich and the poor be part of the same body, so the rich must form the means by which the gifts of God are transmitted to the poor. In this way, the inequities of wealth distribution are addressed, but these are not the terms used by Holcot. Instead, the body metaphor is taken very literally as a digestive system, where a blockage can cause an abscess, avarice being a spiritual version of this abscess.[107] *Moralitates* is another collection of quotations from well-established authorities, but again there is the notion that the rich have an obligation: wealth is justified only if it is distributed to the poor.

Holcot's *Super libros sapientie* is a commentary on the *Book of Wisdom*, a work believed to have been written by King Solomon as advice to rulers, which was accepted as canonical by the Catholic Church but considered apocryphal by the Protestant Churches. Holcot, however, had contemporary monarchs in mind, for in Lectio LXXIV he describes the oaths made at the coronation of the King of England, one of which is to restrain greed and injustice.[108] Justice is dealt with more than once and considered from two different points of view: the first lecture is from that of Christian doctrine and the second from Aristotelian ethics. For example, Lectio XXIV begins with the statement that justice leads to immortality but that injustice brings death, and in support, Holcot brings in the doctrine of original sin (injustice originated with Adam), the practice of the cardinal virtues and many quotations from Augustine.[109] Lectio CIX is a discussion of Aristotle's distinction between commutative and distributive justice and the practice of justice both as a virtue and for the good of

---

[106] Robert Holcot, *Heptalogus* (Paris: Regnault Chaudiere, 1517), sig. B.iii^{v}.

[107] Holcot, *Heptalogus*, sig. B.iv^{r}.

[108] Hester Goodenough Gelber, "Blackfriars London: The Late Medieval *Studium*", in *Philosophy and Theology in the Studia of the Religious Orders and at the Papal and Royal Courts*, ed. Emery Kent, William J. Courtenay and Stephen M. Metzger (Turnhout: Brepols, 2012) 177.

[109] Robert Holcot, *Super libros sapientie* (Reutling, 1489), Lectio XXIV [no pagination].

the community. Holcot concludes that legal justice is for the benefit of the community and a useful weapon against avarice, and this shows that he believed that secular legislation had a role in the suppression of vice and economic injustice.[110]

The Oxford theologian John Wyclif (*c.* 1329–1384), best known for his denial of transubstantiation and his radical view that the Church should revert to the poverty and humility of its beginnings, is orthodox on the matter of the Ten Commandments and the seven deadly sins. Avarice, the fifth of the seven deadly sins, means worshipping worldly goods above worshipping God and so the avaricious person is no better than an idolator or pagan.[111] However, his tract in English on the Commandment against theft does have oppression of tenants by lords as well as unfair trading and usury as examples. Wyclif's position, echoing Augustine and William of Ockham, is that those who do not serve God have no right to own goods or property:

> So eche man in his degree is boundoun to serve God. And yif he wante this service, he is no lord of goodis bi no trewe title. For he that stondith in grace is verrey lord of thingis; and whoever failith by defaute of grace, he failith reght title of thing that he occupieth, and unableth himsilf to have the goodis of God.[112]

Wyclif again displays conventional views about economic ethics in Chap. XXVI of his *Tractatus de Mandatis Divinis* and again criticises lords: those who oppress their tenants are just as guilty of theft as when they levy excessive taxes on the poor and impose fines without mercy.[113]

Wyclif set down his ideal of good lordship in *Of seruantis & lordis hou eche schal kepe his degree*, a tract composed in the aftermath of the Peasants' Revolt of 1381. Wrongs were done by both lords and peasants

---

[110] Holcot, *Super libros sapientie*, Lectio CIX [no pagination].

[111] John Wyclif, "On the Seven Deadly Sins", in *Select English Works of John Wyclif*, vol. 3, ed. Thomas Arnold (Oxford: Clarendon Press, 1871), 149.

[112] John Wyclif, "VII Mandatum", in *Select English Works*, vol. 3, 88.

[113] Wyclif, *Tractatus de Mandatis Divinis*, ed. Johann Loserth and F.D. Matthew (London: C.K. Paul for the Wyclif Society, 1922, repr. New York, Johnson, 1966), 369–370. See also Wyclif's sermon on the Seventh Commandment, in *Select English Works*, vol. 3, 88.

and to correct such ills, peasants should obey their lords but lords should follow this prescription. They

> schulden knowe goddis lawe & studie it & meyntene it, & distroie wrong & meyntene pore men in here right to lyue in reste, pees & charite, & suffre no men vunder colour of hem to do extorcions, bete men, & holde pore men out of right bi strength of lordschipis.[114]

Lords should exemplify virtuous living to their servants and tenants and punish any wickedness. More importance should be given to sins against God than to "falsnesse of dispit don ayenst nere owene person or worldly profit". Similarly, such people should be loved and rewarded for their "holy lif and truethe" rather than some personal advantage or profit the lord happened to gain from their good behaviour. Oppression and extortion by the lord's stewards and other officials should not be tolerated.[115] For Wyclif, original lordship was that held by Adam before the Fall; civil lordship and ownership of property came about because of original sin, and it can only be maintained by force.[116] Wyclif argued that civil lordship had to proceed from righteousness or it could not be with God's approval, an idea taken from Augustine and used by William of Ockham. However, Wyclif was a great deal more radical than Ockham in saying that the sinful were unworthy of civil lordship, because he added that lordship could be taken away from them.[117] The true basis for lordship was justice: "true civil lordship presupposes the disposition of the virtue of justice in such a lord" which is over and above any law of inheritance or purchase.[118]

Justice was also the basis for the ownership of goods. In support of this idea, Wyclif quotes from the Bible ("Seek first God's Kingdom and

---

[114] John Wyclif, *Of seruauntis & lordis hou eche schal kepe his degree*, in *The English Works of Wyclif*, ed. F.D. Matthew (London: Kegan Paul, Trench, Trubner & Co. for EETS, rev. 1902), 230.

[115] Wyclif, *Of seruauntis & lordis*, 238–239.

[116] Introduction to "John Wyclif on Civil Lordship (Selections)", in *The Cambridge Translations of Medieval Philosophical Texts: Vol. 2: Ethics and Political Philosophy*, ed. Arthur Stephen McGrade, John Kilcullen and Matthew Kempshall (Cambridge: CUP, 2001), 589.

[117] Introduction to "John Wyclif on Civil Lordship", 590; William of Ockham, *A Short Discourse*, 96.

[118] "John Wyclif on Civil Lordship", 595, 596.

his justice, and all these things will be added to you") and from Jerome ("The whole world of riches belongs to the believer").[119] In his tract in English on the seven deadly sins, Wyclif regarded the carrying out of justice as essential, strongly urging lords to know God's law better than their subjects do:

> And for thei schulden passé comynes in knowyng of Gods lawe, thei schulden teche comynes to holde rightwisenes. And this is tho cause why God approves this state, and gives hom worldly worschip with powere and rentis; and if thei leven this office, thei forfeten ageyns God, and serven Gods enmye, and ben Gods traytoures. And so to hor servauntis schulden thei have charite, ne punische hom in no wey, ne take of hom no servise bot of way of charite and profite to hor soule. And as God lufs more mon then mon schulde luf God, so lords of hor godenesse schulden luf more hor servauntis then hor tenauntis loven hom, for this is Gods lawe. And for luf dos mony thinges, for hit is not ydel, then lords schulden helpe hor tenauntis, and defende hom in right.[120]

Justice is required for social harmony, but showing justice and benevolence towards tenants and servants is also obeying God's will. The reason God gave landowners their powers and rents is so that they could fulfil it.

The English thought surveyed up to this point is conventional on matters of practical economic ethics; the exceptions are commentaries by Ockham and Wyclif on the behaviour of lords and their rights to own land. The late fourteenth century seems to have been rather less productive in terms of major or original thought about economic ethics. Ideas tended to be repeated, an example being John Eyton of Repingdon's *Tractatus de usura*.[121]

In regard to two subjects pertaining to economic ethics, justice and lordship, there is greater divergence amongst English theologians and philosophers. Justice was handled in different ways by Wyclif, Holcot and Burley. Wyclif saw justice as God's law, and to carry it out was to do His will. Burley's exposition of it was strictly within Aristotle's view of it in Book

[119] "John Wyclif on Civil Lordship", 628 (Matthew 6:33); 629 (Jerome's Letter to Paulinus).
[120] Wyclif, "On the Seven Deadly Sins", 146.
[121] John Eyton, *Tractatus de usura*, in Oxford, Merton College, MS 112, folios 60r–65r.

V of the *Nicomachean Ethics*, whereas Holcot considered justice from the point of view both of obeying God's law and of justice being for the common good. Neither justice nor the common good was controversial, but criticisms of lordship, amongst other of their ideas, brought both Ockham and Wyclif into conflict with the Church. Ockham was called to the papal court in Avignon to defend his teachings on several topics and then obliged to flee, and Wyclif was declared a heretic after his death. Followers of Wyclif were purged from Oxford and thereafter there was great emphasis on preserving orthodoxy. New fellowships in theology were created at Cambridge with the same objective of preventing heresy.[122] However, it is remarkable that although the influential Peter the Chanter criticised abuses of purveying, no English philosopher or theologian of the fourteenth century did so. This was left to William of Pagula, John Bromyard and Thomas Docking, whose works are discussed in the next chapter. Criticism is also found in *The Book of Vices and Virtues*, the English translation of Laurent d'Orleans's *Somme le Roi*, which will also be discussed in Chapter 3.

Moral philosophy seems to have gone into a decline in England in the fifteenth century. Although moral philosophy was taught and debated at both Oxford and Cambridge, comparatively little was actually written.[123] The historian William Courtenay has discussed the lack of any philosophers or theologians of any standing after 1350, apart from Wyclif, and the apparent decline of philosophy and theology in England until the introduction of humanism into the universities in the sixteenth century. His research has indicated that although logicians and theologians were still active in the late fourteenth century much of their surviving work was introductory material for students or was focused on much narrower topics such as the meaning of particular terms or the truth of particular propositions. The reason for this situation could have been the isolation of England from the interchange of intellectual ideas with the rest of Europe, more particularly France, owing to the Hundred Years' War. This is discounted by Courtenay but he acknowledges that the repeated visitations of the Black Death after 1349 could have had an impact on

[122] Alan B. Cobban, "Theology and Law in the Medieval Colleges of Oxford and Cambridge", *Bulletin of the John Rylands Library* 65 (1982): 72–77.

[123] Leader, "Philosophy at Oxford and Cambridge": 33.

the sheer numbers of masters and students in England and hence the volume and quality of work produced. Courtenay says another factor could have been the growing importance of law which overtook theology as a subject for higher study at Oxford and Cambridge.[124] Perhaps this was the most likely reason, for while the study of natural and moral philosophy and metaphysics, as preparation for the study of theology, all declined in England, they continued to flourish in France, Germany and Italy. However, moral philosophy was taught outside the main universities of Oxford and Cambridge at the *studia* of the Franciscans and Dominicans, and also in monasteries, and it seems likely that such knowledge informed the sermons and pastoral handbooks produced in the fourteenth and fifteenth centuries.[125] It is possible, also, that after Wyclif, theologians avoided controversy and speculation; for example, Thomas Gascoigne, for a while chancellor of Oxford University, focused his attention on preaching and prepared a compendium for preachers variously titled *Dictionarium theologicum* or *Liber veritatem*.[126]

Conclusions

Neither medieval nor classical thinkers had our modern notion of an economic sphere, instead regarding economic activity as an area where human beings carried out monetary transactions or traded goods or services, and those humans were vulnerable to the temptations of the devil or to immoral or ignoble desires. Thus, economic activity needed guidance by the Church and from moral principles to ensure that individuals made the correct choices, much as they would be guided in the matter of marriage or of bringing up their children. Therefore, "economics" was part of moral philosophy and theology and, for the present day, the term "economic ethics" is more appropriate than "economics". The term "eco-

[124] William J. Courtenay, *Schools and Scholars in Fourteenth-Century England* (Princeton: Princeton University Press, 1987), 327–328, 336, 346–347, 358, 366–368; Cobban, "Theology and Law", 57–77.

[125] Leader, "Philosophy at Oxford and Cambridge", 37–39; Gelber, "Blackfriars in London", 165–180.

[126] Christina van Nolcken, "Gascoigne [Gascoygne], Thomas (1404–1458)", *ODNB* (accessed November 2012).

nomics" might not have been used until after *Oeconomica*, a work attributed to Aristotle, was anonymously translated into Latin at the end of the thirteenth century and again by Leonardi Bruni in *c.* 1429.[127] Bartolomé Clavero, a Spanish historian and anthropologist, has used the term "economy of charity", which is a useful shorthand for the moral obligation of those with superfluous wealth to give to the poor and, in so doing, both practise charity and make restitution of their excess.[128]

From the point of view of both medieval theologians and classical philosophers, money-making for its own sake is the motivator of unjust pricing and usury. In medieval times, the gaining of excess profits was seen to be at the expense of others' needs. In other words, the individual good overrides the common good. The terms "common good", "common profit" or "common weal" can be linked to justice since justice was acting for the good of many rather than for the good of one. Balance and justice can be recovered by the offender restoring what was taken unjustly, but ideally offences such as deceitful trade, unfair pricing or usury should be avoided by taking heed of moral instruction. Theologians warned that offenders broke the Commandment against theft and displeased God or were guilty of the sin of avarice and in danger of eternal damnation.

The ideal that those who had excess wealth should give it to the poor, thereby avoiding damnation, was also a way of ensuring that everyone should have enough to meet their needs, a balancing out via an "economy of charity" so that social order and stability were maintained. It is evident that medieval theologians did not share the modern belief in endless economic growth; instead, they experienced shortages of staple foods through poor harvests or animal diseases, lacking the technology to overcome such hazards. There were periods of relative prosperity, but interruptions due to wars, plagues or natural disasters would have made it difficult for medieval theologians and philosophers to conceive of a continuing upward trajectory of economic growth. Wealth had its limits and therefore excess wealth could be acquired only at the expense of others.

---

[127] Bernard G. Dod, "Arisoteles latinus", in *The Cambridge History of Later Medieval Philosophy*, ed. Norman Kretzmann, Anthony Kenny and Jan. Pinborg (Cambridge: CUP, 1982), 64; Wood, *MET*, 52.

[128] Jacques Le Goff, *Money and the Middle Ages: An Essay in Historical Anthroplogy* (Cambridge: Polity, 2012), 147.

However, needs were hierarchical; those in the higher social ranks had greater economic needs than those at the lower end of society. The body politic model and the argument that leaders needed more resources to defend society against its enemies were used to justify inequality and economic imbalance. Another argument, which we have seen put forward by Duns Scotus, was that division of ownership was necessary because of the Fall and humankind's corrupt nature and it could be implied that economic inequality or injustice is a consequence of this. Yet there were expectations that kings, lords and landowners should abide by the virtue of justice, for although warnings about unjust pricing, deceitful trade and usury might have been aimed largely at merchants, some theologians saw unfair taxes and tolls as further instances of theft or avarice and equally worthy of condemnation.

Some theologians' and philosophers' comments on practical economic ethics were limited to fair exchange in buying and selling and to usury, probably because these topics were the ones discussed by Aristotle. The work of Duns Scotus and Walter Burley falls into this group. William of Ockham and John Wyclif went beyond this limitation in their criticisms of the basis of lordship. Peter the Chanter had a much broader coverage than most; indeed, his works on practical economic ethics are closer to a priest's manual than an academic treatise, as we shall see more clearly in the next chapter.

Evidently, theologians and philosophers considered economic ethics to be of great importance: it mattered how individuals behaved and they should be reminded that avarice was a mortal sin and that acts of charity and almsgiving, and living according to the virtues, should be the goals of a just society. Furthermore, they had a wider perspective of economic activity than the marketplace. The ethical concepts discussed in this chapter were shared by many theologians and philosophers, but it is not the case that they were peculiar to academic discourse while other sections of society remained ignorant. The next chapter will be concerned with how lay society in late medieval England was made aware of them.

3

The Translation of Economic Ethics into the Daily Practices of the Laity

The last chapter showed that many theologians and philosophers understood that there was more to economic ethics than offences by merchants and usurers. However, the question remains as to how their understandings might have been conveyed to the rest of society. Here, the clergy had an important role as pastors of their flocks, preachers and confessors. This chapter examines a variety of texts, some of which were compiled or translated into Middle English and some of which remained in Latin and were in circulation in late medieval England. The examination comprises extracts from some religious tracts and the relevant parts of most surviving pastoral manuals, whether for confessors or preachers or for the laity to read for themselves. It also includes sermons, guides for the conduct of rulers or of others in positions of authority, and popular books of wisdom. The large number of surviving copies of some manuals indicates substantial usage by both clergy and laity, and some sermons and books of wisdom were printed, indicating a high level of demand from lay readers. Although some pastoral manuals were written earlier (for example, Robert of Flamborough's *Liber poenitentialis*, which was written between 1208 and 1213, had a chapter on each vice with questions for the priest to ask

J. Hole, *Economic Ethics in Late Medieval England, 1300–1500*,
Archival Insights into the Evolution of Economics,
DOI 10.1007/978-3-319-38860-1_3

penitents), the main impetus for the writing of pastoral manuals came from the decrees of the Fourth Lateran Council of 1215, which put much emphasis on the care of the soul. One of its stated objectives was to stamp out vices and foster virtues amongst the laity. Annual confession was instituted and so more emphasis was placed on the education of parish priests who were to instruct their parishioners, prior to confession, in Church doctrine. To enable this, manuals appeared with material for preaching sermons and for moral and religious instruction, along with treatises on the Commandments and the virtues and vices. Many were written in the vernacular for the laity or for the less well-educated clergy. In 1281, the Constitutions of John Pecham or Peckham, Archbishop of Canterbury, ordered that such instruction be increased to four times a year.

For the benefit of their readers, most manuals were furnished with a good number of quotations from biblical and patristic sources. Later manuals—that is, those compiled in the fourteenth and fifteenth centuries—added references to Aristotle's thought. The ideas of Albertus Magnus and Thomas Aquinas about economic ethics, both of which were heavily influenced by Aristotle, took time to appear in English confessional handbooks and pastoral manuals. In the fourteenth century, although there are difficulties in precisely identifying sources, the authors of such works still tended to quote from older authorities: *Speculum Christiani*, for example, which was written in the second half of the fourteenth century, quoted from Robert Grossteste's sermons. By the early fifteenth century, Aquinas's ideas are very apparent in *Dives and Pauper* but these were transmitted via quotations from John of Freiburg's *Summa Confessorum*, into which Freiburg copied and adapted parts of Aquinas's *Summa Theologiae*.

It is significant for this enquiry into the nature of economic ethics that many confessional manuals described the sin of avarice and its countervailing virtues. It is also relevant that many pastoral manuals described the particular kinds of avarice which those in particular occupations might be prey to, ranging from society's rulers to merchants and servants, and that some had questions for the priest to ask their penitents which related to their status or occupation. Handbooks written for a lay readership showed the Church's objective of intensifying awareness of economic ethics, for without the presence and exhortation of a priest, readers were urged to examine their consciences about a range of business transactions.

There is direct evidence that pastoral manuals were written for those in the laity who could not understand Latin. Towards the end of *The Pricke of Conscience*, the author explains that he has drawn his material from certain books unknown to those who understand only English and that he chose its title because he wanted his readers' consciences to become "tendre" and prompt them to meekness and the fear of God.[1] The prologue of *Cursor Mundi* tells the reader that the book has been translated into English for the common folk of England to understand it better.[2] Robert Mannyng of Brunne's *Handlyng Synne* was written for "lewde men" and in verse for the better instruction of those who would listen rather than read.[3] *A Myrour to Lewde Men and Wymmin* has many Latin quotations but the author states that his purpose is to show not very well-educated and "middling" men and women whether they are on the path to hell or the path to heaven and to know the difference between vice and virtue.[4]

Pastoral manuals written for the laity, guides to conduct and books of wisdom served to remind the more literate members of society about practical economic ethics, whereas manuals for the priesthood and sermons were ways of passing on those teachings to the unlettered as well as the lettered in late medieval England. Education of the masses was important to the Church, as evidenced in the statutes drawn up by the Bishop of Salisbury (*circa* 1217–1219, a few years after the Fourth Lateran Council of 1215), which stress the importance of religious instruction in "domestico ydiomate" and Archbishop Peckham's later instruction that sermons also be delivered in the vernacular.[5] A good number of sermons addressed

[1] *The Pricke of Conscience: A Northumbrian Poem*, ed. Richard Morris (Berlin: A. Ascher for the Philological Society, 1863), 257.

[2] *Cursor Mundi*, ed. R. Morris, vol. 3 (London: Kegan Paul, Trench, Trubner & Co for the EETS, 1893), 1660, Appendix III.

[3] *Robert of Brunne's 'Handlyng Synne', A.D. 1303*, ed. F.J. Furnivall (London: Kegan Paul, Trench, Trubner & Co. for EETS, 1901), 2–3.

[4] *A Myrour to Lewde Men and Wymmin: A Prose Version of the Speculum Vitae ed. from B.L. MS Harley 45*, ed. Venetia Nelson (Heidelberg: Carl Winter Universitatsverlag, 1981), 71.

[5] *Councils and Synods with Other Documents Relating to the English Church, Vol. II*, ed. F.M. Powicke and C.R. Cheney (Oxford: Clarendon Press, 1964), Part 1, 61 and Part 2, 901.

matters of economic morality: excess wealth, avarice or covetousness and how these should be overcome. Some attacked economic injustices by landowners, merchants and other classes of society. This chapter includes some Latin sermons because sermons tended to be recorded in that language even though they might have been given in English.

Pastoral manuals, devotional tracts and sermons can be grouped as serving the same purpose of general moral and religious instruction. Guides to conduct were written with advice about economic ethics for a more defined audience, that of rulers, estate managers and legal officials: examples cited in this chapter are Walter of Henley's *Le Dite de Hosbonderie*, the anonymous *Hosbonderie* and *Seneschaucie*, the *Speculum Justiciarorum* and *De Placitis et Curiis Tenendis* for justices and manor court officials, respectively. Advice on economic ethics was also given to kings or princes, and so this group includes the two versions of William of Pagula's *Speculum Regis Edwardi III*, Walter of Milemete's *On the Nobility, Wisdom and Prudence of Kings*, the anonymous *The Three Consideracions Right Necesserye for the Good Governaunce of a Prince*, Thomas Hoccleve's *Regiment of Princes* and Sir John Fortescue's letter to the Prince of Wales of 1470–71. Their common link is that all were written for those exercising authority and again demonstrate that economic ethics were applied not only to merchants but to those wielding royal power and to public officers of various kinds. A further category, books of wisdom, had a more general readership, but as collections of sayings on a very wide range of topics, they also included advice concerning economic ethics. This group includes two compilations of philosophical writings widely read in late medieval England: the *Distichs* or *Sayings of Cato* and the *Dictes and Sayings of the Philosophers*.

The first part of this chapter deals with the criticisms of economic immorality put forward in pastoral manuals, religious tracts, sermons, guides to conduct and books of wisdom. The second part considers the various remedies proffered by those sources. In regard to the criticisms, it is important to emphasise that the concerns of theologians about excess wealth, the nature of avarice and how avarice leads to economic injustice were reiterated or expounded in a large number of these texts and that their purpose was to raise awareness of how immorality or sin could occur in daily life. Many kinds of economic immorality were cited, going beyond the realm of the marketplace.

Criticisms

Excess Wealth and Social Inequality

The doctrine that excess wealth conflicts with the teachings of Christ, which was discussed in the previous chapter, appears in many works.[6] Robert Mannyng of Brunne's *Handlyng Synne*, written in the early fourteenth century, rails against the wealthy: "Ye ryche men, ye ryche purchasours, /Ye wene that al the worlde be yours".[7] Wealth should not exclude the consideration of others, especially the poor. The word "father" in the Lord's Prayer teaches us that God gives to many, not just one; that we are all brethren, great and small, rich and poor; and that we must hate pride, wrath and avarice for these bring us out of fellowship.[8] A variety of animal images to express the wickedness or burdens of excess wealth are used in Lollard sermons: a rich man is like a "moldwarpe", black by wickedness and blind by ignorance; a covetous man is like a sumpter horse who loses the treasure he carries after he has broken down with work.[9] In striking fashion, an anonymous sermon uses the analogy of Ptolemy's theories of planetary movement. When planets are in the lower part of their epicycle, they move according to the movement of the heavens; when in the upper part, they move against it; thus, men who have fewer worldly goods and are poor live and move in accordance with heavenly things and are virtuous, whereas those who are wealthy forget God and succumb to the lusts of the flesh.[10]

The same idea that the poor are more virtuous than the rich is found in the anonymous treatise, *Dives and Pauper*, written at the beginning of the fifteenth century. Pauper argues that the rich man is in greater peril of his soul than the poor man: whereas the material needs of the poor man are little beyond food, drink and clothing, the rich man needs a large household with

---

[6] For example *The Pricke of Conscience*, 37–38; Richard Lavynham, *A Lityl Tretys on the Seven Deadly Sins*, ed. J.P.W.M. van Zutphen (Rome: Institutum Carmelitanum, 1956) 21–22.

[7] *Handlyng Synne*, 196.

[8] *Dan Michel's Ayenbite of Inwyt*, vol. 1, ed. P. Gradon (London: OUP for EETS, 1979), 102.

[9] *Lollard Sermons*, ed. Gloria Cigman (Oxford: OUP for EETS, 1989), 144–147.

[10] Sermon no. 41, in *Middle English Sermons*, ed. W.O. Ross (London: OUP for EETS, 1940), 249–250.

servants and requires the services of labourers, craftsmen and lawyers. He has to maintain his social standing by holding feasts and by giving to both friends and enemies, for which a great deal of money is needed. Hence, there is a danger of covetousness developing. Dives's objections that Solomon prayed to God to give him neither wealth nor beggary (quoting from Proverbs 30:8–9) and that it is more blessed to give than receive (quoting from Acts 20:35) so that the rich may give more than the poor are rebutted by Pauper on the grounds that the rich man's soul is so taken up with his material needs that there is no room for the love of God.[11]

Quite apart from wealth absorbing space in the human spirit, *Jacob's Well*, an anonymous collection of sermons dating from the early fifteenth century, declares that wealth, like seeds heaped up, will rot but if sown abroad will increase and multiply.[12] However, the wealth sown abroad should be done so wisely: prodigality or wastefulness is sinful for all excess riches belong to the poor. For their part, the poor should not be covetous but should be content with their lot. Indeed, the solution for both rich and poor is to be poor in spirit.[13]

From the comments cited above, which are typical of the genres discussed in this chapter, all agree that excess wealth should be given to the poor, whereas *Jacob's Well* states that excess wealth rightfully belongs to the poor. Yet there remains the question of deciding the level of need and whether what was defined as need could vary according to social status. Alexander of Hales's notion of superfluity was discussed in the previous chapter, which gave a justification for the wearing of rich vestments, and some manuals and treatises are prepared to make concessions where the issue of excess wealth is concerned. Richard Lavynham's *A Lityl Tretys on the Seven Deadly Sins* allows the gathering of wealth to cover the costs of maintaining a household and poor relief. It cites the "compendio theologie"(the *Compendium Theologiae* was written by Hugo Ripelin of Strasbourg, a pupil of Albertus Magnus), as well as Albertus Magnus himself, Thomas Aquinas and Augustine's statement that Christ made Judas the keeper of the purse in order to give money to the poor (the

---

[11] 'Holy Poverty' version A, in *Dives and Pauper*, vol. 1, part 1, 58–59, 63.

[12] *Jacob's Well* (Brandeis), 134–135.

[13] *Jacob's Well* (Brandeis), 306, 307–308.

statement about Judas as the purse-keeper also appears in *Jacob's Well*).[14] Both *Handlyng Synne* and *Dives and Pauper* also insist on almsgiving but distinguish between types of households. *Handlyng Synne* recognises that those with families have greater need for wealth than those without and furthermore that an allowance should be made for those who need to maintain a certain position in society: priests or persons with "no charge of cyld ne wyff … nede nat to have tresourye But after manhede & curteysye".[15] The corresponding passage in *Manuel des Pechiez*, upon which *Handlyng Synne* is based, omits this notion altogether, showing that Robert Mannyng himself felt it was important to allow for differences in levels of wealth, so that persons of social standing could maintain a lifestyle that befitted their status and display this status according to the expectations of others. In *Dives and Pauper*, Dives argues that the rich have need of their wealth: in addition to having large household expenses, kings, princes and lords have to keep funds "to wachyn men of arms in defens of the rewme & of here lordchepe". Pauper agrees that extra wealth for such purposes is necessary and does not have to be given to the poor, but superfluous wealth above and beyond such needs must be given to others "for alwey the comon profyt owyth to ben chargyd mor than the profyt of on persone".[16]

In this way, the works cited above deal with the problem of unequal wealth by saying that the retention of any excess is denying the needs of the poor as well as endangering the soul. They are also aware that the social hierarchy, which requires the maintenance of the status appropriate to each level, is vital. Underlying this is the notion of the body politic discussed in the previous chapter, in which John of Salisbury saw that each member of the body had a role and that the lowest levels of society needed to be cared for so that they could maintain the upper levels. Discontent with one's lot, however, endangers this harmonious system: warnings about the mortal sin of avarice are an attempt not only to discourage unethical behaviour but to ensure that each person should know his or her place.

[14] Lavynham, *A Lityl Tretys*, 6; Leo M. Carruthers, "Richard Lavynham and the Seven Deadly Sins in *Jacob's Well*", *Fifteenth Century Studies* 18 (1991): 21–22; *Jacob's Well*(Brandeis), 119.

[15] *Handlyng Synne*, 196–197.

[16] Seventh Precept, cap. xii, in *Dives and Pauper*, vol. 1, part 2, 160–161.

Sermons also justified acceptance of inequality. Economic justice did not mean equality of wealth, only that each should have what is due to their station in life. Social harmony was to be maintained by each member of society remaining in the estate they occupied at birth; to desire more material goods was covetousness and disruptive to social order. So despite attacks on avarice, the social hierarchy was still favoured since it was how social unity was maintained, with the higher levels attending to justice and the lower carrying out their various functions in a proper manner. A classic example is seen in the sermon given by Thomas Wimbledon, titled *Redde rationem villicationis tue*, which deals with the command to give an account of one's stewardship on the day of reckoning or the Day of Judgement. It was given to what was probably a very large audience, at St Paul's Cross in London, in or about 1388. It became very popular, with several copies made, and was reprinted several times in the sixteenth and seventeenth centuries.[17] Wimbledon invokes John of Salisbury's theory of the body politic and gives it theological weight by quoting Christ's parable of the "householdynge man" rewarding his vineyard workers for their labour. He also quotes Avicenna, who pointed out that man cannot live by himself, thus corn has to be made into bread, wool into cloth, meat and fish have to be cooked, and therefore growers, craftsmen and merchants are necessary. Every man must "trauayle acordyng to his degre". All of these directives are supported by references from the Bible.[18] To ensure that these precepts are obeyed, all will be called to give an account on Judgement Day, but represented by bailiffs. Two of them, one representing priests with care of men's souls and the other temporal lords with governance over people, will answer for themselves and for others. They will be asked why they have entered into their office: was it for worldly profit or to help people, destroy falsehood and foster the truth? If it was for worldly profit, they are tyrants "as the phylosophre seyth".[19] The second question they will be asked is how have they ruled?

---

[17] Luke 16:2; "Descriptions of the Manuscripts and Prints", in *Wimbledon's Sermon*: *Redde Racionem Villicationis Tue*: *A Middle English Sermon of the Fourteenth Century*, ed. I.K. Knight (Pittsburgh: Duquesne University Press, 1967), 3–22.

[18] I Corinthians 7:20–24, II Timothy 4 (incorrectly), I Peter 2:18, I Thessalonians 4:6, Psalms 81:3–4 and Proverbs 4:27. See also Nancy H. Owen, "Thomas Wimbledon's Sermon: *Redde Racionem Villicacionis Tue*", *Medieval Studies* 28 (1966): 179–180.

[19] Owen, 'Thomas Wimbledon's Sermon', 183.

Have they treated rich and poor equally?[20] The third question is how have they lived? Have they themselves been guilty of the crimes for which they have punished others or instructed others not to do? The third bailiff represents everyone else, who must give an account of what they have received from God: have they obtained any worldly goods by extortion, "raveyne", usury or deceit?[21]

This evidence suggests that economic ethics and the notion that they applied to all classes of society were very important in late medieval England. As well as reminding people that they should not have wealth in excess of their station and to give any surplus to the poor, the commonly invoked three estates theory and body politic theory could have been attempts to preserve the traditional order in the face of the greater social mobility of the late medieval period.[22] Lollards who preached sermons also supported the existing social order, justifying it in much the same way as orthodox preachers. For example, one declared that the social order was necessary because the labour of the "comyne peple, whos occupacions stondeth in grobbyng about the erthe" was needed to sustain knights and clerks.[23] Ambition for a better standard of living was condemned because of its tendency for social and economic disruption. Knights' pride in their ancestry was criticised, but those who ape them must have acquired the means to do so by dubious means: "a mene bacheler" and "dyuerse squyers also, whiche ben come vp of non olde auncetrie, but bi extorcions crepen so highe".[24] No longer satisfied with their ancestors' pewter ware, these people must be served on silver, have fine clothes trimmed with fur and pearls, and have many retainers and horses, but to maintain all of this, they must rob their neighbours or enter into extortion or fall into great debt.[25] Social mobility was disrupting not only the established hierarchy but the traditional expectations of the wealth

---

[20] Owen, "Thomas Wimbledon's Sermon", 184.

[21] Owen, "Thomas Wimbledon's Sermon", 185.

[22] For an extended discussion of the prosperity brought to some after the Black Death, see Philippa C. Maddern, "Social Mobility", in *A Social History of England 1200–1500*, ed. Rosemary Horrox and W. Mark Ormrod (Cambridge: CUP, 2006), 113–133.

[23] *Lollard Sermons*, 86.

[24] *Lollard Sermons*, 138.

[25] *Lollard Sermons*, 138–139.

that each level was entitled to. Suspicion of the lower orders was also revealed in this sermon: if they had improved their standard of living, then it could not have come about by honest enterprise.

The Sinful Nature of Avarice or Covetousness

Definitions of avarice by Church authorities, examples of which were examined in Chapter 2, are re-affirmed in pastoral manuals, both for the priesthood and for the laity. *The Book of Vices and Virtues*, a fourteenth-century English translation of *Somme le Roi*, cites Paul's saying that avarice is the root of all evil.[26] *Fasciculus Morum*, a preachers' handbook dating from the early 1300s, cites Augustine (from *On Genesis*) that avarice is the desire for something greater than its real value, and, again showing concern with maintaining social order, Peter Lombard's declaration (from *The Sentences*) that avarice can be revealed in the strong desire for a high position in the world.[27] *Speculum Christiani*, dating from the 1360s or 1370s, has a chapter on avarice that consists almost entirely of quotations from Paul, Jerome, Gregory, Ambrose, Seneca, Robert Grosseteste and Isidore of Seville.[28] Quotations from authorities were a way of making it evident that avarice was not something that had been recently invented but rather was a concern going back centuries and identified by many as one with serious implications. Other works may not cite specific authorities but affirm that avarice is against God's will or the seriousness of its nature.[29]

Several manuals describe the nature of avarice by means of analogies. John de Burgo's *Pupilla Oculi*, written in 1384, compares avarice with idolatry and disease: the multiplication of riches does not quell avaricious

---

[26] *Vices and Virtues*, 30.

[27] *Fasciculus Morum: A Fourteenth-Century Preacher's Handbook*, ed. S. Wenzel (University Park: Pennsylvania State University Press, 1989), 313.

[28] *Speculum Christiani*, ed. G. Holmstedt (London:, Humphrey Milford, OUP for EETS, 1933), 66.

[29] *Fasciculus Morum*, 371; *Handlyng Synne*, 198–201; *Regimen Animarum*, in Oxford, Bodleian Library, MS Hatton 11, fol. 74r; *Ayenbite of Inwyt*, vol. 1, 34; *The Lay Folks' Catechism*, ed. T.F. Simmons and H.E. Nolloth (London: Kegan Paul, Trench & Trubner for EETS, 1901), 92; *A Myrour to Lewde Men and Wymmen*, 208.

desire for it is like one suffering from dropsy who tries to quench his thirst as the swelling grows.[30] *Jacob's Well* has covetousness as one of the layers of ooze or "wose" in the well that is the corrupt human being. For fear of poverty, the covetous man, instead of trusting in God, gathers a muck heap, like a porcupine gathering a heap of apples in an orchard with its sharp prickles.[31] *A Lityl Tretys on the Seven Deadly Sins* uses the porcupine image and also an image of serfdom, remarking that such gatherers are tenants of the devil performing their obligatory services to their lord.[32] *Jacob's Well* uses the porcupine story as well adding that by such gathering, a heap of treasure falls happily into the fiend's keeping, and such keepers are servants of the fiend, quoting from a tale in Ranulph Higden's *Polychronicon* about a fiend being seen in charge of King Richard's treasury.[33] The images of illness, corruption, filth and serving evil are all extreme and used to emphasise the doctrine of avarice as a mortal sin leading to eternal damnation.

A number of sermons closely follow the descriptions of the nature of avarice used by theologians or found in the pastoral manuals. One anonymous sermon uses Augustine's definition of it as an all-consuming and endless desire, whereas two more employ the image of dragons to represent the seven deadly sins, one of which is avarice.[34] Avarice was sometimes described as a form of idolatry in pastoral manuals, but one anonymous sermon goes so far as to define it as heresy: heresy is living against the faith "and good maner", an example being gathering wealth; therefore, a covetous man is a heretic and will be damned. This is followed by the story of a usurer who refused to make restitution on his deathbed because his wife and children would be in penury: the man died and went to hell and is considered a fool for caring more for his family

[30] John de Burgo, *Pupilla Oculi*, Strasbourg, Goetz, 1514, fols. CLXVI, CLXIX. For further discussion of the analogy between dropsy and avarice, see Richard Newhauser, "The Love of Money as Deadly Sin and Deadly Disease", in *Zusammenhänge, Einflüsse, Wirkungen: Kongressakten zum ersten Symposium des Mediävistenverbandes in Tübingen, 1984*, ed. Jörg O. Fichte, Karl Heinz Göller and Bernhard Schimmelpfennig (Tubingen: Walter de Gruyter, 1986), 315–326.

[31] See *Jacob's Well* (Brandeis), 117.

[32] See Lavynham, *A Lityl Tretys*, 6.

[33] *Jacob's Well* (Brandeis), 117.

[34] *A Late Fifteenth-Century Dominical Sermon Cycle*, vol. 1, ed. S. Morrison (Oxford: OUP for EETS, 2012), 139–140 and vol. 2, 413, 441.

than for his soul.[35] Again, like the manuals, other sermons compare avarice with animal behaviour or with physical illness. The Augustinian friar John Waldeby (1315–*c.* 1372) compared avarice to an illness and the riddance of it to a doctor performing a phlebotomy or blood-letting, and it is in this fashion that the devil exits from the rich man, whereas John Felton's *Sermo de innocentibus* likens the behaviour of avaricious and covetous people to the rapacity and injustice of wolves and the worldly love of apes.[36] More imaginative use of analogy is found in an anonymous sermon on Proverbs 30:18–19 which speaks of the difficulty of understanding the ways of an eagle, a serpent and a ship on the sea. The eagle represents pride, the snake covetousness or avarice and the ship the great men, the lords on great estates, who oppress the poor. Just as a serpent moves his head up and his tail down but wriggles his middle parts from side to side, the covetous man's tongue and countenance profess virtue while his nether part works in the opposite direction of worldly goods and money-making. The middle part moves to the right for pleasure and to the left by slander and detraction.[37] The sea represents the world and the ship bears the great men who support and sustain their officials to oppress and despise the poor, who are the small fish living in the water of hardship and suffering. These liveried officers, either by a legal deception or by physical violence, put the poor out of their house and land.[38] The imagery of this sermon certainly reinforces the message of the theologians about wealthy lords who sustain themselves by oppressing the poor.

Showing that criticism of economic malpractice extends well beyond merchants and into the rural scene is a Lollard sermon which uses the analogy of a school of avarice where all men go to learn. Covetousness is a schoolmaster whose students include great lords who learn how to oppress their people with great taxes and tallages, "smallere men" such as knights and squires who "ouerledyth" their poor tenants and "semple" neighbours with heavy fines and threats. The sermon censures deceitful merchants and artisans but also husbandmen who destroy their neighbour's

---

[35] Sermon no. 37, *Middle English Sermons*, 210–211.

[36] Cambridge, Gonville and Caius College, MS 334/727, fol. 154v; H.L. Spencer, *English Preaching in the Late Middle Ages*, Oxford, Clarendon Press, 1993, 344–345.

[37] Sermon no. 42, *Middle English Sermons*, 264–265.

[38] Sermon no. 42, *Middle English Sermons*, 266.

crops, mow his meadows or take his pasture or let their animals cause damage without making amends.[39]

Some pastoral manuals distinguish between avarice and covetousness, recognising that the latter is innate and hard to suppress but that the former is a conscious decision to adopt a parsimonious lifestyle. According to *Handlyng Synne*, covetousness is a desire for things that we all have which can lead to liberality or good things, but avarice is actually worse than covetousness because it is the desire to retain wealth.[40] Adding to the argument that covetousness is less serious than avarice, *Jacob's Well* allows that whereas some kinds of covetousness are mortal sins, others are merely venial. Coveting another's goods is a mortal sin, and coveting "vnlefull thynges" such as "a benefyse, or another estate, or degre, vnrightfully" is a mortal sin.[41] Coveting things of your neighbour's that could do the neighbour harm is a mortal sin, but "yif it be but a lytel harm, as an appyl or swich an-other smal thyng" that you know would not displease your neighbour, then it is a venial sin.[42] Striving after excessive wealth is a deadly sin, but if the love of God takes precedence then it is a venial sin: "And yif thou haue & kepe myche riches, wyth an vnordynat loue that sumdel lettyth the fro largenes of expunsys, so vertu be sauyd & almes dede, it is venyal synne".[43]

Thus, labouring in order to become disproportionately wealthy is a sin that can be mitigated by giving to the poor and with the proviso that the love of God comes first. This seems to recognise how economic ethics were accommodated by the wealthy in society, and this will be examined further in Chapter 7. Nevertheless, the warning that avarice is a mortal sin that corrupts the soul and turns people away from God needed to be restated in many ways in order to get the attention of lay society. The Church evidently hoped that all those engaged in any sort of monetary gain and those in possession of worldly goods and wealth would be able remind themselves that they should act in an ethical manner. At the same

[39] *Lollard Sermons*, 142–143.

[40] *Handlyng Synne*, 196.

[41] *Jacob's Well* (Brandeis), 135.

[42] *Jacob's Well* (Brandeis), 136–137.

[43] *Jacob's Well* (Brandeis), 136–137.

time, Church teachings offered a mitigating element to those who were wealthy, to offset the general condemnation of the attachment to wealth.

Avarice as the Cause of Economic Injustice

Avarice, the desire to obtain more wealth, leads to deceit and many other misdeeds. Some works list particular instances of avarice, whereas others have it broken down into subdivisions, and both display a wider range of offences than usury or deceitful trade. Alexander Carpenter's *Destructorium viciorum*, a treatise dating from *c.* 1429, lists ravine, falsity (of witnesses, accusers and executors, for instance) and injustice before he mentions fraud by merchants and usury.[44] *Cursor Mundi*, a thirteenth-century English poem written for the laity, says that covetousness is an evil sin which brings much grievance, from which comes "blindnes" (delusion or the inability to perceive the truth) and treason, ravening, theft and extortion.[45] Works following the subdivision method are the *Ayenbite of Inwyt*, the Kentish English translation of *Somme le Roi*, and *The Book of Vices and Virtues*, the Midlands English version, which give avarice ten roots or boughs. The *Ayenbite of Inwyyt* has usury, theft, robbery, making false legal claims, sacrilege, simony, "chapfare", "wycked crafte" and wicked games.[46] *The Book of Vices and Virtues* has the same offences, adding "malignite" or various sorts of evil behaviour that might be engaged in to make a profit.[47] Whichever approach is used, whether listing or subdivision, the purpose is to demonstrate that avarice leads to a multitude of offences as well as its widespread nature.

Indeed, to some writers, the whole of England is given over to theft and avarice. A short passage in *Speculum Christiani* headed "*Peccati Britonum et causa deposicionis eorum*" lists many sins, among them giving false witness and covetousness, but four seem to be of particular concern and

[44] Alexander Carpenter, *Destructorum viciorum* (P. Levet, 1497), Part IV, Chaps. V, VI, VIII, IX, XVIII, XIX.

[45] *Cursor Mundi*, vol. 3, 1541.

[46] *Ayenbite of Inwyt*, vol. 1, 34–35.

[47] *Vices and Virtues*, 30.

these include false withholding of wages, extortion and oppression.[48] At the end of the section in *Dives and Pauper* on the Commandment against theft, Dives declares that the whole nation must be guilty of covetousness and theft for simony "regnyth" amongst the clergy, usury amongst the merchants and the wealthy, ravine and extortion amongst lords and great men, and robbery and "mycherye" (petty theft) "amongis the pore comounys".[49] *The Book of Vices and Virtues* says that all manner of people can be avaricious: "prynces and prelates, clerkes, lewed, & religious".[50] Likewise, John Bromyard in *Summa Praedicantium* writes that avarice is found in all parts of society: the clergy, the laity, merchants and artisans. Examples include the following: lawyers and bailiffs profit from their work; the poor steal; the middling people are usurers or they hold back their crops when the poor are starving; and lords make false purveyances from their neighbours and bring litigation to the king's court to enrich themselves.[51] An example of how avarice amongst the rich could disrupt society can be found in a sermon preached at St Paul's Cross in London in 1406 by the Wycliffite William Taylor.[52] Taylor blamed excess wealth and the greed of the lords for economic disruption and deprivation. If the rich gave away their superfluous wealth, "we shulden not haue fallun into so manye inconuenyentis as we ben now". If lords were self-sustaining and content with their income from rents, "the comyntee of the puple shulde haue be myghty and sufficient in husbondderie and marchaundise to susteyne hemsilf, to paye the lordis hir rentis and othere thingis that ben due to hem" and to sustain the clergy.[53] All of these examples show that avarice was not limited to merchants. The strong impression is both that economic ethics is a matter for the whole of society and that each section of society contributes to the lack of morality in their particular ways.

As an example of how a priest might investigate these offences, the *Pars Oculi* of William of Pagula's *Oculus Sacerdotis* (written *c.* 1320) sets out the varieties of avarice he should consider: whether anything has been

[48] *Speculum Christiani*, 220.

[49] Seventh Precept, cap. xxviii, in *Dives and Pauper*, vol. 1, part 2, pp. 209–210.

[50] *Vices and Virtues*, 30.

[51] Bromyard, *SP*(*1*), p. 79v.

[52] *Two Wycliffite Texts*, ed. Anne Hudson (Oxford: OUP for EETS, 1993), xiii, 12–13.

[53] *Two Wycliffite Texts*, 17.

acquired unjustly through theft, ravine or extortion; whether greed is present in acquisition; whether the parishioner is generous in giving or sparing in what he retains; whether the parishioner has been involved in usury, simony or other fraudulent business. If he is a judge, he should be asked about corrupt arbitration. Other questions should be asked about false witnessing and the execution of wills.[54]

It is also significant that both the *Magna Carta* and the *Carta de Foresta* are reproduced in *Oculus Sacerdotis* and in its variant *Regimen Animarum* (the versions are the reissues of the charters by Edward I).[55] These charters were inserted into the text because those who infringed upon them were subject to excommunication *ipso facto*, as declared by Archbishop Boniface in the constitutions of Canterbury in 1253.[56] Archbishop Stephen Langton, who was involved in the drafting of the *Magna Carta*, had already taken this action, and in 1279, Archbishop Pecham ordered that copies of the charter be placed in every cathedral and collegiate church.[57] In the third chapter of *Jacob's Well* dealing with *sentencie*, those who violate the terms of the Great Charter (*Magna Carta*) and of the Charter of the Forests (*Carta de Foresta*) are subject to cursing and excommunication.[58] The *Carta de Foresta* sets out the regulations concerning economic exploitation of royal forests as sources of food and fuel, whereas the *Magna Carta* dealt with such matters as taxation without consent and unjust fines, both of which again indicate the broader, non-market side of economic ethics. Other manuals in this survey do not contain these charters but the clergy were reminded of them in *Instructions for Parish Priests*, in which John Mirk remarked that many more causes for excommunication could be found in the Charter of the Forests and the Great Charter.[59]

---

[54] *Oculus Sacerdotis*, MS Rawlinson A361, fol. 6v.

[55] *Oculus Sacerdotis*, MS Rawlinson A361, fols 30v–32r; fols 32r–33v; *Regimen Animarum*, MS Hatton 11, fols 50v–51r.

[56] *Regimen Animarum*, MS Hatton 11, fol. 51v.

[57] R.H. Helmholz, "Magna Carta and the *ius commune*", *University of Chicago Law Review* 66, (1999): 362–363.

[58] *Jacob's Well* (Brandeis), 17.

[59] John Mirk, *Instructions for Parish Priests*, ed. E. Peacock (London: Kegan Paul, Trench, Trubner & Co for EETS, 1902), 24.

The themes of economic injustice through avarice and covetousness continue in the late fifteenth century. A boy bishop's sermon given at St Paul's in London during the reign of Henry VII spoke of the negligence by spiritual leaders and the familiar topic of current moral degeneracy. In the temporal sphere, many sins prevail, for lechery is called pleasure, robbery and deceit are called "chevesaunce", extortion is called lordship and usury no sin at all.[60]

Particular Kinds of Economic Injustice

Many of the instances of avarice cited in pastoral manuals—such as the use of false weights and measures and the sale of faulty goods—concern merchants and traders.[61] My intention in this section, however, is to focus on those instances which could involve other kinds of participants, who might be landowners or employers of labour on manorial estates. In other words, their financial transactions might not strictly be described as commercial, but they were part of the economic activity that took place in late medieval England.

Non-payment of Debts and Usury

There were many in late medieval society, besides merchants and traders, who engaged in transactions involving credit. They were reminded that failing to repay monies owed, using a pledge without consent, and falsely withholding wages were all considered to be theft or ravine. Those who do not repay their debts are guilty of theft according to *The Middle English Treatise on the Ten Commandments* and of ravine according to *The Book of Vices and Virtues*.[62] *Handlyng Synne* states that using things taken as a pledge for a loan without the permission of the borrower is

---

[60] *Two Sermons Preached by the Boy Bishop*, ed. John Gough Nichols (London: Camden Society, 1875) 6–7.

[61] For a discussion of these sources, see Davis, *MMM*, 49–55.

[62] Royster, "A Middle English Treatise on the Ten Commandments: Part 1: Text and Notes", *Studies in Philology* 6 (1910): 30; *Vices and Virtues*, 34–35.

both usury and theft, as is keeping them beyond the term of the loan.[63] Similarly, those who withhold the wages of servants or hired workmen are guilty of theft or ravine according to *The Middle English Treatise on the Ten Commandments*, *The Book of Vices and Virtues*, *Of Shrifte and Penance*, the second part of *Jacob's Well* and *Handlyng Synne*.[64]

Usury was another practice which could involve landowners. Usury is condemned in every pastoral manual as either a form of avarice or an instance of theft.[65] It is not simply a matter of lending money at interest but unjustly profiting from a wide range of transactions which could involve goods, land or services as well as money. Also, it can be more than just dealings between merchants. In *Memoriale Presbiterorum*, both knights and merchants are to be questioned about usury, although merchants are to be interrogated about several varieties of it.[66] It is evident that William of Pagula believed that landowners could be involved in usury: in *Oculus Sacerdotis*, he argued that if usury were permitted, the wealthy would devote more of their attention to the profits to be made from usury than to farming. The poor would starve and food prices would be driven up, which would be the most serious consequence of usury.[67] Both of these sources show that writers recognised that landowners, as well as merchants, were implicated in usurious transactions.

Several manuals divide usury into categories. *Fasciculus Morum* gives it six forms: the first is taking income for something used as a pledge or living off a hostage's expenses; the second is a usurer buying something for less than it is worth and then selling it back to the purchaser at a much higher price (which is sometimes referred to as a *chevisance*); the third is an unwritten contract which involves the payment of "bounties" which are really interest; the fourth is a partnership agreement which is

[63] *Handlyng Synne*, 85.

[64] Royster, "A Middle English Treatise on the Ten Commandments", 30; *Vices and Virtues*, 34–35; *Of Shrifte and Penance*, 61; *Jacob's Well* (Salisbury), fol. 198r; *Handlyng Synne*, 87.

[65] For example, *Of Shrifte and Penance*, p. 61; Royster, "A Middle English Treatise on the Ten Commandments", 29; Mirk, *Instructions for Parish Priests*, 12; *Ayenbite of Inwyt*, vol. 1, 9; Thomas Docking, *De Decem Praeceptis*, in Oxford, Bodleian Library, MS Bodley 453, fols 50v–90v.

[66] M.J. Haren, "The Interrogatories for Officials, Lawyers and Secular Estates of the *Memoriale Presbiterorum*", in *Handling Sin: Confession in the Middle Ages*, ed. Peter Biller and A.J. Minnis (Woodbridge: York Medieval Press, 1998), 145, 147.

[67] See the translation in Shinners, J., and W.J. Dohar, *Pastors and the Care of Souls in Medieval England* (Notre Dame, IN: University of Notre Dame Press, 1998), 149.

for profits alone, without taking any risks of losses; the fifth are penalties set not to ensure that a debt is repaid on time but merely for gain; the sixth is a rich man taking labour from the poor instead of interest or getting a friend to lend with interest on his behalf.[68]

Some less usual examples of usury are to be found. *Jacob's Well* has selling a sick animal as healthy as a form of usury, as does *The Book of Vices and Virtues*.[69] According to the *Ayenbite of Inwyt*, "chafferers" or usurers do not replace dead animals, a reference to *métayage*, whereby the farmer pays rent to the landowner who provides the animals and seed. The *Ayenbite* also mentions buying crops when they are still in the ground and buying corn when it is cheap and selling when it is dear and adds that chafferers take advantage of their poor neighbours in hard times and make them do three pence worth of work for one penny.[70] Other guilty parties are those who support usurers or get others to commit usury on their behalf: the *Ayenbite of Inwyt* refers to "master usurers", great men who support Jewish moneylenders and "caorsins" (another term for usurers, possibly due to the fact that originally some moneylenders came from Cahors). *The Book of Vices and Virtues* attacks masters for using their apprentices or servants as agents for usury.[71] *Vices and Virtues* also says that lords who support and maintain usurers (here described as Jews and Saracens) are also guilty of usury.[72] *Jacob's Well* states that the letting of houses to any aliens who are known usurers, so that they can practise usury there, is forbidden in canon law (the *Extravagantes*).[73] All of these examples show that those involved in usury directly could be landowners or property owners just as easily as merchants and were regarded as equally guilty. The same applied to great lords who provided support and protection for usurers.

Learned discussions of usury were available in tracts aimed at laypeople. The approach of *Dives and Pauper* is to cite numerous authorities. It has several chapters devoted to usury, which frequently cite Aristotle and John of Freiburg's *Summa Confessorum*. The usurer is selling both

---

[68] *Fasciculus Morum*, 349, 351.

[69] *Jacob's Well* (Salisbury), fol. 198r; *Vices and Virtues*, 31–32.

[70] *Ayenbite of Inwyt*, vol. 1, 36–37 and vol. 2, note 127.

[71] *Ayenbite of Inwyt*, vol. 1, 35 and vol. 2, note 127.

[72] *Vices and Virtues*, 31–32.

[73] *Jacob's Well* (Brandeis), 33.

the thing he lends and the use of the thing, because he charges more for its use which is really selling the thing twice.[74] Aristotle's passages in Book V of the *Nicomachean Ethics* and Book III of the *Politics* are quoted on the matter of money being for exchange only and that the lender should be returned only "the euene value".[75] In addition to the *chevisance*, charging more for delayed payment is usury, but transactions in which there is doubt over the value (of, for example, bushels of wheat) at the time when payment is due are not classified as usury.[76] For authorities on doubt about the future value, Pauper cites both John of Freiburg's *Summa Confessorum* (which was largely reliant on the work of Thomas Aquinas) and the *Extravagantes* of the *Corpus Iuris Canonici*. The *Summa Confessorum* is again the authority for classifying a buyer paying less for a purchase in advance as a usurer.[77] Likewise, a kind of forward selling agreement to avoid price rises and falls is also usury.[78] There is a distinction between legitimate stockpiling and hoarding to make a profit: if someone buys corn or other "nedful thingis" in a time of plenty in order to sell at a profit in time of dearth, it is sinful. Pauper quotes Proverbs 11:26: "He that hydyth whete in time of hungyr he schal ben cursyd amongis the peple".[79] If, however, it is done "pryncipaly for comoun profyt" to save people from starvation, as Joseph did when governor of Egypt, then it is lawful. *Handlyng Synne* also condemns profiteering from holding back corn in times of dearth, thus harming the poor.[80]

What is clear from all of these works is that usury was not an offence committed only by merchants, nor does it relate only to money-lending but to a large range of transactions where excessive profits might be made, such as underpaying labourers, selling something for much more than it is worth or speculatively withholding goods in order to increase prices. Authors could have been familiar with all of these manifestations of usury

[74] Seventh Precept, cap. xxiv, in *Dives and Pauper*, vol. 1, part 2, 196–197.
[75] Seventh Precept, cap. xxiv, in *Dives and Pauper*, vol. 1, part 2, 197, 206.
[76] Seventh Precept, cap. xxv, in *Dives and Pauper*, vol. 1, part 2, 199.
[77] Seventh Precept, cap. xxv, in *Dives and Pauper*, vol. 1, part 2, p. 200.
[78] Seventh Precept, cap. xxv in *Dives and Pauper*, vol. 1, part 2, p. 200.
[79] Seventh Precept, cap. xxvi in *Dives and Pauper*, vol. 1, part 2, pp. 201, 202.
[80] *Handlyng Synne*, 178.

through their reading of learned works or even have observed some from their own experience.

Ravine, Extortion and Unjust Acquisition: The Abuses of Lords and Gentry

Lords or other members of the landowning class are accused of theft or avarice for a variety of offences involving the abuse of their powers over their tenants for their own economic gain. In many manuals and treatises, one kind of economic injustice by lords or landowners is forcing their tenants to pay heavy fines and taxes. For Thomas Docking, they are guilty of theft.[81] Lords who increase "custome" or rents or take unreasonable fees from towns are guilty of theft according to *Handlyng Synne*.[82] In *Regimen Animarum*, lords who introduce their own private customs or laws and bring charges against people are guilty of avarice; Richard Laynham says "bringerys vp of newe customys, of taskys & talyagis" are "tyrauntis & extorsioneris"; Alexander Carpenter declares that laws and customs which lead to extortion from the poor are a type of ravine. They expel truth and justice and persecute the servants of God, and over-taxing of tenants and extortion are condemned in *Jacob's Well*.[83] In the *Memoriale Presbiterorum*, knights are to be asked whether they have exacted excessive tallage and other taxes from their tenants, especially the poor, and it is added that a knight ought to know that by divine law, anything more than what is owed to him by right or by custom is ravine. Another money-raising venture knights are to be asked about is whether they have an unlicensed chapel on their manor from which the offerings go into their own pockets rather than to the mother Church.[84] *Jacob's Well* states that lords who prevent the debts of their dead tenants from being paid, or who take the goods of the intestate pretending that they were owed larger amounts in rents and amercements, will be cursed

---

[81] Docking, *De Decem Praeceptis*, MS Bodley 453, fol. 50v.

[82] *Handlyng Synne*, 84, 79.

[83] *Regimen Animarum*, MS Hatton II, fol. 73v; Lavynham, *A Lityl Tretys*, 9; Alexander Carpenter, *Destructorum viciorum*, part IV, Chap. V; *Jacob's Well* (Brandeis) 131–133.

[84] Haren, "Interrogatories", p. 143.

and subject to excommunication: such things are forbidden by the constitutions of Archbishop John Stratford.[85] Lords who prevent their tenants from attending church courts or otherwise interfere with the judicial process of those courts are also subject to excommunication.[86]

Apart from exploiting their tenants, lords can profit themselves by acquiring land for nothing or by forcing the owner into debt. Bromyard describes an unjust acquisition of land: it sometimes happens that an inheritance such as a town, lordship or manor is divided between daughters, or for some other reason, and a tyrant in the adjoining land acquires it. If the tyrant cannot prevent the rightful holder from having his share of the estate, he maliciously devises some ways for him to be indicted or accused, reported to lords of towns and judges, attached and imprisoned, so that it will be necessary for him to sell his inheritance, either for nothing or to be bound by a mortgage so wickedly increased that he can never recover his part.[87] An anonymous sermon asserts that a covetous man seeks to control the country by being "a grett purchesoure", obtaining a poor man's croft by extortion: "Suche a man among grett men and lordes is a grett felowe" but by his poor neighbour "he settis no price". Should anyone reproach him, he treats them with derision, but God will take vengeance upon these "man qwellers and deceytfull men and thise exstorcioners". Other sermons attacking rapacious lords can be found in other collections.[88]

Fasciculus Morum and John Bromyard describe what they believe is the attitude of rapacious lords and how they justify themselves. *Fasciculus Morum* says that in Ireland and Wales those who steal their neighbours' livestock are called thieves but in England "the noble are called *shaveldours* and *riflers*" and "imagine that whatever they do, they do with right and reason".[89] For example, a poor widow is forced to exchange

[85] *Jacob's Well* (Brandeis), 20–21; Item 7 of "The Constitutions of Archbishop Stratford, A.D. 1343", in *A Collection of the Laws and Canons of the Church of England*, vol. 2, trans. John Johnson(Oxford: John Henry Parker, 1851), 389.

[86] *Jacob's Well* (Brandeis), 25–26.

[87] Bromyard, *SP(2)*, 285r.

[88] Sermons no. 36 in *Middle English Sermons*, 203. Also sermon no. 40, 238-239; *A Late Fifteenth-Century Dominical Sermon Cycle*, vol. 1, 23–24 and *Lollard Sermons*, 222, 224.

[89] *Fasciculus Morum*, 341.

her acre of land for a piece that is less valuable, yet the person who gives her that land claims he is doing her a favour.[90] Bromyard, in his chapter on robbery, writes that oppressive lords and their officials collect tallage from their subjects, explaining them as ancestral customs and giving such excuses as great expenses, defending the state, a just war, or preventing unjust suffering occurring. However, there is no just cause and often the reason is their own high expenditure on an overabundance of great horses, equipment for tournaments and jousts, extravagant feasts, novelties and great retinues which they have in times of peace as well as war. Their rapacity is the major reason for the poverty of others, yet they pretend that there would be no rapacity if others were not rapacious. But there would be no injustices by them if their expenses really were just. They ask for help and then may extort or rob because middling people will not give willingly: it is evident from lords' rejection of small offerings from a town or village that they desire a large amount of money, and to feed this their officials impose very heavy punishments and unreasonable fines on the guilty. The subject of unjust taxation seems to be of great concern to Bromyard, for it reappears in his chapter on rulers.[91]

Thomas Brinton, Bishop of Rochester, attacked the great magnates for being parasites. One of his sermons, which might have been preached during a procession held on 17 July 1377, the day after Richard II's coronation, would have had a large and wealthy audience. According to Brinton, the sins of the rich and the magnates are worse than those of the middling people or the poor: whereas the middling people commonly live honestly of their own labour, magnates commonly live off others, by acts of violence, robbery, exactions and extortions, dubious titles and pleasurable expenses, to the extent that those who would be otherwise rich men are otherwise paupers.[92] During Lent in 1374, Brinton addressed his Rochester congregation with a sermon about the many wrongdoings of the rich and powerful, including lack of impartial

[90] *Fasciculus Morum*, 343.

[91] Bromyard, *SP(2)*, 284v; *SP(2)*, 302r.

[92] *The Sermons of Thomas Brinton, Bishop of Rochester (1373–1389)*, vol. 1, ed. M.A. Devlin (London: Royal Historical Society, 1954), 198.

justice. He observed that, in church courts as much in secular courts, the character or disposition of a minister or official tends to follow that of his lord. For example, if a lord was pure, pious and just, then usually his seneschals, judges, bailiffs, notaries and other ministers would be pure, merciful, kind, affable and just. If, however, the lords were cruel, unjust, avaricious and unmerciful, oppressors of the poor and despoilers of the people, then such ministers would act for themselves or for their lord, not for the common good. Instead of ruling the lord's subjects justly and wisely, they do so in order to make a profit, and instead of punishing the guilty, collect and extort money and commit other offences.[93] Brinton's sermon again shows how the Church viewed the avarice of lords, accusing them and their officials of living off the poor for their own gain.

The depredations of bailiffs and other officials of magnates were widely recognised and condemned.[94] The *Memoriale Presbiterorum* concludes that seneschals and bailiffs "are exceedingly cavilling and altogether given to avarice and falsity and led by blind greed which is the worst of all evils; nor do they care for God or for holy church or its ministers, but only for securing profits and rewards"; in *Cursor Mundi*, bailiffs will be asked by their priests about lying and deceit and the stealth that commonly follows, and wrongdoing by stewards and bailiffs is also mentioned in *Of Shrifte and Penance*.[95] Thus, bailiffs, stewards and other estate officials were commonly attacked and, as will be seen in Chapter 5, were the subject of a number of petitions. Pastoral manuals, sermons and other texts recognised that lords and landowners, and their officers, were also guilty of avarice and provided plentiful evidence and examples of the kinds of abuses in existence.

---

[93] *The Sermons of Thomas Brinton*, vol. 1, 139.

[94] *Regimen Animarum*, MS Hatton II, fol. 73v; Docking, *De Decem Praeceptis*, MS Bodley 453, fol. 49v; *Speculum Laicorum* , 17; *Dives and Pauper* Seventh Precept, cap. xi, vol. 1, part 2, 157; *Vices and Virtues*, 34 ; *Handlyng Synne*, 178–79; *Jacob's Well* (Brandeis), 61.

[95] Haren, "Interrogatories", pp. 135, 137–41; *Cursor Mundi*, vol. 3, 1517; *Of Shrifte and Penance*, 80–81.

Purveying Abuses: Economic Injustice by Lords and Monarchs

Purveying abuses were particular to those in positions of high authority, extending right up to the king. Although some purveyors were profiting themselves, critics believed that sinful officials were reflecting the moral state of their masters.

Thomas Docking condemns purveying abuses: those whose officials extort from the poor by buying victuals that could be sold in the common market are sinful. It is stealing from the poor because it is not at the market price but the price that pleases them, or they never pay at all.[96] John Bromyard writes that the powerful enrich themselves by false procuring as well as by tallage, taking forced loans without repayment and other offences.[97] Purveyors, along with other officials, are accused of plunder and extortion in *The Book of Vices and Virtues*.[98] In 1406, William Taylor's sermon alluded to protests and demonstrations by those who were unpaid for their victuals by lords' purveyors.[99]

The most extended attack on purveying abuses was by William of Pagula. Pagula, the canon lawyer and author of the priest's manual, *Oculus sacerdotis*, was also the author of the very different *Speculum Regis Edwardi III* or *Mirror of Edward III*. His two versions of the *Speculum*, written in the 1330s, are both very strong reminders to the king of his duties as a monarch and of the economic injustice resulting from abuses by his royal purveyors. The king is supposed to protect the poor, not steal from them, and to restrain his household expenditure. If purveying came to an end, the peasants would have enough to plant for the next season's crops and increase their production of food. The king should respect the rights of his people, for it is by their assent that he rules, implying that a ruler deemed a tyrant will be deposed.

Pagula's first version of the *Speculum* appeals to justice which "never sells another's goods but gives to each one what is his own; it neglects its

---

[96] Docking, *De decem praeceptis*, MS Bodley 453, fol. 50v.

[97] Bromyard, *SP*(*1*), 17v.

[98] *Vices and Virtues*, 34–35.

[99] *Two Wycliffite Texts*, 18.

own utility so that it might serve the communal equity".[100] Pagula adds that God loves the just, quoting the Psalms, St Cyprian, Gregory, Seneca and other sources and asks:

> But how is it either justice or equity these days to buy something for a lesser price than the seller wishes to sell them for, and contrary to consent ... For where there is no consent, there is no selling but extortion, no justice but seizure, no equity but falsehood and iniquity.[101]

Here, Pagula clearly expresses one of the principles of just pricing, that it should be with the consent of the seller, which was disregarded by royal purveyors. Taking goods without consent is theft, and theft "destroys in humanity the foundation of justice and goodness". Such robbers are "worse than any beasts, for one robber devours an entire land, just like an evil prince" and they will be damned.[102] For example, servants of the royal household took wagons and horses from poor people in the area of Windsor forest and paid them nothing for carrying firewood.[103] In another, two scouts, one after the other, entered a village each with a signed paper with an unknown seal in order to requisition servants and horses. The villagers were intimidated and paid them to leave, but to no avail.[104] Pagula could well have been drawing on his personal experience as vicar of Winkfield in Berkshire, just a few miles from Windsor Castle, where the king frequently stayed.

Pagula's solution for the king's salvation is that he immediately orders that anyone in his household who takes anything against the owner's will shall be hanged.[105] As a warning, Pagula contrasts the behaviour of Henry III, who paid for his provisions, with the behaviour of Edward III's late father and alludes to the fate of Piers Gaveston, Hugh Despenser and

[100] William of Pagula, *Mirror of Edward III*, First Version, in *Political Thought in Early Fourteenth-Century England: Treatises by Walter of Milmete, William of Pagula and William of Ockham*, ed. and trans. Cary J. Nederman (Turnhout: Brepols, 2002), 73.

[101] *Mirror of Edward III*, First Version, 74.

[102] *Mirror of Edward III*, First Version, 79.

[103] *Mirror of Edward III*, First Version, 87.

[104] *Mirror of Edward III*, First Version, 90.

[105] *Mirror of Edward III*, First Version, 93.

Roger Mortimer. The king is urged to keep the common law and pay the market price.[106]

The second version of the *Speculum* frequently reminds the king that he is mortal and cries shame on the fact that once people know the king is visiting, they hide, consume or otherwise dispose of their poultry and goods beforehand, in case they should lose them.[107] The king's over-consumption potentially leads to dire poverty: a royal official buys a hen from a poor woman for half its value, and while the king fills his stomach, the woman has no eggs to feed her children.[108] The king is urged to pay his debts before making generous gifts and to consider the value of keeping a war horse, the cost of which is the equivalent of maintaining four or five paupers, and Pagula repeats a common estimate that the king's debts, and those of his father and grandfather, are three times the value of his assets.[109] Pagula quotes from and recommends that the king read the advice of the saintly Louis IX to his son, pointing out that Edward is ungrateful for what God has given him, as evidenced by the purveying abuses: "You ought to know that as liberality is a sign of nobility, so robbery is a sign of barbarism".[110] The king is warned about the fate of his father, for "excess expenditures" bring not only "the destruction of the kingdom" but also the hatred of his people: "For I want you to know that you do not have the love of the English people as a good king should have".[111]

These are severe criticisms. The historical context of the purveying issue will be discussed in Chapter 5. The point to bear in mind here is that Pagula saw the king as ultimately responsible, that his own prodigality was to blame for the hardships and injustices inflicted on the poor by his purveyors.

[106] *Mirror of Edward III*, First Version, 98, 101, 103.

[107] William of Pagula, *Mirror of Edward III*, Second Version, in *Political Thought*, 109.

[108] *Mirror of Edward III*, Second Version, 131.

[109] *Mirror of Edward III*, Second Version, 115, 117, 129.

[110] *Mirror of Edward III*, Second Version, 126.

[111] *Mirror of Edward III*, Second Version, 129, 134.

Other Non-mercantile Types of Misconduct

There was also the potential for economic abuses by legal professionals and people resorting to courts of law. *The Ayenbite of Inwyt* has various abuses of the legal system as the fourth branch of avarice. Seven kinds of people are involved, including those who use corrupt judges, those who hire false witnesses, those who make false claims or accusations, judges who are not impartial but influenced by love or hate, and judges who sell their verdicts and so damage the poor.[112] *Memoriale Presbiterorum* states that lawyers and church court officials are to be asked by their priests whether they have ever given false advice or delayed cases unnecessarily for monetary gain and whether they have ever taken a lower fee in order to undercut their colleagues or taken a higher fee which was well in excess of the labour, effort and costs required for the case.[113] The *Speculum Justiciarorum* or *Mirror of Justices*, dating from the late thirteenth or early fourteenth century, was written out of concern that justices were acting for monetary gain or self-interest, or trying to please the powerful, rather than following the written laws, and sets out to correct this by relating English common law with the law of the Old and New Testaments and patristic writings.[114] However, unlike in the pastoral manuals, there are no citations of any passages from any of these sources. Corrupt judges and bribery are also condemned in sermons.[115]

Among laypeople who abuse the processes of law, villeins are held in suspicion. In the *Memoriale Presbiterorum*, the confessor is warned that rich villeins are less concerned about sinning than noblemen and tend to think that a money payment can settle any wrongdoing. They have a reputation for making false accusations and stealing their neighbours' land by removing the boundary marks.[116] *Handlyng Synne* says that those "fals husbandys" who take someone else's land or furlong for ploughing

---

[112] *Ayenbite of Inwyt*, vol. 1, 39–40; see also *Jacob's Well* (Brandeis), 130–131); *Of Shrifte and Penance* 80, 81.

[113] Haren, "Interrogatories", 133.

[114] *The Mirror of Justices*, ed. William Joseph Whittaker (London: Bernard Quaritch for the Selden Society, 1895), 1, 3.

[115] See Sermon nos. 21 and 36, *Middle English Sermons*, 122–125, 202.

[116] Haren, "Interrogatories", 153–157.

are guilty of theft, and *Jacob's Well* says villeins should neither plough over boundary marks nor argue about them.[117]

Most of the lower orders are subject to doubt about their loyalty and honesty. *Cursor Mundi* advises that ploughmen should be asked whether they are better at tilling their own earth than tilling that of the men who hire them.[118] *Handlyng Synne* says labourers are guilty of theft if they withdraw customary labour or quibble over the days or hours; *Of Shrifte and Penance* says that a man who works slowly might be doing harm to his lord, and *A Middle English Treatise on the Ten Commandments* states that a labourer who spends two days working on a task where only one day is necessary is guilty of theft.[119] *Cursor Mundi* advises that workmen should be asked by their priests about lying, deceit and stealth.[120] Servants are to be questioned by their priests about fraud and theft according to the *Memoriale Presbiterorum*, and theft by servants from their masters is condemned in *Handlyng Synne* and *Of Shrifte and Penance* and twice in *Jacob's Well*.[121]

Both *The Book of Vices and Virtues* and *Jacob's Well* list certain occupations as branches of avarice or covetousness. *The Book of Vices and Virtues*'s "schrewed" or wicked crafts include prostitution and professional fighting. Gambling gives rise to many sins: not only covetousness, swearing and wasting time but instant usury.[122] *Jacob's Well*'s "craft of foly" adds jugglers, fake cripples, begging intruders, public buffoons, heralds at arms, professional tournament champions, workers who take more than they are worth and executioners.[123] Although executioners seem a strange inclusion, the underlying rationale appears to be that these occupations exhibit idleness or contribute nothing to the common weal.

[117] *Handlyng Synne*, 87; *Jacob's Well* (Salisbury), fol. 198r.

[118] *Cursor Mundi*, vol. 3, 1517.

[119] *Handlyng Synne*, 85; *Of Shrifte and Penance*, 61; *A Middle English Treatise on the Ten Commandments*, 30.

[120] *Cursor Mundi*, vol. 3, 1517.

[121] Haren, "Interrogatories", 149; *Handlyng Synne*, 84; *Of Shrifte and Penance*, 61; *Jacob's Well* (Brandeis), 128; *Jacob's Well* (Salisbury), fol. 198r.

[122] *Vices and Virtues*, 41–42.

[123] *Jacob's Well* (Brandeis), 134–135.

Remedies

So far, this survey has dealt with portrayals of the sinful nature of avarice and its various manifestations, but important parts of economic ethics consisted of promoting the positive ideals of justice and equity and of good lordship. There is an interrelationship between these three ideals, and the rest of this chapter will explore how justice and equity were conceived in these works and how lords were meant to exemplify them.

The Virtues of Justice and Equity

Speculum Christiani explains that justice means giving every man his due and in helping to sustain "nedy wreches".[124] One of its many quotations is from Book V of the Book of Wisdom:

> Ryghtful men schal myghtyly stande to-gedre in grete stedfastnes aghens hem that haue anguyshed and trobledde hem cruelly, and aghens hem that falsly haue take a-way here true labours and her truly goten gudes.

Speculum Christiani also has quotations on doing justice from Seneca, Jerome, several from Augustine and Gregory, Bernard of Clairvaux, Paul and John Chrysostom.[125] *Jacob's Well* addresses the nature of justice with quotations from a number of authorities, including Ambrose, Augustine, the gospels and Deuteronomy. The author uses "ryght", the Middle English term for justice, throughout. For example: "Ambrose seyth ryght is to gyve to yche persone his owyn thyng and to yeldyn to yche wyght that thyng whiche he is worthy to have"; and, based on Matthew 7:12, "Restore to hym that thou hast takyn unryghtfully as ye woldyn others dedyn to you do ye to hem".[126]

[124] *Speculum Christiani*, 46, 48; similar words appear in Thoresby's *Lay Folks' Catechism*. See *The Lay Folks' Catechism*, ed. T.F. Simmons and H.E. Nolloth (London: Kegan Paul, Trench, Trubner for EETS, 1901), 80.

[125] *Speculum Christiani*, 236–240.

[126] *Jacob's Well* (Salisbury), fol. 137v; fol. 138r.

Thus, in *Speculum Christiani* and *Jacob's Well*, justice is seen as serving God rather than, as in Aristotle's view, as the supreme virtue. Yet because justice is giving each his or her due, it is also seen in a number of pastoral manuals as maintaining the social order. *The Book of Vices and Virtues* says justice is for orderly living among others, saying that according to "Ploteus", all four virtues must be possessed by a ruler in order for him to be worthy of that role. The text marvels that heathen philosophers, who knew nothing of the true grace of God, "clombe thei vp to the hil of parfightnesse of lif bi strengthe of here owne vertue".[127] Yet, calling on Paul's words asserting that charity is greater than faith or hope, these virtues are seen as nothing without charity. Furthermore, Augustine defined the four cardinal virtues as four kinds of love, and where God is loved, justice is serving God.[128] The *Ayenbite of Inwyt* also marvels at the heathen thinkers but adds that God teaches the four cardinal virtues a hundred times better than the old philosophers. Yet it maintains that justice is a man who sits in order and in right state, implying that justice is maintaining the natural hierarchy, a view which is repeated in *The Myrour to Lewde Men and Wymmin*.[129] To the quotation from Plato about orderly living among others, the *Ayenbite of Inwyt* adds that the just man reveres those above him, loves his equals and gives grace to those beneath him. It also describes the four virtues as a sound building, for the four virtues of prudence, temperance, justice and fortitude are the four towers that make the four corners of the good man's house strong. The metaphor of the building with four towers is also used in *Speculum Vitae* and the *Myrour to Lewde Men and Women*.[130]

The expectation was that those in the higher orders of society were responsible for meting out justice to those below and to their peers.[131] *Dives and Pauper* declares that the duty of lords and the wealthier members of society was to rectify such instances of theft as the use of false weights and measures, deceptive trade and workmanship, idle labourers, ravening

[127] Similar words are in the *Speculum Vitae*, the verse version of the *Vices and Virtues*. See *Speculum Vitae: A Reading Edition*, vol.1, ed. R. Hanna (Oxford: OUP for EETS, 2008), 73, 74.

[128] *Vices and Virtues*, 124–125 .

[129] *Myrour to Lewde Men and Women*, 90.

[130] *Ayenbite of Inwyt*, vol. 1, 124, 125–126;. *Speculum Vitae*, vol. 1, 67; *Myrour to Lewde Men and Women*, 88).

[131] Haren, "Interrogatories", 143; *Cursor Mundi*, vol. 3, 1517.

and extortion, "for riche men and lordys in this world ben Godys balyys & Godys reuys to ordeynyn for the pore folc & for to susteynyn the pore folc".[132] Yet God's reeves and bailiffs should be merciful and forgive their subjects the debts which are owed, both to God and to the bailiffs, "for God is so gret a lord & so ryche that ther may no man don hym fraude of his good ne hyndryn ne lessyn his lordschepe".[133] *Jacob's Well* describes the rewards to be gained in heaven through the exercise of justice: each person shall have a crown of gold with four precious stones representing the four virtues, the stone of justice set at the back of the crown.[134]

Some texts consider the notion of equity or fairness as underlying the carrying out of justice and in that way are closer to the thought of Aristotle. For example, *The Book of Vices and Virtues* says that "euenhede" or equity is how right and true judgements are made, "without bowynge to that on side or to that other".[135] In *Speculum Vitae*, fairness or "evenhede" is a gift of the Holy Spirit (part of the Gift of Knowing) but is also the use of reason: "Evenhede es a vertu of skille that acordes Resoun with Wille".[136] On the other hand, *Jacob's Well* turns its discussion about "euenhede" or equity into a ruling about aspirations to higher positions in the social order, which would disturb the natural hierarchy because desiring to be equal with one's neighbour is standing on even ground, but desiring to be superior means that the ground is uneven. Therefore equity fails.[137] *Jacob's Well* adds that equity provides a reason for the wealthy to give to the poor and needy: "Thi ground is noght levelyd evene ne pleyn for equyte wolde that thou schuldyst partyn of thi good with thi neyghbour in nede".[138] It is also why justice should be impartial.[139]

The notions of justice expressed in these works are that it is serving or obeying God, quoting biblical or Church authorities rather than classical thought. This may be because the authors wanted to convey the idea that

---

132 Seventh Precept, cap. iv, in *Dives and Pauper*, vol. 1, part 2, 137.

133 Seventh Precept, cap. xi, in *Dives and Pauper*, vol. 1, part 2, 159.

134 See *Jacob's Well* (Salisbury), fol. 138v.

135 *Vices and Virtues*, 152–158.

136 *Speculum Vitae*, vol. 1, 159.

137 *Jacob's Well* (Salisbury), fol. 141v.

138 *Jacob's Well* (Salisbury), fol. 142r.

139 *Jacob's Well* (Salisbury), fol. 142r.

doing justice was God's will and therefore such acts had divine sanction and to link this to the roles of lords and rulers, who could be described as God's bailiffs in their ministrations. However, equity was also important because it contained the notion of impartiality, essential for true justice. Although *Speculum Vitae* described it as a gift of the Holy Spirit, there is a sense that equity is an attitude of mind, the use of reason. Yet it is clear from the passage from *Jacob's Well* that equity meant accepting one's social status: one should remain a servant or be on a par with one's fellows and not aspire to mastership or lordship.

The virtues are also proclaimed in a number of sermons.[140] However, there is more evidence of the widespread dissemination of the virtues in popular books of sayings or books of wisdom. *The Distichs of Cato*, dating from the third century, was used both as a Latin textbook and as a guide to morals in medieval schools and thus was a significant part of the education of the literate classes. Chaucer described the carpenter in *The Miller's Tale* as a man of little education—"He knew nat Catoun, for his wit was rude"[141]—and quotations of Cato's wisdom are found elsewhere in the *Canterbury Tales*: *The Merchant's Tale*, *The Nun's Priest's Tale* and *The Canon's Yeoman's Prologue*.[142] Furthermore, Caxton printed four different editions of Cato's sayings. Of the many manuscript versions, one is *Le Livre de Catun*, which has what appear to be the original Latin lines and additional explications in Anglo-Norman.[143] "*Equum iudica*" advises impartial justice to rich and poor.[144] Further advice is to avoid excessive consumption and to be neither a spendthrift nor a miser.[145] One should be munificent, but wasting one's gains is to be avoided, for this will lead to the suffering and ruin of others, ravine and theft.[146] Those who would

[140] For example, sermon no. 37, *Middle English Sermons*, 213; *A Late Fifteenth-Century Dominical Sermon Cycle*, vol. 1, 60.

[141] *The Miller's Tale*, in *Riverside Chaucer*, 68.

[142] *The Merchant's Tale*, in *Riverside Chaucer*, 156; *The Nun's Priest's Tale*, 255; *The Canon's Yeoman's Prologue*, 271. "Caton the grete clerke" is also quoted in *The Castle of Perseverance*. See *Four Morality Plays*, ed. Peter Happé, Harmondsworth, Penguin, 1979, 114.

[143] *Le Livre de Catun*, ed. Tony Hunt, London, Anglo-Norman Text Society, 1994. This edition uses London, British Library, MS Harley 4657, which dates from the early fourteenth century.

[144] *Le Livre de Catun*, 13.

[145] *Le Livre de Catun*, 27.

[146] *Le Livre de Catun*, 32, 35.

be happy should despise riches because those who admire them are always greedily begging for them.[147] Yet liberality is urged, for what is the point of wealth if one is still a miser?[148] The existence of the *Distichs of Cato*, its widespread use as an educational text and its continuing popularity amongst book buyers show that literate people, beyond the clergy and the nobility, had some awareness of the virtues of liberality and justice. The promotion of the virtues in pastoral manuals demonstrates that they were an important part of economic ethics, the positive values that society should adhere to.

Kings and Economic Justice

Advice concerning economic ethics, this time directed towards a more specific audience, that of kings, can be found in texts belonging to the genre of advice to princes. In *On the Nobility, Wisdom and Prudence of Kings*, which was written in the 1320s, Walter of Milemete advises the king not to appoint the avaricious and covetous to his council as counsellors or to associate with them in any way for they act only for their own gain. Instead, he should practise the virtue of justice and "direct the great men of his land that they should not destroy their tenants nor extort their goods through unjust lordship".[149] The king should also practise temperance—for "one who is continent abstains from excess victuals"—and liberality, the mid-point between prodigality and avarice.[150] Thomas Hoccleve, in *The Regiment of Princes*, which was composed between 1410 and 1411 and dedicated to Prince Henry, later Henry V, advises him that a covetous king would never be trusted by his people and that tyranny results from a king constantly demanding money from his subjects.[151] Hoccleve's *Regiment* was based partly on the *Secreta secretorum*, attributed at the time to Aristotle, and partly on Giles of Rome's *De*

[147] *Le Livre de Catun*, 36.

[148] *Le Livre de Catun*, 39.

[149] Walter of Milemete, *On the Nobility, Wisdom and Prudence of Kings*, in *Political Thought*, ed. Nederman, 47, 51.

[150] *On the Nobility, Wisdom and Prudence of Kings*, 52, 53.

[151] Hoccleve, *Regiment*, lines 4012–4025, 4516–4519.

regimine principum, which, like *Somme le roi*, was written for Philip III of France. The avaricious are "To whom noon habundance may souffyse", and Hoccleve gives a grim warning of the consequences should the king be gripped by avarice:

> Thus may thy style likned be to thefte:
> As a theef in this world is hangid heere
> For good which that he of the peple refte,
> So shalt thow hange in helle and bye it deere.[152]

Hoccleve evidently felt it was his place to lecture the king about the mortal dangers of avarice and the harm it would bring to his people. The king should counter avarice with liberality and give more than others in his kingdom.[153]

In *The Donet*, Reginald Pecock agrees that superfluity or extravagance should be avoided by rulers: a prince should govern "bi resoun and bi feith, and by law is therupon maad to the comune and to ech otheris helpe, forthering and profite".[154] He also agrees that besides upholding the law, the ruler should be content with his own income and should tax his people unless it is needed by or for the profit of the community, and not without common assent.[155]

The mid fifteenth-century English tract, *The Three Consideracions Right Necesserye for the Good Governaunce of a Prince*, translated from a French work of the preceding century, raises the issue of just pricing. It is possible that over-spending by Henry VI was a factor influencing the circulation of this work in English. In discussing the prince's rents and revenues, the anonymous author advises that royal purveyors should take nothing from his subjects unless it is "at a just and convenable prys and with oute longe creaunce or delay of payment". Not only will failure to do so be sinful, but the king risks social disorder: "for that that faileth in the heede or

[152] Hoccleve, *Regiment*, lines 4475, 4495.

[153] Hoccleve, *Regiment*, lines 4645–4655.

[154] Reginald Pecock, *The Donet*, ed. Elsie Vaughan Hitchcock (London: OUP for EETS, 1921, repr. New York, Kraus, 1971), 75.

[155] Pecock, *The Donet*, 76.

in the chief is nat well kept ne susteyned in the membrys".[156] Following on from this invocation of the theory of the body politic, the poem also appeals to the Bible. The prince should follow the words of Christ to Peter in the gospel of John: "Petre, yf thou love me, feede and norissh my shepe, that is to say my peeple", and thus "no man shulde be governeure of his peeple but yf he love God, and also but yf he will pasture and noryssh his peeple in peas, love and good justise".[157] Therefore, as well as ensuring that the just price be paid for purveyances, the king should ensure the social and economic well-being of all members of society. By doing so, he would be acting for the love of God.

In 1470–1471, Sir John Fortescue wrote to Edward, Prince of Wales about the nature of good government, and this advice was sent to the Earl of Warwick, who had restored Henry VI to the throne. Fortescue urged that a council be established to provide continuing advice on economic policy—"the good politike wele of the londe"—and to consider "what lyvelod the king hathe for the sustenacion of his estate".[158] Goods for the king's household should be paid for immediately, which would be not only less expensive but also more beneficial to the poor: "And the king shall have therby alway the market at his gate to his grete profute but to moche more profute of the pore peopull". Such an action would also be pleasing to God "that hathe no prince excused of paying his dettes".[159] Fortescue warned of the danger to a king's reputation if he borrowed but failed to repay his creditors. He had a hard-nosed view of economic and political reality and how a king could be deserted in favour of powerful lords: "for his subgiettes willin rather goo wyth a lorde that is riche and may pay their wages and expences thann with their kyng that hathe nought in his purs".[160] Fortescue also warned about the consequences if

---

[156] "The Three Consideracions Right Necesserye for the Good Governaunce of a Prince", in *Four English Political Tracts of the Later Middle Ages*, ed. Jean-Philippe Genet (London: Royal Historical Society, 1977), 185.

[157] "The Three Consideracions", 190.

[158] "Articles sent by Edward, Prince of Wales, to the earl of Warwick concerning the government of England, written by Sir John Fortescue, 1470–71", in *The Politics of Fifteenth-Century England: John Vale's Book*, ed. Margaret Lucille Kekewich et al. (Stroud: Sutton, 1995), 223.

[159] "Articles sent by Edward, Prince of Wales", 224.

[160] "Articles sent by Edward, Prince of Wales", 231.

"the commones of Englande wer made pouere as biene the commones of France". Quite apart from the risk of a rebellion:

> Also it is the kinges honour and also his office to make his reaume riche, and it is his dishonour whanne that he hathe but apore reaume, of which men wil saye that he reigneth but upon beggeres, yit it were moche gretter dishonour yif he founde his reaume riche and than made it pouer. And it is also gretly ageinste his conscience that oughte to defende hem and their goodes, yif he toke from hem theire goodes withoute lawfull cause.[161]

The widely circulated late fifteenth-century work, the *Dictes and Sayings of the Philosophers*, also recognises the importance of maintaining a sound economic order: "Susteyne and love also thos that be the grete multiplyers that is to saye the comones" whose labour sustains the kingdom, the people and the knights and "the houses full of richesse, wherefore suche thinges wol be gretely kept and cherissed".[162] It also stressed the relationship between good government and economic prosperity: "And the knightys been mainteyned by moneye and money cometh of the peple, and the people is governed by Justice without whiche no Royaume may prospere".[163]

Milmete, Hoccleve and Pecock adopt a more traditional ethical view in their urging of the role of moderation and reason in the king's economic management. *The Three Consideraciones* and the *Dictes and Sayings* promote prosperity because prosperity amongst a king's subjects is conducive to the maintenance of the social hierarchy, peace and order. Fortescue pointed out the practical and political benefits for a ruler if he maintained prosperity in his kingdom, but described this as a matter of honour. Thus, different viewpoints are presented in these texts, but they can all be regarded as expressions of economic ethics, the ideals to which a king should aspire.

---

[161] "Articles sent by Edward, Prince of Wales", 241.

[162] *The Dictes and Sayings of the Philosophers*, trans. Earl Rivers (London: William Caxton, 1477, repr. London: Diploma Press, 1974), 21.

[163] *Dictes and Sayings*, 92.

Good Lordship Versus Bad Lordship

In addition to moral advice to kings and princes, there was advice to lords concerning impartiality in justice and the upholding of the virtues. Pauper urges princes, lords and leaders of the people to do justice: "to you it longith to knowyn ryghtful doom to demyn what is good & what is wyckyd, what is trewe & what is fals".[164] According to Bromyard, the role of lords is to judge and therefore they themselves must be just. A way of finding signs of nobility in acts of government and judgements is to ask whether they eradicate slavery and cruelty or eradicate mercy and kindness.[165] The late thirteenth-century *De placitis et curiis tenendis* advises the holder of pleas and manor courts to refuse bribes and gifts and to maintain the poor. In sentiments similar to those of *Jacob's Well*, his justice and mercy will be rewarded in the afterlife:

> his judgment shall endure for ever, and his name shall be in praise, and so from his little bailiwick he shall be transferred to a kingdom by Him who taketh the needy from the dust and lifteth up the poor out of the mire, and so he may sit with princes and hold a throne of glory.[166]

The administration of impartial justice, the rejection of bribes and truly helping the poor are all important principles of economic ethics that lords should uphold.

Good lordship, like the common good, can be regarded as a political concept but it does have relevance to economic ethics, both because of lords' role as arbiters and dispensers of economic justice and because lords themselves were meant to be beyond the temptations of avarice. According to *The Book of Vices and Virtues*, the ground of true lordship is virtue: humankind was given lordship over all other creatures but it was lost through sin and the only way it can be recovered is through virtue. This virtue is defined as self-control, control of the body and the heart. Kings and barons might have kingdoms, castles and cities, but in their

[164] Fifth Precept, cap. vii, in *Dives and Pauper*, vol. 1, part 2, 14.

[165] Bromyard, *SP(2)*, 109v.

[166] *The Court Baron*, ed. F.W. Maitland and W.P. Baildon (London: Bernard Quaritch for the Selden Society, 1891), 69–70.

hearts they are not lords for they are moved by anger, ill-will, covetousness or other desires they cannot fulfil. John Bromyard also says that nobility requires many virtues: wisdom especially for those who rule.[167]

Presenting a slightly different argument from *The Book of Vices and Virtues*, Pauper states that God gave Adam and all humankind lordship over other living things, but this is not a justification for temporal lordship, which is "ordeyned and foundyn of man be weye of synne and of coueytise". Dives retorts that if all were poor, Pauper himself would suffer. Pauper responds that if all were rich, then who would work in the fields or manufacture goods?[168] Lordship and the gulf between rich and poor are justified if they are a "propre dispensacioun ordeyned of God", but those who obtain their wealth and lordship by covetousness are tyrants and ravenors.[169] The rich and powerful are ordained by God to govern the poor, and, somewhat conveniently, because they own more goods than the poor, they save the poor from the sin of pride and other vices.[170]

Specific advice to lords about their economic dealings with their tenants was also given. John Bromyard writes of the duty a lord has towards his subjects because his land and wealth are God-given. Those who believe that they can take from their own subjects, because all their subjects own belongs also to them, are stealing. These subjects are assigned to the rich for their care, like a ward to a guardian. Lords live by the labour of their subjects, and because they have care of them, receiving a stipend from God in the form of villages or towns, lands and rents, there is a kind of compact whereby the subjects are bound to serve the lord faithfully and perform whatever customs they are obliged to render, while the lords are obliged to minister to their subjects and pay them good salaries. Those lords who rob from their subjects have broken this compact ordained by God and will be judged before Him. Theft by the powerful is also wrong for another reason: Bromyard refers to Book 6 of John of Salisbury's *Policraticus*, which asserts that if the head of the body politic is unwell, the disorder affects the other members of the body, who cannot tolerate it

---

167 *Vices and Virtues*, 83–84; Bromyard *SP(2)* 108r.

168 'Holy Poverty', version A, in *Dives and Pauper*, vol. 1, part 1, 63.

169 Seventh Precept, cap. v, in *Dives and Pauper*, vol. 1, part 2, 139.

170 Seventh Precept, cap. v, in *Dives and Pauper*, vol. 1, part 2, 140.

without great suffering.[171] Lords who offend in this way do so to maintain an opulent or extravagant lifestyle, justifying their excessive spending by attributing it to their blood or the status they were born into. If they are asked why they spend more on horses, food, clothes and the pomp of this world than their land, rents and revenues are worth, their response is that for honour, family, blood and status they must show liberality. Bromyard argues firstly that it would be better and wiser to lose the aforesaid honour than to live unjustly. Secondly, he maintains that such expenditure does not show liberality or nobility but the vilest sin and the fiery devil because it says in the *Decretum distinctione* (Distinctiones of Gratian's *Decretum*) 86c that liberality is fine or beautiful and requires no superfluous expenditure. Certainly, giving to actors, illegal hunters and shameful persons is not liberality but vice.[172] Thomas Docking attacks the higher clergy for their lavish lifestyle in a similar fashion: they use their benefices to maintain prostitutes, horses, great households and fine clothing. They are not feeding the poor but actors, jesters and huntsmen; they are surrounded by gold, silver and giltware.[173] Indeed, if all thieves in England were hanged, few or none of our bishops would be left.[174] Here, it is clear that liberality does not mean going beyond the bounds of moderation and that a lord's excessive expenditure is violating a contract with God.

Bromyard argues that such excesses can lead to a range of social and economic problems. He reiterates the point that the nobility are appointed by God, quoting Deuteronomy: "I took the chief of your tribes men, wise men and known, and made them heads over you … And I charged your judges [to] judge righteously between every man and his brother, and the stranger that is with him".[175] He compares subjects with domestic fowl and animals, malefactors with game and wild birds, and nobles or leaders with hawks or falcons and hunting dogs. The game and wild birds are seized and punished, whereas the domestic fowl and animals provide the fixed rents, incomes or revenues for the nobles' sustenance.

[171] Bromyard, *SP*(*1*), 306v, 307r

[172] Bromyard, *SP*(*1*), 308v.

[173] Docking, *De Decem Praeceptis*, MS Bodley 453, fols 53r–53v.

[174] Docking, *De Decem Praeceptis*, MS Bodley 453, fol. 53v: "si omnes fures essent suspensi, pauci vel nulli prelati nobis in anglia nobis remanerent".

[175] Deuteronomy 1:15–16.

Those who plunder their subjects are not noble birds or dogs but kites, foxes and wolves. Those who live in palaces and live extravagantly take from the towns unjustly and leave them in ruins and poverty, with hardly enough bread and cold water.[176] Many nobles by name or title have lived ignobly and their punishment often happens in this world as much as in the eternal because they face impoverishment, disinheritance and community disturbance or disorder. Impoverishment results from their debts to merchants and other creditors, caused by their extravagance and ostentation.[177]

Lords' officials were also given advice about justice and moderation in managing estates. Walter of Henley gave advice about observing moderation, acting prudently when it came to finances and treating tenants fairly. His *Le Dite de Hosbondrie* was written in the late thirteenth century but may well have continued to be used in the fourteenth and fifteenth centuries, for it was printed by Wynkyn de Worde as *The Boke of Husbandry*.[178] Usury and *chevisances* were to be avoided, for "he who borrows from another robs himself", which again shows that agents operating in the rural sector could be engaged in those sorts of financial arrangements, as well as merchants.[179] Walter also advises against fining tenants too heavily, for this brings animosity, and gifts should be made to the poor. Following the argument of theologians discussed in Chapter 2, Walter states that gifts to the poor are necessary because God has lent the landowner his wealth.[180] *Hosebonderie*, an anonymous treatise also dating from the thirteenth century, advocates just pricing on lords' estates. A smith should be paid according to prices paid elsewhere, and seneschals and bailiffs should oversee that their subordinates do not deal in any

---

[176] Bromyard, *SP(2)*, 109r.

[177] Bromyard, *SP(2)*, 110v.

[178] Dorothea Oschinsky, *Walter of Henley and Other Treatises on Estate Management and Accounting.* Oxford: Clarendon Press, 1971.

[179] Walter de Henley, *Le Dite de Hosebondrie*, in *Walter of Henley's Husbandry together with an Anonymous Husbandry, Seneschaucie and Robert Grosseteste's Rules*, ed. Elizabeth Lamond (London: Longmans Green , 1890), 4.

[180] Walter de Henley, *Hosebondrie*, 5.

goods "unless by tally and good witness".[181] Thus, the officials of lords, like their masters, were reminded of the principles of economic ethics.

Making Restitution, Punishment and Spiritual Discipline

According to Alexander of Hales and Aquinas, making restitution is an important principle of economic ethics. Pastoral manuals advised making restitution directly to the affected party where it concerned selling faulty or overpriced goods, using false weights and measures, usury and forestalling, as well as the unjust acquisition of land and property.[182] An inheritance that was gained partly through usury, ravine, theft or any other fraud had to be restored and restitution made of property wrongfully withheld from the owner as well as the profits gained therefrom.[183] Another way of making restitution was by giving alms to the poor.[184] However, the alms had to come from the offender's own money or goods, not from ravening, theft or usury.[185] Whereas almsgiving and the works of mercy could have been generalised acts of charity, restitution meant making good for specific wrongs, often to specific parties.

A specific ecclesiastical punishment, excommunication, was decreed for the practice of usury and the use of false weights and measures. Usury was the most serious offence, on a par with murder, arson and heresy: both *Cursor Mundi* and *Instructions for Parish Priests* say that usury was one of the sins that could be dealt with only by the bishop.[186] Both a usurer and the borrower or other person supporting or dealing with them faced serious consequences. Usurers could not receive communion until they had made complete restitution, nor could they make offerings, and nor could they be buried in consecrated ground. Their wills had no validity.

---

[181] Walter de Henley, *Hosebondrie*, 63.

[182] Seventh Precept, cap. x, in *Dives and Pauper*, vol. 1, part 2, 153–155.

[183] *Jacob's Well* (Brandeis), 199, 200, 202; any land, houses property or money unjustly acquired must be restored before the offender can receive absolution, *Speculum sacerdotale*, 71.

[184] Mirk, *Instructions for Parish Priests*, p. 52.

[185] *Cursor Mundi*, vol. 3, 1565.

[186] *Cursor Mundi*, vol. 3, 1488; Mirk, *Instructions for Parish Priests*, 54–55.

Dives and Pauper devotes much of chapter xxvii of Commandment VII to the punishments for usurers.[187] Usurers also risked social ostracism: *Handlyng Synne* has a tale that in a certain town a man was found to be a usurer and "They helde hym vyler than a Iew" and his house was known as the home of the fiend.[188] The ritual of cursing, which was carried out in churches two or three times a year, included usurers in a list of those who were subject to excommunication. Priests were told "Thou shall pronounce this idous thing/With crosse & candell and bell knylling", and after the articles of the sentence of cursing and excommunication have been read out, the priest should throw down the candle and spit on the ground and then the bells should peal.[189]

Other offences committed by the avaricious and covetous were not subject to excommunication or cursing, but plenty of exempla warning of eternal punishment appeared in confessional handbooks and other works. A good example is a story repeated by John Bromyard from one of Peter Damian's sermons about unjust land acquisition: an angel took an inheritor to hell and showed him a pillory, above which were three hooks and three people hanging, one above the other. The one in the lowest position suffered more, for the drops of foul matter ran down from those above. There was also an empty hook. The angel explained to the inheritor that his ancestors were hanging there and that the empty hook was for him if restitution was not made.[190]

Other ways of attacking avarice were by almsgiving and by spiritual discipline, voluntary poverty or fasting: *Fasciculus Morum* says contempt for the world and voluntary poverty uproot avarice; fasting is favoured by *Speculum Sacerdotale* and John Mirk; the contemplation of mortality is recommended by *Regimen Animarum*, and Alexander Carpenter, who has no fewer than 68 chapters devoted to avarice, describes many different remedies.[191] Calling upon the individual's conscience was another:

---

[187] *Fasciculus Morum*, 353; *Dives and Pauper*, vol.1, part 2, 203–206.

[188] *Handlyng Synne*, 92.

[189] Mirk, *Instructions for Parish Priests*, 21, 24.

[190] Bromyard, *SP*(*1*), 18r–18v.

[191] *Fasciculus morum*, 383, 387; *Speculum Sacerdotale*, ed. Edward H. Weatherly (London: OUP for EETS), 92; *John Mirk's Festial*, vol. 1, ed. Susan Powel, (Oxford: OUP for EETS, 2009), 80; *Regimen Animarum*, MS Hatton II, fols 73v–75r; Alexander Carpenter's *Destructorium Viciorum*.

readers of *The Pricke of Conscience* were warned that on Judgement Day there would be fifteen accusers, including conscience, sin, angels, demons, martyrs, God and the Trinity. Conscience will reveal all wrongdoings and their sins will betray the wicked.[192]

The significance of teachings about restitution for our understanding of economic ethics is that they were related to distributive justice, in returning what was due to the aggrieved party. In restoring what had been taken unlawfully or by deceit, a kind of order, or the original state of affairs, was returned. This, in turn, can be linked to the ideal of a harmonious society which obtained before the depredations of the avaricious happened, the kind of world that existed before the Fall of humankind.

Conclusions

The ideals of economic ethics such as moderate or reasonable wealth, justice, charity, lordship and the good order of society and the contrasting evils of avarice and prodigality and its manifestations in deception, usury, extortion and abuse of purveying are themes which appeared in a range of sources: pastoral manuals, sermons, guides to conduct, and books of wisdom.

James Davis has argued that there was an interplay between the moral advice of the Church and secular legislation, which he based on the assertion that Church moralists frequently "drew directly upon statute law as an exemplar of practical order".[193] In my own research, I have found that there is evidence for such "interplay" in William of Pagula's insertion of the *Magna Carta* and the *Carta de Foresta* in his influential priest's manual *Oculus Sacerdotis*, which also appear in the variant of *Oculus Sacerdotis* known as *Regimen Animarum*. Their presence is due to the fact that those charters were required to be distributed to every cathedral and collegiate church in the realm. However, I have found that although many of the authors of confessional manuals show awareness of numerous types of marketplace fraud in their framing of the questions to be put to penitents,

[192] *Pricke of Conscience*, ed. Morris, 147–148, 151, 161, 181–183.
[193] Davis, *MMM*, 30.

they do not cite a particular statute but instead remind penitents that deceit could be a breach of the Commandment against theft or that false weights and measures and usury are condemned in Deuteronomy.

Notions of avarice, prodigality, liberality, justice, charity and good lordship, originating from theological or philosophical sources, were conveyed to the laity in a variety of ways, some employing more abstract arguments, others the everyday imagery of birds and animals, illness or disease more readily understood by lay readers or hearers.

The underlying connection between avarice, justice, charity, the common good and good lordship is in the concept of order versus disorder. Avarice, including ambition for a higher station in life, destabilises society by leading to crimes such as extortion and usury, while excess wealth, without charity and almsgiving, leads to an imbalance where the rich prosper at the expense of the poor. Justice is restoring order, bringing reason and conscience together and giving everyone his or her due. This order, however, is ordained by God and therefore serving justice is serving God. Restoring the correct balance between rich and poor is also serving justice and God, although correct balance does not mean equality but what each station in life should be properly accorded.[194] The term "common good" was used less often in pastoral manuals, sermons and guides to morality but was implied in passages declaring that a ruler should care for the good of all his subjects. The theories of the three estates and the body politic were employed in both pastoral manuals and sermons in order to justify the maintenance of the social order, probably because the growing prosperity of merchants and traders brought concerns that their ambitions would upset the traditional and God-given hierarchy.

Yet an important matter shown in this chapter is that notions of economic ethics were applied to all classes of society from the king downwards, not just to merchants, artisans and victuallers. Members of the ruling class and legal and estate officials were criticised for their rapacity and reminded of their responsibilities regarding the administration of economic justice. Indeed, it could be the case that injustices by rulers and lords, such as excessive fines and fees, had a wider impact on the

[194] For a much fuller discussion of the ideal of balance, see Joel Kaye, *A History of Balance, 1250–1375*. Cambridge: CUP, 2014.

economic welfare of the poor than deceitful traders in urban centres. Concern with rapacious lords is very significant in these works, and this can be explained by the fact that the economy of late medieval England was still mostly rural. The avaricious behaviour of lords or gentry and their officials would have affected many more people than overpricing or deceptive trading by merchants, artisans and victuallers in towns or at fairs. Given that many of the works discussed reached a wide lay readership and that sermons reached an even larger audience, confining economic ethics to the latter is too narrow a view.

The next chapter will examine the presentation of issues relating to economic ethics in literary works of the fourteenth and fifteenth centuries. Literary works have at times a more complex approach than pastoral manuals through their use of fictional forms. They also take the discussion well beyond merchants and traders into the realm of lordship, kingship and the rural scene.

4

Wealth and Lordship in Late Medieval Literature

I have examined economic ethics in late medieval England from the point of view of theologians and philosophers, the authors of pastoral manuals and guides to conduct and sermons. Incorporated into those texts were condemnations of avarice, usury and prodigality; praise for the virtues of liberality, moderation and justice; and promotion of the concepts of the just price, good lordship and the common good. In order to convey meaning and relevance to their readers or hearers, writers looked to the secular world for illustrations. As I have shown, they not only drew upon the activities of merchants and usurers, craftsmen, traders and labourers but also considered examples drawn from landowning and noble levels of society.

I am drawing upon literary evidence in this chapter because many fourteenth- and fifteenth-century literary works were informed by ideas that were similar to those found in theological and pastoral works, but they were able to explore problems of economic ethics in different ways. I have argued that economic ethics were intended to apply to all members of late medieval society, but in this chapter I do not intend to discuss the criticisms of idle labourers, fraudulent traders, or usurers or the good or

J. Hole, *Economic Ethics in Late Medieval England, 1300–1500*,
Archival Insights into the Evolution of Economics,
DOI 10.1007/978-3-319-38860-1_4

bad images of merchants in late medieval English literature as they have been very well addressed elsewhere.[1] Instead, I will focus on the portrayal of lords and rulers, both as offenders and as ethical role models. The literary works I examine here are also concerned with questions about good lordship and justice, so they are important for examining economic ethics as they affect the elite, landowning classes. It is also significant that those classes were largely the audiences for these works. Authors had the opportunity to use these more literary genres to make their criticisms directly to their readers and to raise issues that concerned them about the role of kings, lords and landowners in economic ethics. Late medieval English writers had concerns about the economic changes that had occurred as a result of the development of markets and commercialisation, changes which had been intensified by the Black Death. John Gower, for one, was concerned about those changes and the impact they had on morality, but he was also concerned about the future of society. In the original version of his prologue to *Confessio Amantis*, which mentioned the sixteenth year of the reign of Richard II, there is a sense of anxiety "What schal befalle hierafterward/God wot".[2] Gower and other writers considered in this chapter expressed their ideas of how the leaders of society could practise economic ethics and of what an ideal society should be.

Three major problems will be investigated in this chapter: firstly, how lords' avarice was criticised but their wealth justified; secondly, the role of kings in economic ethics; and, thirdly, how lords and knights failed to meet ethical expectations. Lastly, two related but differing visions for a socio-economic future will be compared and contrasted. These topics are addressed, in different ways, in two works by Chaucer (*The Parson's Tale* and a poem on the "golden age"), John Gower (*Confessio Amantis* and the *Mirour de l'Omme*), John Lydgate (*The Fall of Princes*), Thomas Hoccleve (*The Regiment of Princes*), William Langland (*The Vision of Piers Plowman*) and the anonymous *Wynnere and Wastoure*.

---

[1] For surveys of the portrayals of deceitful trade and usury in late medieval English literature, see Chap. 1 "Images of Market Trade" in Davis, *MMM*, 34–136; David Aers, "Justice and Wage-Labor After the Black Death: Some Perplexities for William Langland", in *The Work of Work: Servitude, Slavery and Labor in Medieval England*, ed. Allen J. Frantzen and Douglas Moffat (Glasgow: Cruithne Press, 1994), 169–190.

[2] Prologue, *Confessio Amantis*, vol. 1, 44.

Gower's *Confessio Amantis* was, apparently, a commission from Richard II, although later Gower dedicated the work to Henry Bolingbroke, Earl of Derby (later Henry IV). In his revised prologue to *Confessio Amantis*, Gower states that he wrote it in English "for Engelondes sake" and that he is concerned that the world is now in many ways "so diversed".[3] Some forty-nine manuscript copies of *Confessio Amantis* survive; it was printed by Caxton in 1483 and was well known in the sixteenth century. The posthumous reputation of Gower's *Mirour de l'Omme* is not so great: only one manuscript copy has survived (Cambridge University Library, MS Additional 3035) but it must be seen as part of Gower's effort to impart his knowledge for the benefit of others. The various colophons to *Confessio Amantis* all state Gower's conviction that he is obliged to impart this knowledge since it is received from God, and the colophons all describe three works: *Mirour de l'Omme*, *Vox Clamantis* and *Confessio Amantis*.[4] *Mirour de l'Omme*, being written entirely in Anglo-Norman, must have been intended for readers in the higher orders of society rather than as a popular work, but it is of interest because of its extensive coverage of issues associated with economic ethics. Its tone resembles that of the *sermones ad status* and its breakdown of the seven deadly sins into various branches is very similar to that found in *The Book of Vices and Virtues* and other guides to conscience.

Hoccleve's *Regiment of Princes* was dedicated to Prince Hal, the future Henry V, and Hoccleve made a copy in his own hand for the prince's brother, the Duke of Bedford. The *Regiment*'s audience, however, was not limited to the royal family, since forty-six copies survive, placing it at the same level of popularity as Lydgate's *Fall of Princes*, Gower's *Confessio Amantis*, Chaucer's *Canterbury Tales* and Langland's *Piers Plowman*.

Lydgate's *Fall of Princes* was commissioned by Humphrey, Duke of Gloucester, in 1431. The Duke had an active role in its production, asking Lydgate to insert a "lenvoie" commenting on the morality involved at the end of each story: that he should "sette a remedie".[5] It took Lydgate eight years to complete this translation of an extended French version of

[3] Prologue, *Confessio Amantis*, vol. 1, 44.

[4] The Colophons, *Confessio Amantis*, vol. 1, 229–233.

[5] *Lydgate's Fall of Princes, Part 1*, ed. Henry Bergen (London: OUP for EETS, 1924), 204.

De casibus illustrium virorum, a work written by Boccaccio around 1358. Lydgate's basis was Laurence de Premierfait's *Des Cas des Nobles Hommes et Femmes*, a second and extended version which he completed between 1405 and 1409 for the Duc de Berry.[6] Not all of the commentaries in *The Fall of Princes* are entitled "envoi" and could be translations from Premierfait's edition, but several were written by Lydgate. In Book II of *The Fall of Princes*, Boccaccio's and Premierfait's examples showing the justified overthrow of a tyrant are replaced with a "Chapitle" on good government where Lydgate rehearsed the principles of the harmonious body politic from John of Salisbury's *Policraticus*.[7] Many of the stories in *The Fall of Princes* concern the despatch of tyrants, so perhaps Lydgate wanted to remind his patron of this well-worn theory of the interdependence of all society's members or perhaps Duke Humphrey had asked that it be included.

The Fall of Princes enjoyed a wide circulation amongst the nobility, for out of thirty-six manuscript copies, either full or partial, several were owned or commissioned by them. Again, like Hoccleve's *Regiment of Princes*, *The Fall of Princes* was not meant to be read only by members of the royal family or the nobility. In his prologue to Book I, Lydgate understands Boccaccio's purpose in writing such a work, which was that the stories were moral exempla to be read by all "the vicious folk off euery comounte".[8] For many ordinary readers, it was Lydgate's "envoi", rather than the narratives, which appealed to them for there are nearly forty additional manuscript copies which contain these alone.[9] The complete work eventually spread beyond the nobility to a wider readership via the printing press. *The Fall of Princes* was twice printed by Richard Pynson (in 1494 and 1527) and reprinted in the mid-sixteenth century by both Richard Tottel and John Wayland. Wynkyn de Worde also printed extracts from *The Fall of Princes*, from both the narratives

[6] "Introductory Note", in *Lydgate's Fall of Princes, Part 1*, xiii.

[7] Jennifer Summit, "'Stable in study': Lydgate's *Fall of Princes* and Duke Humphrey's Library", in *John Lydgate: Poetry, Culture and Lancastrian England*, ed. Larry Scanlon and James Simpson (Notre Dame, IN: University of Notre Dame Press, 2006), 222; *Lydgate's Fall of Princes, Part 1*, 221–225.

[8] *Lydgate's Fall of Princes, Part I*, 6–7.

[9] A.S.G. Edwards, "The Influence of Lydgate's *Fall of Princes c.* 1440–1559: A Survey", *Medieval Studies* 39 (1977): 431.

and the "envoi", as pamphlets in 1519, titled *The Proverbs of Lydgate.*[10] Therefore, a wider range of readers of Lydgate's *The Fall of Princes* would have learned of the curative powers of justice and of how important it was for society's rulers to possess this virtue and to apply it with impartiality to all. They would have read Lydgate's warnings about the future reputation of society's leaders if they were avaricious and of the fate of tyrants, examples of which are discussed later in this chapter.

The Vision of Piers Plowman was another popular work. Scholars have maintained that the B-Text of *The Vision of Piers Plowman* was copied mainly in London and that Langland avoided using many dialect terms to ensure that it could be understood by the city's geographically varied population and also by people in the Midlands. William Palmer, a London rector, and Thomas Roos, a mercer, both left copies in their wills and this suggests its appeal to both clergy and laity. It had fallen out of favour by the mid-fifteenth century and was not printed by Caxton or other early printers.[11] However, A.V.C. Schmidt comments that sixty manuscripts of *The Vision of Piers Plowman* survive (that is, of the A, B and C versions) and adds that it was revived as a best-seller after its printing in 1550.[12]

Some of Chaucer's lyrics, including *The Former Age* and the *Parson's Tale* from the *Canterbury Tales*, both of which are cited in this chapter, were circulated separately. Some of the lyrics were circulated in Chaucer's lifetime. Selections from the *Canterbury Tales* and the *Tales* as a whole were copied in the century after Chaucer's death. Although they originally were written to entertain the court of Richard II, they later reached a wider audience, particularly after their printing in 1478 by William Caxton.[13]

---

[10] *Lydgate's Fall of Princes, Part 4*, ed. Henry Bergen (Washington:, Carnegie Institution, 1927), 106, 123.

[11] Caroline Barron, "William Langland, a London Poet", in *Chaucer's England: Literature in Historical Context*, ed. Barbara A. Hanawalt (Minneapolis: University of Minnesota Press, 1992), 92, 99.

[12] *Vision of Piers Plowman*, xx.

[13] Julia Boffey, "The Reputation and Circulation of Chaucer's Lyrics on the Fifteenth Century", *Chaucer Review* 28 (1993): 23–40; A.S.G. Edwards, "Chaucer from Manuscript to Print: The Social text and the Critical Text", *Mosaic (Winnipeg)* 28 (1995): 1–12.

Criticism of Lords and Justifications of Wealth

The uneven distribution of wealth was generally accepted as part of God's disposition of resources and responsibilities, yet lords, too, could be guilty of avarice. Gower's Anglo-Norman work *Mirour de l'Omme*, written between 1376 and 1379, deals with at least as many issues concerning economic ethics as his better-known *Confessio Amantis*. In the *Mirour de l'Omme*, Gower justifies the economic inequality between lords and others by arguing that God did not make some people poor because he was unable to make everyone wealthy but because he wanted to test the lords' devotion to him: whoever is both wealthy and just has deserved great favour and will have eternal reward. He does not conclude, like John Bromyard, that lords who are unjust have broken their compact with God, nor does he take up Wyclif's controversial argument (discussed in Chapter 2) that lords who have not lived up to ethical standards should have their lordships taken away. Yet Gower is still critical of lords, attributing wars, along with the ruin of the poor and the breakdown of law and order, to the covetousness of some lords. His explanation of such evil is that lords have such power over people, those people have to follow their governance.[14]

Therefore, the evil in the world is brought about by lords: Gower might be thinking of the deeds committed by lords' retainers, such as extortion, bribery and corruption in the law courts, entering properties "with force and arms", which were the subject of many complaints in late medieval England.[15] If people are bound to follow their lords and forced to do their will, no matter how evil it might be, lords clearly have a great deal to answer for. Gower, with a good sense of caution, did not identify particular offenders, instead attributing the very worst kinds of behaviour to the lords of Lombardy.[16] Probably Gower had heard of the deeds of the Visconti and other tyrannical lords via contacts in London, where many Lombard merchants were based. Or he might have read Chaucer's *Complaint Unto Pity*, in which he referred to the "tyrauntes

[14] *Mirour de L'Omme*, 256, 257.

[15] See the first version of Gower's prayer for England at the end of Book 8 of *Confessio Amantis*, vol. 1, 221).

[16] *Mirour de L'Omme*, 256.

of Lumbardye".[17] Gower's caution is a contrast to the *Second Shepherds' Play*, in which, apart from the fact that it would be strange for shepherds to be aware of practices in Lombardy, there is a sense that the oppression the shepherds complain of is by local lords. The shepherds claim they are over-taxed by "thyse gentlery-men".[18] The shepherds also complain about the behaviour of lords' retainers, who make threats when purveying for their masters (the issue of purveying abuses will be discussed more fully in the next chapter). Parliament tried to address this problem but placed the blame upon those retainers who were pretending to be acting for a lord. It determined that badges should be worn only by retainers in service for life and by means of an indenture and that a valet or an archer should be living in the lord's household for a least a year.[19]

The Commons had asked, at the Parliament held at Cambridge in 1388, that the giving out of badges be abolished. Unfortunately for them, the subsequent Statute of Livery and Maintenance (1399) was not so comprehensive, citing livery only and restricting the giving out of livery to those at the rank of banneret or higher. This compromise obviously suited the Lords since they could continue to issue badges to whomever they pleased. Further complaints were made by the Commons, and the issue was brought to a head again during the reign of Henry IV.[20] The problems being addressed by legislation were abuses of a version of feudalism termed "bastard feudalism" by historians.[21] Michael Hicks suggests that a system of retaining involving indentures and fees was stimulated by the wars of Edward I in the 1290s and that it was more prevalent in the north, where magnates relied on what forces they could gather in Yorkshire, as well as closer to the Scottish border, to protect against any

---

[17] Phillipa Hardman, "Chaucer's Tyrants of Lombardy", *Review of English Studies*, New Series, 31 (1980): 172–178; Chaucer had also visited Lombardy. See David Wallace, *Chaucerian Polity: Absolutist Images and Associational Forms in England and Italy* (Stanford: Stanford University Press, 1997), 31–40.

[18] *The Wakefield Pageants of the Towneley Cycle*, ed. A. C. Cawley (Manchester: Manchester University Press, 1975), 43.

[19] *Parliament Rolls*, Richard II, January 1390.

[20] *SR*, vol. 2, 74–75; Nigel Saul, "The Commons and the Abolition of Badges", *Parliamentary History* 9 (1990): 302–315.

[21] Michael Hicks, *Bastard Feudalism* (London: Longmans, 1995), 12. The term was first used by the Reverend Charles Plummer in 1885.

incursions by the Scots.[22] This might explain why the *Second Shepherds' Play*, which was performed at Wakefield, complained about the economic injustices committed by retainers. Retainers could commit crimes with or without their lord's approval, but whichever the case, lords were held responsible for their behaviour.[23] An earlier statute (1346) ordered lords to dismiss "bearers and Maintainers of Quarrels and Parties" who had been "maintained and borne by Lords", but it seems without much effect. The issue arose again in 1461: Parliament noted that those problems were continuing and it was recorded that articles were to be proclaimed throughout the realm and that Edward IV would hear petitions from affected parties.[24]

Langland has a description of an abuse of livery and maintenance in *The Vision of Piers Plowman*, a work contemporary both with Gower's *Mirour de l'Omme* and with his later work *Confessio Amantis*.[25] A petition is brought to Parliament by Pees, a husbandman, against Wrong, who could be an oppressive lord.[26] Wrong, "a wikked luft", colludes with the worldly lawyers to offer a bribe to the king via the good offices of Lady Mede. The king, however, orders the imprisonment of Wrong.[27] Lady Mede then offers gold to Pees, which he is tempted to accept, but a furious protest by Reason, citing all the greed and corruption in the land, puts an end to that manoeuvre.[28]

Lady Mede represents many things: venality, corruption and the easy world of giving and taking bribes as opposed to the world of true labour for true or eternal reward, which was earned for labouring for God.[29] Lady Mede, though seemingly not from the nobility (Mark Ormrod has

---

[22] Hicks, *Bastard Feudalism*, 78, 82–83.

[23] Hicks, *Bastard Feudalism*, 125, 127.

[24] *SR*, vol. 1, 304; *Parliament Rolls*, Edward IV, November 1461, membrane 17, item 38.

[25] *The Vision of Piers Plowman* has three main versions (A, B and C texts) generally thought to range in date from the 1360s to the 1390s. See Lawrence Warner, *The Lost History of Piers Plowman: The Earliest Transmission of Langland's Work* (Philadelphia: University of Pennsylvania Press, 2011), 13–14. For the purposes of this chapter, Schmidt's second edition of the B-Text is used.

[26] *Vision of Piers Plowman*, passus IV, 55–56.

[27] *Vision of Piers Plowman*, passus IV, 56–57.

[28] *Vision of Piers Plowman*, passus IV, 57.

[29] James Simpson, "Spirituality and Economics in Passus 1–7 of the B Text", *Yearbook of Langland Studies* 1 (1987), 83–103.

suggested that Lady Mede was based on Alice Perrers, the mistress of Edward III), behaves as a wealthy lord might do in many respects and represents the power of money.[30] She is a corrupting influence on the judiciary when she is brought for judgement at Westminster, giving gold and silver cups, ruby rings and money to the judges who come to give her comfort over her fear of the king. She also gives valuable gifts to the canon law clerks, promising that she will have their names called at the consistory court and assuring that their lack of learning will be no impediment to their advancement.[31] Then a friar comes to hear her confession, in return for money, which exemplifies Langland's objections to the mendicant orders and to the materialism of the Church in general but is also Langland's realistic view of the ease with which the wealthy can make amends and proclaim to all their generosity and piety. After promising to act as her loyal agent, the friar suggests she pay for a stained glass window at his Church, saying that with her name engraved upon it she can be sure of eternal salvation. Mede responds by offering to do even more, for if she pays for it all, everyone "shall see I am suster of youre house".[32] Langland represents this as pure hypocrisy: "An aventure pride be peynted there, and pomp of the worlde".[33]

"To be cursed in consistorie [Mede] counteth noght a russhe" for she provides copes and coats for the court officers and "She is assoiled as soone as hireself liketh".[34] Thus, excommunication or other penalties of the church courts are meaningless, for Mede and others like her can simply buy absolution. Conscience's tirade reveals the absolute power of those with money in the figure of Lady Mede and echoes the many condemnations of the pastoral manuals. Her actions ruin all: the poor have no hope of winning through litigation for "Lawe is so lordlich, and looth to maken ende" without bribes.

Nevertheless, Mede justifies both herself and the value of being able to reward people, to the king. She accuses Conscience, her antagonist,

---

[30] Mark Ormrod, "Who Was Alice Perrers?" *Chaucer Review* (40) (2006): 219–229.

[31] *Vision of Piers Plowman*, passus III, 38.

[32] *Vision of Piers Plowman*, passus III, 39–40.

[33] *Vision of Piers Plowman*, passus III, 40.

[34] *Vision of Piers Plowman*, passus III, 43.

of cowardice and disloyalty to the king because in the past he had urged him to abandon his claim to France, "the richeste reaume that reyn overhoveth". This might be a reference to the Treaty of Bretigny of 1360, when Edward III renounced his claim to the French throne and gave up some of his territories in exchange for Guienne, Gascony, Calais and others.[35] Lady Mede plainly regards the acquisition of France as wealth potential, and the abandonment of the claim a missed opportunity for gathering more and distributing it. To her, Conscience's arguments are unrealistic: Mede firstly points out that the king needs to reward those who serve him and secondly questions how people could be employed and make a living without any reward.[36]

The early fourteenth-century *Wynnere and Wastoure* presents another debate about the justification of wealth, also adjudicated by the king, and taking place between two opposing characters. Wynnere the merchant and Wastoure the aristocrat represent avarice on the one hand and prodigality on the other. Wynnere believes himself to be "a wy that alle this werlde helpis" and proceeds to attack Wastoure's profligate way of life, spending everything that Wynnere gathers while failing to maintain his own land and property. Wynnere is there to teach lords how to live on much less and spend little, for those such as Wastoure "this lande will he stroye".[37] Wastoure rejects Wynnere's version of moderation with the retort that Wynnere has used his savings to fill his wide houses with wool sacks, bend his roof beams under the weight of so many hanging hams, and stuff silver coins into coffers. Wynnere should let the people and the poor have part of that silver, and, as befits those who commit avarice, Wastoure declares that Wynnere will be hanged in hell if he spares nothing for them. Wynnere's defence is to accuse Wastoure of other sins—pride, gluttony and lechery—but he also urges him to protect his finances by increasing his revenue: "Rayse vp thi renthowses, ryme vp thi yerdes".[38] Wastoure maintains that feasts and fine food help the poor.[39] Wynnere

[35] *Vision of Piers Plowman*, passus III, 46.

[36] *Vision of Piers Plowman*, passus III, 47.

[37] *Wynnere and Wastoure*, 9.

[38] *Wynnere and Wastoure*, 10.

[39] *Wynnere and Wastoure*, 11.

remains on the offensive, describing all the rich and succulent food that Wastoure consumes and contrasting it with his own modest diet.

Wastoure supports the inequities of the social order as a natural hierarchy that should be left as it is.[40] The poor will get some morsel of meat and surely a winner needs a waster, for what annoys one man gladdens another. Wynnere, however, rejects the idea that spending by the rich will create wealth for the poor. Wastoure gives a final spirited defence of the noblemen's less cautious way of life, telling him to "Take the coppe as it comes, the case as it falles".[41] This is an echo of Jesus's advice in the gospels: "Take no thought for the morrow".[42]

Chaucer's *Canterbury Tales* contain both satire and serious concern about avarice. The hypocrisy and cant in the Pardoner's sermonising about avarice, and the miller's money-making schemes in the *Reeve's Tale* and those of the summoner in the *General Prologue*, are designed both to entertain and to provide insights about contemporary morality. Serious intent helps to explain the significant change in style and format in the final tale by the Parson, which is a lengthy sermon on preparing for confession and the seven deadly sins. Because of its nature, there is no debate about the uses of wealth but a series of declarations. It is noteworthy that the Parson's first example of avarice is not deceitful merchants and usurers but landowners:

> Of Coveitise comen thise harde lordshipes, thurgh whiche men been distreyned by taylages, custumes, and cariages, moore than hire duetee or resoun is. And eek taken they of hir bonde-men amercimentz, whiche mighten moore resonably ben cleped extorcions than amercimentz.[43]

Stewards justify such actions on the grounds that a "cherl" owns nothing that is not his lord's, a belief also expressed by landowners in some of the cases to be discussed in the next chapter.[44] The Parson disagrees; citing Book IX of Augustine's *De civitate Dei*, he says lords have done wrong

[40] *Wynnere and Wastoure*, 13.

[41] *Wynnere and Wastoure*, 15.

[42] Matthew 6:34.

[43] *Parson's Tale*, in *Riverside Chaucer*, 313.

[44] *Parson's Tale*, 313

because they have taken away things that they never gave. Furthermore, quoting Genesis 5, he declares that slavery or thraldom is sin, so it is not natural that there be lords of thralls; it is only so as a result of original sin.[45] Yet the Parson still upholds the law which says that bondmen's worldly goods belong to their lords, but they should be taken only when needed for defence of the territory.[46] Siegfried Wenzel has shown the close relationship between parts of the text of the *Parson's Tale* and a number of treatises, particularly Raymond of Pennaforte's *Summa de poenitentia* and Peraldus's *Summa de vitiis et virtutibus.*[47] The *Parson's Tale* thus presents as conservatism and orthodoxy, a morality and a view of economic ethics which Chaucer appeared to embrace. It could have been a prologue to Chaucer's own renunciation of some of his works.[48]

Both *The Vision of Piers Plowman* and *Wynnere and Wastoure* show awareness that people need to make a living and that lords and other rich people can, by spending and giving rewards, support the livelihoods of many. The ethical issue for William Langland is whether those rewards are fair, in the sense of being proportionate and in the sense that they were given for honest labour, not as bribes or for corrupt behaviour. Lady Mede represents the giving of rewards for undeserving and corrupt purposes and her possession of wealth is highly questionable.[49]

Both Gower and Chaucer are critical of personal gain by lords and its impact on society. They focus less on bribery and corruption and are more concerned with the misuse of lords' power and the opportunities provided thereby for extortion and oppression. Chaucer's Parson believes lords should take from their tenants only if their goods are needed to help with the defence of their lives and property, whereas Gower sees the impact of lords' avarice greatly expanded by the depredations of their retainers. Both, however, are conservative when it comes to the matter of economic inequality and the role of lords in the social order, believing

---

[45] *Parson's Tale,* 314.

[46] *Parson's Tale,* 314.

[47] Siegfried Wenzel, "Notes on the 'Parson's Tale'", *Chaucer Review* 16 (1982), 252.

[48] Richard Newhauser, "The Parson's Tale and its Generic Affiliations", in *Closure in the Canterbury Tales: The Role of the Parson's Tale,* ed. David Raybin and Linda Tarte Holley (Kalamazoo, MI: Medieval Institute Publications, 2000), 76.

[49] *Vision of Piers Plowman,* passus II, 27.

that it is divinely ordained. The Parson rests his argument on the oft-repeated theory of the three estates, whereas Gower argues that wealth was given by God to some in order to test their devotion to him. Therefore, although both Chaucer and Gower would agree that lords should use their wealth for the good of others, they do not go so far as to make this a condition for their possession of it.

Langland does focus on bribery and corruption, the misuse of wealth and lordship in his characterisation of Lady Mede, but her fate is unknown after her trial. It appears that Langland, too, would not suggest, as Wyclif did, that lords should have their lordships, and hence their source of wealth, taken away from them if they were sinful. For the author of *Wynnere and Wastoure*, the issue is the use and justification of wealth by lords as well as merchants, but there is no proposal that either should be punished for misuse by being divested of it. Overall, the purpose of the criticisms is reform, not revolutionary change. Owing to the great power of lords and their affinities, criticism of a particular lord's ethical behaviour was a perilous undertaking, but so was criticism of a particular king. The next section reveals how criticisms of the monarch's attitude to economic ethics were presented.

The Role of Kings in Economic Ethics

In *The Regiment of Princes*, Thomas Hoccleve has real concerns about the prodigality of kings and the distress and the disorder it can bring about.[50] But the king "ne rekkith" the ways in which he wreaked economic damage, and this imputed ignorance is part of the prevailing tendency to blame corrupt officials rather than the king himself. As we will see in the next chapter, many petitions concerning purveying abuses speak of evil officials acting on the king's behalf and assume the king was unaware of what had been done in his name. Certainly, some officials were indeed profiting themselves in acting as purveyors, but according to contemporary critics, the root of the problem, the reason why purveying abuses occurred in the first place, was the king's own failure to control his expenditure.

[50] Hoccleve, *Regiment,* lines 4019–4025.

Hoccleve then discourses upon the virtue of largesse and the vice of prodigality. According to Aristotle, largesse is first considering what can be afforded and giving only to the deserving poor:
Aristotle of largesse tellith this:

> Who vertuously large list to be,
> Considere first of what power he is
> And eek the tymes of necessitee,
> And, as the men deserven, so be free;
> Geve in mesure unto the indigent
> And the worthy, and that is wel dispent.[51]

The king must steer a path between liberality or wise largesse and prodigality or foolish largesse. If he spends more than his land "may to souffyse or atteyne", he shall "be destroyed aftir the sentences of Aristotle".[52]

Hoccleve's sense of urgency could have been compounded by memories of the excesses of Richard II and his awareness of the fact that Henry IV was in financial difficulties. Henry IV was obliged to request Parliament for grants to meet a number of expenses: the Glendower rebellion in Wales, Scottish border raids, problems in Ireland and the defence of Calais, the need to enlarge his affinity and the rising costs of his household. Parliament was critical but in general acceded to Henry's requests. In turn, Henry was aware that he needed to co-operate with Parliament.[53] In January 1404, the Commons asked Henry for an explanation of all his costs and he responded by asking both Lords and Commons not to hold anything back but to give their good counsel "as they should wish to reply before almighty God". This brought a positive response from the Commons.[54] In the "Durham Newsletter", Sir Arnold Savage, speaker of the Commons, felt free to inquire about specific items: that Henry had spent £50,000 on "various ladies of the realm" through letters patent,

---

[51] Hoccleve, *Regiment*, lines 4124–4130.

[52] Hoccleve, *Regiment*, lines 4404–4417.

[53] Gwylim Dodd, "Conflict or Consensus: Henry IV and Parliament, 1399–1406", in *Social Attitudes and Political Structures in the Fifteenth Century*, ed. Tim Thornton (Stroud: Sutton, 2000), 119, 126, 133, 134–135.

[54] *Parliament Rolls*, Henry IV, January 1404, Item 10.

that one Francis the Lombard received £8,000 through letters patent, and that one of the royal ministers owed £6,000 for purveyances.[55]

The contrast with Richard II's attitude could not be more marked. In January 1397, the Commons asked that "the great and excessive charge of the king's household should be amended and reduced". The king reasserted his God-given rights, declaring to the Lords that "by descent and inheritance" he wished to have "the regality and royal liberty" of his crown:

> the king took great offence and affront in that the Commons who were his lieges should wrongly take upon themselves or presume any ordinance or governance of the king's person, or his household, or other persons of standing whom it should please him to have in his company.

The king ordered that the identity of the petitioner be revealed to him and the Commons complied, making an abject apology.[56]

Richard II's household expenditure had more than doubled in the 1390s, from £16,000 per annum in 1389 to nearly £38,000 in 1396, and by 1398 his expenditure exceeded his income by £11,000. Part of this expenditure was related to Richard II's attempts to compete with the nobility by creating his own affinity and paying fees to knights and esquires.[57] Hoccleve, however, saw that it was necessary for the king to spend in order to expand his power and influence and thus he extolls largesse or liberality.[58] This view was perhaps not shared by the Commons in Parliament, who saw only prodigality in the financial excesses of Richard II. Yet to Hoccleve, and indeed to most theologians, avarice is far worse than prodigality: it must be eschewed by a king because he was placed on his throne to help those in distress.[59] The king's liberality can benefit many others, but avarice benefits none.

Gower looks at the issue of spending from the point of view of household governance. Although he tends to place the blame for over-spending

[55] *Parliament Rolls*, Henry IV, January 1404, Appendix 1.

[56] *Parliament Rolls*, Richard II, January 1397, items 14–16.

[57] Nigel Saul, *Richard II* (New Haven: Yale University Press, 1997), 259.

[58] Hoccleve, *Regiment*, lines 4652–4659.

[59] Hoccleve, *Regiment*, lines 4635–4641.

on royal officials rather than the monarch himself, Gower believes that over-spending can be corrected if the king ensures that honesty prevail within his household. Book 7 of *Confessio Amantis* concerns the education of a ruler according to what is believed to have been the Aristotelian education of Alexander the Great, which is divided into theoretical and practical education. The practical part, "toward the governance of kinges", covered ethics, economics and politics. Whereas "Policie" is how a ruler is to govern his realm in times of either war or peace, "Iconomique" is to teach honesty among members of his household.[60]

Langland's approach to the question of royal over-spending is different: to him it is not so much the level of spending, but how it can be justified. In *The Vision of Piers Plowman*, Langland has a spendthrift monarch who, like Richard II, justifies his high levels of borrowing, taxation and purveying by his status. A king makes the claim in the text that since he is the "heed of lawe" and protector of the Church and the Commons, the Spirit of Justice allows him, since he is judge of all, to take from both. He never asks for or borrows more than he needs for his status. Conscience replies that the king may take what he needs but on the condition that he can defend and rule his kingdom "in reson, right wel and in truthe".[61] Good government or defence of the realm thus permits the king to borrow, be granted high taxes and procure what goods he needs. Implicit in this rationale is its counter, which is that a corrupt and badly governed society removes the right of the king to take from his subjects.

Most of the cautionary tales in Lydgate's *The Fall of Princes* concern characters from mythology or the classical past who indulged in misgovernment and tyranny, extortion and avarice, but he also gives medieval examples of misrule: the Emperor Andronicus Comnenus of Byzantium, Charles of Anjou, and Duke Gaultier of Florence.[62] After the story of Andronicus, Lydgate declares in his "Lenvoye" that justice requires that

---

[60] *Confessio Amantis*, Book 7, vol. 3, 302.

[61] *Vision of Piers Plowman*, passus XIX, 345.

[62] *Lydgate's Fall of Princes, Part 3*, ed. Henry Bergen (Washington, DC: Carnegie Institution, 1923), 957–960, 972–976, 991–998.

evil princes who use tyranny and extortion have an evil ending.[63] As if to ensure that it is not forgotten, the words "evil ending" are repeated at the end of all the stanzas citing those rulers' other misdeeds. To Lydgate, rulers must be guided by the virtues and be mindful not only of their rewards in heaven but of their posthumous reputations. In his final letter to his patron Duke Humphrey of Gloucester, Lydgate hopes that virtue will guide him to heaven and reminds him, that like those in the book, he will be judged by those who read of his deeds.[64]

Hoccleve's and Lydgate's works, belonging to the advice to princes genre, advocate that kings ensure an abundance of goods and wealth for all and represent the administration of justice as another important component of kingship. Gower and Langland are both concerned with the king's own expenditure and its effect on the livelihoods of others but view it from two different angles. Gower sees it as a matter of household management, whereas Langland is prepared to support high levels of royal expenditure provided that it can be justified by matters of national importance such as the defence of the realm. All of the writers discussed consider economic ethics to be of primary importance to the monarch, and Lydgate, in particular, demonstrates the damage and loss that result from a tyrant's misdeeds, including the fall of the tyrant himself. None of these writers criticised the monarch directly; rather, they took care to present their works as advice on how an ideal standard of kingship could be attained and the consequences if it was not. The use of characters from mythology or the classical or more recent past assisted that purpose in much the same way as the exempla were used in the pastoral manuals. Also, advice for princes was intended to have universal application; all readers should be wary of profligacy and maladministration. Given the wide circulation of these works in manuscript and printed form, readers must have appreciated the moralising about the expectations of kingship and the impact their poor financial management could have on the economic life of all.

[63] *Lydgate's Fall of Princes, Part 3*, 961.

[64] *Lydgate's Fall of Princes, Part 3*, 1019–1020.

The Failures of Knights and Lords

We have seen that lords were criticised for their avarice, extravagance and wasting of wealth, but both lords and knights were criticised for failing to live according to the ideals associated with their roles as protectors of society. In the *Canterbury Tales*, any notion of wealth is absent from Chaucer's portrayal of the "verray, parfit gentyl knyght", who had a modest bearing and was not expensively dressed: his tunic was stained where his armour had been worn. His life had been devoted to fighting in many campaigns, some against heathen Turks.[65]

To Gower and Langland, life was better in the past: they look back to times when they believed the feudal order offered more certainty and security. As far as Langland is concerned, knights, as lords of their manors, have a role to play in protecting the livelihoods of their tenants and saving them from destitution. Reflecting the ideas of John Bromyard in *Summa praedicantium*, Piers the ploughman tells of a lord or landowner's covenant with God which dictates how he should behave towards his tenants. The knight promises to try to improve on his past behaviour and in return, Piers says he will work to feed them both, in the hope that the knight will protect him from dishonest idlers or wasters who hunt across his land, destroying hedges and stealing his crops.[66]

Piers's expectation is that the knight will also assist by hunting the hares, foxes and other animals that damage his crops. This type of compact is very like the feudal bond in which knights or lords offer protection in exchange for labour. Langland sees it as a workable system provided that bondsmen are not exploited. Piers is willing to comply with a feudal type of arrangement and to provide his labour on the condition that he is treated with mercy. He asks that the knight not charge his tenants excessive fines, nor ill treat his bondsmen "And though ye mowe amercy men, lat mercy be taxour/And meekness thi maister … And mysbede noght thi bondeman".[67]

---

[65] *General Prologue*, in *Riverside Chaucer*, 24.

[66] *Vision of Piers Plowman,* passus VI, 96.

[67] *Vision of Piers Plowman,* passus VI, 96–97.

In the *Mirour de l'Omme*, Gower remarks that the knights of late medieval England have fallen well below their chivalric ideals. Instead of going to fight in foreign wars or defending people's rights, a knight gets involved in legal disputes in the hope of material gain, preying like a raven upon the poor.[68] Such a knight is dismissed by Gower as a "chivaler de haie" and without honour. Knights should not be involved in commerce, for it is not in accordance with the strict observance of knighthood.[69] Gower ignores the fact that in late medieval England, knights were also landholders, who needed to earn income from their estates and to do so they needed to maintain and improve their properties and sell grain, wool or other produce. Instead of acknowledging that, he invokes the Roman law, the "law of the emperor", which states that a perfect knight cannot be a merchant or a trader, because their love of money makes them lose their appetite for battle. Whoever does not take up arms for fear of losing money will lose his honour and privileges.[70]

Gower does not express this extreme view in *Confessio Amantis*, but he still presents an idealised view of economic conditions. He recalls a time when "the world stod thane in al his welthe": not only was there plenty and riches but justice was upheld and everyone obeyed the law and knew their place.[71] The claim that everyone was more prosperous in this idealised past ignores the state of the peasantry in many parts of the country prior to the Black Death. "The world" might be, rather, the relative prosperity of Gower's own landowning class before they suffered a fall in land rents and the rise in labourers' wages which came afterwards. His attitude strongly resembles the position taken by those who drew up the Ordinance and Statute of Labourers (in 1349 and 1351), which ordered that wages and prices be fixed at pre-1349 levels.

In *The Regiment of Princes*, Hoccleve, instead of railing against knights for their failure to adhere to the ideals of chivalry, blames lords for some

[68] *Mirour de l'Omme*, 261.

[69] *Mirour de l'Omme*, 263.

[70] *Mirour de l'Omme*, 262. The Justinian Code states that neither soldiers nor allies should attend to their own houses or other possessions, but this was written in a time of emergency, for the preamble expresses concern with the defence of the Byzantine Empire against the barbarian hordes. See *Corpus iuris civilis*, vol. 3, ed. R. Schoell and W. Kroll (Berlin: Weidmann, 1895), 549–551.

[71] *Confessio Amantis*, vol. 1, 47–48.

of the social and economic changes that had occurred in late medieval England. He takes particular objection to the wearer of a fur-trimmed scarlet gown with sleeves trailing the ground (known as a "houppelande"). The gown he estimates to be worth £20, and to Hoccleve it is an "abusioun" for a number of reasons. Hoccleve believes the wearer would have spent all of his income on his appearance and on trying to impress others. This man is a waster and, being of lower social status, an apparent flouter of the sumptuary law of 1363: "So poore a wight his lord to countrefete/In his array, in my conceit it stynkith".[72] Hoccleve blames lords for this state of affairs, for they let their employees "Usurpe swich a lordly apparaille". Another new fashion is the tippet, a long decorative attachment to the hood, which to Hoccleve is "a foul waast of clooth". The whole business of excessive clothing is repugnant. Hoccleve urges lords to

> In Goddes name, putte it in exyl;
> It is a synne outrageous and vyl;
> Lordes, if ye your estat and honour
> Loven, fleemeth this vicious errour.[73]

Money spent on opulent clothing has further ramifications. Those who indulge themselves in such a manner cannot afford to maintain a large household and this means that fewer servants can be employed: "now housholdes ben ful sclendre and lene" compared with "In dayes olde, when smal appareille/Souffysid unto hy estat or mene".[74]

Langland also remarks on the reduction in household expenditure compared with former times, when the lord dined in his hall and fed many. The rich tend to eat in others' houses or by themselves in private rooms rather than in their own hall, thus avoiding having to provide meals for large numbers of people. In former times, food was set aside for the poor and carried out to them from the hall, as instructed by Robert Grosseteste in Walter of Henley's *Hosbonderie*.[75] The newer and less

[72] Hoccleve, *Regiment*, lines 428–431, 435–437.

[73] Hoccleve, *Regiment*, lines 459–462.

[74] Hoccleve, *Regiment*, lines 491–494.

[75] Anne M. Scott, *Piers Plowman and the Poor* (Dublin: Four Courts Press, 2004), 197.

charitable practice could have resulted from cost-conscious merchants becoming lords of the manor or from the decline in some landowner incomes after the Black Death.

In various ways, lords of the manor have failed to maintain ethical standards: knights have diverted their attentions to gathering material wealth instead of pursuing chivalric causes, and lords have encouraged imitators to waste their resources on conspicuous consumption and they no longer provide food from their tables for the poor. Lords, like kings, are looked to for moral leadership: Gower, Langland and Hoccleve all look to the past for a remedy, believing that if a strict social hierarchy is maintained and the virtues encouraged, the problems created by avarice can be overcome.

The Ideal Society: Social Order and the Virtues

We have seen how writers were disappointed with the ethical leadership of kings and lords and looked to the past for examples of how the ideals of kingship and lordship should be practised. In this final section, I examine how authors of literary works envisaged economic well-being for all.

Chaucer's *The Former Age* begins with his imagination of the prelapsarian world described by John Duns Scotus and William of Ockham, except that it is the discovery of precious metals rather than original sin that brings ruin to humankind. Duns Scotus, Ockham and Chaucer were probably imagining the Garden of Eden as described in Genesis. Chaucer could have been influenced by Boethius, since *The Former Age* resembles Chaucer's poem *Boece*, which is his translation of Boethius's *Consolation of Philosophy*.[76] *The Former Age* recalls the "blisful lyf" of people who did not need to labour, because everything was provided, and corn sprang from the earth without sowing. Everyone slept in caves, with only grass or leaves for bedding. There were neither towers nor walls, for there were no wars.[77] This pre-monetary paradise ended when humankind discovered precious metals and jewels:

[76] A.V.C. Schmidt, "Chaucer and the Golden Age", *Essays in Criticism* 26 (1976): 99–115.

[77] *The Former Age*, in *Riverside Chaucer*, 651.

But cursed was the tyme, I dar wel seye,
That men first dide hir swety bysinesse
To grobbe up metal, lurkinge in derknesse,
And in the riveres first gemmes soghte.
Allas, than sprong up al the cursednesse
Of coveytyse, that first our sorwe broghte.[78]

Prior to this discovery, there was absolute equality and no need for quarrels since all people cherished one another. Again, like Duns Scotus and Ockham, Chaucer imagined that there was no need for a hierarchy with its lordship, tallage and tyranny:

Unforged was the hauberk and the plate;
The lambish peple, voyd of alle vyce,
Hadden no fantasye to debate,
But ech of hem wolde other wel cheryce;
No pryde, non envye, non avaryce,
No lord, no talyage by no tyrannye …[79]

Gower has a similar vision in *Confessio Amantis* at the beginning of Book 5 on avarice. Genius describes a world where all goods were held in common; then along came Avarice and so began the strife and division that still pervade the present. When avarice came, that was when "men knewen the moneie … And of comun his propre made".[80] Gower, like Chaucer, imagines towns without walls and a world without strife before the discovery of money.[81] Because of their belief in man's fallen nature, it is doubtful that either Gower or Chaucer held that a return to common ownership was possible. They saw common ownership as belonging to a lost age, where it had been the basis of peace and order. Gower does not go as far as Chaucer: he does not speak of there being no need for a hierarchical order if everyone's needs are met, for such a viewpoint would

[78] *The Former Age*, 651.
[79] *The Former Age*, 651.
[80] *Confessio Amantis*, Book 5, vol. 3, 35.
[81] *Confessio Amantis*, Book 5, vol. 3, 42.

be at odds with his ideas of a socio-economic order, a harmonious body politic, within which each person accepted his or her status.

Lydgate avoids the myth of common ownership and instead imagines a time when the virtues reigned. In his vision, as in the theories of the three estates or the harmonious body politic, there are knights, merchants and tradesmen who all perform their allotted tasks and do not aspire to anything more. In Book III of *The Fall of Princes*, Lydgate reflects on Boccaccio's anger about corrupt judges in which he harks back to a "goldene world[e], flouryng in vertu", a time when there was no livery and maintenance and no extortion, and merchants' profits were always just and artificers were never idle.[82]

Langland also envisages a role for the virtues but they are an accompaniment to living in an order sanctioned by God. In *The Vision of Piers Plowman*, Langland combines the diversity of gifts described in I Corinthians 12:4 with a version of the harmonious body politic. No one should despise any other. Of this new kingdom, Grace makes Conscience the king and Craft or Skill his steward, Piers Plowman his "procuratour" (that is, his reeve and registrar to receive what is owed and his (honest) purveyor). Piers the ploughman will be a tiller of the truth with the gospellers Matthew, Mark, Luke and John as four oxen and Augustine, Ambrose, Gregory and Jerome as four plough-horses for harrowing, and this also suggests that Langland saw agricultural work as "honest labour". Alongside the powers given by these biblical and patristic authorities, there are the "cardynale vertues", for Grace gave Piers four seeds to sow: prudence, moderation, fortitude and justice.[83] *The Vision of Piers Plowman* looks forward to heavenly rewards for those who are prepared to uphold economic justice. The rich are advised to be merciful to the poor because Christ was merciful, and the judgements they make at court will be judged of them in the afterlife.[84]

The virtues are meant to be practised in order to be absorbed into one's character, but Langland expresses a degree of scepticism. He draws attention to the unwillingness of some members of society to undergo

[82] *Lydgate's Fall of Princes, Part 2*, ed. Henry Bergen (London: OUP for EETS, 1924), 417.
[83] *Vision of Piers Plowman*, passus XIX, 337–338.
[84] *Vision of Piers Plowman*, passus I, 25.

ethical reform, showing that Piers's vision does not appeal to some of the characters in the text. One of those who refuses to be ruled by either justice or conscience is a brewer, who wants to continue selling dregs and drawing thick and thin ale at the same time. A vicar says that he has never met anyone who could tell about the cardinal virtues or who placed any value on conscience.[85] Langland includes landowners in this inveterate group. A lord makes fun of the virtues, calling wisdom or prudence the Spirit of Understanding, by which his auditor or steward records what is owing to him, and equating fortitude with force, by which his officials collect the manorial revenue.[86] Langland thus recognises the importance of the virtues in regulating individual behaviour but sees that they will be bypassed in favour of self-interest and monetary gain by many people.

Lady Mede represents a number of sins and an immoral, worldly society where everything is done for a reward or a fee. Her richly attired appearance and corrupt behaviour are the very opposite of the honest simplicity of Piers Plowman. However, Langland seems to be recognising the reality of material needs in the discourse between Lady Mede and Conscience. When accused of many misdeeds by Conscience, Lady Mede defends herself to the king by pointing out that "It bicometh to a kyng that kepeth a reaume/To yeve [men mede] that mekely him serveth", as do emperors and lords, the pope and prelates, and all other orders of society depend on fees.[87] But Conscience insists that the true reward is God's gift of life in heaven to those who have worked well on earth "with right and with reson" and "useth noght the lyf of usurie".[88] Thus, Langland is aware of society's flaws and material needs. His vision seems to be less of a bucolic golden age than one of honest toil for fair rewards, where all abide by right, reason and conscience.

The notion of the just price is criticised by Langland. Secret bribes and fees are not fair rewards. Exchanges should be fair but Langland sees the pitfalls of the just price in recognising that it is judged and administered by the fallible. This is a criticism of the theories of Peter the Chanter,

[85] *Vision of Piers Plowman*, passus XIX, 342.

[86] *Vision of Piers Plowman*, passus XIX, 344–345.

[87] *Vision of Piers Plowman*, passus III, 46–47.

[88] *Vision of Piers Plowman*, passus III, 47.

William of Auxerre, Hostiensis and others that a good and wise man or a third party could determine the just price. Here, Langland reiterates Aquinas's conception of the just price and the ideas of other theologians that prices should be fixed in a public space rather than a private one by saying that wages are reasonable if they can be measured against the cost of materials and labour and that prices are reasonable if they are calculated freely and openly.[89]

But Langland parodies some of the negotiations required to reach the just price. When on his way to confess to Repentaunce, Gluttony is diverted to a tavern where a game takes place involving the exchange between two men of a hood and a cloak. The cloak is deemed to be worth more than the hood, but the recipient has to be satisfied: if he regrets the exchange, he has to buy Gluttony a drink. The valuation process involves a group of assessors and an umpire when they fail to agree.[90] Davis points out that the setting of a tavern, usually a place of ill repute for moralists, and the engagement of traders and craftsmen, often regarded as deceitful, in the just price negotiations, indicate that Langland was questioning whether the ideal of the just price could be achieved. As well as being sceptical of the idea that "a good or wise man" could determine the just price, Langland was ridiculing Aquinas's theory, based on Aristotle's definition, that the just price had been reached when an exchange was to the advantage of both the buyer and the seller. Davis believes that Langland wished to demonstrate both "the potential corruptibility of scholarly ethics in exchange" and "the conflict between moral ideals and practical behaviour".[91] This is further evidence of Langland's belief, and Chaucer's and Gower's as well, that owing to their corrupt and fallen nature, many in society were incapable of behaving in an ethical manner.

Langland's answer to the vagaries of just pricing or defining a fair reward is to live in moderation. Lady Holi Chirche teaches that immoderate living is unnecessary since God commanded the earth to provide wool, linen

[89] *Vision of Piers Plowman*, passus III, 48.

[90] *Vision of Piers Plowman*, passus V, 78–79.

[91] Davis, *MMM*, 68–69.

and food, enough for everyone to live "in mesurable manere".[92] Measure is the basis for Langland's remedy, his model for how economic ethics should work, for some have too much wealth and others too little. His main concern is that some wealth be given to the poor. Those with wealth should be governed by reason, and wealth should be managed by "Kynde Wit" or common sense. Kynde Wit will give as it is needed, for "housbondrie" or thrift, and reason and common sense all go together.[93] In *The Fall of Princes*, Lydgate also writes of the ideal of living in moderation. "The compleynt off Bochas upon the fall of Adam" is Boccaccio's censure of humankind for its covetousness, fraud and extortion and his exhortation for it to be content with sufficiency.[94] Boccaccio praises poverty, but by poverty Boccaccio intends sufficiency, living according to one's needs, in between the extremes of absolute poverty and excess wealth.[95] *Wynnere and Wastoure* presents a different view: if merchants spend as lords do, wealth "trickles down" and everyone prospers. This could be the poet's vision of how society should be, which at the same time justifies the wealth of lords. Amongst the authors discussed here, Langland is the one who gives the most detailed consideration to economic ethics and how they might be applied. He sees how many kinds of people would be reluctant to practise the cardinal virtues or apply the concept of the just price in an open and disinterested manner. His recommendation is to live in moderation and to accept the God-given order of society. Similar ideals are expressed by Chaucer, Gower and Lydgate in their visions of a golden age where all of humanity had sufficiency: because there was no desire for more, there was no avarice. On the other hand, subsistence was the reality for many. Yet the attitude of Langland and his contemporaries towards change was that the hierarchical order was natural and change and mobility were alien.

[92] *Vision of Piers Plowman*, passus 1, 14–15.

[93] *Vision of Piers Plowman*, passus 1, 17.

[94] *Lydgate's Fall of Princes, Part 1*, 23, 25.

[95] *Lydgate's Fall of Princes, Part 1*, 177.

Conclusions

Langland, Chaucer, Gower, Lydgate and Hoccleve are all conservative commentators on economic ethics. Russell Peck has commented that as a social critic, Gower intended "not to undermine social structures but rather to show the faults of men who corrupt them", an observation which could be made about the other authors.[96] I argue that their conservatism is the influence of Church teachings and that, like preachers, they felt an obligation to criticise unethical behaviour and promote ethical solutions. They all felt that order should be not only maintained but strengthened, and this could mean a return to both a pre-commercial world which might be feudal in its manner of social organisation and a world in which all abided by the teachings of the Church about avarice and lived according to the virtues of justice and temperance. Economic ethics were intended to have universal application, and all of the authors examined here were concerned with the role of kings, lords and knights. They saw society's leaders appropriating the goods and money of their subjects or dependents to satisfy their greed or prodigality and creating much distress. They also exhorted leaders to live according to the virtues, to provide for and protect their subjects and to bear in mind their reputations and the fate of tyrants.

[96] Russell A. Peck, *Kingship and Common Profit in Gower's 'Confessio Amantis'* (Carbondale and Edwardsville: South Illinois University Press, 1978), xiv, xx.

5

The Application of Theory: The Language of Economic Ethics in Statutes and Petitions

Chapter 4 showed that extortion and oppression by lords and rulers were strongly criticised in literary sources. Authors advocated living according to the virtues of justice and moderation or according to the ideals of kingship, lordship or knighthood, which they believed had been neglected. In doing so, they were articulating many of the same criticisms and principles of economic ethics which featured in pastoral manuals and sermons. It is significant that some of those literary works were popular and read by a broader range of society than their royal or noble patrons, but the question remains as to whether those particular ethical principles relating to economic life had any impact or application in secular society. Did they, for example, influence how regulations were worded and applied? What do the written petitions of those with grievances reveal about their expectations of justice, the common good and good lordship and their actual experiences? To answer these questions, this chapter investigates three kinds of evidence: statutes regulating economic activity in late medieval England; petitions against economic abuses; and cases involving abuses of the right of purveying, extortion by lords and their officials, unreasonable tallage, fines and tolls, and land enclosures.

J. Hole, *Economic Ethics in Late Medieval England, 1300–1500*,
Archival Insights into the Evolution of Economics,
DOI 10.1007/978-3-319-38860-1_5

Purveying abuses are a very good example of economic injustice by lords and kings and will be analysed as a case study later in this chapter. I am building upon the work of J.R. Maddicott in order to show that the long-standing debate about purveying had ethical aspects, which covered the responsibilities of the king, the extent of his financial needs, and the damage to the economy which resulted from his excessive spending or lack of proper management or both. Maddicott studied the impact on the poor of taxation and military service as well as of purveying. He referred to the protests about purveying made by William of Pagula in *Speculum Regis Edwardi Tertii* or *Mirror of Edward III*, which was discussed in Chapter 4, as well as cases recorded by inquiries and cases put forward in petitions. From those sources, Maddicott found that the effects of purveying on peasants could be devastating. He identified three factors which contributed to the economic injustice of purveying abuses: firstly, the fact that purveying was an arbitrary exaction and not, like taxation, subject to parliamentary consent; secondly, the government's inability to control local officials; and, thirdly, the ability of the more wealthy to bribe purveyors to escape their exactions.[1] Scrutinised from the perspective of economic ethics, purveying abuses contradicted the principle of the just price, the use of bribery gave the wealthy a major advantage over the poor, and avarice led to the corrupt behaviour of purveyors. This chapter will argue that legislators and petitioners operated within the same conceptual framework as theologians and the authors of pastoral manuals and literary works.

Regulating for Economic Injustice

This section deals with the role of Parliament in economic regulation and investigates whether any of the statutes it framed used moralising language. Maurice Keen has pointed out that Parliament was established primarily to uphold the legal rights of both the king and his subjects and

[1] Maddicott, "The English Peasantry and the Demands of the Crown, 1294–1341", in *Landlords, Peasants and Politics in Medieval England*, ed. T.H. Aston (Cambridge: CUP, 1987), 300, 303–304.

"not designed to foster the public welfare".[2] Nevertheless, public welfare featured a good deal: the king's financial needs made it necessary for him to summon Parliaments, so enabling the Commons to get their petitions attended to in exchange for granting funds. For instance, in 1401, the Commons moved that grants not be finalised until all their petitions had been dealt with, and Henry IV found that he had to agree with their proposal.[3]

There are two main sources from which moralising language appears in Parliament. The first are the speeches made by Chancellors or those who spoke in their place, reminding lawmakers to uphold moral principles. In these instances, justice is spoken of in a more general sense than economic justice, but it is reasonable to assume that it was part of what was intended, especially when speeches also referred to prosperity or redressing hardship as worthy objectives. In his opening speech to the king and Parliament of September 1429, the Chancellor and Archbishop of York spoke of lack of faith and fear of God as the causes of much wrongdoing and suffering but added justice as the basis of prosperity and of support for the government.[4] In January 1431, the canonist William Lyndwood spoke in the Archbishop's place "in fine fashion" on the three pairs of virtues which should support the realm: union and unity, peace and tranquillity, and justice and equity. According to Lyndwood, it was the decline of those virtues which had led to so much distress: unity was undermined by those with ambitions for power above their own status; peace and tranquillity, by those who spread rumours and untruths; and justice and equity, by those who engaged in dubious legal claims or who oppressed the poor.[5] In May 1432, the opening speech by the Lord Chancellor, the Bishop of Bath and Wells, again referred to justice and quoted both "the prophet" and Aristotle: "Now kings, understand, be well-informed, you who rule the land, serve the Lord with fear". The Bishop called upon subjects, in turn, to obey the king and to observe the king's laws "which is, according to Aristotle, the salvation of every city and

[2] Keen, *England in the Later Middle Ages: A Political History*, 2nd edn. (London: Routledge, 2003) 2.

[3] Keen, *England in the Later Middle Ages*, 252, 271.

[4] *Parliament Rolls*, Henry VI, September 1429, membrane 15, item 3.

[5] *Parliament Rolls*, Henry VI, January 1431, membrane 10, item 4.

realm". Here, the Bishop's view of justice was in its retributive sense and he put the fear of God above all virtues. The Bishop had evidently given a lengthy exposition, for the rolls note that he had quoted many authorities and given many examples and narratives to illustrate his points without troubling to record them all. He concluded by announcing that the king had summoned Parliament to redress the economic hardship and suffering of his subjects.[6] Justice appeared again when the Bishop spoke of good governance by the king in January 1437, using the royal crown as a symbol, where, as in *Jacob's Well*, the crown was supported by the four virtues. Good governance was linked to prosperity, for he gave as one of the reasons for summoning Parliament the need to determine how the merchandise of the realm "can better and more profitably be sold, sent abroad and exported for the royal profit and common good of the same realm".[7] The Bishop again spoke on the theme of good governance fostering prosperity in January 1442, this time using the imagery of the throne of Solomon.[8] The Parliamentary Rolls reveal no further speeches by the Chancellor relevant to economic ethics until November 1485, when John Alcock, Bishop of Worcester, chose his theme from Psalm 44:5, "Strive to prosper, go forth and triumph". Following the ideals of the *res publica*, he reminded members of Parliament that they were elected not for their own private gain but for the public realm and the common good.[9]

The second source from which moralising language came was parliamentary petitions. Early parliamentary statutes were initiated by the king and his justices, but by the reign of Edward III they were based largely on petitions. Individual petitioners seeking redress for some particular or private grievance from the king would approach the Commons for support, or the Commons themselves might present their own petition, which might be of a general nature. Both kinds of petitions were drafted by professional scriveners, but by the fifteenth century, the Commons discussed the form their own petitions should take and their clerk prepared the final versions. The final version became the bill that would be

---

[6] *Parliament Rolls*, Henry VI, May 1432, membrane 14, items 1, 4.

[7] *Parliament Rolls*, Henry VI, January 1437, membrane 8, item 5.

[8] *Parliament Rolls*, Henry VI, January 1442, membrane 15, item 1.

[9] *Parliament Rolls*, Henry VII, November 1485, part 1, membrane 1, item 1.

submitted to the Lords for acceptance or rejection.[10] The wording of such bills was evidently given a good deal of consideration, and it seems that members of the Commons saw fit to add moral condemnations to their grievances where they thought the matter was urgent. It is also likely that their clerk made some contribution to the wording, since he was a man who would have had some form of clerical training or been a member of the lower clergy.[11]

Examples of statutes with moralising language include those which sought to regulate wages and prices. Usage of such terms as covetousness, private gain, oppression, greed, excessive wages, and damage to the people or to the common weal suggests that their purpose was to urge local authorities to act according to their conscience. For example, the Statute of Labourers of 1351 decried the malice of servants who refused to work without outrageous wages and, for their own advantage and out of their greed, had been demanding two or three times the amount they had been paid in the twentieth year of the king's reign, before the plague, which harmed the great and impoverished all the commonalty.[12] That covetousness brought about unjust behaviour was a teaching found in many of the pastoral manuals surveyed in Chapter 3.

Other statutes reflect the moralists' condemnation of private gain to the detriment of others. The *Statutim de Pistoribus* lists punishments to be inflicted on bakers and brewers who broke the assize, and on butchers and other victuallers who sold unwholesome wares, without moralistic language. However, its clause dealing with forestallers of victuals is strongly condemnatory, probably because the artificially raised prices in one market could affect prices in many others. A forestaller should not be tolerated in any town, for he is an oppressor of the poor who for his own greed and profit prevents others from buying and who, by telling merchant strangers that they should sell at higher prices, deceives all with

[10] Ronald Butt, *A History of Parliament in the Middle Ages* (London: Constable, 1989), 580–585.

[11] J.H. Denton, "The Clergy and Parliament in the Thirteenth and Fourteenth Centuries", in *The English Parliament in the Middle Ages*, ed. R.G. Davies and J.H. Denton (eds) (Manchester: Manchester University Press, 1981), 89. The same procedure for redrafting of petitions continued in the fifteenth century. See A.R. Myers, "Parliamentary Petitions in the Fifteenth Century", *English Historical Review*, 52 (1937): 385–404, 590–613.

[12] *SR*, vol. 1, 311.

art and ingenuity. A forestaller is an enemy of the whole county and the country.[13] The Statute of Westminster of 1330 also cited the greed and wilfulness of taverners, who at that time were not regulated like sellers of bread and ale. Taverners were not only selling bad wine but failing to comply with reasonable or just pricing—that is, allowing for the import price and transport costs but little in the way of excess profit—to the great damage of the people.[14] A statute of 1389 cites poorly dyed and damaged cloth being sold—"*a grantz deceyte perde et damage du poeple*"—and a statute of 1391 described the sale of corn, wine and ale by false measure as "*a tres grant damage et oppression de toute la commone poeple*".[15] The language of economic ethics was certainly used to justify the legislation in these instances.

Later statutes appealed to the ideals of equity, reason and conscience. The reason for this change of language could be the wording of the original parliamentary bills or petitions on which they were based, which like Chancery petitions, were appealing to a prerogative body. Gwylim Dodd explains this more fully in his description of a petitionary culture in Parliament and of how petitions were created and worded.[16] A statute of 1489 fixed the maximum price of woollen cloth: those who sold at more than sixteen shillings per broad yard had gained "unreasonable lucre" which was to the "damage" of the buyers and the people and "ayenst equite and gode conscience".[17] Similarly, an ordinance of the same year fixed the price of hats and caps to prevent their being sold "to the grete charge and damages of the Kingis subjettes and ayenst all gode reason and consciens".[18] The ideal of equity, discussed in Chapter 2, was the maintenance of balance and reciprocity and underpinned notions of what was reasonable or unreasonable. Conscience was supposed to remind people of what was right or reasonable as readers of pastoral manuals and guides to morality already knew.

---

[13] *SR*, vol. 1, 203–204.

[14] *SR*, vol. 1, 264.

[15] *SR*, vol. 2, 64, 79.

[16] Gwylim Dodd, *Justice and Grace: Private Petitioning and the English Parliament in the Late Middle Ages* (Oxford: OUP, 2007).

[17] *SR*, vol. 2, 533.

[18] *SR*, vol. 2, 534.

The fact that members of the Lords in Parliament, and very likely most members of the Commons, were landowners, made it less likely that bills which might affect their economic interests would be passed into law. Furthermore, lords in Parliament scrutinised and amended any pending legislation.[19] Lords and knights' rights to control the livelihoods of their tenants preceded the foundation of Parliament and were enshrined in the *Magna Carta*.[20] Exceptions included a statute of 1275 against charging excessive tolls in market towns and several acts or ordinances excluding lords from the right of purveying, which will be discussed in the context of the case study later in this chapter. None of those acts used the moral language of statutes which regulated markets, wages and prices, indicating a level of caution in drafting legislation which tried to restrict the economic offences of lords. Therefore, it is of some interest that a late fifteenth-century act against enclosures employed the same kind of language as an act against usury. The 1487 act against usury (later repealed) sought to reform "all corrupt and unlefull bargaynes":

> For so much as ymportable damages losses and enpov[er]ysshing of this realme ys had, by dampnable bargayns groundyt in usurye, colored by the name of newe Chevesaunce, cont[ra]rie to the lawe of naturell justis, to the comen hurt of this land and to the greate displesur of God.[21]

The 1489 act against enclosures, titled an *Acte Agaynst Pullyng Doun of Tounes*, begins with:

> The Kyng our sovereign Lord, havyng a singuler plesure above all thinges to avoide such enormitees and myschefes as be hurtfull and prejudicall to the commen wele ... remembreth that amonge all othre thinges gret inconvenyences daily doth encreace by desolacion and pulling down and wilfull waste of houses and Townes ... and leying to pasture londes whiche custumeably have ben used in tilthe.[22]

---

[19] Chris Given-Wilson, "The House of Lords, 1307–1529", in *A Short History of Parliament*, ed. Clyve Jones (Woodbridge: Boydell, 2009) 23.

[20] *Magna Carta*, ed. David Carpenter (London: Penguin, 2015) 111-115.

[21] *SR*, vol. 2, 514.

[22] *SR*, vol. 2, 542.

Like the activities of forestallers, the impact of enclosures had wider ramifications than the waste of land and buildings. Because of fewer crops being grown, there were idle labourers "and begynnyng of all myschefes daily doo encreace", and the decline in arable farming led to a decline in the population of towns and the emptying of churches. In fact, the whole kingdom was affected:

> the defence of this land ageyn oure ennemyes outwarde febled and impaired; to the great displesure of God, to the subvercion of the polecy and gode rule of this lond.[23]

The moralising language sets the act against enclosures apart from the neutral wording of the legislation against excessive tolls and lords' engagement in purveying, which were cited previously. The concern about the spread of poverty and possible unrest was primary, and as the king was obliged to provide peace and security for his realm, the interests of landowners, whether of the more powerful nobility or the gentry, on this occasion were over-ridden. Although enclosures were lucrative for some landowners and benefited England's wool trade, the interests of those who profited had to give way to the national interest. Judging by the increased numbers of them in succeeding centuries, the act's attempt to control enclosures had little effect, but its intention was moral in that it saw the wider effects of the "myschefes" of some landowners on many others and the harm to "the commen wele".

In conclusion, there are examples of statute law on economic matters which share the language of economic ethics. In the words of the act against enclosures and in other statutes, there is a strong echo of the moral language of the pastoral manuals, which was used to emphasise the seriousness of the offences concerned. In the fourteenth century, to ensure that such words were heard throughout the realm, copies of statutes and ordinances were sent for proclamation in not only county courts but also market towns.[24] It seems likely that this practice continued in the

---

[23] *SR*, vol. 2, 542.

[24] J.R. Maddicott, *The Origins of the English Parliament 924–1327* (Oxford: OUP, 2010), 370; Norman Doe, *Fundamental Authority in Late Medieval English Law* (Cambridge: CUP, 1990), 132.

fifteenth century or at the very least that interested parties had the opportunity to have copies made. The *Modus tenendi parliamentum* stated that copies of rolls should be made available to anyone at a charge of one penny per ten lines.[25] However, it seems that there was relatively little in the way of statute law that might impinge upon the economic interests of landowners, and those with complaints resorted to petitions in order to seek redress.

Seeking Redress for Economic Injustice

Plaintiffs who sought redress might take action through the courts of Common Pleas or the King's Bench, but these were common law courts. Those who had found that common law had no remedy for their grievance or that it had failed them in some way would petition the Court of Chancery, the King's Council, and Parliament. The focus in this section is on petitions brought to them because they all acted as prerogative courts with the power to make judgements based on ethical principles. How Chancery (the court of the Chancellor) operated and how petitions to it were framed will be considered first.

Chancery has been described as "a court of conscience", and appeals to conscience, reason, equity or other ethical concepts formed part of the petitions it received.[26] The Chancellor, being an officer of the king and part of his council, could act according to prerogative rather than common law.[27] Very few records of judgements by Chancery exist and therefore the rationale used to reach its decisions is not available. However, the Chancellor was usually a bishop or an archbishop who would have been familiar with the meaning and application of concepts such as conscience, justice and right which petitions commonly employ.[28] From his clerical training and knowledge of biblical and theological texts, the Chancellor

[25] Chris Given-Wilson, "The Rolls of Parliament, 1399–1421", *Parliamentary History* 23 (2004): 57–72.

[26] J.H. Baker, *An Introduction to English Legal History* (London: Butterworths, 1990), 118.

[27] T.S. Haskett, "The Medieval English Court of Chancery", *Law and History Review* 14 (1996): 255.

[28] Haskett, "The Medieval English Court of Chancery": 267–268, 275–276, 311–313.

should have understood why it was important to apply them.[29] Cases brought to Chancery might lack documentary evidence and this is a further reason for a petitioner to appeal to the good conscience of the court. For example, a petitioner might have paid a debt but have no written record of a contract or of his repayment, yet the court of Chancery might be persuaded to act to ensure that he was not penalised. However, if such a judgement was made, it was not meant to be generally applicable as a principle or to form a precedent, as the judgement was strictly for that particular petitioner.[30]

Many fifteenth-century petitions used "conscience" as a standard to which to appeal. For example, William Brigge, a Norfolk parson, claimed that his opponents in his land dispute had done so "ayens conscience"; William Lomnour petitioned for his opponents in a disputed inheritance to be examined "and do and resceive as feith and good concience requirith"; and Robert and Agnes Bale, regarding a disputed will, claimed that all the money, jewels and household goods belonged to them "of right and after consciens".[31] Petitions from this period, from the 1430s to 1460s, used "as faith, reason and conscience requireth" or very similar words. For example, a Chancery petition dating from 1465 to 1467 claimed that Robert Richard arranged to pay £10 for his manumission from the manor of Sutton which was owned by the monastery at Ely. Richard entered the service of Thomas Lamport, who in due course received this payment but kept it for himself and charged Richard a further five marks. Richard left the service of Lamport "for lack of resonable sustenaunce, as wille as clothyng" and entered the service of William Fylddyng, squire. So far, the language is matter-of-fact but Lamport was described as being "of grete malyce and ongodly delyng, ayenst alle trouth and gode consience" when he delivered the payment to the prior at Ely, who then refused to deliver the manumission.

[29] T.S. Haskett, "Conscience, Justice and Authority in the Late Medieval English Court of Chancery", in *Expectations of the Law in the Middle Ages*, ed. Anthony Musson (Woodbridge: Boydell, 2001), 160.

[30] Haskett, "The Medieval English Court of Chancery": 252–253; Dennis Klinck, *Conscience, Equity and the Court of Chancery in Early Modern England* (Farnham: Ashgate, 2010), 24–26.

[31] *Select Cases in Chancery A.D. 1364 to 1471*, ed. W.P. Baildon (London: Bernard Quaritch for the Selden Society, 1896), 130, 137, 143.

Richard had no remedy at common law and on his behalf William Fyldding and William Alberd, a yeoman, asked the Chancellor to summon the prior to appear before him "and therin to be ruled as gode fayth and consciens requyreth".[32] The language used in all of these examples strongly suggests that the writers knew that the Chancellor's court would consider recognised breaches of ethical standards and might respond appropriately. There is plenty of evidence in these petitions to support Norman Doe's declaration that conscience was "a distinct moral force known directly, principally through the pulpit and the confessional, by the ordinary citizen".[33]

Dennis Klinck has observed that in earlier petitions, dating from the late fourteenth century, pleas "for the love of God and in the way of charity" appear more often than for "conscience".[34] Examples are petitions concerning oppression and extortion by one Sir Richard Champernoun in Devonshire, trespass with force and arms in Bristol, and damage to a ship on the river Thames.[35] Two undated petitions, addressed to the Bishop of Exeter who was Chancellor between 1396 and 1399, used different wording. One, concerning an enfeoffment, pleaded "To the honour of God, and in salvation of right, and maintenance of peace and love", the other "to the honour of our Lord Jesus Christ".[36] Historians have not suggested any reasons why the change in practice occurred, although it could be speculated that by the fifteenth century the authors of those petitions using "conscience" had assimilated the concept, not only from the pulpit and the confessional as suggested by Doe but from works such as *The Pricke of Conscience* or *Piers Plowman*. Nevertheless, the appeals to the love of God or to charity, or to conscience, were all appeals to ethical principles. Another aspect of chancery petitions is their appeal to the grace of the Chancellor not only to carry out justice but, as a leading figure in the Church, to identify immorality and lack of conscience. Timothy Haskett argues that the Chancellor was an embodiment

[32] *Select Cases in Chancery*, 154–155.
[33] Doe, *Fundamental Authority*, 132.
[34] Klinck, *Conscience, Equity and the Court of Chancery*, 14.
[35] *Select Cases in Chancery*, 11, 13, 15.
[36] *Select Cases in Chancery*, 64, 84.

of two forms of grace: "the king's grace in the doing of what is just; but he also manifests the grace of God in showing the respondent his error, his breach of conscience".[37] Klinck argues that conscience had a more objective meaning in the late medieval period and quotes Sir John Fortescue's definition as the knowledge of God's will.[38] Petitions to Chancery concerned many instances of economic injustice and provide the primary examples of appeals to ethical ideals; however, petitions to other bodies also employed ethical language, as will be seen below.

The King's Council was, like Chancery, a body for receiving petitions for cases in which redress through common law either had failed or was not possible.[39] The Council, as well as its function of providing advice and counsel to the king, gave directions to lower courts. Where it heard cases itself, these were more likely to involve persons of prominence or very serious matters such as treason or heresy, but cases concerning economic justice were given attention. The composition and number of members of the Council varied according to the decision of the monarch or, in the case of his minority, that of his regents but would include the Chancellor and treasurer, justices and exchequer officials, lords and knights.[40] Petitioners would ask for the exercise of the special powers of the King's Council, and, as they would at Chancery, pray "for God and charity" or "for the sake of pity".[41]

A good example of an appeal to economic ethics, and of the king responding in the manner required, is a petition to the King's Council of 1378 by the citizens of Norwich, who asked that the city's council and bailiffs be given the power to amend and improve "remedies and ordinances for the good government of the town & of victuals". According to "good faith & reason for the common profit of their town", the petitioners found that their existing regulations were inadequate and that it

[37] T.S. Haskett, "Access to Grace: Bills, Justice and Governance in England, 1300-1500", in *Suppliques et Requetes: le Gouvernement par la Grace en Occident (XIIe–XVe Siecle)* ed. Helene Millet (Rome: Ecole Française de Rome, 2003), 305.

[38] Klinck, *Conscience, Equity and the Court of Chancery*, 17.

[39] James F. Baldwin, "The King's Council and Chancery, II", *American Historical Review* 15 (1910): 745.

[40] James F. Baldwin, *The King's Council in England During the Middle Ages* (Oxford: Clarendon Press, 1913), 65, 101, 106, 264–265, 271, 275.

[41] Baldwin, *The King's Council in England*, 283.

was "most accordant with good faith & profitable for the King our lord & for his people" that they should be able to change them as needs arose "& as shall seem good to them for the common profit of the people". The petitioners asked that "for God & in way of charity" they not pay a fine for the articles granted to them by Parliament. The endorsement noted that this was duly effected and that such articles would be "most accordant with good faith & reason & most profitable for the good and peaceable government of the town".[42] The use and repetition of terms such as "profitable" and "peaceable" were also part of the citizens' strategy of persuading the monarch that granting their request would be in his interest as well as theirs, in that he received additional monies and they gained greater autonomy in their city governance. They would also have been aware that their charter of liberties could be taken from them by the king if they failed to maintain peace and good order.

A further example is a petition about avaricious behaviour made at the end of the fifteenth century to the King's Council, which at that time met in the Star Chamber. The lead miners of Yorkshire brought a case to the Star Chamber in 1499 in which they complained that the merchants of York were not using the statutory weights but ones "after there pleasour" and for their own singular profit. The petition was addressed to the king and the lead miners presented themselves as the king's poor subjects who had suffered as a result of the merchants using their own authority instead of the king's. It alleged that with "there cuvetus myndes", the Mayor and Common Council of York, the authorities in charge of the crane, made the miners pay 14 pence as a weighing fee, which used to be 2½ pence and which was levied "contrary to Right and conciens".[43] Both of these petitions show the application of ethical language in a way that would suit the petitioners' interests: in the case of the City of Norwich, it was an appeal to good governance, the common profit, peace and order, whereas the Yorkshire lead miners attacked the greed of the City of York, which had abused its authority for its own gain.

---

[42] *Records of the City of Norwich, Vol. 1*, ed. William Hudson (Norwich: Jarrold & Sons, 1906), 64–65.

[43] *Select Cases before the King's Council in the Star Chamber A.D. 1477–1509*, ed. I.S. Leadam, vol. 1 (London: Bernard Quaritch for the Selden Society, 1903), 69–71.

Petitions to the king via Parliament also appealed to grace and justice. A petition to the king relied on the principle that the king was the ultimate provider of justice, a disinterested party concerned for the good of all his subjects, an ideal promoted in much of the advice to princes discussed in Chap. 4.[44] A petitioner to Parliament might ask the Commons to intercede on his behalf, the Commons being possessed of wisdom and justice. A petition of 1414 from Thomas Paunfeld, who described himself as a free tenant of the king on the manor of Chesterton in Cambridgeshire, addressed it "To the worshipful and wyse syres and Wyse Communes", saying that he was unable to pursue his cause "saue in this heye Court of rightwisnesse". Paunfeld claimed that he had been falsely accused of trespassing and outlawed and "my pore persone that am goddes cristene creature" was now imprisoned. Therefore, he continued, "I beseche yow that ye wole prayen to oure liege lord the kyng of his special grace" for a remedy.[45] Such a request for intercession suggests that the king was believed to have special powers. In some contexts, the king was believed to have a direct and special connection with God and could intercede on his subjects' behalf. The king was regarded as "the vessel of God's grace"; thus, the petition was very like a prayer. The petition to the king also provided an avenue to "a 'purer' form of justice far more closely aligned to a moral imperative than the 'ordinary' justice offered by the king's lower courts" in that it was an appeal to the king's conscience and his sense of equity and fairness.[46]

An appeal to the king in Parliament could be made on behalf of others or for the general good rather than the good of an individual as described above. In November 1381, soon after the Peasants' Revolt, Sir Richard Waldegrave, Speaker of the Commons, made a speech to the king and lords in Parliament, listing "grievous oppressions throughout the coun-

[44] Paul Brand, "Understanding Early Petitions: An Analysis of the Context of Petitions to Parliament in the Reign of Edward I", in *Medieval Petitions: Grace and Grievance*, ed. W. Mark Ormrod, Gwilym Dodd and Anthony Musson (Woodbridge: York Medieval Press, 2009), 113, 117.

[45] *An Anthology of Chancery English*, ed. John H. Fisher, Malcolm Richardson and Jane L. Fisher (Knoxville: University of Tennessee Press, 1984), 198–200, citing Kew, The National Archives, SC8/23/1143 A; Gwylim Dodd, "Thomas Paunfield, the 'heye Court of rightwisnesse' and the Language of Petitioning in the Fifteenth Century", in *Medieval Petitions: Grace and Grievance*, 222–241.

[46] Dodd, *Justice and Grace*, 285.

try", including the "outrageous" number of servants in the king's household and in the king's courts, and "the poor Commons" being "robbed and destroyed" by royal and other household purveyors, subsidies and tallages. "For these reasons the said Commons are brought into greater poverty and hardship than they ever before", and this was the reason for their revolt. The king and lords were asked to remove "evil officers and counsellors" and replace them with "worthier and more virtuous ones". The increased taxes and other impositions had achieved nothing for the defence of the realm, and meanwhile the Commons could no longer live in honour and prosperity, with the risk of greater turmoil in the future if no good and due remedy was provided.[47] The levying of the third poll tax, which affected all classes of society, was the immediate cause of the revolt, but the peasants had also been suffering at the hands of lords and landowners who wished to extract as much revenue as possible from their tenants. At Mile End, the rebels asked for not only the ending of serfdom but also for a uniform rent of four pence per acre of land.[48] Waldegrave had blamed the realm's problems on Richard II's advisors and was no doubt hoping that the king's own sense of economic justice would prevail. All of these examples show a clear expectation that it was the king's role to give redress.

Petitioners to the king and to Parliament described themselves as the deserving poor in the hope that they would obtain a positive response to their appeals to charity.[49] For example, John and Alice atte Woode of Gloucestershire petitioned Parliament in 1402 concerning "the extortions and oppressions" committed by James Clifford and Anselm Gyse. John atte Woode alleged that he was imprisoned for felony for three and half years, during which time Clifford and Gyse took over his and Alice's property and destroyed the trees on their land. The king, "considering the great and horrible trespasses, oppressions and false conspiracies", commissioned an inquiry. This inquiry was, however, stacked against the atte Woodes, who then asked the Parliament to summon two of the commissioners, who were in London, to answer for their actions. According to

[47] *Parliament Rolls*, Richard II, November 1381, membrane 11, item 17.

[48] Nigel Saul, *Richard II* (New Haven: Yale University Press, 1997), 56, 68; Christopher Dyer, "The Social and Economic Background to the Rural Revolt of 1381" in his *Everyday Life in Medieval England* (London: Hambledon and London, 2000), 191–219.

[49] Dodd, *Justice and Grace*, 286.

the atte Woodes, the officers at Gloucester were of "the covin and affinity" of Clifford and Gyse "and have been so procured by them" that justice was impossible there. The atte Woodes were now ruined and impoverished and had no means by which they could fund legal action or support their children and so called on Parliament to help "for the love of God and in the way of charity".[50]

Petitions contained hyperbolic language, such as, perhaps, "the great and horrible trespasses" described above, in order to persuade the king and Parliament that the petitioner's cause was a deserving one. In a petition to the Star Chamber in about 1494, John Culford claimed he had increased the value of his tenancy at Brynkworth and John Wotton, the kitchener of the Abbot of Malmesbury, with his "covetous disposicion and royall power" and the aid of armed servants, forcibly removed Culford and his wife and all their goods from their house. Culford alleged they even threw a child lying in its cradle into a fire. He could not return "an occupie his husbondry as your true subgiet aught to doo which is contrary to your lawes & peax right and conscience", language denoting the fundamental order and harmony of the properly ordered realm under God. Culford was "not of power" to sue Wotton at common law and called on the "blissid charitee and pitee" of the king to summon Wotton to Westminster so that he might have "restytucion". Wotton subsequently denied the violent invasion and throwing the child into a fire, claiming that Culford had refused to pay pannage for his swine that were grazing on waste ground belonging to the Abbey and that the manor court had determined that Culford should forfeit his house and land.[51] The allegation that a child was thrown into a fire seems excessive and might have been an attempt to invoke outrage or additional "charitee and pitee" with its hint of the massacre of the innocents by Herod. The petitioners seemed to feel that claiming ruin and poverty as the result of someone else's covetousness was not enough and that more needed to be said in order to obtain redress.

---

[50] *Select Cases before the King's Council 1243–1482*, ed. I.S. Leadam (Cambridge, MA: Harvard University Press for the Selden Society, 1918), 86–92.

[51] *Select Cases before the King's Council in the Star Chamber*, vol. 1, 45–49.

Dodd has outlined a formula for petitioning which began with describing the seriousness of the petitioner's situation and then the power and misdeeds of his opponent and lastly emphasising a link between the petitioner's situation and some matter of more general concern. For example, a petitioner, like John Culford, whose petition was described above, might claim that he was reduced to poverty as a result of being defrauded or physically attacked, which was against the king's peace. The thrust of the claim, apart from the allusions to covetousness and child murder, was that an action against the king's peace was an attack on the king himself and a disruption of the divinely ordained ideal of order. A petition from a town, asking for the right to collect certain rents for defensive purposes, might claim that the security of its trade would benefit its hinterland or the entire county and, ultimately, the king.[52]

An example of this kind of approach, in this case the loss of royal revenues, was taken by Sir John Fastolf. Fastolf knew the importance of describing a complaint as "oppression" and "grievance", getting the right legal advisers to prepare a petition, and obtaining the support of others. Further weight (both literally and metaphorically) would be added by attaching the seals of respected men. He had heard from his friend John Botewryght about "the grete extorcion" by the Duke of Suffolk, who had taken away 140 acres of pasture at Swaffham, which was part of the royal demesne. Fastolf advised that Botewryght get "the avice of som lerned man to put theyr opressions and greuauncez in wryting" and get the bill sealed with the seals of "such gentlemen that have lyvelode there" and of other respected men and send it to the king and the lords of his council: "And then it ys and woll be of more credence to the Kyng and the lordys then a simple letter". Fastolf believed that the loss of the pasture would be "grete disheritaunce" to the king as well as bringing "fynell destruccion of the tenauntes there".[53]

Petitioners with claims of economic injustice which could not be resolved by common law could seek redress by imitating a prayer for intercession or a prayer for a special dispensation of grace or charity, which tended to be

---

[52] Dodd, *Justice and Grace*, 297–301.

[53] *Paston Letters*, vol. 3, 112, no. 996, Letter from Sir John Fastolf to Thomas Howes of 20 December 1450.

a feature of fourteenth-century petitions. Later petitions appealed to conscience, justice and reason, but all petitions had expectations that the king, the chancellor or Parliament would respond to the language of economic ethics. This language was familiar to those who had been questioned by their confessors, heard sermons, or read guides to conscience or other kinds of pastoral literature. This familiarity was probably widespread. Haskett suggests that, based on the dialectical variations from the English used in documents issuing from Chancery, petitions to Chancery were written in many different parts of England, probably by local lawyers.[54] Petitioners hoped that the avaricious who sought to profit themselves at the expense of others would be punished and that the losses they had suffered as a consequence of deceit, oppression or extortion would be restored. To obtain the desired outcome, they needed to present themselves as the deserving poor in need of charity or to have been treated unjustly by persons without a sense of morality or a conscience. The following case studies will show how ethical principles and expectations of justice were brought into consideration in specific instances of economic malfeasance.

Case Studies

There are a number of kinds of non-mercantile economic injustice that occurred in late medieval England: the selection made here is of purveying abuses, instances of extortion and oppression and land enclosures. Petitions, statutes and other records are analysed for the presence of the language of economic ethics, in terms of both the complaints and the responses.

Abuses of Purveying

In Chapter 3 on pastoral manuals and sermons, it was shown that notions of "extortion" and "ravine" were used mostly to condemn lords' behaviour. Because of their position in society, both lords and kings could use

---

[54] T. S. Haskett, "Country Lawyers? The Composers of English Chancery Bills", in *The Life of the Law: Proceedings of the Tenth British Legal History Conference*, ed. P. Birks (Oxford, 1991, repr. London, Hambledon Press, 1993), 9–23.

their power over others to deprive their subjects, or inferiors, of their possessions and justify extortion or "ravine" by their high status. The ancient right of prise or purveying by kings was one means by which extortion and oppression could and did occur. Under the guise of purveyance, lords also took goods, produce and livestock without payment and sometimes by force, even though they were prohibited by statute from doing so.

Therefore, purveying abuses are good examples of breaches of economic ethics, and I focus on them here because the ethical aspects have been overlooked in most studies of purveying. Maddicott's analysis of the effects of purveying abuses has ethical implications, even if he did not phrase his findings in precisely those terms. He studied the impact of taxation and military service, as well as of purveying, on the poor between the end of the thirteenth century and 1341 and, as discussed previously in this chapter, found three factors in purveying abuses which I have classified as kinds of economic injustice: that it was without consent; the deceit and corruption of local officials; and the use of bribes by the more wealthy to avoid the purveyances.[55] Christopher Given-Wilson and Gerald Harriss have both examined purveying but from organisational and political points of view rather than an ethical one.[56] Wendy Scase ventured into the historical and regulatory background in her comparison of a satirical poem with the condemnations of William of Pagula, whose *Speculum Regis Edward III* was discussed in Chapter 3. Her focus was complaint literature and as part of her analysis she examined some legislation to control purveying abuses.[57] My reason for the examination of purveying in this thesis is different, stemming from the fact that Pagula and Peter the Chanter (as discussed in Chapters 2 and 3) classified under-payment or non-payment by purveyors as theft. Furthermore, as shown in Chapter 4, both Hoccleve's *Regiment of Princes* and Lydgate's

[55] Maddicott, "The English Peasantry and the Demands of the Crown": 300, 303–304.

[56] Christopher Given-Wilson, "Purveyance for the Royal Household, 1362–1413", *Bulletin of the Institute of Historical Research* 56 (1983): 145–63; G.L. Harriss, *King, Parliament and Public Finance in Medieval England to 1369* (Oxford: Clarendon Press, 1975), 104, 110–111, 124–126, 164–165, 247–249, 376–383.

[57] Wendy Scase, "Satire on the Retinues of the Great (Ms Harley 2253): Unpaid Bills and the Politics of Purveyance", in *Studies in Late Medieval and Early Renaisance Texts in Honour of John Scattergood*, ed. Anne Marie D'Arcy, Alan J. Fletcher and V.J. Scattergood (Dublin: Four Courts Press, 2005), 305–320.

Fall of Princes linked purveying abuses to the king's excessive living, for which the antidote was for the king to live in moderation and to take no more than was needed, which are two other ethical considerations. These examples raise the question of whether purveying abuses were recognised from ethical points of view in the legislation.

Abuse of the right of prise or purveying was a long-standing issue, addressed in clauses 28, 30 and 31 of the *Magna Carta*, in which the king declared that none of his bailiffs or constables should take crops or any other chattels, horses and carts or wood without paying for them immediately.[58] Edward I purveyed large amounts of supplies from many English counties for his military expeditions, and by 1297 the burdens were so heavy that a petition to the king claimed that his demands and failure to pay had brought about widespread poverty. Purveying on such a scale was unsustainable.[59] Statutes in 1275 and 1297 had recognised the problem and ordered that all "prises" be paid for within forty days, on pain of imprisonment or fines or both, but made exception for "antient" prises due to the king, the castle or the lord of the castle. This distinction made the law virtually inoperable.[60] The use of the word "prise" was common in royal writs in the thirteenth century, and perhaps because it had become associated with excessive taking, it was replaced by "purveyance", suggesting provision by the king's subjects even though it amounted to the same thing.[61]

Prises or purveying continued at high levels in the fourteenth century. When there were no military campaigns, it became the practice to continue with purveying to supply the king's household which moved around the country.[62] From parliamentary petitions and the wording of statutes, it seems that very often the goods, produce or livestock were taken more or less by force, either at a low price or with no payment at all. The many petitions to the king blamed the deprivations brought by

[58] Helmholz, "Magna Carta and the *ius commune*", *University of Chicago Law Review*, 66 (1999) : 333–334.

[59] Michael Prestwich, *War, Politics and Finance Under Edward I* (Totowa, NJ: Rowan & Littlefield, 1972), 118–129.

[60] *SR*, vol. 1, 28, 34–35, 116.

[61] Prestwich, *War, Politics and Finance*, 131.

[62] Given-Wilson, 'Purveyance for the Royal Household', 145.

purveying on the avaricious behaviour of the purveyors. For example, mentions of petitions brought in April and July 1309, April 1343 and October 1362 are made in the parliamentary rolls.[63]

A statute of 1300 spoke of "great Grievance in the Realm, and damage without Measure" caused by the great prises which were occurring in many parts of the country, and in 1311 an ordinance referred to "Prises and divers Oppressions" fearing that "the People of the Land will rise". The king was urged to live of his own resources and to make no prises other than those "anciently due and accustomed".[64] Royal writs attempted to relieve the burden, particularly on the poor: for example, in September and November 1303, no corn was to be taken from people who had goods worth less than ten shillings.[65] Evidently, purveyors disregarded such constraints, for the 1330 statute of purveyors in the reign of Edward III noted that "the People hath been greatly grieved" because corn, hay, livestock and victuals had been taken by purveyors for the king and his family without payment or at far less than their value. In an effort to ensure just pricing, the statute ordered that everything be appraised "by the Constables and other good Men of the Towns" and that payments be made "before the King depart out of the Vierge" (the verge was an area of twelve miles' radius from wherever the king's household happened to be staying).[66] In 1331, as an attempt to ensure payment, another statute ordered that tallies be made and sealed in the presence of both constables and purveyors.[67] By 1354, it was reported that many people who were given tallies had long and costly journeys to claim payment, and it was ordered that purchases under 20 shillings be paid for immediately and larger amounts be paid within three months at a more convenient time and place.[68] In 1337 and 1340, more statutes dealt with "the great grievances" caused by the keepers of the king's horses and the problems with

[63] *Parliament Rolls*, Edward II, April 1309; Edward II, July 1309; Edward III, April 1343; Edward III, October 1362.

[64] *SR*, vol. 1, 137, 159.

[65] *CPR* (*Edward I*), vol. 4, 159, 201.

[66] *SR*, vol. 1, 262.

[67] *SR*, vol. 1, 266.

[68] *SR*, vol. 1, 347–348.

purveying of fodder and stabling.[69] Evidently, these attempts to control abuses were only partially successful, for complaints by the Commons continued. In April 1343, the Commons petitioned the king for a remedy

> against the outrageous grievances and oppressions done to the common people by the king's purveyors and others of the king's officers, since if God and you do not provide swift remedy, your people will be completely destroyed by them, as their malice increases from day to day.[70]

The moralistic language gives a sense of exasperation at the failure of all the previous attempts at regulation to control the greed and selfishness of purveyors and expresses the Commons' belief that such behaviour was a manifestation of ill will or evil. Such evildoers should be punished by God, and the king should enact his role as the dispenser of justice. By October 1341, the king had received frequent complaints that purveyors and keepers of horses had committed "undue excesses" such as stabling horses inside people's houses, insulting and beating the residents and extorting money from them in order to "bring grooms and harlots with them to live with them on such extortions". The king ordered the sheriff of Nottingham to proclaim that purveyors not only were forbidden from taking anything without paying an agreed price but also should "bear themselves modestly".[71] The king had charged the sheriffs of Gloucester, Hereford, Worcester, Oxford and Berkshire to purvey for corn and other victuals "to his best advantage and the least damage to his people" but in May 1346 those counties had complained about the behaviour of these clerks and their officials who had "borne themselves ill … compelling the poor and simple men not having victuals to supply … but sparing the wealthy altogether to extort money from them to be released in this behalf".[72] There is more evidence in the 1350s, this time from Leicestershire, of individuals using their position as purveyors to profit themselves.[73]

---

[69] *SR*, vol. 1, 277, 288.

[70] *Parliament Rolls*, Edward III, April 1343, membrane 3, item 29.

[71] *CCR* (*Edward III*), vol. 6, membrane 23d.

[72] *CPR* (*Edward III*), vol. 7, 113.

[73] *CPR* (*Edward III*), vol. 9, 161.

By 1362, the purveying issue was so sensitive that a statute ordered "that the heinous Name of Purveyor be changed, and named Buyer … and that the Takings be made in a convenient and easy Manner, without Duress, Compulsion, Menace or other Villainy".[74] The use of the words "heinous", "menace" and "villainy" show how difficult it had been to control abuses by individual purveyors. The statute tried to enforce the ethical ideal of moderation: royal takings or purchases should be made where and when there was plenty of supply and no more than was needed for the two households (that is, the households of the king and of the queen). A further effort at major reform was the reduction of the number of buyers and the review of their commissions, to be sealed with the Great Seal, by Chancery, every six months. Again, the ideal of just pricing was brought to the fore: no one was "bound to obey to the Buyers of other Lords against their Agreement and Will" nor obey the buyers for king and queen "unless they make ready payment".[75] Official appraisers, such as lords, constables or other good men, were—without duress—ordered to set a price for corn, which should be "as commonly runneth in the next Markets".[76] The principles of just pricing were to be observed.

It was also acknowledged in the statute that lords had been engaging in purveyances. Henceforth, purveying was banned except for the king and queen's households: "no Lord of England, nor none other of the said Realm" shall henceforth make purveyances. This was another aspect of purveyance that was difficult to control. In October 1377, the Commons complained to Richard II that, under the guise of purveying, nobles and lords were driving out inhabitants and taking their goods, and the problem was continuing for some years after that, as confining purveying to the royal households was upheld in statutes in 1383 and in 1400 in the reign of Henry IV.[77] The Commons probably did not wish to name particular lords, given their position of power, and it was rare for a lord to acknowledge that they, like the king, were also in the habit of taking goods without paying. There are two exceptions. Firstly, in August

[74] *SR*, vol. 1, 371.

[75] *SR*, vol. 1, 365, 371, 373.

[76] *SR*, vol. 1, 319.

[77] *Parliament Rolls*, Richard II, October 1377, membrane 15, item 116.

1419, the Duke of Exeter's receiver wrote to the people of York letting it be known that any monies owing for victuals or merchandise would be paid "or if they canne complayne upon the sayd Duc or eny of hys sayd officers for eny extorsion done unto hem on the sayde dukes behalf".[78] Secondly, in February 1445, the Commons complained in Parliament that the purveyors of the Duke of Gloucester had been taking goods without payment. On that occasion, they might have felt able to do so because by then the Duke had fallen into disfavour.[79]

In disregard of the 1362 statute, royal purveyors were still not paying for their takings in the fifteenth century. Appeals to Henry IV invoked the ethical ideal of the common good and emphasised the economic hardship suffered by many of his subjects. In September 1402, the Commons requested that the statute be upheld, "for the salvation of the common good of our said lord the king and of his people of his realm" for the "poor Commons have still not been paid, to the great destruction and impoverishment and suffering of your said Commons; and hence there is great clamour among your said Commons throughout the realm".[80] Plainly, the appeals had little success for the matter came up again in March 1406: it was alleged that purveyors for the king's household "have taken for your use, from year to year, and day to day, from the time of your coronation until now, from the poor lieges and Commons" the livestock, corn, straw and hay of many counties without paying. And

> the said poor Commons have pursued and daily pursue the treasurer of the said household to have payment … [and all they get is] tally sticks, tallies and bills, to the complete ruin and destruction of your said poor Commons, to the extent that they have nothing on which to live and are left beggars.[81]

The language used here — "ruin", "destruction" and "beggars"— was to show that the king was failing in his duty to protect his subjects.

---

[78] *York Memorandum Book, Part II (1388–1493)*, ed. M. Sellers (Durham: Surtees Society, 1915), 83.

[79] *Parliament Rolls*, Henry VI, February 1445, membrane 3, item 47.

[80] *Parliament Rolls*, Henry IV, September 1402, membrane 6, item 81.

[81] *Parliament Rolls*, Henry IV, March 1406, Part 1, membrane 8, item 107.

Purveying was less of an issue for the Commons during the reign of Henry V, probably because the king was absent for extended periods on military campaigns and was drawing his supplies from the French. There are just two entries in the parliamentary rolls, one dating from May 1413 which concerns the correct measures to be used for purveying corn for the king's household and the other from March 1416 which limited the amounts that could be purveyed to the household and ordered that prompt payments be made.[82] Neither recorded a complaint about abuses, but it is likely that abuses were occurring and that these regulations served as reminders about correct procedures. Similar reminders were made in the earlier years of Henry VI's reign, in November 1422 and in July 1433, but in September 1429, the Commons petitioned about the effects of soldiers' taking supplies in Kent, Sussex and elsewhere while on their way to France. In the hope that there would be a response on moral grounds, they pleaded for help from the king "For God and in the way of charity".[83]

Henry VI made additional efforts to deal with the injustices of purveying and its effects on the economic well-being of his subjects. In December 1438, he responded to a petition from the City of London, which had prayed for "the king's consideration for the present dearness and scarcity of corn, and the multitude of inhabitants of the said city and of them that daily flock thither".[84] Henry VI tried to ensure that all would be provided for and that there would be enough corn for the royal household, for the City of London and for the growers. He wrote to the commissioners appointed to acquire corn for the king, ordering them not to interrupt supplies destined for the City of London but still to ensure that "reasonable provision" was made for the king "and enough kept to serve his subjects in Norfolk and Suffolk, both for their food and for sowing their lands".[85] Yet Henry could control neither his expenditure nor the depredations of his purveyors: in November 1439, the

[82] *Parliament Rolls*, Henry V, May 1413, membrane 3, item 42; and Henry V, March 1416, membrane 4, item 38.

[83] *Parliament Rolls*, Henry VI, November 1422, membrane 5, item 42; Henry VI, September 1439, membrane 6, item 45; and Henry VI, July 1433, membrane 4, item 54.

[84] *CCR* (*Henry VI*), vol. 3, 199.

[85] *CCR* (*Henry VI*), vol. 3, 200.

Commons were again complaining, despite the grant of a large amount of money to the crown. Although there were no moral criticisms of purveyors recorded, the Commons pointed out that the king would be aware "of grete murmour and clamour … for non paiment of the dispensis of his household".[86] In 1441–1442, Parliament reiterated that "every of the King's liege People" had the right to resist purveyors and that a purveyor could not take them to court, on pain of a fine of £20, but in 1445 the Commons alleged that "the poor People be not able, nor dare make Resistance … nor sue them by the Law".[87] It was not until the reign of Edward IV that serious and thorough efforts were made to control household expenditure and to prevent abuses of the system.

Although there were instances of purveyors acting for private gain, non-payment, under-payment or delayed payment probably caused the most damage to those affected. The principal reason for these abuses was the failure by successive kings to live of their own resources or to heed the advice of the moralists that they should live in a way appropriate to their status but with no excessive expenditure. Ordinances to contain expenditure by the royal household had been drawn up in 1318 and 1323, presumably to little effect.[88] Similarly, an ordinance of 1445, following a petition by the Commons in Parliament, had little effect owing to Henry VI's lapse into insanity, but some of its provisions were incorporated into the household book of Edward IV.[89] This is an unfinished work, compiled *circa* 1471–1472, which might have been a draft for an official manual, but it sets out in detail how the various social ranks and officials visiting the household should be provided for, how the number of visitors should be controlled, and how provisions coming into the household should be verified and paid for.[90] Clearly, its author saw extravagant living and wastefulness as an ethical issue, for among its introductory readings is a passage on proportionality rather than foolish excess, and the nature

---

[86] *SR*, vol. 2, 213, 320, 327; *Parliament Rolls*, Henry VI, November 1439, membrane 14, item 16.

[87] *Parliament Rolls*, Henry VI, January 1442, membrane 6, item 25; Henry VI, February 1445, membrane 10, item 25.

[88] T.F. Tout, *The Place of the Reign of Edward II in English History*, 2nd edn. (Manchester: Manchester University Press, 1936), 261.

[89] A.R. Myers, "Some Household Ordinances of Henry VI", in his *Crown, Household and Parliament in Fifteenth-Century England*, ed. Cecil H. Clough (London: Hambledon, 1985), 234–237.

[90] A.R. Myers, introduction to *The Household of Edward IV: The Black Book and the Ordinance of 1478*, ed. A.R. Myers (Manchester: Manchester University Press, 1959), 13–28, 33.

of liberality and magnificence, with reference to Book IV of Aristotle's *Nicomachean Ethics*.[91] Edward IV's ordinance of June 1478 declared that he was "right desirous to sette withynne our household a politique, raisonable, and vertuouse guyding in euery behalf", alluding to "certayne enormytees and mysseguydinges" discovered in the household accounts. Very much in the style of the pastoral manuals, the ordinance declared that the king was concerned to avoid the two vicious extremes of avarice and prodigality and he wished that the household be guided by the virtue of liberality. The household overall would be governed by "equyte and rightwisenesse" as "the grettest renommed vertue[s]".[92] References to the virtues had not previously appeared in the wording of statutes about purveying, and their presence in Edward IV's ordinance may reflect his own wish to live up to the ideals of kingship.

Robert Mannyng, in *Handlyng Synne*, argued that those of higher estate needed to maintain their standing and to have the capacity to give rewards for service or distribute largesse.[93] This argument surely applied to kings, but when it came to over-indulgence or the pleasing of favourites at the expense of the king's subjects, there were objections made in Parliament on important issues of economic deprivation, the harm done to "the poor Commons" and the corruption and greed of purveyors. There were plenty of officials ready to obtain the supplies the king desired, but there were many who saw it as an opportunity for private gain. There were also persons acting as purveyors who had not been accredited, as the statute of 1362 which sought to correct this implied. Instances where fair prices were not paid and people were forced to sell or were given no payment at all were tantamount to theft. Most critics attributed the blame to the purveyors themselves or the king's evil counsellors, but William of Pagula did not shrink from accusing Edward III of theft since the king was ultimately responsible. The purveying abuses were an exploitation of the ancient right of prise, according to which the king had a right to take goods from his subjects in time of need. The following case study is of how lords of the manor perceived the issue of taking others' goods.

---

[91] *The Household of Edward IV*, 86.

[92] *The Household of Edward IV*, 211–212.

[93] *Handlyng Synne*, 196–197.

Extortion and Oppression by Lords and Gentry

Attention has been drawn to the fact that lords, as well as royal households, engaged in the right of prise or purveying, even when they were not legally entitled to do so. There is evidence that lords regarded taking goods from an unfree tenant on one of their manors as a long-established right. In addition, a lord might make whatever exactions or tallages he deemed fit. As discussed in Chapter 2, the early thirteenth-century English theologians Robert of Courson and Robert of Flamborough believed that arbitrary tallages were morally wrong, that all tallages needed to be justified and that unjust tallages should be remedied. Robert of Flamborough proposed that the lord support those whom he reduced to penury, and Robert Courson advocated the building of poor houses and providing infrastructure.[94] The consciences of lords had to be relied upon in this matter, and so it was that many fourteenth- and fifteenth-century treatises and pastoral manuals, which were discussed in Chapter 3, condemned the taking of a villein's goods as theft and demanding excessive tallage as extortion. For example, Thomas Docking's treatise on the Ten Commandments condemns such lords as guilty of theft.[95] *Handlyng Synne* declares that lords who increase "custome" or rents or who take unreasonable fees from towns are also guilty of theft.[96]

Lords were therefore the subject of criticism by moralists but in practice lords might have regarded themselves as having the right, under feudal law, to take from their bonded tenants. Hence, they were not infringing on anyone's rights, nor were they breaching any ethical code. Historians have different perspectives on this issue. Paul Hyams affirms that "The lord could take anything his villein held, and the villein had no redress in royal courts": if there was any court action, "there was no case to answer once the plaintiff had been proved a villein".[97] John Hatcher quotes the statement in the *Mirror of Justices* that anything acquired by

[94] J.W. Baldwin, *Masters, Princes and Merchants: The Social View of Peter the Chanter and His Circle*, vol. 1 (Princeton: Princeton University Press, 1970), 237–238.

[95] Thomas Docking, *De Decem Praeceptis*, in Oxford, Bodleian Library, MS Bodley 453, fol. 50v.

[96] *Handlyng Synne*, 84, 79.

[97] P. Hyams, *King, Lords and Peasants in Medieval England: The Common Law of Villeinage in the Twelfth and Thirteenth Centuries* (Oxford: Clarendon Press, 1980), 20.

a serf belonged to his lord, but points out that in practice taking a serf's belongings was limited to the taking of a heriot or a proportion of goods when a serf died. Furthermore, villeins were allowed to buy and sell land if they paid a fine and their right to make wills was frequently recognised.[98] Christopher Dyer asserts that "lords only interfered with peasant goods in extreme situations", such as a rebellion. The claim of the right to a serf's property was a routine "bluster" of lawyers, who were aware that lords' franchises could be enquired into by royal commissions and that serfs were entitled to protection if they could prove they lived on lands that were once part of the royal demesne. This meant that tenants' rents and services could not be altered by the current lord.[99] The royal commissions referred to by Dyer were presumably the *Quo Warranto* proceedings, which investigated the claims made concerning rights to land, or possibly the general eyres or commissions of oyer and terminer, both of which had fallen into disuse by the mid-fourteenth century.[100] After this period, presumably, serfs who could satisfy the royal demesne condition could apply to royal courts.

It appears that lords did not see themselves as exploiters of the poor and believed their tenants were merely performing their feudal obligations in exchange for access to land and so-called protection, regardless of whether or not they could afford the rents and services required.[101] If this was the case, then it is perhaps not so surprising that the charges against them of extortion and oppression appeared so frequently in pastoral manuals and sermons. Lords needed to be made aware that continuing to practice such rights in an unrestrained or unreasonable fashion brought economic damage and hardship to the poor. It is possible that some lords took goods and livestock from their tenants as a way of supplementing their incomes, or, perhaps, as punishment for non-payment

[98] John Hatcher, "English Serfdom and Villeinage: Towards a Reassessment", *Past & Present* no. 90 (1981): 8–10.

[99] Christopher Dyer, "The Ineffectiveness of Lordship in England, 1200–1400", *Past & Present*, (2007) Supplement 2: 75; John Hatcher and Mark Bailey, *Modelling the Middle Ages: The History and Theory of England's Economic Development* (Oxford: OUP, 2001, repr., 2009),104.

[100] Richard W. Kaeuper, "Law and Order in Fourteenth-Century England: The Evidence of Special Commissions of Oyer and Terminer", *Speculum* 54 (1979): 738.

[101] Dyer, "The Ineffectiveness of Lordship": 79–80.

of fines or failure to perform services. Another practice regarded as extortion and oppression was excessive or arbitrary tallage, but again, historians disagree about the protection afforded to tenants by the custom of the manor, a topic which will be discussed in the next chapter.

Free tenants who had had goods and livestock taken by their landowners petitioned Chancery. In two cases dating from the mid-fifteenth century, the landowner's defence that he believed the free tenant was his villein or bondsman indicates that he felt it was his right to do so. John Bysship of Hampshire said he was imprisoned after John Wayte and other armed men broke into his house and took his goods and chattels. Wayte responded that Bysship was his bondsman and denied any wrongdoing.[102] Laurence Kylwyth of Cornwall claimed to have been treated in similar fashion by Henry Bothrygan, squire, who said Kylwyth was his bondsman.[103] In such cases, the plaintiff declared themselves to be of free condition and it was often recorded by the clerk that a subsequent jury trial found this to be true, the defendant found guilty and a fine and arrest ordered.[104] Lawyers acting for lords might have interpreted Bracton's statement—"By a bondsman, even another's whom we possess in good faith, we acquire, because we believe him to be ours, having no intimation of the opposite"—as meaning that anything acquired by the villein was therefore acquired by the lord.[105] The free tenants were obviously anxious to have it on record that they were free men, not villeins, but they were also acting in the belief that they had suffered economic injustice.

Many lords, regardless of whether they were favoured by the king, may have been simply too powerful to be sued for their unethical behaviour by action through the law courts. It was when deeply unpopular royal favourites were judged to be disrupting good order that accusations of

---

[102] *Select Cases in Chancery*, 134–136.

[103] *Select Cases in Chancery*, pp. 151–153.

[104] *Court of Common Pleas: The National Archives CP40 1399–1500*, London, Centre for Metropolitan History, 2010, available through British History Online <www.british-history.ac.uk>, CP40/568 rot. 059; CP40/571 rot. 520 and 531; CP40/663 rot. 344; CP40/667 rot. 305d; CP40/669 rot. 241d; CP40/674 rot. 213; CP40/743 rot. 214; CP40/745 rot. 108; CP40/873 rot. 457.

[105] Henry de Bracton, *On the Laws and Customs of England*, vol. 2, trans. Samuel E. Thorne (Cambridge, MA: Belknap Press with the Selden Society, 1968), 135–136.

economic injustice came to light. In 1321, Parliament, both the Lords and the Commons, judged that Edward II's favourites the lords Despenser should be exiled, alleging many wrongdoings. The words "malveistees" (evil deeds) and "coveteise" are used several times in the document entitled *Exilium hugonis le despens patris et filii*. Among their misdeeds was their seizure of the land of others by means of false accusations, very much in the manner described by John Bromyard in his *Summa Praedicantium*. The Despensers used their position to advise the king to assume "the lands and chattels of Sir Hugh Audeley the Son, and they forejudged him of his Lands without due Process according to the Law of the Land, through covetousness", and "by other false compassings" they obtained the lands of Sir Roger Damory.[106] The Despensers were accused of persuading the king to impose unreasonable fines and forfeitures so that "through covetousness" they could obtain the lands. The lands of Master John de Mowbray in Gower, and others, were obtained in this way "to the Damage and Dishonour of our Lord the King … [thereby] causing the King to deny Right in Parliament, contrary to his Oath".[107] Their influence on the king was seen to be evil, and in the same way as described in the confessional manuals, the covetousness of the Despensers was the driving factor. For instance, the Despensers were accused of taking bribes "through their evil covetousness": anyone who sought an audience with the king had to pay Hugh Despenser the younger, and therefore their avarice impeded access to the king and possibly barred the way to those who might have been seeking justice. Hugh Despenser the younger had accumulated large amounts of money from estates which his accusers said he acquired unjustly. He deposited nearly £6,000 with Italian merchants (the Bardi and the Peruzzi) most of which was derived from revenue from his estates.[108] For instance, he took John de Lachele out of Colchester gaol, where he was imprisoned for a trespass against Lady de Merk, and forced him to sell his land to him. This was done before Lady de Merk had received her damages of 1,500 marks.[109] Perhaps the most serious

[106] *SR*, vol. 1, 183.

[107] *SR*, vol. 1, 183–184.

[108] E.B. Fryde, "The Deposits of Hugh Despenser the Younger with Italian Bankers", *Economic History Review*, New Series 3 (1951), 344–362.

[109] *SR*, vol. 1, 184.

accusations were that the Despensers had corrupted the king by their evil advice and counsel and brought him dishonour. Parliament wanted to inflict the ultimate punishment on the Despensers and needed to show that it was necessary. Similarly, the Lusignans had been attacked as favourites of Henry III, and deeming them evil and immoral made them deserving of punishment.[110] Both cases are examples of ethical language being used to strengthen the case against political opponents.

In cases in which great lords were still in positions of power, actions through the common law courts or via petitions to the king, Parliament or Chancery were aimed at their retainers. A notorious example is William de la Pole, Duke of Suffolk. The Duke was very powerful, firstly serving as a steward of the household of Henry VI in 1433 and then expanding his influence and control, after Henry's minority ended in 1436, to the point where he managed the king's business without the input of the King's Council. His domination of East Anglian courts would have been very difficult to resist and did not cease until his banishment in 1450.[111] Sir Thomas Tuddenham and John Heydon were adherents of the Duke of Suffolk and their actions on his behalf brought them into disputes with the Pastons and Sir John Fastolf. They were also the subject of complaints by the Mayor and Aldermen of Norwich, for the Duke of Suffolk was an enemy of not only the Pastons and Sir John Fastolf but also the City's government. A jury presentment by the Conesford Ward in Norwich accused Tuddenham, Heydon and others of conspiring to "maintain together all plaints and matters in the Counties of Norfolk Suffolk and Norwich" in order to get the decisions they wanted and extort money. In 1435, they made William Grey Mayor instead of the one duly elected. In 1438, they threatened to make the Duke of Suffolk "the heavy lord" ("gravem dominum") of the City, falsely accused the Mayor and Commonalty of insurrection, which came with a fine of over £40, and falsely accused Robert Toppes and others of treason. They threatened Toppes with hanging and forfeiture of his lands unless he paid £15 to the King via the Duke of Suffolk. The Mayor and Commonalty

[110] Further details are in J.R. Maddicott, "Magna Carta and the Local Community 1215–1259", *Past & Present*, no. 102 (1984), 54–61.

[111] R.L. Storey, *The Reign of Henry VII* (London: Blandford, 1968), 33–34.

were forced to pay 1,000 marks. The presentment claimed that "many other oppressions and extortions" amounted to the value of £20,000.[112] Thus, the presentment could accuse Tuddenham and Heydon of extortion and oppression but not their patron.

Stronger language concerning Tuddenham was employed in a petition to Parliament by the town of Swaffham in 1451. This described Tuddenham, who had been lord of the manor of Swaffham for many years, as "a common extortioner" and asked that he be imprisoned. The petition pointed out that "if a common thief was so often indicted or accused" he would not be put on bail or mainprised but sent to prison to await trial. Tuddenham would never appear at a commission of oyer and terminer to answer to the indictments. The sense of moral outrage was strong. Not only had Tuddenham committed great wrongs and been sinful, but the jury of the local assize had been intimidated by his "horrible menaces".[113]

Sir Thomas Tuddenham was not the only member of the gentry accused of unethical behaviour. Some examples of cases concerning others, dating from the mid-fourteenth century, are outlined here. There are several cases recorded in the Close Rolls and the Patent Rolls of gentry landowners taking goods and chattels, often invading properties with force and arms, but such actions were mostly the results of disputes over land title with the plaintiffs. The examples given here are instances of economic injustice in which landowners extorted money or otherwise mistreated their tenants. In 1353, it was alleged that John Fitz Wauter in Essex used his steward and other employees to charge excessive amercements, take produce and livestock and take goods in the common market at Colchester against the will of the sellers. Fitz Wauter himself had taken livestock, kept them at his manors and had received the proceeds of extortion.[114] In 1359, the king ordered further inquiries to be made concerning allegations of "oppressions, extortions and excesses" done by John de Gildesburgh of the manor of Brumpton in Somerset "on the tenants of the manor and wastes and destructions of houses and gardens

[112] *Records of the City of Norwich*, 346–347.

[113] *Parliament Rolls*, Henry VI, November 1450, appendix.

[114] *CPR* (*Edward III*), vol. 9, 412–414.

therein". Gildesburgh had earlier appeared in court "to shew cause why the manor should not be resumed and he to make restitution to the tenants of moneys received by extortion, and satisfaction for his oppressions" but he denied all charges.[115] Sir Robert Darcy was accused of many extortions and acts of violence in Lincolnshire, but in September 1360 he was pardoned for his good service to the Duke of Lancaster in France.[116] The source for this material is the *Calendar of Patent Rolls*, which does not always reveal all of the original text, but the summarised entries give some indication that concepts of economic ethics were employed. It is of further significance that although the entries in the Patent Rolls were administrative records, not petitions, the clerks used "extortion" and "oppression" as common terms.

Actual cases of lords being accused of unethical behaviour are relatively few, probably for the reason that lords were powerful. On the downfall of the few, the notions of "evil" and "covetousness" were employed to ensure that their punishment was justified. On occasion, the gentry were attacked for abuses of their lordship and accused of "extortion and oppression", the language of economic ethics. Quite apart from the legal barrier preventing their unfree tenants from access to courts outside their own manor, even the free tenants would have taken large risks in seeking redress for economic injustice. Smaller targets, as it were, appeared much more frequently in allegations and some examples of these are discussed in the following section.

Extortion by Officials, Unreasonable Tolls and Fines

Criticisms of the covetousness of royal or lords' officials were made just as frequently as criticisms of merchants, market traders and usurers in pastoral manuals, as was shown in Chapter 3. *Handlyng Synne* censured counsellors, false accounters and covetous stewards, as well as judges who charged outrageous amercements, especially against the poor.[117] *Jacob's Well* similarly condemned foresters, beadles, bailiffs and any other officials

[115] *CPR* (*Edward III*), vol. 11, 281.
[116] *CPR* (*Edward III*), vol. 11, 463.
[117] *Handlyng Synne*, 178–179.

who profited themselves from gathering taxes.[118] Officials also came under severe criticism in *Speculum Laicorum*, in *Regimen Animarum*, and in Thomas Docking's *De Decem Praeceptis*. The *Memoriale Presbiterorum* described seneschals and bailiffs as "exceedingly cavilling and altogether given to avarice". It instructed priests to ask bailiffs whether they have ever paid a fee to a lord or a middleman or an annual amount to a lord for holding his bailiwick. If they have, this inevitably means that the poor in his bailiwick will suffer, for the bailiff will harass them for the additional money.[119]

Both a 1275 statute and a 1311 ordinance had the same concern about the economic harm caused to others as the result of greedy officials. Both were amplifying clause 20 of the *Magna Carta*, which stated that free men should be fined only for a major offence and a villein an amount that would not destroy his livelihood, and in both instances the fines were to be imposed on the oath of trustworthy neighbours.[120] The 1275 statute ordained that individual officials should not profit by charging fines and amercements at their own whim. Its clause XVIII ordered common fines to be assessed before justices in the eyre, for sheriffs and "baretors" or cheats had been imposing fines that were "unjustly assessed … so that the sum is many times increased … to the great Damage of the People" who had been paying such fines many times over without being acquitted.[121] Clause XXXI was concerned with excessive tolls in market towns: should these be imposed, then the franchise will be taken back by the King or if it is a lord's town, the lord will do likewise. If a bailiff should impose a fine without the authority of his lord, "he shall restore to the Plaintiff as much more for the outrageous taking … and shall have forty days imprisonment".[122] An ordinance of 1311 recognised that high customs and tolls would damage trade and sought to abolish the creation of

[118] *Jacob's Well* (Brandeis), 61.

[119] M.J. Haren, "Interrogatories for Officials, Lawyers and Secular Estates of the *Memoriale Presbiterorum*", in *Handling Sin: Confession in the Middle Ages*, ed. Peter Biller and A.J. Minnis (Woodbridge: York Medieval Press, 1998), 135, 137–141; see also *Cursor Mundi*, vol. 3, 1517; *Of Shrifte and Penance: The ME Prose Translation of 'Le Manuel Des Peches'*, ed. K. Bitterling (Heidelberg: Winter, 1998), 80–81.

[120] *Magna Carta*, ed. David Carpenter (London: Penguin, 2015), 47.

[121] *SR*, vol. 1, 31–32.

[122] *SR*, vol. 1, 34.

new tolls and any increases in old ones on a range of goods.[123] The 1275 statute attempted to control the avarice of officials by threatening punishment, and the authors of the pastoral works cited above warned them to examine their consciences.

The same principle of the 1275 statute that amounts should be agreed by all in order to be fair and just and that tolls and fines should not be taken arbitrarily was behind a complaint in 1326 by the "middle people" of Norwich to the King's Council. Bailiffs and the rich had resumed collecting tallages and fines from them, even though they had promised the king's justices that they would no longer do so "without the common assent of them all" and were now, without any royal warrant, demanding 200 marks and threatening even larger amounts.[124] Similarly, in 1398, a presentment to the King's Bench alleged that Walter Topcliffe, steward of the liberty of the town of Gainsborough, exacted heavy fines, which were according to "his own will" ("ad voluntatem suam propriam") rather than on the advice of assessors, implying that the individual will was against the common good. Also, he charged market stallholders and boat owners tolls that were a great deal higher than they were used to, he charged tolls from carters from outside the town who had hitherto paid nothing, and he charged fees on merchandise brought to town regardless of whether it was a market day or not. Topcliffe amassed "twenty shillings to be levied on market days every year at Gainsborough by extortion" ("per extorsionem") plus another twenty shillings from the merchants.[125] Topcliffe's acting according to his own will was a breach of his duties and was also yet another example of the selfishness of the avaricious person who thinks only of their own profit. In 1399, the Commons petitioned that sheriffs of counties who were responsible for collecting the fee farm had been giving "a great Parcel of Profits of the same … severally to Lords and other the King's liege people" with the result that the farm could not be paid "without doing Extortion … in great Oppression and Hindrance".[126] Thus, we have a real instance of precisely the kind of behaviour that *Memoriale*

[123] *SR*, vol. 1, 159.

[124] *Records of the City of Norwich*, 61.

[125] *Select Cases in the Court of King's Bench under Richard II, Henry IV and Henry V*, ed. G.O. Sayles (London: Bernard Quaritch for the Selden Society, 1971), 92–94.

[126] *SR*, vol. 2, 115.

Presbiterorum said confessors should ask bailiffs about (that is, whether they had ever given part of their official receipts to other parties).

Most sheriffs were representatives of royal power and, in their oath of service, swore to protect the king's interests and treat the people in his jurisdiction with impartiality, without regard to wealth or status, and to refuse any bribes or favours.[127] They were not supposed to use their positions of authority to profit themselves. There is evidence that such activity by sheriffs was regarded as extortion and oppression by secular authorities as well as the Church. A commission of oyer and terminer was ordered in October 1314 to determine whether Gerard Salveyn (formerly sheriff of York), his bailiffs and other officials had, since the beginning of Edward II's reign, employed such means as false accusations, imprisonment, and "intolerable distraints made for unjust causes, and extortions of divers sums of money".[128] In March 1315, a commission of oyer and terminer was ordered concerning allegations that Hugh Daudele, who had been sheriff of Shropshire, sheriff of Staffordshire and a royal representative in Montgomeryshire, "had greatly oppressed the people of those parts by false indictments...heavy ransoms, intolerable distraints and extortion". A few days later, another commission was ordered to investigate complaints of "malpractices and oppressions" by Gerals Salveyn, formerly sherriff of York.[129] Sheriffs, like lords, were in positions of power and could use it to profit themselves at others' expense.

Other official appointees who were alleged to have profited themselves were to be investigated in commissions of oyer and terminer held in the reign of Edward III. Thomas de Grenefeld, who had been a coroner in York, was accused of refusing to carry out his duties "without extorting grievous ransoms from the people", and around the same time (December 1340) commissions of oyer and terminer were ordered for London and thirty counties to hear grievances about oppressions by ministers and justices from the start of Edward III's reign.[130] A month later, three of the commissioners were asked to look into the activities of numerous named appointees, including such well-known figures as William de la Pole,

[127] *SR*, vol. 1, 247; see also Richard Gorski, *The Fourteenth-Century Sheriff: English Local Administration in the Late Middle Ages* (Woodbridge: Boydell, 2003), 114.

[128] *CPR* (*Edward II*), vol. 2, 242.

[129] *CPR* (*Edward II*), vol. 2, 312.

[130] *CPR* (*Edward III*), vol. 5, 106, 110–113.

John de Pulteney, William de Shareshull and John de Stonor. These men, "by the common report and clamour of the people" and according to allegations made in a number of petitions, had broken their oath of office and "borne themselves in divers manners fraudulently and unfaithfully to their offices". The king had them arrested.[131] Terms such as extortion, oppression and fraud in the wording of the instructions to the commissioners indicate moral opprobrium and that the persons accused, even if they were of higher rank, were considered to be little better than deceitful traders in the marketplace.

The same kinds of accusations about abuse of power for personal profit were made in the late fourteenth century. A certain John Skipwith, who had been sheriff of Lincoln two years earlier, was the subject of a number of Chancery petitions in 1397. Firstly, Sybil, the widow of Sir Robert Darcy, alleged that Skipwith had forcibly taken the land that was her dower and had kept the profits for seven years or more and given her little or nothing from them. Sybil would have sued Skipwith at the King's Bench in Lincoln but found no lawyer willing to represent her "for fear of the malice of the said John" ("pur doute et malice du dit Johan"). Then John de Rouseby of Bardney petitioned Chancery that Skipwith, while sheriff, had arrested and imprisoned him. Skipwith refused to release Rouseby unless he gave him his land or 10 marks. Rouseby paid 40 shillings "to the great damage of the said suppliant and against right and reason" ("et encountre droit et resoun"). Rouseby prayed the Chancellor for a remedy "for God and in the way of charity, considering that the due effect of the common law is so overborne by the said John Skipwith and his supporters in the county of Lincoln and elsewhere". Skipwith seems to have been something of a menace, as there are other petitions complaining of his armed bands forcibly entering properties, of his making a false arrest to extort large sums of money, and of his threatening behaviour making action through the common law courts impossible. Chancery responded by instructing the justices of the assize at Lincoln to investigate all of the petitions presented and reply promptly, "so that we may proceed in the matter as of right and according to the law and custom of our realm of England ought to be done".[132]

---

[131] *CPR* (*Edward III*), vol. 5, 110–111.

[132] *Select Cases in Chancery*, 29–34.

The above words signify that Chancery believed that such behaviour, if it could be shown to have occurred, could be dealt with by the forces of common law. In its judgements, Chancery itself was careful to refrain from using the moralising language of the petitions but there are examples of fifteenth-century legislation which do not. In 1430, an ordinance described extortion by sheriffs in Herefordshire, who had been holding unauthorised inquiries and inquests and wrongfully taking the fines and amercements for their own use, as "the great Mischiefs and importable Oppressions daily done to the King's liege People". They were forbidden from taking such "heinous" and grievous amercements, on pain of a fine of £40.[133] A statute of 1444 referred to the "perjury, extortion and oppression" practised by sheriffs, bailiffs and other officials. Sheriffs were forbidden to "let to ferm" their counties, bailiwicks, hundreds or wapentakes or to make false imprisonments "for their Reward or Profit". Henceforward, they must let prisoners out on bail on sureties.[134] The next clause of the statute dealt with the matter of sheriffs levying more money than was needed for the wages of the knights of the shire "keeping and [retaining] great part of the Money to their own Use and Profit, to their Officers and Servants, to the great Loss of the common People".[135] A clause in a later statute (1449) called over-charging by customs officers "contrary to all Law and Conscience".[136] In 1455, an ordinance regarding officers of the Exchequer receiving "great and [excessive] Gifts, Fees and Rewards" from sheriffs and others for entering pleas and judgements as "against all Reason and Conscience" and "to the Great Damage and Destruction of all the said Accomptants, and all the people aforesaid".[137] The terms "reason", "conscience", "extortion", and "oppression" are the moralising language of the petitions and the pastoral manuals as well as of the literary works discussed in the last chapter.

Despite the legislation, corruption by officials persisted in the late fifteenth century. For example, in 1476, Thomas Yotten, the Common Clerk of York, was found to have been guilty of "excessive takyngs of money, misguideing of the books, accomptes and other evidences". Yotten was

[133] *SR*, vol. 2, 266.

[134] *SR*, vol. 2, 334–335.

[135] *SR*, vol. 2, 336.

[136] *SR*, vol. 2, 356.

[137] *SR*, vol. 2, 372–374.

removed from his post by Richard, Duke of Gloucester.[138] The persistence of excessive fines and false accusations in order to extort money by sheriffs might have been due to the fact that they were unpaid. To address this problem, Edward IV introduced "tallies of reward" whereby sheriffs could draw their annual expenses out of the revenue they collected. The allowances varied from £340 for the largest county of York to £13 6 s 8 d for the smallest county of Rutland.[139] Yet this seems to have had little effect: in 1495, *An Acte agaynst Shreifs and Undershreifs* began "Whereas great extorcion is yerely used and had within divers counties … by the subtile and untrue demeanour of Shriefs, Undershriefs, Shire Clerkis or any other officers". These officials were entering "false playnts" in which the defendants were never summoned or attached and did not know of any suit against them. Yet the amercements were entered in the books year after year "ingroced to amounte to greate and importunable sommes of Money, which … be yerly levyed of the pouer Commons". This was condemned by the statute as "the expresse pillage and empoverysshing of the seid Commons".[140]

The language directed at corrupt sheriffs and officials was very similar, whether in petitions or in statutes, and also similar to that used in accusations of avaricious behaviour made against lords and gentry, but there was additional concern that sheriffs were officials of the king. The common theme was selfish gain at the expense of others, whether they were poor tenants on a manor or townspeople being forced to pay high fees and fines. Lords and officials could have a particular role in spreading corruption and it was able to continue unabated because many of those who suffered were intimidated if they sought redress in common law courts. To many, such as William Langland and John Gower, it seemed the whole of society was corrupt.

Enclosures

Another type of activity which sometimes led to economic deprivation was the enclosure of arable lands for pasture. Major sources of information about enclosures which had taken place by the mid-fifteenth century

[138] See *York Civic Records, Vol. 1*, ed. Angelo Raine (Yorkshire Archaeological Society, 1939), 9–10.
[139] Storey, *The Reign of Henry VII*, 141.
[140] *SR*, vol. 2, 579.

and those which occurred in the late fifteenth century are the protests by a contemporary, John Rous, about enclosures in Warwickshire and the presentments made to the inquisition or *Domesday of Inclosures*. Some historians have debated the impact that such enclosures had on the rural economy as a whole or the lives of the poor. Edwin Gay disputed the statistical analysis made by I.S. Leadam in the tabulations provided in his 1897 edition of the records of Domesday and queried the extent of arable lands that had been enclosed and their impact.[141] In a later article, Gay tried to estimate the total number of enclosures nationwide, not just the counties covered by the Domesday, going back to 1455, and calculated that the overall number was probably no more than 5 per cent of total agricultural land. He loftily concluded that therefore it was

> surely nothing very alarming. The gradual displacing of the agricultural population ... at the rate of 7,000 or even 10,000 every thirty years, would doubtless cause a certain distress in a body politic of England's dimensions in the sixteenth century. With the ignorance and hidebound conservatism of the English peasant, such a change would be more bitterly resented, the ill effects of such an uprooting more pronounced, than a similar social adjustment in the much more fluid industrial population of to-day.[142]

Eric Kerridge also disputed Leadam's conclusions about the extent of enclosures because his evidence was relying on the presentments to the Domesday of Inclosures rather than actual judgements. Several defendants at the Domesday rebutted claims on legal grounds, and prosecutions were never made.[143] Fryde disagreed, saying that most of the presentments were found to be true and that the failure to prosecute could have been for political or legal reasons. He argued that the total number of enclosures was probably far greater than those alleged in the

---

[141] *The Domesday of Inclosures 1517–18 Being the Extant Returns for Berks, Bucks, Cheshire, Essex, Leicestershire, Lincolnshire, Northants, Oxon and Warwickshire by the Commissioners of Inclosures in 1517 and for Bedfordshire in 1518*, ed. I.S. Leadam, 2 vols. (London: Longmans Green, 1897); Edwin S. Gay and I.S. Leadam, "The Inqusitions of Depopulation in 1517 and the 'Domesday of Inclosures'", *Transactions of the Royal Historical Society*, New Series 14 (1900): 231–303 (which consists of Gay's critique, a rebuttal by Leadam and a final rejoinder by Gay).

[142] Edwin S. Gay, "Inclosures in England in the Sixteenth Century", *Quarterly Journal of Economics* 17 (1903): 588–589.

[143] Eric Kerridge, "The Returns of the Inquisitions of Depopulation", *English Historical Review* 70 (1955): 212–228.

presentments to the Domesday, because "One must assume considerable hesitations of juries in presenting some notoriously violent and dangerous notables".[144] Hilary Turner has investigated an allegation ("reputational damage") concerning an enclosure in the early sixteenth century and found it to be untrue.[145] However, given the prevalence of the practice known as livery and maintenance by lords and of bribery and corruption of juries in late medieval England, Fryde's conclusion is a reasonable one to draw. Yet the overall impact is difficult to assess without a very large number of local studies; the few which have been completed are outlined here.

Christopher Dyer conducted research into deserted villages in the West Midlands and concluded that although Rous had been mistaken about the causes of desertion in some cases, "his evident anger at the destruction of the villages must have been provoked by a real problem", having found records which substantiated Rous's claims.[146] Donald Leech has documented a long-running dispute over enclosures of common land outside Coventry, where craftsmen who had had grazing rights there claimed they were at a disadvantage.[147] Harold Fox's survey of enclosures in medieval Devon, on the other hand, is a study of changing land use without referring to the gains or losses of particular parties.[148] Similar kinds of local studies have been made by Cora Weaver and Nicholas Amor.[149] Dyer's and Leech's studies did investigate the impact of enclosures upon tenants, but the main interests of Fox, Weaver and Amor were changes in land use.

---

[144] Fryde, *Peasants and Landlords*, 203, 204.

[145] Hilary L. Turner, "Reputational Damage: William Willington and the Supposed Enclosure of Barcheston", *Midland History* 37 (2012): 222–239.

[146] Dyer, "Deserted Medieval Villages in the West Midlands" in his *Everyday Life*, 35.

[147] Donald Leech, "'By the Evidence of this City': Enclosing Land and Memory in Fifteenth-century Coventry", *Medieval History Journal* 15 (2012): 171–196.

[148] Harold Fox, "The Chronology of Enclosure and Economic Development in Medieval Devon", *Economic History Review*, 28 (1975): 181–202.

[149] Cora Weaver, "From Private Pursuit to Public Playground: The Enclosure of Malvern Chase", *Transactions of the Worcestershire Archaeological Society*, 3 (1998): 207–219; N.R. Amor, "Late Medieval Enclosure: A Study of Thorney, near Stowmarket, Suffolk", *Proceedings of the Suffolk Institute of Archaeology and History* 41 (2006): 175–197.

My focus here is on land enclosures as an ethical issue; in other words, on those enclosures which involved evictions or otherwise damaged the livelihoods of others. Enclosures as an economic activity that could harm the poor were not specified in the fourteenth- and early fifteenth-century pastoral manuals, sermons and literature and this is probably because enclosures as a widespread movement seem to have begun at a later period, from the mid-fifteenth century onwards. Earlier examples are a petition to Parliament of November 1330, which alleged that Sir Roger de Mortimer enclosed some common pasture with an embankment at King's Norton Wood, and records from the end of the fourteenth century of peasants enclosing land in Arden, Warwickshire.[150]

In 1459, John Rous, an Oxford-educated priest in a chantry founded by Richard Beauchamp, the Earl of Warwick, saw the economic and social damage enclosures had caused in Warwickshire. He submitted a petition to Parliament while it sat at Coventry. Unfortunately, the petition has not survived and there was no response from Parliament. Twenty-seven years later, Rous wrote in his *Historia Regum Anglie*: "My labour then was quite in vain, and so I presented petitions to several parliaments afterwards ... but to no effect". He raised the issue again, hoping that "frequent reading of it by the nobility may stir their hearts to the praise of God and the great profit of the commonwealth". He described those landowners who enclosed lands for sheep farming as "internal enemies of the kingdom" and "lovers and inducers of avarice", who by expelling the many inhabitants of towns, villages and hamlets murdered the poor and brought about starvation. Rous listed sixty-two villages and hamlets that had been destroyed in Warwickshire and argued that the lack of rural inhabitants meant a lack of demand for goods from the towns. He warned that the trade of the whole kingdom would be destroyed if no action were taken to check this avarice. Rous declared that the enclosers were sinning "grievously" by depriving many poor people of their livelihoods, reminding them that they depended on the common people in evoking the image of the body politic, "for the common folk carry the burden, even though

[150] *Parliament Rolls*, Edward III, November 1330, E.175/2/216, membrane 3 [dorse], item 62; Andrew Watkins, "Peasants in Arden", in *Daily Life in the Late Middle Ages*, ed. Richard Britnell (Stroud, Sutton, 1998), 88.

lords provide the leaders".[151] Rous also attacked the enclosers in his earlier history, written between 1477 and 1485, of the Earls of Warwick. In the English version, known as the Yorkist roll, he claimed: "They destroy the realm and cause derth of corne". He alleged that towns' abilities to pay their tenths were severely affected, their income being only 100 marks a year instead of £200 because of the damage to trade from enclosures.[152] The deleterious effects of the enclosure movement on the body politic were also pointed out by John Russell, Bishop of Lincoln and Lord Chancellor, in one version of a speech drafted for the intended Parliament of Edward V in June 1483.[153] The impression is that as Rous's appeals to the consciences of enclosers were ignored, Russell's speech would have encountered the same fate had Parliament met on that occasion.

The surviving returns to Chancery from the Domesday or inquisition of enclosures of 1517–1518 covered nine counties, dating back to 1485. Not all enclosures were for pasture; some were for arable farming, and not all enclosures involved eviction of tenants.[154] Yet some of the allegations made in the presentments to the 1517 inquisition describe weeping people being thrown off the manor and being reduced to extreme poverty, sometimes leading to their deaths. For example, a case quoted by Fryde describes how, on 11 August 1495, Thomas Pigott, a sergeant at law and lord of the manor of Dodershall in Buckinghamshire, expelled twenty-four tenants from their messuages, a total of 120 people, who were reduced to extreme poverty and so died.[155] The same fate befell tenants of Sir Ralph Shirley at Rakedale and Willow in Leicestershire in November 1495, of Sir John Villars at Brooksby in the same county in December 1492, of Robert Brudnell at Holyoak, also in Leicestershire, in December 1496 and of John Ashby at two hamlets in Northamptonshire

[151] John Rous, *Historia Regum Anglie*, ed. T. Hearne, extracts translated and reprinted in *English Historical Documents, Vol. 4: 1327–1485*, ed. A.R. Myers (London: Routledge, 1969, repr. 1995), 1029–1030.

[152] John Rous, *The Rous Roll*, ed. Charles Ross (Gloucester: Sutton, 1980), paragraph 30; Nicholas Orme, "Rous, John (*c.* 1420–1492)", *ODNB*.

[153] *Grants Etc. From the Crown During the Reign of Edward the Fifth*, ed. John Gough Nichols (London: Camden Society, 1854), li.

[154] *The Domesday of Inclosures*, vol. 2, 502–509, 521, 570–579, 591; R.H. Hilton, "A Study in the Pre-history of English Enclosure in the Fifteenth Century" in his *The English Peasantry in the Later Middle Ages* (Oxford: Clarendon Press, 1975), 167-168.

[155] Fryde, *Peasants and Landlords*, 192, citing *The Domesday of Inclosures*, vol. 1, 162–163.

in May and December 1489.[156] As Fryde pointed out, it is noteworthy that most of these particular evictions occurred in winter, which showed that the landowner was more concerned about the crops being harvested beforehand than the welfare of his tenants.[157] However, other landowners were prepared to be more ethical: Fryde cites an interesting case of the vicar of Quinton in Warwickshire writing to the President of Magdalen College, Oxford, in the 1480s. The college owned the manor but its farmer had expelled tenants and ploughed up fields for pasture and Quinton was now in a state of decay. The vicar advised the President that it would be better to support and help a community than one man—"yowr tenantes rathere than a strong man, the pore and innocent for a gentylman or a gentylman's man"—and urged that the farmer be replaced by a group of the tenants, and this duly occurred in about 1490.[158] No doubt, the College saw this as an opportunity to improve the condition of its manor, but this could have been achieved by replacing the farmer with another gentleman. Instead, it decided to take the ethical option of making amends by helping the poor.

Parliament's belated response to enclosures was the 1489 *Acte Agaynst Pullyng Doun of Tounes*, which was referred to previously. It recognised the destructive impact of enclosures on the rural economy, ordering that offenders lose half of their annual profits to the crown and be obliged to spend those proceeds on repairs to ruined buildings.[159] In the same year, a statute concerning the Isle of Wight noted that farms had been engrossed or amalgamated and turned to pasture. The population had fallen, and as the main concern with the Isle was that it should be well populated so that it could be defended against the French, it was ordained that no one person should have a farm worth more than 10 marks a year, on pain of forfeiting the lease and a fine of £10. However, the legislation was less draconian in that those who had paid entry fines, built upon or improved the land "shall be recompensed … as right and good conscience requyren".[160]

---

[156] *The Domesday of Inclosures*, vol. 1, 229–230, 234, 237, 295–296.

[157] Fryde, *Peasants and Landlords*, 200, 204–208.

[158] Fryde, *Peasants and Landlords*, 202–203; Dyer, *Everyday Life*, 39.

[159] *SR*, vol. 2, 542.

[160] *SR*, vol. 2, 540.

The movement toward land enclosures which affected the poor or the rural economy was, like deceitful trade or profiteering from the powers given to sheriffs or royal purveyors, a problem that was difficult to control. Critics tried to show that enclosures were made for private gain and against the common weal. Their appeals to conscience, using the language of economic ethics, were made in the hope that the perpetrators would see the error of their ways.

Conclusions

Some historians have argued that poems and other literary works were part of a literature of complaint, that they were demonstrating the sinful nature of humankind rather than describing actual situations in which social or economic damage was inflicted. Richard Newhauser has described the authors of these works as theodiceans, for their descriptions of evil and moral decline are there to demonstrate that God will eventually carry out divine justice.[161] Joseph Keller describes many poems as catalogues of complaints: the world is seen in terms of vices and virtues, and the triumph of vice over virtue is a sign that the apocalypse is near.[162] Such views give the impression that authors were simply carrying on a literary tradition of complaint, or, if they were clergymen, it was part of their mission to emphasise the sinful nature of humankind. To some extent that is true, but such complaints had roots in the many struggles of those who believed they were entitled to justice for the wrongs committed against them. Those who sought redress in the law courts or via petitions to Chancery or to Parliament for extortion or unjust land acquisition did not venture to prophesy the end of the world, but they often used the same kind of moralistic language in order to draw attention to their causes. If in some cases they did not accuse their opponents of avarice or covetousness, they often used the terms oppression and extor-

[161] Richard Newhauser, "Historicity and Complaint in *Song of the Husbandman*", in *Studies in the Harley Manuscript: The Scribes, Contents and Social Contexts of British Library MS Harley 2253*, ed. Susanna Fein (Kalamazoo, MI: Medieval Institute Publications, 2000), 204.

[162] Joseph R. Keller, "The Triumph of Vice: A Formal Approach to the Medieval Complaint Against the Times", *Annuale Mediaevale* 10 (1969): 12–37.

tion to emphasise the social and economic impact. They might also draw attention to the impact on broader society or on the economy or to how rapacity was the very opposite of the common good.

Opportunities for avaricious clerks, sheriffs and justices to enrich themselves expanded with the growth of bureaucracy and are the reason so much of the complaint literature and the pastoral manuals is concerned with corrupt officials, extortion and oppression, just as much as they were with the perceived growth of avarice brought about by increased commerce. No doubt, some authors wished to demonstrate that the end of the world was nigh, but their immediate desire was to have readers or hearers look to their consciences. The appeals to conscience and warnings of avarice were intended to have the same effect on great lords, the gentry, lawyers and officials as on merchants and traders who were engaging in usury, excessive pricing or selling faulty products. Many statutes and ordinances sought to regulate and punish errant traders, bailiffs, sheriffs, purveyors and other officials but also to prevent unethical behaviour from occurring by using moralising language.

The subject of consumption, often over-consumption, by royal and aristocratic households and the attendant injustices was as important an issue for Parliament as it was for William of Pagula, John Bromyard and other theologians. Central to the abuses of prises or purveying was the resulting deprivation of the common people. The size of noble and royal households and their retinues was the underlying problem: certainly, the size of retinues and the scale of lavish feasting were criticised in sermons by Thomas Brinton, who accused magnates of living off the labour of others. If the household needs of lords and kings were less or could be supplied from their own estates, there would be less need for purveying and, consequently, fewer officials likely to act dishonestly for their own financial gain. The greater the king's requirements for money, victuals and other goods, the greater the number of officials needed to obtain them. Although taxation and purveyances continued, the successes in the war in France and the flows of revenue therefrom after about 1350 helped to ease pressures on English inhabitants, at any rate until the increases in the reign of Richard II, culminating in the poll tax.[163] Parliamentary

[163] Maddicott, "The English Peasantry and the Demands of the Crown", 285–357.

records show that the king was appealed to on moral grounds, using such terms as "reason", "conscience" and "charity", the "common profit" or the "common weal".

The activities of the landowning classes were harder to control by legislation, given their position within the existing power structure. Although some of the gentry were prosecuted in the courts for the unjust treatment of their tenants, a much more difficult target was a powerful member of the nobility, against whom the common law was ineffective. Individual lords seemed to be beyond reach, unless, like the Despensers, they were accused of the crime of treason. Sometimes, allegations were made after they had died. For example, some years after William de la Pole, the Duke of Suffolk, had died, George Heath, who had been made the inheritor of a property in Norfolk by an inquisition led by the Duke, recalled being summoned into his presence, the Duke saying that if Heath would "not be reuled by hym he shulde be so hevy lord unto him that he shulde not be able to bere it". The Duke then made George swear with his hand on a missal and "swere to make noon estate nyver relese withoute his advise, and he wolde see that [he] shulde be savyd harmless". Heath, "for fere therof" obeyed.[164] McFarlane concluded that most people felt that lords were far too powerful to be petitioned against, sued in a court of law or crossed in any way: taking such action was something that should never be attempted.[165] Thomas Denys, the coroner of Norfolk, was imprisoned in the Fleet in 1454 on the basis of what he claimed were false allegations, among them that he and his wife had been petitioning against lords: "one James Cook, a seruant of myn … hath accused and diffamed me and my wyf of settyng vp billes agayn lordis, that, Almyghti God I take to record, I not am ne neuer was gilty therof".[166] Sir John Fastolf's servant, Henry Windsor, feared that his observations about lords' activities after the first battle of St Albans might subject him to retaliation if his letter happened to fall into the wrong hands: he asked John Bokkyng

[164] Colin Richmond, "Sir John Fastolf and the Land Market: An Enquiry of the Early 1430s Regarding Purchasable Property", in *East Anglia's History: Studies in Honour of Norman Scarfe*, ed. Christopher Harper-Bill, Carole Rawcliffe and Richard G. Wilson (Woodbridge: Boydell, 2002), 109.

[165] McFarlane, *Nobility of Later Medieval England*, 124–125.

[166] *Paston Letters*, vol. 2, 88, no. 492, Letter from Thomas Denys to John Paston I of 8 April 1454.

and William Worcester to destroy his letter after reading it "for I am loth to write anything of any lord …".[167]

If lords were going to be opposed over land acquisitions, then the plaintiff had to be one of their peers. McFarlane cites a letter to William Wayneflete, Bishop of Winchester, from Gervas Clyfton, an esquire, informing him that his manor of Briggeford in Nottinghamshire had been invaded by a group acting in the name of Lord Lovell, who had installed new tenants. Clyfton explained that if he had had written authority from Winchester, he would have turned the tenants out, "Bot as it is now, considering he [i.e., Lovell] is a lorde, I may not soo deale".[168]

This chapter has shown that the wording of statutes, advice to legislators and petitions contained the same moral language and concepts used in Church instruction, appealing to notions of justice, right and conscience, and that such language was applied in instances of economic injustice that were outside as well as inside the marketplace. Petitions to Parliament, concerning the Lusignans and Despensers, and those from the urban governments of Norwich and Swaffham, concerning Tuddenham and Heydon, show familiarity with the language of economic morality. The use of such terms as "extortion", "horrible menaces" and "sinfully" mirrors that of the pastoral literature and shows that the laity, too, regarded ethics as playing a fundamental role in economic affairs.

William de la Pole, Duke of Suffolk, was the subject of, or the force behind, many allegations of economic injustice, yet he adhered to the conventional pieties. Close to dying, he wrote to his son that he should endeavour to please God, eschew the company of proud or covetous men and seek out the good and virtuous.[169] Such sentiments suggest a level of compartmentalisation, given William's own rapacity. It will be the task of the next chapter to investigate whether any responsible individuals had qualms about their actions and what their reactions were to economic ethics.

[167] *Paston Letters*, vol. 3, 159, no. 1026.

[168] McFarlane, "The Wars of the Roses", in *England in the Fifteenth Century: Collected Essays*, ed. G.L. Harriss (London: Continuum, 1981), 250.

[169] *Paston Letters*, vol. 3, 82–83, no. 980, Letter from William, Duke of Suffolk, to his son John of 30 April [1450?].

6

Lords of the Manor: Rapacious or Reasonable?

Late medieval England was highly dependent on rural production to provide not only food but also important commercial products such as timber and wool. Such production was highly dependent on the labour provided by servile or unfree tenants (villeins) or by hired labour. At the same time, lords were dependent on their estates for their income. The argument put by moralists in Chapter 3 was that income from their own estates was not sufficient for many lords, as a result of their indulgence in excessive consumption and profligacy. Their remedies of increasing land rents, entry fines, amercements and a range of feudal fees and charges led to economic hardship for many of their tenants, particularly the poor. Chapter 5 gave some examples of petitions complaining about extortion and oppression by some landowners or their officials or retainers. The historian Rodney Hilton's explanation was that it was a matter of necessity for lords to get their rents by physical force or threat.[1] For K.B. McFarlane, it was a matter of "lordly high-handedness or extortion

[1] R.H. Hilton, "Peasant Movements in England before 1381", *Economic History Review*, New Series, 2 (1949): 120.

J. Hole, *Economic Ethics in Late Medieval England, 1300–1500*,
Archival Insights into the Evolution of Economics,
DOI 10.1007/978-3-319-38860-1_6

in which neither tenants nor servants were spared".[2] Examples he gave are the illegal land acquisitions of Ralph, Lord Cromwell (d. 1455), Sir John Fastolf's pursuit of debtors, and the practice of some landlords, such as Humphrey, Duke of Buckingham, in the 1440s, of threatening or even imprisoning their own receivers to ensure that they pursued tenants owing rents or services.[3]

A question remains, however, as to whether such rapacity or "harsh efficiency" (to use McFarlane's expression) was a common, even routine, occurrence in the rural economy or something which manifested itself relatively rarely. Did lords consider their own financial needs as paramount and exploitation of tenants as a matter of right, or is there evidence of their being reasonable or pragmatic? Is there any evidence of lords' awareness of the economic deprivation resulting from their harsh measures? The answer to this second question can be found in some wills, which will be considered in the second part of this chapter.

Evidence from Manors

Rents and Entry Fines in General: The Problem of Determining Whether or Not They Were Excessive

In order to assess whether or not lords in general were exploitative, it is necessary to investigate the levels of rents and entry fines, the extent of the burden of services on unfree or bonded tenants versus the number of free tenants, the amount of poverty among tenants and how the poor tenants were treated, the level and frequency of amercements, and the protection against exploitation afforded by custom. Furthermore, there is the very important extrinsic factor of the population losses caused by the Black Death and their impact on rents. In considering all of these matters, I shall be drawing on the records of individual manors as examples but also on wider-ranging studies by historians.

[2] K.B. McFarlane, *The Nobility of Later Medieval England* (Oxford: Clarendon Press, 1973), 49.
[3] McFarlane, *Nobility of Later Medieval England*, 49, 50, 213, 223.

Throughout England, villein holdings tended to be of a standardised acreage as this made the task of assigning services and rents to each holding more convenient. The annual payments by villeins could be regarded as a rent package, consisting of cash and services, whereas rents from free tenants consisted of money payments only. Beyond this generalisation there was much variation. Rents overall could vary from one part of the country to another: in Suffolk, cash rents in 1300 averaged five pence per acre as opposed to an average of seven pence elsewhere. In Suffolk, the lower rents were compensated by a higher amount of labour services, for on the smaller manors, labour services tended to be about 30 per cent of the total rent package as opposed to 10–20 per cent elsewhere.[4] Entry fines (the amounts paid by both free and unfree tenants when acquiring a piece of land) also varied considerably and within the same part of the country. In Suffolk, five pence per acre was paid at Walsham High Hall between 1318 and 1327, but 36 pence per acre on the adjoining Walsham manor between 1327 and 1329. The latter may reflect high demand for land. Higher entry fines were sometimes imposed when land was transferred *inter vivos* (that is, during the lifetime of the tenant rather than on his or her demise).[5]

What kind of land was most in demand? The *Inquisitiones post mortem*, conducted when the lord of the manor (or manors) who held land from the king died, contain valuations. Should the heir be under age or, if female, not yet married, the lands were temporarily retained by the king, along with the revenues, and the royal escheators or valuers would make their assessments before the land was granted to the tenant's heir. A survey of ten counties which provided agricultural supplies for London, based on the reports of *Inquisitioness post mortem* from 1270 to 1339, indicated that, in general, land was valued in terms of its being a production resource; arable areas had the highest value, and within the arable category, land with soils easier to cultivate was valued the most.[6]

[4] Mark Bailey, "Villeinage in England: a Regional Case Study, c. 1250 –c.1349", *Economic History Review*, New Series, 62 (2009): 435, 437.

[5] Bailey, "Villeinage in England": 444.

[6] Bruce M.S. Campbell, James A. Galloway and Margaret Murphy, "Rural Land-use in the Metropolitan Hinterland, 1270–1339: the Evidence of *Inqusitiones Post Mortem*", *Agricultural History Review* 40 (1992): 17.

Examples of Rents and Entry Fine Assessments: Wakefield and Halesowen

The manor of Wakefield in Yorkshire (owned by the Warenne family and later by the Duke of York) was extremely large, covering 100 square miles or 26,000 ha, in comparison with most manors, which covered only six square miles or 1,554 ha. Its lands and population varied from arable and relatively high density to upland grazing and low density.[7] In the Wakefield court rolls, rents and entry fines are listed only in relation to land area, without an exact location or a description of the type of land (whether arable, meadow or pasture). Prior to the Black Death (in 1331), the rolls contain the entry fine information but not the rents: for example, four acres for two shillings, one acre plus one rood (a quarter of an acre) for 12 pence, three acres for 18 pence. On the other hand, new acres from the lord's waste attract a higher entry fine: two shillings and six pence for one acre or two shillings for one and a half acres. Meanwhile, an entry fine for a toft (the site of a house plus outbuildings) and a bovate (between 10 and 20 acres) was reduced "because the land was poor", and 10 acres of land untenanted for 12 years because of the poor soil attracted a fine of only two shillings.[8] Examples of where the land was probably of higher value are a messuage (land with a house and outbuildings) and two acres for two shillings, and four and a half acres for five shillings.[9] On the face of it, this seems reasonable because account was taken of the condition of the land. It is possible that while the new acres from the lord's waste had a higher entry fine, they might have been let for a lower annual rent, and the entry fines for the lands with poor soil were discounted.

After the Black Death, there are more instances of reasonableness in Wakefield. Rents were "levied in part'" for eight decayed holdings in the Sowerby district in 1352. For example, a holding of three acres held by

[7] Introduction, *The Court Rolls of the Manor of Wakefield from 19 October 1436 to 9 September 1437*, ed. Brian J. Barber (Leeds, YAS, 2014), 7, 11.

[8] *The Court Rolls of the Manor of Wakefield from October 1331 to September 1333*, ed. Sue Sheridan Walker (Leeds: YAS, 1983), 16–17 (Court held at Wakefield, 8 November 1331); 22 (Halmote held at Brighouse 19 November 1331).

[9] *Court Rolls of the Manor of Wakefield from October 1331 to September 1333*, 19 (Halmote held at Halifax, 18 November 1331).

service for 18 pence per year was in decay and was demised to another to hold for 14 pence per year, and a holding of 15 acres and three roods formerly held by service of 21 pence per year was demised for 18 pence per year.[10] Yet the lord's income began to improve: by the first half of the fifteenth century, some of the poorer-quality grazing areas within Wakefield were more lucrative and this was possibly due to an increase in sheep-farming. Also, Wakefield contained extensive woodlands and so offences such as poaching, taking timber and illegal grazing contributed significantly to income from amercements.[11]

Rapacity was followed by reasonableness at the ecclesiastical manor of Halesowen in Worcestershire. Halesowen covered some 10,000 acres or 4,000 hectares and, like Wakefield, covered woodland as well as arable lands with different types of soils. During the thirteenth century, when the population was considerably higher than after the Black Death, the Abbot of Halesowen had doubled entry fines to 13 shillings and four pence for a virgate (about 25–30 acres), six shillings and eight pence for a half virgate, and three shillings and four pence for a quarter virgate. Zvi Razi suggests "As the rate of entry fines was equivalent to two years' rent, it is likely that the annual rent was also doubled".[12] Apparently, these entry fines were still lower than those on the Winchester and Glastonbury estates (also owned by the church). Evidently, the latter were considered to be market value, whereas at Halesowen entry fines were fixed for customary or bonded tenants. However, when a tenement was acquired by someone who was not an inheritor, they rose dramatically. For example, in 1294, Thomas Robin of Oldbury paid £6 13 shillings and four pence, not six shillings and eight pence, for a half virgate, and in 1301, William Lee paid £2 seven shillings for a quarter virgate.

The high rents and entry fines had consequences. During this period of higher population combined with a shortage of land, some tenants who

[10] *The Court Rolls of the Manor of Wakefield from October 1350 to September 1352*, ed. Moira Habberjam, Mary O'Regan and Brian Hale (Leeds: YAS, 1987), 23–24 (Court of the Countess de Warenne held at Wakefield 3 March 1351).

[11] Brian J. Barber, Introduction to *The Court Roll of the Manor of Wakefield from 19 October 1436 to 9 September 1437* (Leeds: YAS, 2014), 19.

[12] Zvi Razi, *Life, Marriage and Death in a medieval Parish: Economy, Society and Demography in Halesown 1270–1400* (Cambridge: CUP, 1980), 5, 9.

were unable to afford them left Halesowen: some 67 departed between 1270 and 1348, but as only departures of the unfree were recorded, the overall number could have been higher.[13] The high levels of rents and services were the source of a long-running dispute between the Abbot of Halesowen and his tenants in the 1270s and 1290s, during which the abbot coerced his tenants, who responded with physical attacks. Eventually, the dispute died down, but there were no more increases in rents and services for some considerable time.[14]

After the Black Death in Halesowen, more land became available for the surviving tenants or for outsiders, but demand was selective. Tenants would pay high entry fines for good land; for example, in 1350, William Hill acquired a virgate for £2 and made a very large profit when he transferred it in 1352 to Roger Hill for £8. Demand for lands of lesser quality or for marginal lands was poor, and the Abbot was obliged to waive entry fines and may have offered lower rents as well.[15] In the 1370s, the abbots of Halesowen tried to compensate for their financial losses by collecting more amercements and raising marriage fines and a range of fees, which led to more acts of resistance and retaliation. By the 1390s, the number of amercements collected declined and entry fines were not so high.[16]

When Wakefield is compared with Halesowen, the secular lord comes across as less rapacious than the abbot. In the first half of the fourteenth century, Halesowen's entry fines were little different from Wakefield's, either five pence or six pence per acre, whereas Wakefield charged entry fines for unspecified acres averaging six pence per acre in 1331. The great difference is in Halesowen's overriding of customary entry fines when a tenement passed to another who was not an inheritor. No such behaviour appears in the Wakefield court rolls. In the end, the abbot of Halesowen's aggressive tactics were counter-productive. Yet it was not only the clerical landlords who were at fault: according to E.B. Fryde, in

[13] Razi, *Life, Marriage and Death*, 29, 30.

[14] Zvi Razi, "The Struggles between the Abbots of Halesowen and their Tenants in the Thirteenth and Fourteenth Centuries" in *Social Relations and Ideas: Essays in Honour of R.H. Hilton*, ed. T.H. Aston et al. (Cambridge: CUP), 164.

[15] Razi, *Life, Marriage and Death*, 111–12.

[16] Razi, "Struggles", 165, 166.

the late fourteenth century, the Countess of Norfolk lost bonded tenants at her manor of Forncett through charging high rents and taxes on top of demands for labour services.[17]

In the period after the Black Death, there are more instances showing that lords were making efforts to keep their tenants. In January 1393, the court of Walsham-le-Willows in Suffolk was waiving entry fines for land: Adam Goodale obtained three acres and three half-roods of the lord's demesne, plus a parcel known as Churchwong, for an annual rent of four shillings and 10 pence, and Alice Smith, as a widow, got two acres or more for four pence a year and one hen and no entry fine.[18] The Greys of Ruthin kept a steady income from their tenants in the 1460s by means of compromise. At his manor of Blunham in Bedfordshire, Edmund Grey increased rents in 1457 but made them both fixed and uniform. In return, in 1471, his bonded or customary tenants were given a charter which allowed them to freely sell their holdings or sell a limited portion of them.[19] As another example of pragmatism, at Elmley Castle in Worcestershire, in 1488, two new tenants were excused entry fines because of the ruinous state of the buildings.[20]

The Burden of Services Versus Numbers of Free Tenants

The economic obligations of villeinage varied also from one place to another. In many manors in Suffolk, they were relatively light. In the first place, free men constituted as much as 80 per cent of total tenants in Suffolk compared with an estimated 40 per cent elsewhere in the country. In Suffolk, villeins tended to be more numerous on manors owned by ecclesiastics such as the Abbott of Bury St Edmunds or the Bishop of Ely or by great lords such as the Earl of Norfolk, but most

---

[17] Fryde, *Peasants and Landlords in Later Medieval England* (Stroud: Sutton, 1996), 247, 248–249.

[18] *The Court Rolls of Walsham Le Willows 1351–1399*, ed. Ray Lock (Woodbridge: Boydell Press, 2002), 185, 186 (Walsham Court 30 January, 1393).

[19] Fryde, *Peasants and Landlords*, 253.

[20] *Court Rolls of Elmley Castle, Worcestershire, 1347–1564* ed. Robert K. Field (Worcestershire Historical Society, 2004), 210, 212.

manors were smaller and held by landlords of lower status.[21] In contrast, over the period 1349–1375, Wiltshire had only 30 per cent free tenants versus about 70 per cent bonded tenants; Devon, as late as the sixteenth century, had 26 per cent free tenants compared with 74 per cent villeins; and there were 39 per cent free versus 61 per cent villein in 1299 in the Midlands estates of the Bishop of Worcester.[22]

By the early fourteenth century, relatively few villeins were actually performing their customary services and were substituting a cash payment.[23] Yet these payments could be considerable: when labour services were commuted to money rents on the Bishop of Worcester's estates, the payments were a good deal higher than for free tenants: in 1299, a free yardland cost three shillings to eight shillings per year compared with a rent around 1300 for customary yardland (roughly equivalent to a virgate) ranging from 10 shillings to £1 six shillings and eight pence. This demonstrates the considerable value of the services the villein had formerly contributed.[24]

When the details of service obligations are available, it is possible to see how much time and effort they could involve. In 1355, the manor of Walsham-le-Willows in Suffolk (owned by a secular lord, Thomas de Pakenham, but enfeoffed to Sir John de Ufford and four others) recorded: "John Wodebite holds a messuage and 24a. of land, and he pays therfore per year 3s. 7$^{3/4}$d; and he will reap in autumn 23 days, and will perform works after Michaelmas ten days; and he will pay in the first year six hens, and in the second year five hens. And he will be reeve and Hayward, and he will plough (?*si jungat*) two days per year, and ten eggs".[25] Simultaneously, Wodebite would have to grow enough crops to feed his family and save enough seed for planting for the next year and be able to produce enough surplus wool, meat or dairy products to pay assorted taxes, rents and fines. At the same manor court, it was recorded

---

[21] Bailey, "Villeinage in England": 433–434, 436.

[22] Fryde, *Peasants and Landlords*, 211; Christopher Dyer, *Lords and Peasants in a Changing Society: the Estates of the Bishopric of Worcester, 680–1540* (Cambridge: CUP, 1980), 72.

[23] Bruce Campbell, "The Agrarian Problem in the Early Fourteenth Century" *Past and Present*, 188 (2005), 7, 9.

[24] Dyer, *Lords and Peasants*, 105–106.

[25] *Court Rolls of Walsham Le Willows 1351–1399*, 44 (High Hall Court 4 November, 1355).

that John Packard, despite having a very small holding ("a third part of a certain messuage in 6a. of land"), was to pay annually 12 pence as well as reap in autumn for six days, give one hen and plough every year for two days.

On the manor of Cuxham in Oxfordshire, owned by Merton College, again services seem onerous. In October 1329, William Wauldrugg, a bonded tenant or villein, had one messuage and half virgate of land (12–15 acres). He was to pay three shillings per year for the messuage and for the land "one quarter of cornet the feast of St Michael and at the feast of St Martin half a quarter of oats/fodder and one peck of corn, and three hens and one silver halfpenny and at the feast of the Birth of our Lord two hens and one cock and two silver pennies for *presantbred* [a customary rent]". Wauldrigg also had to work every other day of the year except for 12 days at Christmas, Easter week, the week of Pentecost and Sundays. This involved using his horse and cart to carry manure, corn, hay or straw and stubble and "all other necessaries" within the limits of the manor and transport corn outside the manor to Henley, about 10–12 miles from Cuxham. On top of this, he was to work for two days in the autumn with two men and one day with one man and plough one rood of land for winter sowing. His tasks included mowing part of a meadow for which he was paid six pence and given part of the grass and a wheat loaf.[26]

Details of services tend to be recorded in a custumal rather than in the court records and as relatively few of these have been published, it is difficult to know whether the burden of services at Walsham-le-Willows and Cuxham was commonly applied. Hatcher asserts that two or more days of services were expected of only a minority of bonded tenants and that there were more counties with relatively light services than there were counties where services of two days or more per week were common. He adds that such services were really recorded as obligations, for their actual performance was increasingly carried out by hired labourers.[27]

---

[26] *Manorial Records of Cuxham, Oxfordshire, circa 1200–1359*, ed. P.D. A. Harvey (London: HMSO, 1976), 657.

[27] John Hatcher, "English Serfdom and Villeinage: Towards a Reassessment", *Past and Present*, 90 (1981): 11.

As we have seen, the proportion of free tenants varied considerably from one part of England to another. An overall average has been estimated at 60 per cent unfree and 40 per cent free in the late thirteenth century, and there was an increase in the number of free tenants in the fourteenth and fifteenth centuries.[28] Bruce Campbell believes that the argument that lords of the manor were rapacious is overstated, since it overlooks the part played by free tenants, who were not subject to servile obligations: mostly their rents were fixed and relatively low, and they could plead in the royal courts for protection. However, lords had the opportunity to charge a higher rent if land formerly held by a free tenant reverted to them and to charge higher rents for land they let from their own demesne or for assarting (uncultivated land).[29]

A very profitable hybrid system operated in Cornwall in the fourteenth century. About one third of all tenants were free in the Duchy of Cornwall, but the Duchy was unusual in that instead of the majority of its tenants being villeins, they were "conventionary", holding land on seven-year leases. The rents they paid were higher than those for free tenants, and both rents and the assession fine they paid on entry could be increased at will. At the end of the seven-year period, the lease could be granted to another: there was no hereditary tenure.[30] In the first half of the fourteenth century, entry fines and rents for conventionary tenants increased by as much as 100 per cent over twenty years. By the mid-fifteenth century, after the Black Death and the resultant decline in demand for land, leases were lengthened to 14 and 21 years, rents were fixed, and, in some parts of the Duchy, assession fines were reduced.[31]

Poor Tenants and Their Treatment

Poor tenants far outnumbered their more prosperous counterparts. Given that some tenants might have had more than one holding, poor tenants

---

[28] Hatcher, "English Serfdom": 7, 15.

[29] Campbell, "Agrarian Problem": 22.

[30] John Hatcher, "Non-Manorialism in Medieval Cornwall", *Agricultural History Review* 18 (1970): 1, 3, 6.

[31] Hatcher, "Non-Manorialsim": 15.

were those who had less than one quarter of a virgate or yardland (less than five acres) and they formed the majority of tenants, whether free or villein. At Halesowen, prior to 1349, the wealthier peasants had a virgate of land, a share in common pasture, and enclosed pasture and meadow-land. They had more livestock and a surplus of produce to sell and were the ones who would lease demesne lands in the post-plague era.[32] Poor tenants had a quarter of a virgate or less, a share in the common pasture and some livestock, while in the middle were tenants with about half a virgate.[33] Between 1270 and 1349, the rich tenants of Halesowen comprised 18 per cent of the total, the middling 39 per cent, and the poor 43 per cent.[34] This is consistent with research by E.A. Kosminsky of the *Hundred Rolls* (a survey of land ownership throughout England for taxation purposes) for 1279–1280 which showed villeins with one virgate or more comprised 26 per cent of the total, middling tenants 36 per cent, and poor tenants 38 per cent. Free tenants had a different distribution: rich tenants were much the same at 23 per cent, but there were fewer middling and a greater proportion of poor tenants.[35]

Thus, the majority of tenants could be classified as poor, whether free or villein. How were they treated by lords of the manor? There are just a few scattered instances showing a charitable attitude. In Wakefield in the mid-fourteenth century, the courts gave consideration to the poverty of some of the tenants:

> "Adam Magotson by the grave [the term used in Wakefield for reeve] surrenders into the lord's hand half a rood with a cottage thereon in Wooldale, which is granted to Matilda daughter of Margery to hold similarly after [the death] of Margery her mother; fine 4 pence, not more because she is a poor little thing [*paupercula*]."[36]

---

[32] Razi, *Life, Marriage and Death*, 74, 76.

[33] Razi, *Life, Marriage and Death*, 78, 79.

[34] Razi, *Life, Marriage and Death*, 84.

[35] Cited in Christopher Dyer, *Standards of Living in the Later Middle Ages; Social Change in England c. 1200–1520* (Cambridge: CUP, 1998), 119.

[36] *The Court Rolls of the Manor of Wakefield from September 1348 to September 1350*, ed. Helen M. Jewell, (Leeds: YAS, 1977), 29 (Court held at Kirkburton 27 November 1348).

In the Wakefield district of Rastrick in 1339, there was a pardon for trespass for Henry Bythebrook because of his poverty.[37] At Warley, again in Wakefield, Adam son of Alexander surrendered three acres with buildings, which were granted to his son John, but John was to pay 12 pence as an entry fine "and not more because he is poor".[38] Apart from Wakefield, in the mid-fifteenth century, Bishop Carpenter of Worcester helped his poor tenants financially; the Duchy of Cornwall occasionally reduced what it termed assession fines or did not increase them if tenants were poor, ill or in their old age, and in 1493 at Elmley Castle in Worcestershire, William Heth was allowed to have a subtenant because of his impoverishment.[39]

The few instances of leniency towards poor tenants suggest that manor officials expected tenants to pay their dues, regardless of their relative wealth. It seems likely that many poor tenants did not plead for a concession or that, if they did, their plea was rejected and they endured hardship as a result. By the late fourteenth century, owing to the population decline after the Black Death, this attitude might have changed: Hatcher and Bailey declare that most fines were extracted from the wealthier villeins, for fear that the less wealthy would leave the manor. Instead, the latter "had to be treated far more lightly".[40] It will be shown below, however, that by the late fourteenth century, amercements and fees were an enlarged source of income for lords of the manor.

Amercements and Other Fines

The court records of the manor of Wakefield have extensive lists of amercements for breaches of the assizes of bread and ale, trespassing, allowing animals to stray, damage to crops, quite apart from criminal offences, making a false claim and so on. It is hard to tell from those records whether

[37] *The Court Rolls of the Manor of Wakefield from October 1338 to September 1340*, ed. Katherine M. Troup (Leeds: YAS, 1999), 68 (Court held at Brighouse 21 April 1339).

[38] *Court Rolls of the Manor of Wakefield from September 1348 to September 1350*, 109 (Court held at Halifax 12 May 1349).

[39] Dyer, *Lords and Peasants*, 206; Hatcher, "Non-Manorialism": 6; *Court Rolls of Elmley Castle*, 215.

[40] John Hatcher and Mark Bailey, *Modelling the Middle Ages: The History and Theory of England's Economic Development* (Oxford: OUP, 2001), 118.

officials were being over-zealous, seeking to maximise the lord's revenue, or whether the number of amercements was simply a factor of the very large area covered by Wakefield and the size of its population. It also has to be allowed that lords of the manor were required by statute to punish breaches of the assizes of bread and ale (selling by short measure or overcharging) by a fine or corporal punishment. Other sources of revenue for lords from villeins were merchet (marriage fines), heriot (payable on the death of a tenant), leyrwrite (a fine for fornication), and chevage (payment for permission to live outside the manor). Villeins could also be fined for failing to perform their service obligations or letting their land or buildings fall into decay. They could be fined for failing to attend the manor court or failing to appoint one of their fellows as a manor official such as a reeve or a hayward. Fines were also imposed for causing damage to bridges or roads, blocking streams or pathways, failing to clear ditches, not using the lord's mill for flour-making, and committing other offences.

Some petitions concerning landowners or their officials charging excessive amercements were mentioned in the previous chapter but it seems that this was more of a problem after the Black Death, when lords were attempting to compensate for falling rental income. Prior to the Black Death, income from all the fines and amercements outlined above would have constituted only a minor portion of the total revenue of lords of the manor. Campbell's survey of the early fourteenth-century *Inquisitiones post mortem* showed that "banalities", which covered tolls paid by markets and fairs, fees from mills and fee farms from towns as well fines and amercements from manor courts, comprised 20 per cent of total income for the great magnates and higher clergy but only seven per cent for gentry landowners and the lower clergy.[41] In 1299, the Bishop of Worcester had 1,346 tenants on his estates, and income from court perquisites was £34 10 shillings: in the years 1376 to 1391, this had risen to over £61, even though the number of tenants could not have risen very much from the low of 781 recorded in 1349.[42] In 1299, on a per-capita basis, the average fine or amercement was about six pence for each tenant; in the late fourteenth century, if the low population of 781 is taken, the average fine or amerce-

[41] Campbell, "Agrarian Problem": 19.

[42] Dyer. *Lords and Peasants*, 121, 238.

ment per tenant would have been about one shilling and six pence. This tripling would have been far less than the annual rents paid by the wealthier tenants but could have disadvantaged poor tenants holding a quarter of a virgate or less. If Hatcher and Bailey's assertion that poor tenants were treated more lightly applied also to amercements, it is hard to find the evidence. Generally, information about the extent of an offender's landholding was not provided in manor court records. It is difficult to know whether lords were prepared to be lenient as a general rule or whether they adopted the position that the punishment should fit the crime.

Tallage

As discussed in Chapter 2, tallage came under criticism from theologians. Their objections were based on its arbitrary nature: a lord could charge his unfree tenants tallage whenever he thought fit and at whatever level he desired because it was part of the principle that whatever property villeins owned, was owned by their lord (tallage did not apply to free tenants). There was no need for a lord to justify tallage.

The records show varying amounts of tallage being charged. At one extreme, in 1299, villeins on the monastic estate of Dunstable in Bedfordshire paid the enormous sum of £60 to rid themselves of any future tallage. Tallage at Halvergate in Norfolk ranged between £10 and £12 per year, then increased to £13, and fell to £8 the year after, while on a neighbouring manor, tallage had been £8 per year for several years, then abruptly increased to £12 .[43] These amounts were for an entire manor or vill, but tallage could be assessed on individual villeins on the basis of the amount of land or number of animals they had. On a smaller scale, in the early fourteenth century, annual tallage ranging from 13 shillings and four pence to 20 shillings was paid by villeins of the manor of Chalgrave in Bedfordshire, which was owned by the Loring family. However, in 1303, the villeins were tallaged individually at one shilling each, which would have been considerably more in total.[44] Tallage was

[43] H.S. Bennett, *Life on the English Manor: A Study of Peasant Conditions 1150–1400* (Cambridge: 1937 repr. Gloucester: Sutton, 1987), 139–140.

[44] *Court Roll of Chalgrave Manor 1278-1313*, ed. Marian K. Dale (Streatley: Bedfordshire Historical Record Society, 1950, ix.

less usual in Suffolk, where it was imposed only annually in the estates of the earl of Norfolk. Most Suffolk manors either did not charge tallage or substituted a smaller "recognition" fine, which in time became a communal fee which villeins negotiated and allocated amongst themselves.[45] This accords with H.S. Bennett's assertion that villeins eventually got tallage changed to an annual customary payment.[46]

A late fourteenth-century example of tallage, probably to supplement manorial income, is from the *Calendar of Inquisitions Miscellaneous*. Apart from "court perquisites", the manor of Dorking in Surrey had land, a mill, a warren, labour services and rents worth just under £10 per year; its woods were worth far more but the trees were felled only every 14 years, and it charged tallage of 24 shillings per year. The manor of Estbecheworth had land, a mill, a warren, labour services and rents worth over £18 per year and charged tallage of 13 shillings and four pence per year.[47]

Were allowances ever made for a poor harvest or any other circumstances which might lead to a villein's loss of income? The records do not reveal much generosity but there is one example in the late thirteenth century in which the tenants of the manor of Drax in Yorkshire had their tallage reduced by one mark (13 shillings and four pence) from £10 because of their poverty.[48]

Exploitation Versus the Power of Custom

Was the custom of the manor an effective protection for villeins against exploitation by their lords? Historians have drawn different conclusions, depending on which manors or estates were under investigation. Those historians who studied ecclesiastical estates, large estates and large manors concluded that, overall, villeins were subjected to heavy economic burdens and exploited by their lords, whereas those who studied estates in the Midlands and in eastern England concluded that

---

[45] Bailey, "Villeinage in England": 449–451.

[46] Bennett, *Life on the English Manor*, 138.

[47] *Calendar of Inquisitions Miscellaneous*, vol. 6 (London: HMSO, 1963), 213.

[48] *Calendar of Inquisitions Miscellaneous*, vol. 1 (London: HMSO, 1916), 154.

overall those burdens on villeins were relatively light.[49] Historians also disagreed about the relative importance of custom. Some argued that custom had equal weight to law and afforded protection to villeins, even when law declared (as in Bracton's *On the Laws and Customs of England*, quoted in Chapter 5) that lords had the freedom to do as they wished and had full power over their unfree tenants. Historians who supported the power of custom believed that lawyers such as Bracton wanted lords to have absolute power. In other words, it was not such much actual law as legal opinion or doctrine, although I would suggest that such opinion was actually the desire to ensure the preservation of the social hierarchy, the order ordained by God, and to demonstrate that law was an expression of God's will. Historians who took Bracton at face value supported the power of law and believed that the unfree tenants were exploited.

Their opposers countered by pointing to what occurred in actual practice; in other words, custom determined what actions a lord could take.[50] Dyer argues that customary law was effective and that lords knew it would be counter-productive to break it because their tenants could form an organised body of opposition.[51] Furthermore, the custom of the manor was not set in stone but arrived at as a result of compromise.[52] Hatcher quotes the statement in the *Mirror of Justices* that anything acquired by a serf belonged to his lord but says that in practice taking a serf's belongings was limited to the taking of a heriot or a proportion of goods when a serf died.[53] Yet when theologians and moralists condemned lords' taking of goods from the poor as *ravine* or theft, they could have been referring

---

[49] John Hatcher, "Lordship and Villeinage before the Black Death: From Karl Marx to the Marxists and Back Again" in *Peasants and Lords in the Medieval English Economy*; *Essays in Honour of Bruce M.S. Campbell*, ed. Maryanne Kowaleski, John Langdon and Philipp R. Schofield (Turnhout: Brepols, 2015), 134 citing Bruce M.S. Campbell and Ken Bartley, *England on the Eve of the Black Death*: *An Atlas of Lay Lordship, Land and Wealth, 1300–49*, Manchester: Manchester University Press, 2009.

[50] J. Hatcher, "Lordship and Villeinage" 113–145.

[51] Christopher Dyer, "Villeins, Bondmen, Neifs and Serfs: New Serfdom in England, *c.* 1200–1600"', in Paul Freedman and Monique Bourin (eds), *Forms of Servitude in Northern and Central Europe*: *Decline, Resistance and Expansion*, ed. Paul Freedman and Monique Bourin (Turnhout: Brepols, 2005), 425.

[52] Dyer, "Villeins, Bondmen", 427.

[53] Hatcher, "English Serfdom and Villeinage": 8.

to this very practice. A heriot could have been more detrimental to a poor tenant: where a better off villein holding a virgate (25–30 acres) might have had two cows and their calves, a pig, perhaps as many as twenty sheep, as well as poultry, a poor tenant with three acres had few resources: possibly insufficient land to feed his family, one cow and in order to make ends meet, may have been forced to work as a hired labourer.[54]

Hatcher says that, furthermore, villeins were allowed to buy and sell land if they paid a fine and that their right to make wills was frequently recognised.[55] This was indeed so, but the fines payable on buying and selling land could be considerable. Hatcher argues that bonded tenants were protected from rises in rents by the custom of the manor, and even tallage was often a fixed annual tax. However it seems, from the evidence above, that there were instances of rises in rents and entry fines before the Black Death and reductions and adjustments afterwards, and that the amounts of tallage could be altered as well. Hatcher goes further and claims that the custom of the manor was to a large extent the custom of the community and that this was necessary for its operation.[56] Thus, both Hatcher and Dyer conclude that the custom of the manor was an effective restraint on lords. However, one wonders whether this community consisted of wealthier tenants, those who were interested in increasing their holdings at lower prices and were willing to allow higher fines and amercements, rather than the tenants as a whole.

Edward Fryde, however, argued that such customs could be altered if the lord saw fit. His research into manor records in many parts of England had shown that lords sometimes disregarded custom by, for example, giving the land occupied by a deceased tenant to someone who was not their next of kin. Customary law, by its very nature, was neither absolute nor uniform, and because the manorial courts were staffed by wealthier villeins who had more to lose from a lord's displeasure, radical changes were possible.[57] Fryde cites a letter of privy seal by Edward III, which reminded officials of his manor of Burstwick in east Yorkshire that

[54] Dyer, *Standards of Living in the Later Middle Ages*, 114, 117.

[55] Hatcher, "English Serfdom and Villeinage": 9–10.

[56] Hatcher, "English Serfdom and Villeinage": 9, 23.

[57] Fryde, *Peasants and Landlords*, 14.

customary tenants expected to be allowed to succeed to the lands held by their family members: at Burstwick, the king had heard that instead the custom was that such holdings were offered to strangers, provided that they could pay the entry fine. Thus, customary or bonded tenants were left in a very uncertain position.[58] Hatcher, on the other hand, is certain that although bonded tenants could be evicted at any time by law, in practice they had security of tenure and eviction was a rarity.[59]

Historians constantly say villeins could call upon the custom of the manor to support their cases in a dispute with their lord, but custom varied from one manor to another, and without the details, it is hard to infer what it might have entailed. Evidently, it was a set of precedents developed by each manor to deal with such matters as land transfers and services. Yet we are told that villeins had custom "on their side" rather than its being on the lord's side. Even though the lord's rights were supported in law and could be physically enforced, tenants "had the advantage of numbers and the knowledge that it was upon their work and co-operation that landlords ultimately depended". Therefore, even before the Peasants' Revolt of 1381, tenants could resist by performing labour services poorly, delaying or withholding the payment or rents and fines, and so on. In the end, it was more economic for lords, and in their own interest, to make concessions than it was to coerce their tenants, "especially for those with limited jurisdictional powers".[60] This implies that the magnates had greater jurisdictional powers than smaller landowners and appears to overlook the fact that it was the magnates who had the largest bodies of retainers capable of threatening tenants or juries at court proceedings.

In conclusion, the changed economic conditions in the second half of the fourteenth century and in the fifteenth century brought financial difficulties to many lords: according to McFarlane, there is little evidence of landlords pressuring their officials to collect rents before the mid-fourteenth century.[61] The substantial fall in numbers of tenants as a result

[58] Fryde, *Peasants and Landlords*, 217.

[59] Hatcher, "English Serfdom and Villeinage": 10.

[60] Bruce M.S. Campbell, "The Land", in *A Social History of England 1200–1500*, ed. Rosemary Horrox and W. Mark Ormrod (Cambridge: CUP, 2006), 225, 226.

[61] McFarlane, *Nobility of Later Medieval England*, 213.

of the Black Death led, as we have seen, to many landowners making concessions over rents and entry fines. Therefore, there are many instances of pragmatism and reasonableness amongst lords but also attempts to recover income by increasing fees, fines and amercements.

When it comes to rapacity or unwillingness to make concessions, there is evidence that ecclesiastical lords, particularly the higher clergy, were at fault. Campbell gave a breakdown of manorial income from the *Inquistiones Post Mortem* of the early fourteenth century, showing that lay landowners were more dependent on revenue from their demesne lands and from rents (76 per cent for the nobility and 92 per cent for the gentry). On the other hand, the ecclesiastical landowners obtained a substantial portion from tithes (20 per cent for the higher clergy and 72 per cent for the lesser).[62] Tithes were compulsory payments, sanctioned in canon law and the Old Testament and regarded as a payment to God. Usually, they consisted of part of the harvest. The existence of this source of income might have led some clerical landowners to be less careful in how they dealt with their tenants. Furthermore, the clergy had no heirs and many of them moved from one benefice to another, perhaps being a lord of a manor for only a few years and less concerned with custom, the economic welfare of their tenants, and good estate management. Certainly, there are plenty of examples of ecclesiastical lords in protracted disputes with their tenants in the thirteenth and fourteenth centuries: the Prior of Halesowen, the Abbot of Ramsey, the Prior of Harmondsworth, the Prior of Bec and the Abbot of Leicester, and in the 1430s the Bishop of Worcester.[63] Both episcopal and monastic estates had had a very long history by the late medieval period, hence their tendency towards conservatism and preserving their traditional rights.

Although negotiation and the recognition of economic reality by lords led to the settlement of disputes in many cases, there were others in which tenants were punished for claiming the rights of royal demesne and refusing servile obligations or withholding rents (or both) due to their lords. A cluster of these claims (17 in total) were made to King Richard II during March and August of 1377 and more followed in

[62] Campbell, "Agrarian Problem": 19.

[63] Hatcher and Bailey, *Modelling the Middle Ages*, 81, 82, 115.

1378. Commissions of inquiry were appointed to distrain offenders or find pledges for rents owing and to imprison those who refused to pay.[64] With only a few exceptions, those claims were brought by tenants on ecclesiastical lands, ranging from remote and larger landowners, such as the Bishop of Winchester, to local churches. On the one hand is the possibility that conditions imposed on those church lands were regarded as particularly irksome by tenants, or that it was a more haphazard and imitative process, where news of what one group of tenants had attempted was passed to another. It also has to be recognised that ecclesiastical landlords comprised a high proportion (45 per cent) of total landowners in the early fourteenth century.[65]

Great lords or magnates also tended to be conservative and were more likely to impose excessive rents and services on their tenants. Magnates had large estates containing several manors and larger sources of income and they, too, were possibly less concerned about the potential loss of tenants who decided they could no longer bear such onerous conditions. The gentry, however, tended to have smaller estates, with just one or only a few manors to rely on for their income. They were more cautious about rent increases and demanding more services from their tenants, preferring to use hired labour rather than risk losing their tenants altogether. There was also the fact that most of their tenants were of the poor to middling variety, holding fewer than 30–40 acres. On the whole, secular lords used law and their manor courts rather than violence to protect their interests.[66]

Even the Bishop of Durham, one of the largest landowners in England (about 37,000 acres), after trying coercion, had to negotiate with his tenants eventually. His halmotes or manorial courts had different customs from the rest of England: instead of the old and infirm voluntarily surrendering their tenancies to an heir, in Durham the land was taken away and given to someone thought to be capable, or an entire village would be made responsible for it. This also happened in the case of a tenant's death, but with the decline in population after the Black Death, the balance of

[64] J.H. Tillotson, "Peasant Unrest in the England of Richard II: Some Evidence from Royal records", *Historical Studies*, 16 (1974):1–16.

[65] Campbell, "Agrarian Problem": 12.

[66] Hatcher and Bailey, *Modelling the Middle Ages*, 115.

power shifted and the Bishop's officers were forced to compromise. Many hundreds of acres were still devoid of tenants and rents were reduced and cash payments taken instead of labour services. In 1357, the bishop appointed a commission to hear complaints about extortion and oppression by his estate officials.[67]

Manor court records lack moralistic language: reasonableness can, with very few exceptions, only be read as springing from self-interest. There are no indications that ethical considerations were involved apart from those few occasions when concessions were made to a tenant's poverty. There is some evidence of consciences being searched towards the end of life, in wills.

Wills

Wills have been studied by historians for evidence of charitable acts and as expressions of piety, insight into moral motivations and the influence of church doctrine.[68] Bequests by the more prosperous in lay society to religious orders, churches and hospitals, distribution of monies to the poor and other worthy causes may have been expressions of personal faith, but they were also formulaic expressions of conventional piety, and the doctrine of purgatory was significant in persuading testators to act

---

[67] R.H. Britnell, "Feudal Reaction after the Black Death in the Palatinate of Durham", *Past and Present* 128 (1990): 28–47.

[68] Davis, *MMM*, 377–380; Jennifer Kermode, "The Merchants of Three Northern English Towns", in *Profession, Vocation and Culture in Later Medieval England: Essays Dedicated to the Memory of A.R. Myers* ed. Cecil H. Clough, 7–50 (Liverpool, Liverpool University Press: 1982), 7–50; J.A.F. Thomson, "Wealth, Poverty and Mercantile Ethics in Late Medieval London", in *La Ville, la Bourgeoisie et la Genese de L'etat Moderne* (*XIIe–XVIIIe Siecles*) ed. Neil Bulst and Jean-Philippe Genet, 265–78 (Paris: CNRS, 1988); J.A.F. Thomson, "Piety and Charity in Late Medieval London", *Journal of Ecclesiastical History*, 16 (1965): 178–195; Sylvia L. Thrupp, *The Merchant Class of Medieval London 1300–1500* (Chicago: University of Chicago Press, 1948), 174–180; Clive Burgess, " 'By Quick and by Dead': Wills and Pious Provision in Late Medieval Bristol", *English Historical Review*, 102 (1987): 837–858; P.H. Cullum and P.J.P. Goldberg, "Charitable Provision in Late Medieval York: 'To the Praise of God and the Use of the Poor' ", *Northern History*, 29 (1993) 24–39; Miri Rubin, *Charity and Community in Medieval Cambridge* (Cambridge: CUP, 1987); P.W. Fleming, "Charity, Faith and the Gentry of Kent 1422–1529", in *Property and Politics: Essays in Later Medieval English History*, ed. Tony Pollard, 36-58 (Gloucester: Sutton, 1984); M.G.A. Vale, *Piety, Charity and Literacy among the Yorkshire Gentry, 1370–1480* (York: Borthwick Institute of Historical Research, 1976).

for the good of their souls.[69] Wills, however, can be regarded also as an expression of economic ethics because many requested settlement of outstanding debts or forgiveness of debts. In addition, wills were a means of making restitution, another principle of economic ethics. Although only a small proportion of late medieval wills have been published, there are enough of them to show that such matters were often of concern, besides the bequests to the Church in order to pay for chantries, to embellish church buildings or to distribute funds amongst the clergy. In addition, gifts to the poor or to prisoners and the establishment of almshouses and hospitals were made as acts of charity, showing that the testator had performed the seven works of mercy in accordance with the Church's teaching.[70] Testators also aided the social and economic life of towns in their charitable giving by leaving money for civic works, such as the repair of roads and bridges or improvements to the water supply.[71]

It was customary for City of London merchants to leave anything from one third to one half of moveable goods to charitable purposes, and sometimes real estate was given away as well.[72] Apparently, it was usual to divide an estate, after funeral expenses had been met, into three if the testator had children and into two if he did not. Charitable bequests and gifts to friends were taken out of the part of the estate reserved to the testator, not the part assigned to relatives.[73] The custom was not peculiar to London but had been part of common law since the reign of Henry II, remaining in force until it was abolished by "various Acts of Parliament" and still observed in the province of York until the late sev-

---

[69] Davis, *MMM*, 378; Vale, *Piety, Charity and Literacy*, 31; Thomson, "Piety and Charity":194; Burgess, "'By Quick and by Dead'": 838.

[70] Burgess, "'By Quick and by Dead'", 837–858; Cullum and Goldberg, "Charitable Provision in Late Medieval York": 24–39; P. Heath, "Urban Piety in the Later Middle Ages: The Evidence of Hull Wills", in *The Church, Politics and Patronage in the Fifteenth Century*, ed. R. B. Dobson, 209-234 (Gloucester: Sutton, 1984); Thomson, "Piety and Charity", 178–195.

[71] Kermode, "The Merchants of Three Northern English Towns", 31–32; Thomson, "Piety and Charity":187–188; *Wills of the Archdeaconry of Sudbury 1439–1474*: *Wills from the Register 'Baldwyne'*, ed. Peter Northeast, 2 vols. (Woodbridge: for the Suffolk Records Society, 2001–2010); John Stow, *A Survey of London*, rev. ed. 1603 (repr. Stroud: Sutton, 1994), 130–136.

[72] Thrupp, *Merchant Class*, 177.

[73] Thomson, "Piety and Charity", 181–182.

enteenth century.[74] Clause seven of the 1225 version of the *Magna Carta* states that a widow "shall have assigned to her for her dower a third of all her husband's land which was his in his lifetime, unless a smaller share was given to her at the church door".[75] It seems likely, therefore, that the division of wills, with perhaps as much as one third or one half being left to charity, was obligatory rather than discretionary throughout late medieval England.

The Evidence of Restitution in Wills

That a testator had searched his or her conscience, and taken economic ethics into consideration, is very apparent where he or she expressed regret for past wrongs and asked his or her executors to make restitution to affected parties. John Chauncey, a gentleman of Northamptonshire (1490s), stated

> I wyll that yf any persone make any righthwys cleym or chealange of any dett wrong or extorcion that shuld be ougth or don by me in my lyfe that myn executors make dewe satisfacdon to hem as rigth and constience requyreth ....[76]

Claimants had to prove that they had been a victim of Chauncey's behaviour, and, although the phrase "as right and conscience requires" is formulaic, Chauncey was prepared for his executors to accept claims going back many years, perhaps his entire working lifetime. The will (1439) of Isabell, Countess of Warwick, instructed her executors to

> Restore and make dewe assithe for all maner land that is holden by me or yn my name wrongfully, yef eny be, (whiche god for-bede and defende); And all-so that they repare all maner extorcion by me doon, yef eny be.[77]

---

[74] Introduction to *Calendar of Wills Proved in the Court of Husting, London, A.D. 1258–A.D. 1688*, ed. Reginald R. Sharpe, vol. 1 (London: Corporation of the City of London, 1889), xxxiii; James Brundage, *Medieval Canon Law* (London: Longman, 1995), 87.

[75] Katherine Fischer Drew, *Magna Carta* (Westport, CT: Greenwood Press, 2004), 141.

[76] *Early Northampton Wills Preserved in Northamptonshire Record Office*, ed. Dorothy Edwards, et al. (Northamptonshire Record Society, 2005), 163, no. 334, Will of John Chauncey, senior, gentleman (1490s).

[77] *The Fifty Earliest English Wills in the Court of Probate, London A.D. 1387–1439 with a Priest's of 1454*, ed. F.J. Furnivall (Oxford: OUP for the EETS, 1882, repr. 1964), 119.

The Countess seemed less certain that any extortion had been done in her name or that she was holding lands that had been acquired wrongfully, but she felt strongly that God would disapprove if either was the case and that she should set her executors to make amends. Sir Hugh Willughby of Wollaton (1448) asked his executors to make restitution to anyone who could prove that "I have taken of ony man withouten rightwes title, or have done any harme be rancour of hert or malice a geyns god consciens and reson".[78] Sir Hugh, like Chauncey, wanted to ensure that his executors received claims with good evidence, but he was plainly anxious that his own desire to wreak damage or revenge upon others might have led to more than land seizures.

The dishonesty and greed of Ralph, Lord Cromwell, were well known.[79] In 1451, Cromwell ordered that his debts be paid and that restitution be made for any injuries he might have perpetrated.[80] In a codicil of 1454, Cromwell ordered that restitution be made to the rightful owners of lands he had acquired through fraud, which were valued by his executors at the large sum of £4,866 13 shillings and four pence, a figure which represents the value of the lands given back, but the value of the total fraudulent acquisitions is estimated to be higher. Lands where a moral claim, but not a legal one, could be established were sold by the executors for a low price rather than returned to their rightful owners.[81] Therefore, with the end of his life approaching, Cromwell knew he had to make restitution for all the economic injustices he had committed, but his efforts appear somewhat limited. Chauncey, Willoughby and the Countess of Warwick seem to have been making genuine efforts to restore the proceeds of wrongdoing to victims.

Some testators remembered a specific injustice from times past. One example concerns regret for having committed usury: Peter Herolf of the manor of Writtle in Essex (1412) lent £10 to a neighbour, Thomas Criour, who enfeoffed Herolf with five acres of his land. If Criour repaid

---

[78] *Testamenta Ebor. II*, 130.

[79] S. J. Payling, "A Disputed Mortgage: Ralph, Lord Cromwell, Sir John Gra and the Manor of Multom Hall", in *Rulers and Ruled in Late Medieval England: Essays Presented to Gerald Harriss*, ed. Rowena E. Archer and Simon Walker (London: Hambledon, 1995), 117.

[80] *Testamenta Ebor. II*, 197.

[81] S.J. Payling, "Inheritance and Local Politics in the Later Middle Ages: The Case of Ralph, Lord Cromwell, and the Heriz Inheritance", *Nottingham Medieval Studies*, 30 (1986) 87.

the loan within ten years, the land would revert to him. In the meantime, Herolf had taken the profits and produce from the five acres, valued at 50 shillings or five shillings per annum effective interest, over the ten-year period: "Yet Herolf, when on his deathbed, was moved by a sound and mature conscience ["sana et matura conscientia"] to hand back the 50 shillings he had earned from the deal".[82] The use of the phrase "sound and mature conscience" suggests that Herolf had absorbed advice that what he had done was a form of usury and wanted to limit the potential harm to the prospects for his immortal soul. Sir William Heron, Lord Say (1404), was also conscientious about his over-payment for his tasks as a "condiour" or conductor of a convoy for the Earls of Arundel and Northumberland and asked his executors to pay them the sums of £5 and £20, respectively.[83]

There are also wills of landowners who felt they should make restitution for keeping the goods of their tenants unlawfully or for withholding wages. In 1407, Sir John Constable of Halsham's will instructed that

> the goods and chattels of certain of my villeins ["nativorum"] which I received into my keeping after their deaths, for the convenience of their sons, and as yet unreturned, shall be paid back to those sons without any decrease. And if I have swindled anyone in either movable or immovable goods, or harmed his body, or kept back the wages of any servant unjustly, I wish that my executors satisfy them faithfully and immediately.[84]

In 1427, Thomas Broke, a landowner from Devonshire, made a will in which he expressed concern for the wrongs he had done to his tenants:

> I bequethe to my poure tenauntes of Holdych, Hotham, Cherd, Cotteleygh, & Wycrofte that haueth yeue to me Capouns & bederpes [days of work performed at harvest] and Plouwys, thoughe they be noughte my tenauntes, I will that myn executours do her gre by god discrecion atte the value of xx li among hame/and if any other man or woman be, that Cane Pleyne hym

[82] Elaine Clark, "Debt Litigation in a Late Medieval English Vill", in J.A. Raftis (ed.), *Pathways to Medieval Peasants*, ed. J.A. Raftis (Toronto, Pontifical Institute of Mediaeval Studies, 1981), 266.

[83] *Testamenta Ebor. III*, p. 27.

[84] Vale, *Piety, Charity and Literacy*, 25, which is a translation of the Latin will found in *Testamenta Ebor. I*, 350.

> that ich haue oppressed hym, or do wrange to him, other yete with my bestys his Corne other his grase, and noughte amendit hit to hym, to amende such trespasses, I bequethe x.li.[85]

Broke also gave £100 to his poorest tenants in areas not already specified and £100 to the poor blind and lame

> and namelych iffych haue do wronge to eny of my tenauntes or mys tak hir good, I will that it be restored to ham. Whether it be Man or woman, by avysement of myn Executours, as they will aunswere to-for god at the dome ....[86]

These two examples show that landowners understood that actions which deprived their tenants of their just rewards were morally wrong and that failing to make amends would risk their immortal souls. In this respect, they were acting in accordance with the advice given by Alexander of Hales and Thomas Aquinas and the pastoral manuals *Dives and Pauper* and *Jacob's Well*, which were discussed in Chapters 2 and 3.

A will which shows how much a past case of economic injustice weighed on the conscience of the perpetrator is that of the merchant, alderman and later mayor of London, Sir Edmund Shaa (1488). Shaa recalled that, forty years earlier, he had helped a landowner relative in Derbyshire with a distraint. He and Richard Shaa took two oxen which he was sure the owner was never able to repossess "and be cause that dede was doon in my wanton dayes whanne I lakkyd discresyon therefor I have a remorce therof now in these dayes being better advysyd". By using the terms "discretion" and "better advised", Shaa presumably meant some form of ethical discernment which would have come with more experience, but that advice could also have come from his confessor, from hearing a sermon or from some texts that he might have read. Perhaps, like Thomas Criour, Shaa felt late in life that he had a sound and mature conscience. Shaa wanted his executors to pay 20 shillings as restitution to the unfortunate tenant if he was still alive or to his family or his executors. It

[85] *Fifty Earliest English Wills*, 27.
[86] *Fifty Earliest English Wills*, 27.

was so long ago that Shaa could no longer remember the man's name or exactly where he lived, so if the task proved to be impossible, his executors were to "take good advise of som sadde doctors of dyvynyte to understond what is best to do wt the said xxs for the wele of the soule of the said man that was distraynyd and for the discharge of my consciens".[87]

How many wills a real reflection of personal desires to make amends? The difficulty with wills is that they were a matter of convention, since they were usually written by notaries, and the primary concern of the charitable portions and bequests to religious institutions was the welfare of testator's soul in the afterlife. There was also the reinforcement of custom which dictated how an estate should be distributed, but some testators used the part of their will available for charitable purposes to make restitution for fraudulent trade or unfair treatment of tenants. Again, this could be a matter of convention, but Thomas Criour's use of "sound and mature conscience" and Edmund Shaa's remorse for the callousness of his youth suggest that both had adopted the Church's teachings about making amends.

Conclusion

Were lords particularly rapacious? The answer seems to depend on which estates and lordships are under consideration. A number of historians have observed that exorbitant rents and heavy labour demands came from conservative or reactionary landowners, who tended to be the great magnates or the higher clergy such as bishops and abbots, and where the number of bonded tenants exceeded free tenants. Yet these were in the minority in terms of the total number of landowners: Campbell's survey, which was based on the returns to the *Inquisitiones Post Mortem* for the early fourteenth century, found over 20,000 landowners, of which only five per cent were the nobility and higher clergy; the rest were the gentry and parish clergy.[88]

---

[87] This will was cited by Sylvia Thrupp (*Merchant Class*, p. 176). The original is Kew, The National Archives, PROB 11/8/187.

[88] Campbell, "Agrarian Problem": 12.

Perhaps it is safe to assume that the great landowners could and did take some liberties with their tenants which the smaller landowners could not. Many historians have said that tenants were not powerless, that bonded tenants responded to economic oppression by means of passive resistance, and that free tenants had access to royal courts or bonded tenants could attempt to gain access by claiming they were tenants of a former royal demesne. The condemnations of extortion and oppression by lords of the manor and the complaints in literary works such as *The Second Shepherds' Play*, discussed in Chapter 4, imply routine exploitation which brought more hardship to poorer bonded tenants. I suggest that the basis for this was not only rents and entry fines but the multiplicity of fees and charges which may have had relatively little impact on the wealthier villeins but a good deal more on their poorer counterparts.

Wills provide some evidence of ethical awareness, but the searching of the conscience occurred when death approached and was motivated by fear of damnation. What considerations were paramount during a merchant's or a landowner's lifetime? Were there any ethical values? The letters and papers to be examined in the following chapter will reveal more.

7

Merchants and Landowners' Responses to Economic Ethics

In Chapters 2, 3, and 4, I presented evidence which showed that ethical notions such as the just price, the common good, good lordship, justice and charity were disseminated, debated and problematised amongst medieval readers and listeners through a wide range of texts, such as pastoral manuals and guides to conscience, sermons and literary works. Chapter 5 showed that such notions reappeared in the framing of petitions and in economic regulation, and Chapter 6 looked at the evidence of landowner attitudes in manor court records and other sources. A question that remains is to what extent individuals were influenced by these notions in their understanding of economic ethics and applied them in their actual economic practices. In particular, were the more prosperous, whether merchants or landowners, influenced by the teachings of the Church concerning excess wealth and avarice? Were there, perhaps, other notions which were more influential in the way they managed their affairs? Were there circumstances in which these overrode the principles of economic ethics? Correspondence and other documents can reveal how economic ethics were perceived and applied in practice.

J. Hole, *Economic Ethics in Late Medieval England, 1300–1500*,
Archival Insights into the Evolution of Economics,
DOI 10.1007/978-3-319-38860-1_7

Historians' studies of letters and papers (of the Paston family, the Cely family, the Armburghs, the Stonors and Sir John Fastolf) have considered their sources from many perspectives.[1] They have considered political affiliations, local power relationships, family relations, legal disputes or business investments, but only rarely the question of economic ethics, which I endeavour to raise in this chapter. The exceptions are K.B. McFarlane and S.J. Payling. McFarlane, while not treating Fastolf's motivations in relation to the principles of economic probity, made an assessment of his attitudes towards wealth-gathering. McFarlane had found, amongst the Fastolf papers, a number of loans to merchants at interest, the records quite openly acknowledging that they were for "*relucrum et incrementum*" or "employ et gayn". Although some of those loans were quite long-term, Fastolf's real aim was to invest in Caister Castle, estates, jewellery and plate for the purpose of display. With echoes of *Wynnere and Wastoure*, McFarlane describes this aim as "a passion for conspicuous waste".[2] Fastolf "aimed less at land and profit than at augmenting his land and fame" and in order to do so "did all that bullying and rack-renting could do to raise the yield of his estates" and entered into business ventures such as shipping.[3] In a similar vein, Payling described Ralph, Lord Cromwell, as "more than commonly rapacious" with his extensive and often illegal land acquisitions.[4] Thus, Fastolf could have been criticised by contemporary moralists for both avarice, by his seemingly never-ending desire for wealth, and prodigality, whereas Cromwell was an exemplar of someone whose greed led him to acquire ever greater wealth. I will consider Fastolf in a separate case study that will permit a closer assessment of his business negotiations and of his attitudes to economic ethics.

[1] For full details, see the Bibliography. Christine Carpenter, "The Stonor Circle in the Fifteenth Century"(2005); E.M. Carus-Wilson "Evidence of Industrial Growth on Some Fifteenth-Century Manors" (1959); Alison Hanham, *The Celys and Their World* (1985); Elizabeth Noble, *The World of the Stonors* (2009); Colin Richmond's three studies *The Paston Family in the Fifteenth Century* (1990, 1996, 2000) and his "The Pastons and London" (2000) and "Sir John Fastolf and the Land Market" (2002); Jonathan Rose, "Litigation and Political Conflict in Fifteenth-Century East Anglia"; Anthony Smith's three studies of Fastolf "Litigation and Politics" (1984), " 'The Greatest Man of the Age'" (1995) and " 'My confessors exorted me gretely therto…'" (2001).

[2] K.B. McFarlane, "The Investment of Sir John Fastolf's Profits of War", *Transactions of the Royal Historical Society*, 5th Series (1957): 100–101, 109.

[3] McFarlane, "The Investment of Sir John Fastolf's Profits", 114.

[4] S.J. Payling, "A Disputed Mortgage: Ralph, Lord Cromwell, Sir John Gra and the Manor of Multon Hall", in *Rulers and Ruled in Late Medieval England: Essays Presented to Gerald Harriss*, ed. Rowena E. Archer and Simon Walker (London: Hambledon Press, 1995), 117.

The Evidence of Letters and Papers

The Ideal of Worshipfulness, Trust, Payment of Debts and the Importance of Shame

How merchants or the gentry responded to or felt about ethical issues in their day-to-day business might well have differed from the conventional pieties expressed in wills. Conventional piety is demonstrated by the fact that Fastolf possessed a psalter, upon which he swore an oath to repay his servant Nicholas Bokkyng, and by so many Paston letters closing with the valedictions "God keep you" or "may Jesus have you in his keeping". Furthermore, both the Pastons and Fastolf had a chaplain for their households (James Gloys and Thomas Howes), so religious observances must have been made. John Paston noted that Fastolf wore a cross around his neck every day and owned a relic, a finger of John the Baptist.[5]

The desire for merchants and the gentry to clear their consciences and to make amends before Judgement Day took precedence at the end of life, but it seems reasonable to suppose that there were other more immediate concerns which demanded attention while they were involved in transactions. Trust and reputation were absolutely necessary to obtain credit, particularly when written instruments were less common than they are today.[6]

A correspondent with William Stonor knew the importance of conscience, both to himself and to his recipient. Sir Richard Graystoke sent a letter to William Stonor, asking him to give the money he owed to the heirs of a John Blackhall immediately, as they were about travel to the north: "therfor I pray yow withowt any delay of or fenying after conscience doo; for, as your neyburs saye, ye be well conscience in such matyrs".[7] Graystoke's appeal to Stonor's conscience shows his own

[5] Colin Richmond, "Religion", in *Fifteenth-Century Attitudes: Perceptions of Society in Late Medieval England*, ed. Rosemary Horrox (Cambridge: CUP, 1994), 198.

[6] Dyer, *A Country Merchant, 1495-1520: Trading and Farming at the End of the Middle Ages* (Oxford: OUP, 2012), 131.

[7] *The Stonor Letters and Papers 1290–1483*, vol. 2, ed. C.L. Kingsford, (London: Royal Historical Society, 1919), 23, no. 181, Letter from Sir Richard Graystoke to William Stonor of 20 April (?1477).

awareness of the ethical practice of paying debts and his expectation that Stonor would adhere to it. He was also appealing to Stonor's sense of his own reputation, according to which he would be discomfited or ashamed if his neighbours knew that he did not honour his commitments. The Cely family was similarly concerned about its reputation. Among wool merchants, honesty was expected by their peers and the reputation of one family member would, by extension, be applied to the others. George Cely wrote to his brother that their father was now at Calais. Their father was regarded as worshipful, and it was in their interest to ensure that this reputation was maintained in Calais "the mor worshyppffull as he ys at Calles, the better belowyd shall we be, and the mor sett by thys actys the world".[8] Their fellow merchants expected payments of debts to be prompt: John Spencer needed to pay Thomas Abram, a London grocer, and asked that George Cely pay him out of funds that he held on Spencer's behalf, ensuring that "ther be no defaut of payment … for I haue fond hym so curtes in his delying that I wold not for twyse the walur he were dysspontyd at the sight of hys byll".[9] Richard Cely the elder urged George to deal with reliable payers at the Calais market: "Borganys man … for ys payment ys goode to me at all tymys befor the day … The man of Lyne ys good payment, and that ys mery for to dele wyt syche men. Take good men and doe the better to hem rader".[10]

That honesty, politeness and prompt payment were highly important for the Celys is further apparent in Richard Cely the younger's exasperation over their unreliable brother Robert. An acquaintance of Richard Cely's godfather had gone surety for Robert for £25 plus another £10 that Robert owed to William Eaton and "Qwat ys mor God know". Richard was against George Cely giving any financial help to Robert: "I awys you to lene hym no mony, ne do no thyng wyth hym byt afor record. Ye knowe the onstedfastenes of hym well inow".[11] The Celys wanted to be

---

[8] *Cely Letters*, 5, no. 4, Letter from George Cely at Antwerp to Richard Cely the younger at Calais, 27 September 1476.

[9] *Cely Letters*, 10, no. 10, Letter from John Spencer at London to George Cely at Calais, 5 November 1476.

[10] *Cely Letters*, 28–29, no. 31, Letter from Richard Cely the elder at London to George Cely at Calais, 25 August 1478.

[11] *Cely Letters*, 44, no. 47, Letter from Richard Cely the younger at London to George Cely at Calais, 9 April 1479.

regarded as successful merchants, as "winners" in the sense that the very opposites of their values were "waste" and sloth. Robert's behaviour had brought accusations of idleness and waste by his father and brothers. Richard Cely the elder had chastised him for his lack of communication and effort in a time when business was slow.[12] On another occasion, Richard Cely the younger told George that Robert had wasted on gambling the money intended for his board and lodging.[13]

Paying one's debts was part of the moral instruction by the Church: those who do not repay their debts are guilty of theft according to *The Middle English Treatise on the Ten Commandments* and of ravine according to *The Book of Vices and Virtues*.[14] In business terms, however, it appears more to be part of being worshipful or being held in good esteem. Thomas Kesten, a fellow wool merchant and friend of the Celys, failed to pay his debts. Richard Cely the elder wrote "I am not wyll plesyd wyt Kesten", because he had not paid another merchant, John Tate, for sarplers of wool.[15] Two years later, Richard the elder disclosed that Kesten owed him personally the large sum of £400 and informed his son George that the money was to be repaid over a period of eight years. The opportunity was taken to make this a highly profitable arrangement for the Celys: Kesten was to send £100 worth of wool and fells to Calais each year and pay all the customs duties, freight and other costs, but he would be paid only £50. Canonists would have regarded this as highly usurious, but perhaps Richard Cely believed such profits were justifiable on the grounds of the potential loss of the £400 owing to him. Interestingly, he still regarded Kesten, apparently an old acquaintance, in a kindly way and trusted him to keep to the agreement.[16] Certainly, Kesten continued to be in debt to

---

[12] *Cely Letters*, 3, no. 2, Letter from Richard Cely the elder at London to Robert Cely at Calais, 5 July 1474.

[13] *Cely Letters*, 29, no. 32, Letter from Richard Cely the younger at Calais to George Cely at Bruges, ?27 August 1478. For a more extensive account of Robert's behaviour, see Hanham, *The Celys and Their World*, 82–91.

[14] Royster, J.F., "A Middle English Treatise on the Ten Commandments: Part 1: Text and Notes", *Studies in Philology* 6 (1910):30; *Vices and Virtues*, 34–35.

[15] *Cely Letters*, 11, no. 11, Letter from Richard Cely the elder at London to George Cely at Calais, 26 January 1476/7.

[16] *Cely Letters*, 45, no. 48, Letter from Richard Cely the elder at London to George Cely at Calais, 15 April 1479. For further details concerning the association between Kesten and the Celys, see Hanham, *The Celys and Their World*, 91–103.

the Celys, for years later he was pleading for extra time to repay his debts and swearing by his Christian faith that he would do so as soon as he could.[17] At this time, he was running a boarding house and, ever hopeful, offered cheap accommodation to the Celys and anyone they might know. Plainly, his reputation as a successful, prosperous and trustworthy merchant was no longer sustainable. He proposed that one way out of his problems might be a good marriage (he was by this time a widower) and asked for the Celys' help because he felt his current penury and indebtedness would prevent it.[18]

A situation in which one was unable to repay one's debts had practical consequences: no merchant would trust Kesten enough to do business with him. Similarly, the landowner Robert Armburgh was aware that if his enemies knew that he was in debt they would hinder his business activities.[19] Here is the potential for a dilemma: on the one hand, the expectations of society about honesty and, on the other, the need to maintain an appearance of reliability. Chaucer drew attention to this in his description of the merchant in the Prologue to the *Canterbury Tales*:

> Ther wiste no wight that he was in dette,
> So estatly was he of his governaunce
> With his bargaynes and with his chevyssaunce.[20]

When, as a creditor, he was faced with the prospect of default, Robert Armburgh felt entitled to write to his debtors, reminding them of former promises they had made. He resorted to moral language, using terms such as "evil", "untruth" and "covetousness" as well as accusing them of shamefulness and supporting his adversaries. Real exasperation led Armburgh to call upon the language of the Church. He appealed to his debtors' sense of personal loyalty as well, arguing that they would be preventing him from maintaining his legal suit against his opponents, and using morally loaded language:

---

[17] *Cely Letters*, 217, no. 219, Letter from Thomas Kesten at Calais to Richard and George Cely at London, 17 May [?1484].

[18] *Cely Letters*, 217, no. 219, Letter from Thomas Kesten at Calais to Richard and George Cely at London, 17 May [?1484].

[19] *Armburgh Papers*, 127–128, Robert Armburgh to William Armburgh, 1 March 1430.

[20] *General Prologue*, in *Riverside Chaucer*, 28.

> Remembre you also how at your excitacion and by your avys and conseill y dede grete cost on worthy persons … nat withstandyng this and alle the grte promesses that ye made me, how evyll ye have payd me my ferme in to this tyme … and therfor, al thinges considered and al maner vntrouthe y cast aside, schameth nat ne hyndre nat your self for covetise of a litil good.[21]

Reputation or worship, which included the ability to meet debt obligations, was a key motivation for the Celys and Thomas Kesten as merchants and for William Stonor and Robert Armburgh as landowners. Armburgh had accused his debtors of evil and immorality, but it seems that he was led to do this for fear of losing his legal battles over lands and properties. Another letter of his about continuing non-payment was a little milder, appealing to the debtors' "good consience and curtesyse".[22] The use of the word "conscience" reflects the influence of the Church, whereas "courtesy" has more secular connotations.

Where reputation or worshipfulness was concerned, the opposite value was shame rather than evil or immorality. Armburgh pleaded with his correspondents to intercede on his behalf to his brother for financial help: "I am lyke for to be suyd of certeyn persones and soule [*sic*] shamyd and hyndrid for gold that I borowyd of hem the last yere".[23] Good reputation was also important to the Pastons: getting into a situation in which debts could not be repaid would bring shame and dishonour.[24] Shame and dishonour would bring unfortunate consequences: Margaret Paston warned John Paston II to spend carefully, for not only would his worshipfulness be threatened but he would risk running down the finances of his friends, who would then become unwilling to help him financially. Furthermore, the Pastons' adversaries would benefit from a situation in which they knew he was impoverished: "if ye take odere hed to your exspences ye

[21] *Armburgh Papers*, 137, Robert Armburgh to Ralph Beauchamp, William Harpour and Richard Barbour, probably late 1432.

[22] *Armburgh Papers*, 149, Robert Armburgh to William Harpour and Richard Barbour, probably late 1433 or early 1434.

[23] *Armburgh Papers*, 112, Robert Armburgh to William Harpour and Richard Barbour, shortly before November 1429.

[24] The preoccupation with shame and honour has been discussed more broadly by Philippa Maddern. See her "Honour among the Pastons: Gender and Integrity in Fifteenth-Century English Provincial Society", *Journal of Medieval History* 14 (1988): 357–371.

shall do your-self and your frendes gret diswurchep and enpoueryssh so them that non of vs shall help othere, to owre elmys grete comfort". Margaret herself had confronted shame by being forced to retrench and break up her household and this caused much consternation: "And at this tyme it compellith me to breke vp howshold and to sogeorn, which I am right loth to haue do if I might othere-wyse haue chosyn, for it caused gret clamour in this town".[25] The shame of being in debt had real disadvantages: the inability to help others in a financial crisis, the exhaustion of the goodwill and trust of friends, and the public dishonour of being unable to maintain a household.

Thus, the retention of lands as the family's livelihood was an important part of being worshipful, which was a guide to action but, as will be shown later, not necessarily one with ethical consequences. Margaret Paston remonstrated with John Paston II for selling Sporle Wood. This was a shameful matter, not only because "your fadre, whos sowle God assoil, cheryssed in euery maner his woodes" but because both friends and enemies would think it was done out of need and that John was a waster. To sell one's own livelihood was shameful: selling the Paston land would make everyone John knew "to purpose the more cruelly ageyn you", but selling part of the Fastolf inheritance, land to which the Pastons did not have good and clear title, would be a practical or sensible action. Sporle Wood was part of the Paston livelihood and Margaret demanded that no more such bargains be made, for she would never do such a thing, even for 1,000 marks. She threatened to withdraw both her moral and financial support: "do as I advyse you … or ell trost neuer to haue comfort of me. And if I may knowe ye be of such disposicion, and I leve ij yere it shall disavayll you in my liffelode ccc marc".[26] By 1477, Margaret was in grave doubt about the future of the Paston estates after her death. The sale of Sporle Wood still rankled, even though the manor had been redeemed by John in 1474, because it showed a lack of respect for his heritage and negligence in selling the family's livelihood to cover

---

[25] *Paston Letters*, vol. 1, 350–351, no. 208, Letter from Margaret Paston to John Paston II of 28 October 1469. Davis originally gave the date as 1470, but this was later corrected (*Paston Letters*, vol. 3, xxviii).

[26] *Paston Letters*, vol. 1, 360–362, no. 214, Letter from Margaret Paston to John Paston II of about 1472.

his overspending. She believed John would sell or mortgage the lands he would inherit from her but this would still be preferable to selling his father's estates. She prayed "God geue yow grace to be of sadde and good dysposyn here-after, to hys plesans and conforte to me and to all yowyr frendys and to yowyr wurchyp and profyte here-after".[27]

In contrast to John Paston II was the ideal of John Paston I, who was well regarded as a squire of worship and a wealthy man who spent carefully. Again, this was a practical or pragmatic value, for such a man would have the resources to maintain his household and to defend his land holdings against the claims of others. The report of some observations by Thomas Billing (the recorder of London) passed on by William Paston the younger, John Paston I's brother, showed approval of "the winner" versus the profligacy of "the waster". A lawyer named Ledam had made some negative comment about John Paston I, and Billing had responded: "Yt is the gyse of yowre contré-men to spende alle the good they haue on men and leuery gownys and hors and harness and end in beggary". The recommended model was John Paston I: "a swyre of wurchyp, and of gret lyuelode, and I wothe he wyll not spend alle hys good at onys, but he sparyt yerely c mark or j c li". Paston was able to "do hys enemy a scherewd turne and neuer fare the warse jn hys howseholde, ner the lesse men a-bowthe hym".[28]

The upholding of worshipfulness could have been something of a veneer, a cover under which to operate according to self-interest and monetary gain. William Paston I, the father of John Paston I, who had added considerably to the Pastons' land holdings, was accused of unethical behaviour as one of the king's justices. In about the year 1433, William Dallyng drew up a draft petition to Parliament alleging that William Paston took "diuerse fees and rewardes of diuerses persones" in Norfolk and Suffolk, including the town of Yarmouth, the Abbott of St Benet's, the Priors of St Faith's, Norwich, Penteney and Walsingham, the town of Lynn, and

[27] *Paston Letters*, vol. 1, 379, no. 227, Letter from Margaret Paston to John Paston II of 11 August 1477; *Paston Letters*, vol. 1, 477, no. 286, Letter from John Paston II to Margaret Paston mentioning the redemption of Sporle manor dated 20 November 1474.

[28] Colin Richmond, *The Paston Family in the Fifteenth Century: The First Phase*(Cambridge: CUP, 1990), 177; *Paston Letters*, vol. 1, 154, no. 83, Letter from William Paston II to John Paston I of July 1454.

of one Katherine Shelton regarding the wardship of Ralph Shelton.[29] In addition, William Paston was accused of making a false prosecution in order to obtain property, very much in the way described by John Bromyard in his *Summa Praedicantium* (discussed in Chapter 3). Juliane Herberd petitioned Henry VI that William Paston, then a serjeant-at-law, had deprived her of her inheritance by turning her off her property at Little Plumstead in Norfolk. William Paston apparently offered Juliane six marks for the land, which "by reson and conscience" she felt was too little. The petition claimed: "And therupon the same William Paston emagined and maligned agayn the same Juliane … and by fals emaginacion sodeynly sent the same Juliane vnto prison to one of the countours of London" and kept her there for thirteen nights. He threatened to keep her there permanently unless she did as he wished. Out of fear, Juliane submitted. Paston made her sign a blank charter and then sent her back to the same prison without paying her anything. Juliane approached the Duke of Bedford for help, but this only resulted in another false charge by Paston and a further term of imprisonment at the Fleet. Sir Thomas Erpingham secured her release but Juliane was sent again to prison at Norwich Castle, this time for three years. In one of her petitions, Juliane claimed she had been deprived of her land for forty years.[30] There is no indication in any of the Paston letters that William's descendants were either aware of or concerned about such allegations. If they were, it makes it even more likely that the Pastons held that being regarded as worshipful would be to their advantage and that a good reputation would help them secure financial assistance or support in legal matters.

It seems that to both merchants and landowners, reputation or worshipfulness was extremely important. For the Stonors and Celys, a reputation for honesty and repaying their debts was vital for their business as merchants. For the Pastons, it was keeping their estates in good order and managing them well, being winners rather than wasters. The Celys disapproved of their younger brother who gambled away his money, while John Paston I was lauded by a fellow lawyer for his prudent spending and there were fears that John Paston II would be a waster. For the Celys, the

[29] *Paston Letters,* vol. 2, 508, no. 869, Petition to Parliament by William Dallyng against William Paston I (draft).

[30] See *Paston Letters*, vol. 2, 509–515.

Pastons and the Armburghs, lengthy delays in payment, or non-payment, of debts would incur the opposite of worshipfulness (that is, shame and dishonour). Their correspondence does not reveal that they thought of it as breaking the Commandment against theft or as something for which they would be judged in the afterlife. They felt that the values of shame, dishonour and worshipfulness were the most important in their dealings with the world around them.

Where Ethics Were Ignored: Distraints, Bribery, Speculation and Chevisances

This section examines instances in which certain actions committed by landowners appeared to be in breach of the ethical standards of the Church. Those instances regarded as unethical were distraints, which could involve inflicting economic hardship on tenants; bribery, which was a corruption of justice; financial speculation, which was profiting from excessive prices without the justifications of reasonable costs; and *chevisances*, which were a disguised form of usury.

The battle to retain their estates led landowners into ethically dubious territory by the standards of the Church. The greatest legal battle for the Pastons was their holding of Caister and other estates in Norfolk and Suffolk, which John Paston I claimed had been bequeathed to him by Sir John Fastolf. Fastolf had made two wills. The first, dated 14 June 1459, differed considerably from the second, dated 3 November 1459, in which John Paston I was the main beneficiary.[31] Paston's claim was disputed and brought strong and violent opposition from both the Duke of Suffolk and the Duke of Norfolk. The Duke of Suffolk's men made incursions into the manors of Hellesdon, Drayton and Costessey, and the Duke of Norfolk's forces besieged and took Caister Castle. The Pastons did whatever was necessary to defend the lands they believed they had inherited from Sir John Fastolf and in such cases of disputed title they disregarded the interests of their tenants. As discussed in Chapter 3, Thomas Docking

[31] For the June 1459 will, see Colin Richmond, "Once Again: Fastolf's Will", *Essays in Later Medieval and Early Tudor England in Honour of Ralph A. Griffith*, ed. Keith Dockray and Peter Fleming (Stroud: Nonsuch, 2005), 115–130.

considered those who sought to pervert the course of justice for monetary or other gain or by threats, as theft in *De Decem Praeceptis*, and bribery and corruption were condemned in *Speculum Christiani*.

An example of disregard for tenants is the Pastons' indulgence in what Colin Richmond has described as "competitive rent-collecting", in which rival owners would attempt to persuade tenants that they were the rightful owners, perhaps using threats. Potentially, this could lead to tenants paying twice or being subjected to violence. Furthermore, there were "tit-for-tat distraints", in which the Pastons indulged in retaliation in kind for distraints made upon their tenants by the Duke of Suffolk or Lord Moleyns.[32] In just one example, in 1465, a certain Piers Waryn, a friend of two of the Duke of Suffolk's officials, Master Philipp and the bailiff of Costessey, had a plough working on the Pastons' land at Drayton. His two plough-horses were taken by Paston servants to Hellesdon to prevent any exploitation of their land. The next day, Master Philipp and the bailiff of Costessey arrived with eight armed men at Hellesdon and took two plough-horses belonging to the parson of Hellesdon worth four marks and two plough-horses worth forty shillings from Thomas Stermyns. The parson of Hellesdon went to see Master Philipp, who told him that if any of John Paston's servants took distraint in Drayton, even if it was only the value of one hen, they would come to Hellesdon and take the value of an ox, and if they could not find an ox, they would break into their tenants' houses and take as much as they could find.[33] Master Philipp also made it very clear that he had the superior armed forces of the Duke of Suffolk to call upon. The Pastons' retaliation to the Duke of Suffolk was necessary to them but involved hardship for both Piers Waryn and the parson of Hellesdon.

The manors of Drayton and Hellesdon were the subject of dispute with the Duke of Suffolk, who, according to John Paston I, claimed that the manors belonged to one Polis and that, because his name was De la Pole, he was the rightful heir. In May 1465, Margaret Paston wrote that John Wykes, Naunton and other Paston servants had taken a distraint of seventy-seven head of cattle at Drayton. The tenants had no money to secure

---

[32] Colin Richmond, "Landlord and Tenant: The Paston Evidence", in *Enterprise and Individuals in Fifteenth-Century England*, ed. Jennifer Kermode (Stroud: Sutton, 1991), 31.

[33] *Paston Letters*, vol. 1, 295, no. 180, Letter from Margaret Paston to John Paston I of 10 May 1465.

their return and were afraid to be bound by obligation to John Paston I. Then William Harleston, an official of Suffolk's, threatened those same tenants with eviction if they did pay: "And that put them in such feere that they drust nothere pay nor be bonden". Harleston went to see Margaret Paston, offering to make an exchange: she should return the cattle, and he would send back what he had taken previously in distraint. However, Margaret refused: "I wold not delyuer hem but by the forme of lawe". Furthermore, she did not obey a replevin until she received one that was with the sheriff's seal.[34] In the meantime, the tenants were caught between the claims of two rival landowners and deprived of the cattle and other goods and chattels they needed to make a living. John Paston I intended to take the matter of the disputed estates to the assizes and meanwhile instructed Margaret to rally the spirits of their tenants: "Neuer the les ye be a gentilwoman, and it is worship for yow to confort yowr tenantis". He asked her to ride to Hellesdon, Drayton and Sparham and speak to the tenants "and byd hem hold with ther old master til I com".[35]

In cases like the above, the lives of presumably innocent tenants were disrupted. There was potential for considerable harm to their economic interests, but what seemed to matter to the Pastons were the claims of the Duke of Suffolk. In such a situation, the tenants were mere instruments in the disputes between rival landowners. Their livestock, goods and chattels could be taken away, but at the same time, the Pastons recognised that those tenants needed reassurance to dissuade them from moving elsewhere.

The Duke of Norfolk was another who engaged in such practices. William Cotting, rector of Brancaster, wrote to the Pastons' servant Richard Calle about the poverty caused and harm done to John Poleyn, one of the Pastons' tenants at Tichewell. Three of the Duke of Norfolk's men, armed with spears, took away three of Poleyn's horses, telling him to "come and trete with my lord of Norffolk". Cotting commented on the lack of any protection for Poleyn and others like him from great lords such as the Duke of Norfolk

[34] *Paston Letters*, vol. 1, 132–33, no. 73, Letter from John Paston I to Margaret Paston, John Daubeney and Richard Calle of 27 June 1465; vol. 1, 301–302, no. 182, Letter from Margaret Paston to John Paston I of 20 May 1465.

[35] *Paston Letters*, vol. 1, 132–133, no. 73, Letter from John Paston I to Margaret Paston, John Daubeney and Richard Calle of 27 June 1465.

> It is a gret peté that ther is non other ordenaunce. Thise poure fermores are liche to be vndo… for swiche an opyn wrong vnremedied knew I never, ne good and trewe men so vnkyndely vexed.[36]

The observation about good and true men suggests that those particular distraints were unjust and purely opportunistic, a way of extorting money as well as the forceful imposition of lordship.

In order to protect their interests, both the Pastons and Fastolf ignored the moral strictures about paying bribes. Despite the Church's condemnation of bribes, Agnes Paston, John Paston II and Sir John Fastolf regarded them as necessary to secure favourable judgements. Bribes were evidently common: Agnes Paston gave an account of a Margaret Talfas who had asked for her advice about whether she should offer a bribe to a sheriff, "and I tolde hire if she dede I supposed she shulde fynde hem the more frendly".[37] The Pastons' disputed Fastolf inheritance obliged John Paston II to make representations at the highest level: the Paston case had been before the King's Council, and the king had to be paid 100 marks and other costs were 40 marks.[38] Sir John Fastolf needed to engage in bribery in a conspiracy and attaint action taken in 1452 by John Andrew, one of the Duke of Suffolk's adherents, against Thomas Howes and John Porter, who was another of Fastolf's servants. Some four years went by, during which time neither Howes nor Porter appeared in court and the sheriff was fined for failing to arrest them. Fastolf responded by giving an official of the sheriff's deputy, who had been seeking to obtain part of the fine from Howes, an embroidered cope. Eventually, Howes and Porter were imprisoned and Fastolf not only wrote to King's Bench Justice Yelverton and to his stepson to approach his father-in-law, another King's Bench justice, but gave Chief Justice Sir John Fortescue an expensive robe of gold cloth and crimson velvet.[39]

---

36 *Paston Letters*, vol. 2, 571, no. 903, Letter from William Cotyng to John Cook for Richard Calle of 9 January 1469.

37 *Paston Letters*, vol. 1, 38, no. 25, Letter from Agnes Paston to John Paston I of 16 November? 1452.

38 *Paston Letters*, vol. 1, 495, no. 299, Letter from John Paston II to Margaret Paston or John Paston III of 27 May 1476.

39 J. Rose, "Litigation and Political Conflict in Fifteenth-Century East Anglia; Conspiracy and Attaint Actions and Sir John Fastolf", *Journal of Legal History* 27 (2006): 58–59.

It seems it was common practice to bribe not only judges and officials but also members of a jury: it was important for Robert Armburgh to know which of them had been corrupted in a case that was to come to the assizes. He asked his correspondent to enquire "whiche ben just men and well consyenssyd and whiche woln takyn mede".[40] These words express the conflict between good conscience and reward so well portrayed by Langland in the figure of Lady Mede that I discussed in Chapter 4. According to John Paston III, there were those who made a living out of accepting bribes. He wrote to his father that two men, who had been present at a previous inquest in London, were reluctant to attend another without payment, saying that the last time they went it cost ten shillings. He also got the impression "that they wold haue had a brybe of yow, besyd th paying for ther issuys, for to haue bedyn at home, for they haue non othyr leuyng but brybys".[41] The expectations of those men makes it clear that it was common practice for litigants to pay the expenses of their witnesses, but the use of the word "bribes" suggests elements of compulsion and falsity. On the other hand, being paid a bribe as well as having their expenses covered was how such witnesses made their living. Whether it was a bribe or just meeting expenses, litigants might have believed such payments were necessary, particularly if they knew that the judges and juries on their case had also been bribed.

Both John Paston I and Sir John Fastolf indulged in the kind of unethical market speculation described in *Dives and Pauper* and many other works. John Paston I was anxious to keep his stocks of malt away from potential buyers. He wrote to Margaret:

> I woll that ye warne both Daubeney and Richard Calle that thei disclose nat what malt I haue. Ne what I shall selle, ne that on marcchaunt knowe nat what an other hath; for ther is gret spies leid here at London for ingrosers of malt to heyghne the prise, hough be it myne is not but of myn owne growing and my tenauntes.[42]

---

[40] *Armburgh Papers*, 143–44, Robert Armburgh to an unknown recipient, probably between 8 July and 6 October 1433.

[41] *Paston Letters*, vol. 1, 526–527, no. 322, Letter from John Paston III to John Paston I of 2 June (probably 1464).

[42] *Paston Letters*, vol. 1, 125–126, no. 71, Letter from John Paston I to Margaret Paston of 14 January 1465.

Paston had bought the malt from elsewhere—he was not the producer—which meant that he could be charged as a forestaller or an engrosser and fined and which would have upset his plans to make a sale. Nicholas Bokkyng, who had been Sir John Fastolf's receiver, revealed in a petition to Fastolf's executors that during the time of a corn shortage he was "willyng to enriche more his said maistre [and] bowte cornes of dyverse pouere men in the Cuntre" to the sum of £224 or more. The profit to Fastolf would be £200 or more, once the corn was sold to Colchester, Manningtree and other places in Essex but the shipments, in the absence of Bokkyng, went through "many mennys handis", and Bokkyng ended up with a loss of 100 shillings.[43] Bokkyng's anxiety was about his financial loss, for which he was claiming restitution after Fastolf's death: the fact that the claim was in relation to forestalling and engrossing did not seem relevant to him. The impression is that, as far as Bokkyng, Fastolf and Paston were concerned, forestalling and engrossing were simply other forms of a money-making operation. The effect that highly priced corn might have on the poor of Colchester and Manningtree was ignored.

Fastolf's efforts to get the best price for his land were not, of course, unethical, but Fastolf's attitude, the importance of his own "profit and avail", is revealed in his report of a discussion he had had with Hugh Acton, Master of the Hospital of St Giles. Acton was negotiating to buy the manor of Mundham for 200 marks. Fastolf wrote "Sende me worde whethyr I hafe made a gode bargeyn", pointing out that the manor had a good clear title and advowson and that he might have kept it. Acton had hoped for a reduced price, but owing to his long-running dispute with the prior of Hickling over outstanding rents, Fastolf was not willing to make allowances for the clergy: "And he wold I shuld hafe do almesse on hem, and relessed hem som money, but ye may sey hym the vntrouth of the Pryour of Hykelyng drawyth awey my deuocion in such causes".[44] Acton was also interested in buying more land from Fastolf called Rees, but Fastolf was opposed to selling it at a price that was less than the value it had accumulated after twenty years. Fastolf calculated that the land was

[43] Oxford, Magdalen College, Fastolf Paper no. 98, Petition from Nicholas Bokkyng to Bishop Wayneflete.

[44] *Paston Letters*, vol. 3, 103, no. 991, Letter from Sir John Fastolf to Howes, Bokkyng and Shipdam of 23 November 1450.

worth more to Acton because it was close to Mundham. He proposed to make an exchange of land instead. Fastolf's servants were to check the accounts of Rees and provide a valuation "as ye and my councell shall well avyse, for my moste proffyt and avaylle".[45] The words "profit and avail" also occur in a letter urging his servants "to solicit and labour the expedicion of my materes comprised in my lettres sent to you seth the fest of Pasch last passed to my moost proffyt and avaylle".[46] Fastolf's uses of "profit" and "avail" seem repetitive since avail could mean profit as well as advantage, but no doubt he wished to emphasise the importance of his own financial success to his servants.

We have seen that appeals to conscience were made in relation to unpaid debts, but conscience did not seem to enter into the equation where lending for profit was concerned, despite the prohibition under canon law. A fourteenth-century example is the Earl of Arundel and Surrey, who in 1350 gave a merchant, Thomas Batsford, £300 "to traffic therewith to the earl's advantage".[47] Again, "advantage" presumably means profit. As already discussed, Richard Cely senior made a highly profitable arrangement for the repayment of his loan to Thomas Kesten and there was no concern about the high rate of interest involved.[48] A speculative venture involving interest appears in the records of Fastolf's Receiver-General, John Kertelyng, from Michaelmas 1433 to Michaelmas 1434, suggesting that this was regarded as normal practice. The records note that £196 13 shillings and four pence had been received from John Wells, citizen and alderman of London. Of this amount, £66 13 shillings and four pence comprised the annual interest of 5 per cent on a loan of £1,333 6 shillings and eight pence contracted with Sir John Fastolf over a period of seven years, the purpose of which was to conduct merchandising.[49]

Although charging any interest on loans (except where damage or loss could be proved) was prohibited in canon law, interest-paying arrangements seemed to be common amongst the merchant community.

[45] *Paston Letters*, vol. 3, 124–125, no. 1005, Letter from Sir John Fastolf to Thomas Howes and John Berney of 28 January 1451.

[46] *Paston Letters*, vol. 3, 84, no. 981, Letter from Sir John Fastolf to Thomas Howes of 7 May 1450.

[47] K.B. McFarlane, *Nobility of Later Medieval England* (Oxford: Clarendon Press, 1973), 90.

[48] McFarlane, *Nobility*, 261.

[49] Magdalen College, Fastolf Paper no. 9.

Venetian merchants charged their English counterparts twelve pence in the pound for immediate repayment of a loan, two shillings if repayment was to be a month later.[50] The Grocers of London charged interest for commercial loans: in the mid-fifteenth century, three merchants of the Staple paid 8.5 per cent for a loan of £477 and another group paid 12 per cent for a loan of £300.[51] The London Court of Orphans was established by the Common Council of the City of London to oversee the property of orphans and appoint guardians. The mayor, aldermen and chamberlain ran the orphans' shares of estates "as a commercial loan fund from which merchants with sound security could borrow at annual interest rates of 10 per cent".[52] Caroline Barron writes that a guardian "was expected to put the money to work to earn interest".[53] Usury was apparently tolerated in Italy, at least among the merchant community, where the Roman law principle of *laesio enormis* was used to justify moderate rates of interest.[54] Fastolf came from a merchant background himself and clearly regarded loans for profit as simply another way to increase revenue.

There do appear to be differing expectations regarding borrowing or lending at interest. While private individuals or merchant organisations charged interest, it seems the king could not ignore the canon law prohibition of usury. The crown took care to avoid accusations that it was repaying loans at interest: the repayments of Edward I, Edward II and Edward III to Italian moneylenders varied from 15 per cent to 150 per cent above the value of the loan, but these were, in the great majority of

---

[50] Wendy Childs, "'To oure losse and hindraunce': English Credit to Alien Merchants in the Mid-Fifteenth Century", in *Enterprise and Individuals*, 71.

[51] Sylvia Thrupp, "The Grocers of London, a Study of Distributive Trade", in *Studies in English Trade in the Fifteenth Century*, ed. Eileen Power and M.M. Postan (1933, repr. New York: Barnes & Noble, 1966), 253.

[52] Vanessa Harding, "The Crown, the City and the Orphans: The City of London and its Finances, 1400–1700", in *Urban Public Debts, Urban Government and the Market for Annuities in Western Europe (14th–18th Centuries)*, ed. Marc Boone, Karel Davids and Paul Janssens (Turnhout: Brepols, 2003), 58, 59; Sylvia Thrupp, *The Merchant Class of Medieval London (1300–1500)* (Chicago: University of Chicago Press, 1948), 107.

[53] Caroline Barron, *London in the Later Middle Ages: Government and People 1200–1500* (Oxford: OUP, 2004), 270.

[54] J.W. Baldwin, "The Medieval Theories of the Just Price ; Romanists, Canonists and Theologians in the Twelfth and Thirteenth Centuries", *Transactions of the American Philosophical Society*, 49(1959): 22–27.

cases, not actual but imputed rates of interest.[55] Gifts were not considered to be against the usury laws and so gifts took the place of interest. For example, Edward III promised the Bardi gifts worth £11,000 on loans totalling £42,000 over the years 1328–1331. Royal grants of land or special trade concessions were made to creditors in some instances, but in most cases, either the precise means of disguising interest payments were deliberately obscured or the records were incomplete.[56] Where records showed that interest was demanded, it was as compensation for damages or as a penalty for delayed repayment. In the first instance, in 1295, the Ricciardi claimed "damages" of 10,000 marks on a loan of 30,000 marks that they had advanced to Edmund of Lancaster, the brother of Edward I, some two years earlier. In the second, dating from 1297, a group of merchants asked the king to repay 4,300 *livres tournois* for a loan of 4,000, which would rise to 4,600 if repayment was not made by 1 January 1298.[57] A claim for damages might have been permissible provided that the interest was calculated from the date of repayment, not the commencement of the loan; in other words, the intention of the lender was not to gain interest.[58] However, it is doubtful whether Italian merchants' primary objective was to earn interest on their loans to the crown. Michael Prestwich has pointed out that, in many cases, they were fortunate if even the principal was returned to them, making it far more likely that they were seeking to gain other kinds of advantages. Some of the rewards they received were manors at low rent, tax exemptions and repayment in wool at fixed prices.[59]

Chevisances provided a means for landowners and merchants to borrow without openly paying interest. This was an arrangement whereby the borrower sold goods to the lender, then bought them back at a higher price, the difference between the selling and the buying price being

[55] Adrian R. Bell, Chris Brooks and Tony K. Moore, "Interest in Medieval Accounts: Examples from England, 1272–1340", *History* 94 (2009): 419.

[56] Bell, Brooks and Moore, "Interest in Medieval Accounts": 418, 422.

[57] Bell, Brooks and Moore, "Interest in Medieval Accounts": 416, 417.

[58] Bell, Brooks and Moore, "Interest in Medieval Accounts": 423.

[59] Michael Prestwich, "Italian Merchants in Late Thirteenth and Early Fourteenth Century England"', in *The Dawn of Modern Banking*, ed. Center for Medieval and Renaissance Studies, University of California, Los Angeles (New Haven: Yale University Press, 1979), 84–85, 87, 92.

effective interest. More complex arrangements sometimes involved third parties or leases of land and the profits therefrom. However, the *chevisance* was frowned upon by the Church as it was a hidden form of usury, and moralising language was used by secular authorities to condemn them. Edward III's writ against usurers, issued in March 1364, urged the Mayor, Alderman, Sheriffs and Commonalty of London to "do your utmost to put an end to the horrible vice and knavery of usury and extortion ('male chevance'), which have been long suffered in our said city".[60] A City of London ordinance declared that although such kinds of contracts were called "exchange" or "*chevisance*", they "might more truly be called 'mescheaunce' or 'wickedness', seeing that it ruins the honour and soul of the agent, and sweeps away the goods and property of him who appears to be accommodated, and destroys all manner of right and lawful traffic". Another declaration against usury and unlawful *chevisance* was made in 1390.[61] Condemnatory terms were used in a proclamation of 1419.[62]

Chevisances were thus perceived to be amongst the worst type of offences, against God and ruining the soul of the agent, but, nearly a century later, the word could be used in the sense of providing help, a remedy or a supply of something.[63] For example, in November 1462, the Chancellor wrote to the Mayor of London, referring to a "chevisaunce of good" needed for the king's army in the threat of a Scottish invasion, assuring the Corporation that if £1,000 or preferably £2,000 could be raised, it would be repaid by means of taxation relief.[64] This case suggests that the Chancellor believed that the defence of the realm was a good enough reason for a *chevisance* and that in this instance it was without its negative and unethical connotations. Another example suggests that

---

[60] *Liber Albus: The White Book of the City of London, compiled A.D. 1419 by John Carpenter, Common Clerk [and] Richard Whitington, Mayor*, trans. Henry Thomas Riley, London, Richard Griffin & Co., 1861, 318.

[61] *Liber Albus*, 319, 344–345.

[62] *Calendar of Letter Books Preserved among the Archives of the Corporation of the City of London at the Guildhall, Letter Book I* , ed. R.R. Sharpe (London: Corporation of London, 1909), 211.

[63] See "chevisance, *n.*", *Oxford English Dictionary*, Online edition, Oxford, 2015, http://www.oed.com.

[64] *The Politics of Fifteenth Century England: John Vale's Book*, ed. M.L. Kekewich et al. (Stroud: Sutton for Richard III & Yorkist History Trust, 1995) 171.

chevisance could have been used as a synonym for a loan. The 1491 will of Thomas, Lord Scrope of Masham, acknowledged the money owing from a *chevisance*. Money had been raised in London for the costs of an overseas trip with the king and needed to be repaid on 9 April in the following year. Lord Scrope of Bolton, his son Henry and one Thomas Trigot were "bond for by obligacion to certayne men of London".[65]

Where *chevisances* were loans disguised as sales, they might have been regarded by the Pastons and others as a discreet way of raising money since there was, as discussed previously, concern about having a good reputation as a person with sound finances. It is also possible that they were used because of fear of prosecution for usury, but the Paston letters do not give evidence of that consideration. William Worcester clearly knew of William Paston's engagement in *chevisances*. After the death of his master, Sir John Fastolf, Worcester compared his own efforts at *chevisance* in London to those of William Paston.[66]

Yet there was concern with risk. John Paston II was warned by his uncle, William Paston the younger, not to borrow £100 from a merchant friend for "that sholde be by weye off chevyshanse and to myn horte", but when John explained that Margaret Paston was his surety, William Paston the younger seemed satisfied that all was well. A *chevisance* could be a dangerous venture if entered into by someone with little collateral. John needed another 100 marks and William offered to arrange another *chevisance*, saying he had some 500 marks' worth of plate as collateral which was at his aunt's home at Warwick's Inn.

> The place at Warwykys Inne is large and my grawnt-dame is agyd; it had been jopartous to leve moche plate wyth hyre, thoghe halffe were hyre owne. But iff I maye doo other wyse I purpose nott to chevyshe any mony by hys meane.[67]

---

[65] *Testamenta Ebor. IV*, 23.

[66] *Paston Letters*, vol. 2, 204, no. 604, Letter from William Worcester to John Paston I of 7 February 1460. It is not clear whether Worcester is referring to William Paston the elder, the father of John Paston I, or the latter's brother William Paston the younger.

[67] *Paston Letters*, vol. 1, 476, no. 285, Letter from John Paston II to Margaret Paston of a probable date of February 1470.

It is evident that John Paston II was anxious about the security of the plate and the safety of his elderly aunt if her house was broken into, but not the immortality of his soul.

Another of John Paston II's considerations was the trustworthiness of a creditor, whether he would take advantage of his greater power to exploit an opportunity and take more as repayment than he was entitled to. With either another *chevisance* or the same one being referred to four years later, it became clear that John Paston II distrusted his uncle William: "I feer that I am lyke to be deseyuyd by hym; by God I had lever than c noblys that I weer qwyte off hym … I am in an agonye wyth hym that vexithe all my spyrytys".[68] Ten years later, a draft bill of complaint accused William Paston the younger of taking goods, produce, timber and livestock from some of the Paston manors, wrongly occupying others and taking the rents, and keeping silverware and coins not rightfully his. John Paston III sought full restoration.[69]

The Pastons regarded *chevisances* as a last resort when they were in financial difficulties, to be avoided if possible because of the financial risk involved. Thomas Daverse advised that he could get a loan on surety for John Paston II: "I truste that I haue studied such a mene that vp-on sureté as ye may make to gete yow an c li. or cc mark to be lante vn-tow yow for an halfe yere with-oute any cheuysshaunc or losse of god by yow".[70] The Pastons' servant, Richard Calle, was obliged to resort to *chevisance* in order to meet expenses, having already borrowed from others: "And all of this twelvemothe I haue not had on peny for my wages. Ther is non of them that hath purveyd nor chewisched halfe so moche as I haue don. Her is no man payd of ther wages, but all spent in howsold".[71] Margaret Paston needed to turn to *chevisance* in order to meet the expenses of John Paston II because income from rents was declining. Her alternative was to increase the rents from the Paston tenants, but this risked losing them altogether. In January 1462, she wrote:

---

[68] *Paston Letters*, vol. 1, 481, no. 288, Letter from John Paston II to John Paston III of 11 December 1474.

[69] *Paston Letters*, vol. 1, 622–626, no. 387, Bill of complaint against William Paston II (draft), 1484.

[70] *Paston Letters*, vol. 2, 379, no. 745, Letter from Thomas Daverse to John Paston II of 29 January 1467.

[71] *Paston Letters*, vol. 2, 395, no. 759, Letter from Richard Calle to John Paston II of 22 May 1469.

> And as for gadyryng of mony I sey nevyr a werse seson, for Rychard Calle seyth he can get but lytyll in substans of that is owyng, nowthyr of yowyr lyuelod nor of Fastolfys. And John Paston seyth they that may pay best, they pay werst.[72]

By 1466, Margaret seems to have been in the same state of exasperation with John Paston II's requests for money as Robert Armburgh had been with his long-standing debtors. She recalled the teachings of the moralists about lavish expenditure:

> yf any thing haue be a mysse any othere wyse than yt howte to haue ben be-fore thys, owthere in pryde ore in laues expencys ore in any othere thing that haue offendyd God, amend yt and pray hym of hys grace and helpe, and entende welle to God and to yowr neybors.[73]

In November 1466, she sent John Paston II £40 in gold royals "which I haue chevysshed and borwed for you". This was necessary because Margaret had already drawn upon her late husband's estate, before his will had been proved at Canterbury

> for as I am enformed be Mayster John Smyth, the chancellere, and othere that we ben all a-cursed that we haue thus mynystred the dedes godes wyth-ought licence or auctorité, and I wene we spede all the wers ther-fore.

Margaret's chief anxiety was the family being cursed and perhaps excommunicated as false executors, rather than the usury laws, although she might have been aware that a case of meddling with an estate prematurely was easier for the Church to identify and punish. The Church's ritual of cursing listed many potential offenders, including "all false executores that maken false testamentes and despose the goodes of him that is dede

[72] *Paston Letters*, vol. 1, 279, no. 168, Letter from Margaret Paston to John Paston I of 7 January 1462.

[73] *Paston Letters*, vol. 1, 333, no. 198, Letter from Margaret Paston to John Paston II of 29 October 1466.

other wise than his will was at his departyng".[74] She begged John Paston II to get a licence from the Archbishop to draw an allowance, "in discharging of my conscyens and yowres, to mynystre a certeyn summe of iij or iiij^{c} marc". John should tell the Archbishop how difficult his financial situation was without that money, the alternative being to ask for higher rents from his tenants: "enfourmyng hym how that your lyffelod hath stond this ij yere in such trobill that ye might right nought haue of it, ner yet can take of it wyth-ought ye should hurt your tenauntes".[75] The main motivation for this request was the Pastons' fear of losing their livelihood, their tenants having moved on, and of ultimately being forced to sell their estates.

Quite apart from her desire not to ask for higher rents from their tenants and risk losing them, Margaret Paston was worried that *chevisances* could harm her reputation, her worshipfulness. On 15 September 1469, John Paston II asked Margaret to send more money and to enter into another *chevisance* if necessary.[76] Margaret replied that she could raise only £10 by way of pledges: "And as fore myn own lyuelod, I am so sympple y payed therof that I fere me I xale be fayn to borrow fore myselfe ore ell to breke vp howshold, ore bothe".[77] A month later, she sent John Paston II the family silver. Margaret regretted that she had not done all that her late husband had requested in his will and considered the idea of another *chevisance* to solve her financial problems. On this occasion, however, she feared a scandal if it became known, perhaps because it would be following fast upon the breaking up of her household or perhaps because she had to borrow in order to carry out her husband's wishes. A solution might be to remove her tenant at Mautby, who was in arrears with his rent, and farm the land herself:

---

[74] John Mirk, *Instructions for Parish Priests*, ed. E. Peacock (London: Kegan Paul, Trench, Trubner & Co for EETS, 1902), 23.

[75] *Paston Letters*, vol. 1, 356–357, no. 210, Letter from Margaret Paston to John Paston II of 25 November 1466. The editor, Davis, originally gave the date as 1470, but this was later corrected (*Paston Letters*, vol. 3, xxviii).

[76] *Paston Letters*, vol. 1, 406, no. 243, Letter from John Paston II to Margaret Paston of 15 September 1469.

[77] *Paston Letters*, vol. 1, 346, no. 205, Letter from Margaret Paston to John Paston II of 22–30 September 1469.

> I haue right not beside my lyffelode that I may make any chevyssans wyth wyth-oute grete slaundere, and my lyffelode encreassith evill for I am fayn to takyn Mautby in myn own hand and to set vp husbandry ther … The fermour owyth me lxxx li. and more.[78]

The Pastons' legal battles over the manors they claimed had been left to them by Sir John Fastolf were expensive to them because they required a great deal of time and effort making representations in London. Giving bribes probably added to the costs. Meanwhile, the money had to be raised somehow. The solution of increasing the rents from their tenants carried the risk of losing them altogether, and the alternative of selling land was a practice they regarded as shameful, amounting to selling one's livelihood. Loss of livelihood here could have signified not just their economic means of making a living but also their social standing and identity. The Pastons' only option was to borrow; if there was nothing that could be given as a pledge for a loan, the Pastons were obliged to turn to the *chevisance*. The hidden interest in such arrangements could have been considerable. Fastolf had a great deal more wealth and apparently saw nothing unethical about investing money with John Wells for a return of 5 per cent, which would have been in conformity with the Roman law principle of *laesio enormis*. However, when the returns were extremely high, such as Bokkyng's attempt to profit from forestalling and engrossing corn in Essex or the Celys' arrangements with Kesten for repayment of their loan, such ventures would be harder to justify in the light of usury's moral prohibition. Perhaps the Celys and the Pastons all believed that one day they would make amends or some sort of formal restitution. In the meantime, they were occupied in making money and paid little attention to ethical considerations, precisely the kind of behaviour criticised and condemned by moralists. On the other hand, they were aware of how they should appear in the eyes of the world and chose to use the moralistic language of pastoral manuals and sermons when it suited their purposes. They had their own ethical system that weighed worshipfulness, reliability and financial probity against worldly shame, dishonour and waste.

[78] *Paston Letters*, vol. 1, 350 –351, no. 208, Letter from Margaret Paston to John Paston II of 28 October 1469. The editor, Davis, originally gave the date as 1470, but this was later corrected (*Paston Letters*, vol. 3, xxviii).

The impression from the writers of these letters is that the doctrines of the Church about avarice and the teachings about the virtues were only partially influential and selectively applied, until death approached.

Sir John Fastolf: Perceptions of Avarice and Its Worldly Justification

The following case study of Sir John Fastolf will demonstrate how his avaricious behaviour was perceived by his contemporaries and how he himself perceived a lack of ethics in others in terms similar to those drawn from moralistic commentaries on economic practice. It will also show how late in life he showed strong awareness of the need to make amends for his own offences, according to approved methods.

Whereas John Paston I was admired for his restraint and shrewdness, Sir John Fastolf was regarded by some of his contemporaries as overly concerned with money-making and as a relentless pursuer of debtors. A few years before Fastolf died, Henry Windsor, one of his servants, wrote to John Paston I: "Hit is not vnknoon that cruell and vengible he hath byn euer, and for the most part withoute pité and mercy". These words suggest that such behaviour had always been part of Fastolf's character and not necessarily attributable to old age and illness. There are records in the Fastolf papers at Magdalen College, Oxford, of Fastolf sueing his bailiffs for being in arrears with their dues and their being sent to prison and of his exacting a very heavy fine for trespassing.[79] For example, John Winter had been employed as Fastolf's agent in France for collection of debts there and Fastolf apparently believed there were some amounts outstanding. In 1447, Winter died, and according to William Worcester, Fastolf had sent to Winter's death-bed for the return of that money: "Sir John Fastolf demaunded m^{1} salux of goolde" that Winter owed him which he had originally received from John Gwyllim, who had been Fastolf's constable at Alençon in 1427, some twenty years earlier (a "salux" was a gold coin struck by Henry V and Henry VI for circulation in their

[79] *Paston Letters*, vol. 2, 145, no. 550, (Davis suggests a date of 1456); McFarlane, *Nobility of Later Medieval England*, 50.

French dominions).[80] However, Fastolf was not the only landowner to press for collection of outstanding rents: from 1440 onwards, the Duke of Buckingham adopted the practice of gaoling his officials if they went into arrears.[81]

Yet Fastolf himself might have been sensitive to perceptions that his primary interest was money and that he had an ungenerous nature. He wrote that he had been told of certain gentleman at a dinner in Norwich: "whiche vtteryd skornefull language of me … seyeng 'War the govnne, war, and goo we to dyner, goo we. Wheere? To Ser John Fastolffez, and there we shall well paye there-fore'". With some sort of retaliation in mind, he asked John Paston I to find out who those people were: "and wyth Goddez grace so purvey for hem as they shall not all be well pleasyd".[82] This probably shows that Fastolf's concern with his reputation was uppermost and that the ethical criticisms of miserliness were secondary.

One of the characteristics of misers was their poor treatment of servants. As we have seen in a number of pastoral manuals, those who withheld the wages of servants or hired workmen were guilty of theft or ravine.[83] William Worcester wrote to John Paston I that he felt Fastolf treated him unjustly: although John Paston I had been pleased to address Worcester as "master", he had not been treated as such by Fastolf, receiving a common household wage and an allowance of five shillings a year. When he raised this with Fastolf, Fastolf replied that he wished Worcester had been a priest so that his income could have been met by a benefice, and so it was that Worcester, not a priest, had to endure a life of poverty, as poor as a serf at the plough. Here, Worcester probably exaggerated in order to amuse John Paston I, and he was less sorry for himself than he was for others in the service of Fastolf: "Foryefe me. I wryte to make yow

[80] Oxford, Magdalen College, MS Southwark 168, Letter from William Worcester, quoted by K.B. McFarlane, "A Business Partnership in War and Administration, 1421–1445", *English Historical Review*, 78 (1963): 301.

[81] McFarlane, *Nobility*, 223.

[82] *Paston Letters*, vol. 2, 110, no. 514, 7 February 1455.

[83] See *A Middle English Treatise on the Ten Commandments*, 30; *Vices and Virtues*, 34–35; *Of Shrifte and Penance: The ME Prose Translation of 'Le Manuel Des Peches'*, ed. K. Bitterling (Heidelberg: Winter, 1998), 61; *Jacob's Well* (Salisbury), fol. 198r; *Handlyng Synne*, 87.

laugh. And Our Lord bring my maistre yn a better mode for othyrs as for me".[84] Yet if it was true that Worcester was unpaid or only partly paid, Fastolf did make some attempt at redress. Writing after Fastolf's death in 1460, Worcester claimed that Fastolf had promised him land.[85] We do not know whether Fastolf took steps to carry out this promise, so it may be simply a case of good intentions.

After Fastolf's death, Nicholas Bokkyng, who had acted as Fastolf's receiver, petitioned William Wayneflete, the Bishop of Winchester, with a long list of "the hurtes grevaunces and losses" he had suffered in the service of Fastolf in the years 1437–1439 and 1442–1443. The Bishop could have received many such claims upon Fastolf's estate, and there is no certainty that Bokkyng's were genuine. Apart from the forestalling losses which were mentioned earlier, Bokkyng, as a riding servant, was given an insufficient allowance for his costs. Fastolf had not taken into consideration the high price of corn, resulting in a loss for Bokkyng of 100 shillings. He had lost more (another 100 shillings?) on sales of wool and barley, a further 106 shillings and eight pence through a shortfall of an allowance for Fastolf's wife Lady Millicent, and 53 shilllings and four pence from a shortfall in the wages he had had to pay to two of Fastolf's servants. His son, John, had received no wages for three years, for which Nicholas Bokkyng asked restitution of 101 shillings and eight pence. Bokkyng had also given 13 shillings and four pence to a penniless French knight whom Fastolf had summoned to London and claimed he was owed 32 shillings from grain sales at Tithewell. He claimed another 52 shillings and three pence for his own lost wages. In 1444, Fastolf had promised to repay Bokking for all outstanding amounts:

> the said knyght promysed feithfully and up on his sawter at heylesdon wyllefully swore on the shrive Thursday whanne he shuld receive the blisseful sacrament that the said Bokkyng shuld have no wrong but in all manere of maters of his accompts that towched conscience he wulde be rewled by maistre John Wygenhale & maistre Richard Purlond.[86]

---

[84] *Paston Letters*, vol. 2, 101–102, no. 506, (Davis suggests a date of 1454).

[85] *Paston Letters*, vol. 2, 204–205, no. 604, Letter from William Worcester to John Paston I, 7 February 1460.

[86] Magdalen College, Fastolf Paper no. 98.

Wygenhale and Purlond might have been auditors, for by Good Friday the accounts were found to be £32 in arrears. Bokkyng was obliged to present himself to two auditors in London who took three weeks to determine that Bokkyng owed Fastolf money rather than the reverse, a sum of £31, which Bokkyng paid. In the meantime, Bokkyng had spent £5 on travel to London and staying there waiting for a verdict and he asked for restitution of this. Bokkyng also claimed for losses when Fastolf's coffers were broken into, a shortfall in the amercements collected by a bailiff—"the auditoris of the said knyght aftrewards of evill will surcharged the said Bokkyng"—and yet more travel expenses, a sum total of £72.[87] Bokkyng's claims painted a picture of a parsimonious master who was difficult to approach on the matter of reimbursements. They could also be regarded as substantiating the comments by William Worcester and Henry Windsor.

Fastolf himself had recourse to the language of the moral handbooks: lands he had legitimately purchased but had become subject to claims by others were a continuing problem. He suffered oppression, extortion and other grievances and the high costs of malicious lawsuits. He complained to his servant Thomas Howes about "the cruell amercymentes and dyuers oppressions don to me, to my tenauntes and to my catell distreyning how oft".[88] There were so many that, a few months later, he was complaining that not all of these injuries had been properly recorded: "And there as it hath ben by negligence of yow ther or of my servauntz here, moo of my greuances and extorcions don to me left out vnremembred".[89] Fastolf also sent to Thomas Howes "a rolle of the grete parte of costes in money leyd owt and payd here in London owt of myne coferys to lerned men and for councell, to diffend the malyciouse and fals processes pursued ageynst me thys x yere day".[90] The quotations show that Fastolf was ready to make use of moralistic language when describing the wrongdoings of others and their impact on his economic affairs.

[87] Magdalen College, Fastolf Paper no. 98.

[88] *Paston Letters*, vol. 3, 85, no. 981, Letter from Sir John Fastolf to Thomas Howes of 7 May 1450.

[89] *Paston Letters*, vol. 3, 87–88, no. 983, Letter from Sir John Fastolf to Thomas Howes of 8 August 1450.

[90] *Paston Letters*, vol. 3, 134, no. 1009: Letter from Sir John Fastolf to Thomas Howes of 24 June 1451.

These perceived injustices may relate to the long-standing antagonism between Fastolf and William de la Pole, the Duke of Suffolk. Richmond has shown that Fastolf suffered from the deviousness of Suffolk in a number of property transactions. In 1434, William de la Pole had sold the manor of Cotton and the estate of Wickham Skeith in Suffolk to Fastolf in order to solve his financial problems, but although Fastolf had paid him in full, the Duke claimed that Fastolf had defaulted and instructed his officials to make distraints. Meanwhile, Fastolf's revenues from Cotton suffered. Fastolf had also bought the estate of Dedham in Essex from the Duke, whose officers occupied both of its manors between 1447 and 1450, doing considerable damage, for which Fastolf was never compensated. Alice Chaucer, the Duchess of Suffolk, maintained her hold over Cotton after her husband's death. The Duke might have been reluctant to let go of Cotton since it was his birthplace, but he had had no previous right to the estates of Drayton and Hellesdon in Norfolk, which he wanted for their high rents, both estates having been improved by Fastolf with new buildings.[91] Clearly, Fastolf regarded such behaviour as dishonest and unethical. In December 1450, he wrote a letter concerning the alleged depredations of Thomas Tuddenham and John Heydon, part of the affinity of the late Duke of Suffolk, who were at that time being supported by Lord Scales: "Wherfor such persones as have founde hem soore greved by extorcion as I have ben". Fastolf called for "justice, reason and conscience" to be "egallie mynistred", fearing that eventually "the pore peple and all the grete part of both shyres of Norffolk and Suffolk be destroyed", declaring that through years of extortion they had been hardly able to maintain themselves, nor pay their rents and taxes, so affecting their landlords' finances.[92] Thus, Fastolf was able to use the ethical terms such as extortion, justice, reason and conscience and the suffering of the poor when it was in his interest to do so.

For Fastolf, good economic management had to underpin the maintenance of livelihood. In January 1451, he instructed his servants to "see that my lyfelode be not minussed by nedelese allouances or make

---

[91] Richmond, *The Paston Family in the Fifteenth Century: The First Phase*, 235–236, 237–238, 239.

[92] *Paston Letters*, vol. 3, 111–112, no. 996, Letter from Sir John Fastolf to Thomas Howes, 20 December 1450.

werkes were no nede ys". He understood the importance of husbanding his resources, for it was the foundation not only of his own livelihood but those of his employees: "At the reuerence of God, tendyr ye thys mater, for it ys the substaunce of my welfare, and of you all".[93] A letter of June 1451 shows that he distrusted his bailiffs and officials at his manors of Caister, Hellesdon, Drayton, Blickling, Saxthorp, "and all such othyre placys where as onye money ys growed and owing for rent, ferme corn, or for conyes wolle, or chatell and wodd and such commoditeez of a maner". He ordered Thomas Howes to receive such revenue directly, "quarterly and dayly as it ys ronne", allowing others to deliver it to him only if he were absent. Fastolf accused his officials of keeping his money for other purposes, such as "to marchaunt wyth my money, or ells pay it in peticions of jtemmys, to my grete damage and hurt, and a grete cause of the diminussying of my lyvelode".[94] "Merchanting", or speculating with money, as already discussed, was something that Fastolf engaged in himself. Fastolf's claim about damage and hurt reveals that potential financial losses were his main concern, not the morality of investing or lending for profit. The same applied to the "petitions of items", which were, presumably, paying for an assortment of expense claims which might or might not have been valid.

Fastolf wanted good standards among his employees and subordinates. For example, he wrote of one of his tenants at Caister: "I vndrestand he ys hald of good rule an gouuernaunce, and a lykly man to do service and stand yn steede at neede, it ys my wille that he contynew and ferme my place stille".[95] He wanted no vicious person either profiting himself or allowing Fastolf's lands and properties to deteriorate. He wrote to Thomas Howes that he had heard "oft tymes manye straunge rapports of demenyng of the gouuernaunce of my place at Castre, and othyr plasys", that his lands had not been improved, and that his wardrobe, wines

---

[93] *Paston Letters*, vol. 3, 124, no. 1005, Letter from Sir John Fastolf to Thomas Howes and John Berney of 28 January 1451.

[94] *Paston Letters*, vol. 3, 132, no. 1009, Letter from Sir John Fastolf to Thomas Howes of 24 June 1451.

[95] *Paston Letters*, vol. 3, 101, no. 990, Letter from Sir John Fastolf to Thomas Howes of 11 November 1450.

and chattels had not been properly managed.[96] Fastolf's increasing frailty prevented him from visiting his manors in Yorkshire, which "resulted in peculation and waste". Apparently, diligence was lacking in the management of these manors, unlike Castle Combe, which although similarly distant from East Anglia, was well governed.[97]

Fastolf is a good example of McFarlane's landowner of "harsh efficiency" in his efforts to recover debts. At the same time, he drew upon the moral language of the petitions, using terms such as "cruel amercements", "great damage and hurt", "extortion", "oppressions" and "viciousness" when describing actions against his interests. He did so to express his moral outrage, but he was also considering the damage of those actions to his own livelihood. It was also to preserve his livelihood that he placed such a high value on good governance.

Fastolf Makes Amends

Three years before Sir John Fastolf died, there was a real concern that he should make arrangements regarding his wealth that would assure him of God's love and a favourable hearing on Judgement Day. Hugh a Fenne, one of Fastolf's servants, wrote to John Paston I:

> Now ser, for Goddis sake … help to sette my maister in a worschepfull dyreccion of his maters to his honour, his profyte, and his hertis ease, the whuch so doon he shall haue the better leysour to dysspose hym-self godly and be-sette his londe and his goodys to the plesour of God and the wele of hos sowle, that all men may sey he deyeth a wyse man and worchepfull.[98]

Hugh a Fenne might not have agreed with Henry Windsor that Fastolf was "cruel and vengible", but he was evidently concerned that Fastolf should arrange his affairs for the benefit of his immortal soul, as indeed should anyone who was nearing death.

---

[96] *Paston Letters*, vol. 3, 86, no. 982, Letter from Sir John Fastolf to Thomas Howes, 27 May 1450.
[97] McFarlane, *Nobility*, 48.
[98] *Paston Letters*, vol. 2, 137, no. 543, 1 March 1456.

There is evidence that during his lifetime, Fastolf had put aside funds for almsgiving. William Worcester noted that John Paston I had recommended that Fastolf needed to have a full record of his income in order to see what could be allocated to household maintenance, legal costs, foreign charges and almsgiving, yet it was the case that household maintenance took up most of the expenses.[99] It seems that Fastolf was aware that he needed to do more to save his soul, for he had promised that his executors would make restitution for any wrongs he had committed. Nicholas Bokkyng's long list of claims for reimbursement has been detailed previously. Fastolf's written obligation, dated 12 January 1450, was cited in his petition, which stated that John Bokkyng was to be paid 500 marks and a reward of £100. Bokkyng was asked why he had not raised all of these matters with Fastolf while he was still alive, and Bokkyng's reply was that he feared Sir John, even though he had made a proclamation at St Paul's about making restitution for any wrongs. Bokkyng said he had received a "sharp & bitter ansuere" from Fastolf while he lay dying in London and the rebukes and the dread that he always had of him discouraged him from doing so.[100] So Bokkyng was now "trustyng in the piteable charite of his noble and discrete executours and also up on an article composed in the said knyghtis laste wille whiche willed that iniuries by hym doon to ony persone shuld be restored". The executors of that will were Sir William Yelverton, the Abbott of Langley, John Paston, Thomas Howes and William Worcester, but their promises had amounted to nothing.[101]

In August 1452, Sir John Fastolf drew up a deed of gift, attached to which was a document expressing his desire that "all manere dettys mesprisions extorcions or wrongis" which anyone could prove he had committed were to be compensated by his executors. He was, perhaps, regretting his treatment of his servants: they should "be rewardid as largely and more than I have devised in my wil and testament late made soo that they with gode governaunce may leve every man aftir his degre the bettyr all ther dayes", especially his "ridynge servauntys" which bring to mind

[99] *Paston Letters*, vol. 2, 170, no. 571, Letter from William Worcester to John Paston I of 20 April 1457.

[100] Magdalen College, Fastolf Paper no. 98.

[101] Magdalen College, Fastolf Paper no. 98.

William Worcester, Nicholas Bokkyng, Walter Shipdam and others, who had spent much time travelling back and forth between Fastolf's estates or to London on his behalf.[102] However, in this same deed of gift, Fastolf was anxious to protest his innocence. Although it was nearly seventeen years after the Duke of Bedford had died, Fastolf insisted that as one of the Duke of Bedford's executors, he had taken nothing from his estate without paying for it.[103] The deed of gift shows not only that Fastolf was abiding by the principles of economic ethics in his intention to make amends but also his great concern about his reputation.

In the June 1459 version of his will, Fastolf's great wish was to establish a college or Benedictine priory at Caister, and he made an arrangement for part of the revenues from his manors to go to his poor tenants after his debts had been paid. He wished his poor relatives to have his moveable goods, but only on the condition that those relatives were well behaved and well disposed towards him, which expressed the common notion of the deserving poor.[104] Yet when it came to any unjust land acquisitions, Fastolf was not prepared simply to return them to the rightful owner: if anyone had a genuine and proven claim to land that Fastolf had bought or that was in the hands of one of his feoffees, that person could buy it back "for a lesse prys than ony other straunge persone".[105] Letting the rightful inheritor have his or her land at a discount does not seem to be in the full spirit of making restitution and resembles the part-way efforts made by Ralph, Lord Cromwell, in his will.

At the same time, Fastolf was anxious that he might be subjected to fraudulent claims. Although he had left France and Normandy nineteen years earlier, Fastolf was worried that his seals and signets might still be in use in those towns and castles where he had been governor or that fraudulent and forged claims might be made on his estate. Those seals and signets had never been returned to him and might still be attached to charters and other kinds of documents, "forged and contrived with

[102] Colin Richmond, "Sir John Fastolf, the Duke of Suffolk and the Pastons", in *Rule, Redemption and Representations in Late Medieval England*, ed. Linda Clark (Woodbridge: Boydell, 2008), 74–77.

[103] Richmond, "Sir John Fastolf, the Duke of Suffolk and the Pastons", 74–77.

[104] Richmond, "Once Again: Fastolf's Will", 124.

[105] Richmond, "Once Again: Fastolf's Will", 124.

oute my knowlage or assent myght be so seled a yens al conscience and trouthe and right wysnesse".[106] Fastolf urged that no one should give any credence to such documents, recalling a slight of some years previously, in which the previously mentioned John Winter had kept a blank letter with Fastolf's seal and never returned it.[107] The issue of his reputation was important to Fastolf, even beyond the grave.

Towards the end of his will, Fastolf repeated the warnings of the pastoral manuals should his executors disobey his instructions regarding the disposal of his worldly goods: "And if it be so that any of myne executoures a tempte maliciously the contrarye in effect he fallith in the sentence of excomunicayon".[108] Finally, he believed that if they dealt with his goods "feythfully by here discrecioun and prudence polletyk" in the same year as his burial and followed his instructions concerning alms for the poor and "dedys of pitye", it would mean "the more hasty delyveraunce of my sowle fro the peynful flames of the Fyer of Purgatory … and so I require hem, as Wysdam, Justyce and conscience to doo for me as they wolde I shuld do for hem in lyk cas".[109] Thus, in the end, although Fastolf was less generous about returning lands to their rightful owners, he believed that his bequests to the poor and the founding of the college at Caister would benefit him in the afterlife. His deed of gift making provision for his underpaid servants was another part of his restitution process, but it is likely that he wished, more than anything else, to be remembered by the members of the college as their benefactor, which indicates his overriding concern with his reputation, this time after his death.

Conclusion

It cannot be said that any of the Pastons, Celys, Armburghs or Stonors were impious or that they were ignorant of the mass of literature about excess wealth and avarice or that they never heard any sermons on those subjects.

[106] Richmond, "Once Again: Fastolf's Will", 127.
[107] Richmond, "Once Again: Fastolf's Will", 127.
[108] Richmond, "Once Again: Fastolf's Will", 128.
[109] Richmond, "Once Again: Fastolf's Will", 129–130.

Even though self-interest might have been the underlying reason, Fastolf appealed to "justice", "reason" and "conscience" in his letter of 1450 about the depredations of Tuddenham and Heydon, and Margaret Paston told her son that his lavish spending, which was depleting her finances, would invoke the displeasure of God. A copy of *The Pricke of Conscience* was left to Agnes Paston by a burgess of Yarmouth in 1434 and this makes it likely that the book was read and known by her husband William or her son John Paston or other members of her family. Certainly, Margaret Paston remonstrated with her son about his lavish spending, saying that it was unpleasing to God, and this shows that she had absorbed this doctrine from some source, even if it was not that particular work.[110] An inventory of John Paston II's books shows a variety of literary, philosophical and devotional works, but unfortunately severe damage has prevented its full extent from being visible.[111] Judging by an inventory of 1448, Sir John Fastolf owned a number of books, among them French versions of Aristotle's *Nicomachean Ethics* and *Le Livre de Vices et Vertues* or *Somme le Roi.* Certainly, the former made some impression on Fastolf: William Worcester recalled him making a distinction between the pursuit of personal glory on the battlefield and a leader who considers the lives of his men, a matter discussed in Book III of the *Nicomachean Ethics.*[112] Fastolf might well also have been familiar with Book V of the *Nicomachean Ethics* and its consideration of fair value and the just price. He also owned a French translation of parts of John of Wales's *Breviloquium de virtutibus*, entitled *Livre des quatre vertus cardinaulx*. William Worcester translated into English, at Fastolf's request, a French version of Cicero's work on old age, *De Senectute*, and a translation from Latin of Cicero's *De amicitia.*[113] Fastolf might also have known Cicero's work on justice, *De officiis*, or known of it through Worcester, who had been educated at Oxford.

---

[110] M. Deanesly, "Vernacular Books in England in the Fourteenth and Fifteenth Centuries", *Modern Language Review*, 15 (1920): 353.

[111] *Paston Letters*, vol. 1, 516–518.

[112] R. Beadle, "Sir John Fastolf's French Books", in *Medieval Texts in Context*, ed. Graham D. Caie and Denis Renevey (Abingdon: Taylor & Francis, 2008), 97, 104, 105, 107.

[113] J. Hughes, "Stephen Scrope and the Circle of Sir John Fastolf: Moral and Intellectual Outlooks", in *Medieval Knighthood IV: Papers from the Strawberry Hill Conference 1990*, ed. Christopher Harper-Bill and Ruth Harvey (Woodbridge: Boydell, 1992), 131, 132.

Fastolf's stepson, Stephen Scrope, translated for him, from French into English, *The Dictes and Sayings of the Philosophers*, the popular compilation (translated by Anthony Woodville, Earl Rivers) cited in Chapter 3 for its content regarding wealth and avarice.[114]

Both the Pastons and Fastolf observed conventional pieties, but these did not always take precedence when involved in land disputes, financial speculation or paying bribes. It looks as though, at times, economic interests were placed in a compartment separate from that of religious beliefs or moral sensitivities. Margaret Paston's concern with keeping the family's estates for future heirs and so maintain the family's honour appears uppermost at times, as does Fastolf's desire for "profit and avail". Fastolf's aim in wealth-getting, with no heirs of his own body, is unclear apart from his wish to found a college, and his efforts to control expenditure and to oversee his accounts were, in part, in order to keep to his almsgiving obligations. So although he was eager to make a profit and pursue unpaid debts, rents and other monies, he followed the prescriptions of the Church regarding the sin of avarice. He may have drawn comfort from the advice that striving after excess wealth is only a venial sin provided that it is preceded by a love of God and almsgiving.[115] The complaints from his employees about their insufficient wages and allowances, however, were couched in the same terms as the petitions and the pastoral manuals, charging him with avarice.

Fastolf, the Pastons and the Celys had their own rationale for what they considered good behaviour: the maintenance of reputation or worshipfulness. The Pastons would have been construed by the Church as unethical in their behaviour towards their rivals. For ignoring the welfare of the hapless tenants who were caught in between the opposing land title claims, the Church would have judged them as guilty of oppressing the poor and of extortion by means of distraints. Furthermore, there is the matter of hidden usury: those who entered into *chevisances* as borrowers were deemed by the Church to be just as guilty as those who profited from them, but there is no evidence in the Paston letters that there was concern about mortal sin, only about security and Margaret Paston's fear of a scan-

[114] Hughes, "Stephen Scrope and the Circle of Sir John Fastolf", 134.
[115] *Jacob's Well* (Brandeis), 136–137.

dal should the purpose of one potential *chevisance*, to carry out the wishes in her late husband's will, become known. On the whole, *chevisances* were just another way of obtaining credit. Many merchants and landowners, apart from the Pastons, were obliged to use credit for many of their transactions, and a shortage of coin might have contributed to the need to turn to *chevisances*.[116] The Pastons' general attitude to *chevisances* seems almost casual when compared with the fury of theologians and preachers, as does Fastolf's loan to John Wells at interest and Nicholas Bokkyng's plan to profit from engrossing on Fastolf's behalf. Fastolf gave alms and it is assumed the Pastons did likewise; otherwise, it seems that the Church's appeal to conscience was largely ignored until nearing death and the fear of an approaching Judgement Day. The Pastons and Fastolf do not represent every one of their contemporaries, but there are indications that people of similar wealth and social standing, such as those in charge of the London Court of Orphans, also ignored the prohibition of usury.

The overall conclusion is that the moral language of sinfulness and evil, extortion and oppression was used in letters when correspondents were trying to persuade or to make a forceful point, as Margaret Paston's remonstrations with John Paston II or Fastolf's complaints about Tuddenham and Heydon attest. When it came to their own behaviour, the rationale applied was one which justified it in terms of profit or worshipfulness. The familiarity with the language of economic ethics indicates that if they had never read the relevant passages in pastoral manuals, they had been instructed by their chaplains or heard sermons about avarice, extortion and economic injustice. Simultaneously, the Pastons and the Celys were concerned with worshipfulness, maintaining their livelihood and sound finances, and Fastolf with good governance and profit and avail. All of these were values which could still be described as economic ethics but which applied strictly to the management of affairs in the secular world. Those values could and did override clerical teachings. Nevertheless, there is plenty of evidence that such people were familiar with the language of economic ethics and were able to draw upon it when it suited their secular interests.

---

[116] Pamela Nightingale, "Money and Credit in the Economy of Late Medieval England", in *Medieval Money Matters*, ed. Diana Wood (Oxford: Oxbow Books, 2004), 53; J.L. Bolton, *Money in the Medieval English Economy: 973-1489* (Manchester: Manchester University Press, 2012), 232–240.

8

Conclusion

A study of the history of economic thought shows a tendency for modern scholars to assume that economics reflect rationality rather than morality. In late medieval times, however, economic thought was subsumed to ethical thought and religious beliefs. In modern times, economic historians have followed the tendency to construct value-neutral spheres within the discipline of economics, despite early work that highlighted the importance of economic morality. Also, most social and economic historians have tended to overlook the fact that economic ethics had a wider application in late medieval England than urban trade. Although some commentators have extended their inquiry beyond the ethics of the marketplace, the sources they have consulted are limited and impressionistic.[1]

[1] McFarlane, *The Nobility of Later Medieval England*, Oxford: Clarendon Press, 1973; Fryde, *Peasants and Landlords in Later Medieval England*, Stroud: Sutton, 1996; Maddicott, "The English Peasantry and the Demands of the Crown, 1294–1341", in *Landlords, Peasants and Politics in Medieval England*, ed. T. H. Ashton, Cambridge: CUP, 1987, 285-359 and "Poems of Social Protest in Early Fourteenth-Century England" in *England in the Fourteenth Century: Proceedings of the 1985 Harlaxton Symposium*, ed. W. Mark Ormrod, Woodbridge: Boydell, 1986, 130–144.

J. Hole, *Economic Ethics in Late Medieval England, 1300–1500*,
Archival Insights into the Evolution of Economics,
DOI 10.1007/978-3-319-38860-1_8

A wider range of contemporary sources needed to be explored, together with a more detailed analysis of the economic ethics that landowners, kings and lords were supposed to practise. Broader applications of economic ethics were embedded in many learned treatises whose original sources were biblical, patristic and classical. Theological and philosophical writers considered the king, lords and gentry, and the officials of all of them, to be engaged in economic activities with ethical ramifications. From the observations made in these texts, there followed criticisms and exhortations to abhor avarice and abide by the ideals of justice and equity, moderation, liberality, charity and the common good. Ideals of balance and harmony were important concepts underpinning much thinking about the good order of society, accompanied by demands to make restitution for economic wrongs and to give alms. Regarding relationships between landowners and tenants, I found evidence that English theologians placed much importance on the ideals of good lordship, particularly the notion that lords and their agents should be virtuous and eschew self-enrichment by means of exploiting the poor.

Although it is important to recognise that medieval theologians saw economic inequality as divinely ordained, they believed that the lot of the poor should not be allowed to deteriorate to a level below subsistence. Disorder would result. To maintain order, all should be satisfied with the level of sufficiency appropriate to their status. Their self-interest should not be pursued to the detriment of others or of the common good.

The Church's teachings about avarice and theft and exhortations regarding the virtues of justice, charity and living in moderation appeared in a large number of normative texts: pastoral manuals, guides to conduct, books of wisdom (many of which were written for a lay readership), and sermons. The ideal of the body politic was frequently used both to justify social inequity and to press home the argument about living harmoniously. Whereas some works had a more learned approach, presenting the concepts of economic ethics in the form of a debate or argument, others employed analogies with which ordinary people could identify. Sermons were a way of delivering moral instructions to a wide audience, which included the unlettered. Extortion and oppression by lords and landowners featured prominently in manuals and sermons, just as frequently as did condemnations of usury and unjust pricing amongst merchants and traders. It is also apparent that particular types of vices or offences were associated with particular social groups or occupations, creating stereotypes that tended to simplify more complex economic realities and their associated ethical problems.

Literary works canvassed social and cultural concerns in imaginative ways. An important concern of these works was that avaricious rulers and their failure to punish avarice could cause severe social disruption and economic hardship. In texts of this kind, appeals were commonly made to the virtues of justice, liberality and living in moderation as remedies. These appeals were accompanied by a deep-rooted conservatism, in which writers looked back to a harmonious golden age when all were provided for or to a former age when knights observed the rules of chivalry and disdained the wealth that came from landowning. Economic injustices were listed among the reasons for the fall of kings. Some works in this vein were popular literature, copied and distributed widely to reach a far greater number of readers than their original royal or noble audience. Their inculcation of economic ethics was augmented by literary strategies: the characters in these works were powerful models or illustrations of good or bad behaviour, and the texts provided moral guidance for readers in their arguments and counter-arguments.

Moralising elements were embedded in regulations and petitions that were responses to economic injustice. The language used in petitions and statutes resembled that of the theologians and the pastoral manuals in its use of such terms as "covetousness", "selfish gain" and "extortion and oppression" to warrant redress or punishment. There were also similar appeals to justice, reason and conscience, the common weal, the love of God, and charity. Statutes were drawn up in a moral environment, and on most occasions the Parliamentary Rolls recorded an address to Parliament by the Chancellor who reminded legislators of their ethical responsibilities. There was ongoing concern about the behaviour of avaricious officials as well as merchants. The exactions of royal purveyors brought questions about the moderation of the king's household needs. Allegations of illegal purveying alluded to the questionable activities of powerful lords, along with general references to lords' abuses of the legal system. Although individuals were rarely named, the complaints demonstrated that the behaviour of lords was as much subject to criticism as that of merchants.

Manorial records showed rapacity amongst some landowners, especially those who felt their position accorded them special rights. A fair proportion of these more oppressive lords were ecclesiastics such as abbots, bishops and priors who were inclined to be coercive or enter into protracted disputes with their tenants. The higher clergy could be accused, and were, by Thomas Docking and later John Wyclif and his followers of failing to practise what they preached. Smaller landowners were more cautious and more ready to make compromises. A number of historians have asserted that relatively wealthy villeins were less affected by their lack of freedom and benefited from fixed rents and the custom of the manor. However, the majority were not so prosperous and subsisted rather than profited. It was the oppression of the poor that theologians, preachers and the authors of pastoral manuals were concerned with. Wills were a means for lords of the manor to make good before Judgement Day. Testators showed concern for some of their past actions, but their displays of conscience have to be regarded as formulaic.

Surviving correspondence of the powerful landowner Sir John Fastolf, of the Cely family of merchants, and of the Stonor, Armburgh and Paston families of landowners reveals more about personal attitudes. Although a landowner might commonly describe his opponents as "extortioners" and "oppressors" who brought hurt and damage to a community as well as to himself, or exhort a family member to live moderately, ethical concepts were also used to assess behaviour in specific instances. These could be characterised as adding the weight of morality to certain situations the writer found disturbing. Often, however, the ethics of people's own conduct were overridden by other considerations, such as worship, reputation and family status, or the need to preserve their livelihoods. It is also significant that these letters show that not only merchants but also the gentry engaged in usury and *chevisances* and did so as a matter of course.

In late medieval England, economic activity was a subject for moral reflection and self-regulation for all social groups. By the written propagation of economic ethics, in a variety of forms, individuals were reminded that their economic activities had an impact on the world around them. Theologians, authors of pastoral manuals and writers of literary works all expressed their views, not of "the economy", but of the "common good" or "common profit", notions which are not ethically neutral terms. They saw the "common good" as something that could be badly affected by actions as various as unfair trading, the charging of interest, deceitful land acquisitions, and over-spending by the crown. Without some connection to the "common profit", individual profit lacked an ethical justification and could be regarded as wrongfully selfish. In the literature of all kinds, the ethical aspect was primary. Despite this evidence, scholars have tended to regard morality as one among a number of factors considered by medieval legislators, which also included, for instance, the needs of the consumer and the effects of natural catastrophes or wars.[2] Such a conclusion, I think, understates the role of moral instruction in the period since the main authorised voice put less emphasis on the needs of the consumer than on the obligation of the wealthy to the poor and the general aim for a harmonious social order. The secular and the religious were not easily separable domains in late medieval England. Catastrophes were perceived as occurring within a moral domain and as the result of the sin of humankind. The provision of practical relief was regarded as a moral act, one of the seven works of mercy.

The appeals to virtue and to practical remedies for abuses found in the many texts that have been discussed in this book show that economic ethical instruction promoted positive values as well as criticisms of wrongdoing. Almsgiving, works of mercy and charitable bequests were recommended ways of addressing the imbalance between rich and poor. Another way of addressing imbalance was to make restitution for unjustly acquired wealth. In addition to such actions, churchmen wanted to reform community mentality. By warning of the risks of hell and purgatory for breaching the Commandment against theft or for committing avarice, the Church hoped to steer the faithful away from selfish gain and private profit. At the same time, the Church promoted the cardinal virtues. All in society were urged to adopt the virtue of moderation, so that the king and the wealthy classes would not waste their riches, while the

[2] Britnell, "Urban Economic Regulation and Economic Morality in Medieval England", in Britnell, *Markets, Trade and Economic Development in England and Europe, 1050–1350,* Farnham: Ashgate, 2009, 7 ; Davis, *MMM*, 136.

less prosperous would be satisfied with their own lot. The rulers of society were urged to administer justice, both in its classical sense of giving each his or her due and of doing the will of God, to ensure that economic grievances were dealt with. Such exhortations to positive virtue had particular relevance to the landowning classes.

The terms "common weal", "common good" or "common profit" are used in many documents, both theological and regulatory. To a large degree, they were used interchangeably and applied in the contexts of national or municipal government. When it came to the relations between a landowner and his tenants or between a great lord and those of his affinity, the notion of "good lordship" came into play. Here, the lord or landowner was not understood as acting for the general good of all but for the good of those in his particular sphere of influence. To some extent, this gave an additional dimension to the ethics of lordship, for a good lord, like the monarch, was expected to act impartially, distribute justice and charity, and provide protection for his subjects. These were the ideals expressed by William of Ockham and John Wyclif and were expectations echoed in petitions and advice literature.

To the Church, economic ethics were relevant to all sections of society, and the obligation to preserve the "common good" fell on all. It was only the honest working poor, living at or below subsistence level, who were not criticised for their greed by commentators. All others in society, from the ruling classes downward, were instructed to guard against their materialistic instincts and desire for greater wealth. Merchants, urban dealers and purveyors were by no means the only groups singled out as failing in this regard. From the numerous forms of moral commentary and social critique analysed in this book, it is apparent that local extortion and oppression by lords or their officials were understood to harm the poor as much as traders selling faulty merchandise, forestallers withholding grain to raise prices, or royal purveyors taking supplies without paying for them. Lords were seen as a more difficult problem: traders, forestallers and purveyors could be legislated against, with varying degrees of success, but the more powerful lords could not be so restrained, and neither could the king. Yet the king, at least, was expected to dispense justice and could be addressed in petitions to Parliament or to the king's Council. The great lords or magnates seemed to be out of reach, to be approached at one's peril, because of their ability to manipulate or evade judicial proceedings and harm the interests of those who tried to oppose them.

Medieval theologians and scholastic philosophers discussed the concepts of economic ethics that originated in the Bible or in classical thought. Their ideas about avarice, excess wealth, the just price and the just wage, usury, justice and lordship, and the ideal order for society were disseminated widely. The presence of these ideas in pastoral or confessional manuals, sermons, guides to conduct, books of wisdom and literary works is evidence that most of society, including the unlettered, encountered them in some form. It is as a consequence of their prevalence that the notions of economic ethics were employed in the wording of regulations, from the Statute of Forestallers (*c.* 1318) to the *Acte Agaynst Pullyng Doun of Tounes* (1489). Legislators were concerned to address hurts and damages to the people or to the common weal and to condemn individuals who were acting only for their own good. Ethical language, appealing to reason, conscience, charity and justice, was common in petitions concerning economic injustices. Such petitions also revealed the expectation that the king, chancellor or Parliament would act according to their consciences and administer justice.

I have perceived little change in the language and concepts of economic ethics in regulation in the period between 1300 and 1500. Marjorie McIntosh drew a similar conclusion from her extensive study of the control of misbehaviour in late medieval and Tudor England. Although she identified distinct phases of concerns over the longer period, regional variation in the types of offences prosecuted and some changes in language usage, there was "considerable consistency within any given period in how social wrongdoing was perceived and conceptualized".[3] McIntosh categorised the perception of offences either as concerns about social harmony or as concerns about public order.[4] These concerns are also implicit in economic ethics. McIntosh suggested that instruction in *The Lay-Folk's Mass Book*, John Mirk's *Festial* and *Jacob's Well*, and dramas such as *The Castle of Perseverance* (which portrayed backbiting and envy, scolding and

[3] Marjorie K. McIntosh, *Controlling Misbehaviour in England, 1370-1600*, Cambridge: CUP, 1998, 12.

[4] McIntosh, *Controlling Misbehaviour*, 9.

spreading malicious gossip as undermining social harmony) helped to shape how laypeople understood and responded to social misconduct.[5] My analysis of a wide range of sources has shown that economic ethics and moral concepts more generally were thoroughly embedded in laypeople's responses to economic behaviour.

The growth of commerce, the demands of labourers for higher wages after the Black Death, and the rapacity of landowners occasioned moral criticism. Other problems that had ethical implications were the growth of royal household spending, and the financing and supplying of military campaigns, both of which brought additional economic burdens to poorer people. The increase in the number of royal purveyors and other officials brought opportunities for inappropriate personal enrichment, compounded, perhaps, by their lack of remuneration.

Purveyors and officials could be controlled, perhaps not very effectively, but the great lords could oppress their tenants at will. Although the less powerful gentry might be named and prosecuted, the lords formed the power structure of late medieval England, equal to and sometimes superior to that of the king. Awareness of this reality formed the basis of late medieval concerns about the responsible exercise of lordship and associated principles of economic ethics.

Writers of moralising works such as *The Book of Vices and Virtues*, *The Fall of Princes* or *The Regiment of Princes* recognised the power of rulers to do good or ill. Instruction in the principles of economic ethics was an important part of the education of the ruling classes, as demonstrated by the frequency with which such works were commissioned by royalty or the nobility. The production of such texts indicates not only that their authors believed their writings had a moral purpose but also that their readers expected moral education.

Wills and letters provide indications that the more wealthy members of society accepted the principles and ideas of economic ethics. Wills show that many in lay society were concerned for their immortal soul and left money for the poor or for good works. Some made restitution for past wrongs. Almsgiving during one's lifetime was widespread.[6] Letters,

[5] McIntosh, *Controlling Misbehaviour*, 188–191.

[6] Dyer, *A Country Merchant, 1495-1520: Trading and Farming at the End of the Middle Ages, Oxford: OUP, 2012*, 208.

on the other hand, show that the ethical obligation to eschew personal gain if it damaged the poor, or the prohibition against earning interest on loans, was sometimes put aside, and values such as worship or reputation, honour and shame took precedence. Trust was also extremely important at a time when documentation of transactions was not routine.[7] All of these codes of behaviour had their ethical value to those in the merchant and gentry society of late medieval England, where risks, not only to personal standing but also to the position of the family, had very serious consequences.

Overall, economic ethics had a wider application than the ethics of the marketplace and were considered fundamental to the success of ideals such as harmony, social order and good government in late medieval England. The significance of these values and teachings has been overlooked or dismissed in recent times by historians, economists and political commentators. To understand and appreciate medieval economic ideas and practices more fully, we need to take account of their ethical dimensions.

[7] Dyer, *A Country Merchant*, 131.

Bibliography

Primary Sources

Manuscripts
Cambridge, Gonville and Caius College
    MS 334/727
London, British Library
    MS Harley 3120
Oxford, Balliol College
    MS 77
    MS 86
Oxford, Bodleian Library
    MS Bodley 453
    MS Hatton II
    MS Rawlinson A361
Oxford, Magdalen College
    Fastolf Papers
Oxford, Merton College
    MS 112
    MS 233

J. Hole, *Economic Ethics in Late Medieval England, 1300–1500*,
Archival Insights into the Evolution of Economics,
DOI 10.1007/978-3-319-38860-1

Southampton University Library
Salisbury Cathedral MS 103

Early Printed Editions

Aegidius Romanus, *De regimine principum.* Venice: Bernadino Guerralda, 1502.
Alexander Carpenter, *Destructorum viciorum.* Paris: P. Levet, 1497.
Johannes de Burgo, *Pupilla Oculi.* Argentoratum: Goetz, 1518.
John Bromyard, *Summa Praedicantium.* Venice: 1586.
John of Freiburg, *Summa Confessorum.* Paris: Jehan Petit, 1519.
Lyndwood, G., *Provinciale (Seu Constitutiones Angliae).* Oxford: excudebat H. Hall Academiae Typographus, Impensis Ric. Davis, 1679.
Robert Holcot, *Heptalogus.* Paris: Regnault Chaudiere, 1517.
——, *Moralitates.* Venice: Simon de Luere, 1514.
——, *Super libros sapientie.* Reutling, 1489.
Walter Burley, *Expositiones Per Decem Libros Ethicorum Aristotelis.* Venice: 1521.

Modern Printed Editions

Alexander of Hales, *Quaestiones Disputate 'Antequam Esset Frater'*, vol. 1, ed. C.S. Bonaventurae. Florence: Quaracchi, 1960.
An Anthology of Chancery English, ed. J.H. Fisher, M. Richardson and J.L. Fisher. Knoxville: University of Tennessee Press, 1984.
Aristotle, *The Nichomachean Ethics*, ed. D.P. Chase. London: J.M. Dent, 1930.
Aristotle, *The Politics and the Constitution of Athens*, ed. S. Iverson. Cambridge: CUP, 1996.
The Armburgh Papers, ed. C. Carpenter. Woodbridge: Boydell, 1998.
Bartholomew of Lucca, *On the Government of Rulers: De Regimine Principum of Ptolemy of Lucca with Parts Attributed to Thomas Aquinas*, ed. J.M. Blythe. Philadelphia: University of Pennsylvania Press, 1997.
The Book of Vices and Virtues, ed. W.N. Francis. London: OUP for the EETS, 1942.
Calendar of Letter-Books Preserved among the Archives of the Corporation of the City of London at the Guildhall, 11 vols, ed. R.R. Sharpe. London: Corporation of London, 1899–1912.

Calendar of Wills Proved and Enrolled in the London Court of Husting, A.D. 1258– 1688, 2 vols, ed. R.R. Sharpe. London: Corporation of the City of London, 1889–90.

The Cely Letters, 1472–1488, ed. A. Hanham. London: OUP for the EETS, 1975.

The Cely Papers: Selections from the Correspondence and Memoranda of the Cely Family, Merchants of the Staple, A.D. 1475–1488, ed. H.E. Malden. London: Longmans Green, 1900.

Christine De Pizan, *The Book of the Body Politic*, ed. K.L. Forhan. Cambridge: CUP, 1994.

Cicero the Philosopher: Twelve Papers, ed. J.G.F. Powell. Oxford: Clarendon Press, 1995.

Corpus Iuris Canonici, Pars Prior, Decretum Magistri Gratiani. Union, NJ: Lawbook Exchange Ltd, 2000.

Corpus Iuris Canonici, Pars Secunda, Decretalium Collectiones. Union, NJ: Lawbook Exchange Ltd, 2000.

Councils and Synods with Other Documents Relating to the English Church Courts, Vol. 2, A.D. 1205–1313, Part 1 1205–65, ed. F.M. Powicke and C.R. Cheney. Oxford: Clarendon Press, 1964.

Councils and Synods with Other Documents Relating to the English Church Courts, Vol. 2 A.D. 1205–1313, Part 2 1265–1313, ed. F.M. Powicke and C.R. Cheney. Oxford: Clarendon Press, 1964.

The Court Baron, ed. F.W. Maitland and W.P. Baildon. London: Bernard Quaritch for the Selden Society, 1891.

Court Roll of Chalgrave Manor 1278 – 1313, ed. Marian K. Dale. Streatley: Bedfordshire Historical Record Society, 1950 (vol.28).

Court Roll of the Manor of Downham 1310 – 1327, ed. M. Clare Coleman. Cambridge: Cambridgeshire Record Society, 1996.

Court Rolls of Elmley Castle, Worcestershire, 1347–1564, ed. Robert K. Field. Worcestershire Historical Society, 2004.

Court Rolls of the Manor of Hales, 1272 – 1307, ed. John Amphlett and Sidney Graves Hamilton. Oxford: Worcestershire Historical Society, 1910 – 12.

The Court Rolls of the Manor of Wakefield. Leeds: Yorkshire Archaeological Society

October 1331 to September 1333, ed. Sue Sheridan Walker. (1983).

October 1338 to September 1340, ed. Katherine M. Troup. (1999).

September 1348 to September 1350, ed. Helen M. Jewell. (1977).

October 1350 to September 1352, ed. Moira Habberjam, Mary O'Regan and Brian Hale. (1987).

October 1433 to September 1436, ed. C.M.Fraser. (2011).
19 October 1436 to 6 September 1437, ed. Brian J. Barber. (2014).

The Court Rolls of Walsham Le Willows 1351 – 1399, ed. Ray Lock. Woodbridge: Boydell Press, 2002 .

Cursor Mundi, ed. R. Morris, 3 vols. London: Kegan Paul, Trench, Trubner & Co for the EETS, 1893.

Dan Michel's Ayenbite of Inwyt, ed. P. Gradon, 2 vols. London: OUP for the EETS, 1979.

The Dictes and Sayings of the Philosophers, 1477, facs. Edn. London: Diploma Press, 1974.

The Distichs of Cato: A Famous Medieval Textbook, ed. W.J. Chase. Madison: University of Wisconsin, 1922.

Dives and Pauper, ed. P.H. Barnum, 3 vols. London: OUP for EETS, 1976.

The Domesday of Inclosures 1517–1518 Being the Returns to Chancery for Berks, Bucks, Cheshire, Essex, Leicestershire, Licolnshire, Northants, Oxon and Warwickshire by the Commissioners of Inclosures in 1517 and for Bedfordshire in 1518 together with Dugdales' Ms. Notes of the Warwickshire Inquisitions in 1517, 1518 and 1549, ed. I.S. Leadam, 2 vols. London: Longmans Green, 1897.

Duns Scotus, *Opera Omnia*, vol. 18. Paris: 1894.

Duns Scotus Vol. II: The Philosophical Writings, ed. C.R.S. Harris. Oxford: Clarendon Press, 1927.

Early Northampton Wills Preserved in Northamptonshire Record Office. Northamptonshire Record Society, 2005.

Eyre of Northamptonshire 1329–30, ed. D.W. Sutherland, 2 vols. London: Selden Society, 1983.

Fasciculus Morum: A Fourteenth-Century Preacher's Handbook, ed. S. Wenzel. University Park: Pennsylvania State University Press, 1989.

The Fifty Earliest English Wills in the Court of Probate, London A.D. 1387–1439 with a Priest's of 1454, ed. F.J. Furnivall. Oxford: OUP for the EETS, 1882, repr. 1964.

Sir John Fortescue, *De Laudibus Legum Angli*, ed. S.B. Chrimes. Cambridge: CUP, 1942.

Four English Political Tracts of the Later Middle Ages, ed. J.–P. Genet. London: Royal Historical Society, 1977.

The Governance of Kings and Princes: John Trevisa's Middle English Translation of the De Regimine Principum of Aegidius Romanus, ed. D.C. Fowler, C.F. Briggs and P.G. Remley. New York: Garland, 1997.

John Gower, *Confessio Amantis*, ed. R.A. Peck, 3 vols. Kalamazoo: Medieval Institute Publications, 2003–06.

____, *Mirour De L'omme (The Mirror of Mankind)*, ed. W.B. Wilson. East Lansing, MI: Colleagues Press, 1992.

____, *The Complete Works of John Gower, Vol. 1: The French Works*, ed. G.C. Macaulay. Oxford: Clarendon Press, 1899.

Henry de Bracton, *On the Laws and Customs of England*, vol. 2, ed. Samuel E. Thorne. Cambridge, MA: Belknap Press with the Selden Society, 1968.

Here May a Young Man See How He Should Speak Subtly in Court, ed. H.M. Briggs. London: Sweet & Maxwell, 1936.

Historical Poems of the XIVth and XVth Centuries, ed. Russell Hope Robbins. New York: Columbia University Press, 1959.

Hoccleve's Complete Works, Vol. 1: The Minor Poems, ed. Frederick J. Furnivall. London: Kegan Paul, Trench, Trubner for the EETS, 1892.

The Household of Edward IV: The Black Book and the Ordinance of 1478, ed. A.R. Myers. Manchester: Manchester University Press, 1959.

Jacob's Well: An English Treatise on the Cleansing of Man's Conscience, Part I, ed. A. Brandeis.London: Kegan Paul, Trench, Trubner & Co. for EETS, 1900.

John Mirk, *Instructions for Parish Priests*, ed. E. Peacock. London: Kegan Paul, Trench, Trubner & Co for EETS, 1902.

John Mirk's Festial, 2 vols, ed. S. Powell. Oxford: OUP for EETS, 2009–11.

John Rous, *Historia Regum Anglie*, ed. T. Hearne. Extracts translated and reprinted in *English Historical Documents, vol. 4 1327–1485.*

John of Salisbury, *Policraticus: Of the Frivolities of Courtiers and the Footprints of Philosophers*, ed. C.J. Nederman. Cambridge: CUP, 1990.

John Wyclif, *The English Works of Wyclif*, 2nd edn, ed. F.D. Matthew. London: Kegan Paul, Trench, Trubner & Co. for EETS, 1902.

____, 'On Civil Lordship (Selections)', in *The Cambridge Translations of Medieval Philosophical Texts: Vol. 2: Ethics and Political Philosophy*, ed. Arthur Stephen McGrade, John Kilcullen and Matthew Kempshall. Cambridge: CUP, 2001, 587–654.

____, *Select English Works*, ed. T. Arnold, 2 vols. Oxford: Clarendon Press, 1869.

____, *Tractatus De Civili Dominio: Liber Primus*, vol. 1, ed. R.L. Poole. London: Trubner & Co. for the Wyclif Society, 1885.

____, *Tractatus De Mandatis Divinis Accedit Tractatus De Statu Innocencie*, ed. J. Loserth and F.D. Matthew. London: C.K. Paul for the Wyclif Society, 1922.

The Lanterne of Light, ed. L.M. Swinburn. London: Kegan Paul, Trench, Trubner & Co. and Humphrey Milford, OUP for EETS, 1917.

A Late Fifteenth-Century Dominical Sermon Cycle, 2 vols, ed. S. Morrison. Oxford: OUP for EETS, 2012.

Le Livre De Catun, ed. T. Hunt. London: Anglo-Norman Text Society, 1994.
The Lay Folks' Catechism, ed. T.F. Simmons and H.E. Nolloth. London: Kegan Paul, Trench, Trubner for EETS, 1901.
Liber Albus: The White Book of the City of London, Compiled A.D. 1419 by John Carpenter, Common Clerk [and] Richard Whittington, Mayor, ed. T.H. Riley. London: Richard Griffin & Co., 1861.
Lollard Sermons, ed. G. Cigman. Oxford: OUP for the EETS, 1989.
Lydgate's Fall of Princes, ed. H. Bergen, 4 vols. London: OUP for EETS, 1924–27.
Magna Carta, ed. David Carpenter. London: Penguin, 2015.
Manorial Records of Cuxham, Oxfordshire, circa 1200 – 1359, ed. P.D.A. Harvey. London: HMSO, 1976.
Medieval Political Theory: A Reader: The Quest for the Body Politic 1100–1400, ed. C.J. Nederman and K.L. Forhan. London and New York: Routledge, 1993.
Middle English Sermons, ed. W.O. Ross. London: OUP for EETS, 1940.
Mirk's Festial: A Collection of Homilies by Joannes Mirkus (John Mirk), Part 1, ed. T. Erbe. London: Kegan Paul, Trench, Trubner & Co. for EETS, 1905.
The Mirror of Justices, ed. W.J. Whittaker. London: Bernard Quaritch for the Selden Society, 1895.
A Myrour to Lewde Men and Wymmen: A Prose Version of the Speculum Vitae, ed. V. Nelson. Heidelberg: Carl Winter Universitatsverlag, 1981.
North Country Wills, ed. J. W. Clay. Durham: Andrews & Son for the Surtees Society, 1908.
The Northern Homily Cycle: The Expanded Version in Mss Harley 4196 and Cotton Tiberius E VII, 3: from the Fifth to the Twenty-Fifth Sunday after Trinity, ed. S. Nevanlinna. Helsinki: Societe Neophilologique, 1984.
Of Shrifte and Penance: The ME Prose Translation of 'Le Manuel Des Peches', ed. K. Bitterling. Heidelberg: Winter, 1998.
Paston Letters and Papers of the Fifteenth Century, ed. Norman Davis, Richard Beadle and Colin Richmond, 3 vols. Oxford: OUP for EETS, 2005.
Peter Lombard, *Libri IV Sententiarum: Liber I et II*, 2nd edn. Florence: Collegii S. Bonaventurae, 1916.
The Piers Plowman Tradition, ed. H. Barr. London: J.M. Dent, 1993.
Plato, *Five Dialogues*, ed. A.D. Lindsay. London: Dent, 1910, reprinted 1938.
——, *Protagoras*, ed. Benjamin Jowett. Oxford: Clarendon Press, 1892.
——, *Republic*, ed. G.M.A. Grube, rev. C.D.C. Reeve. Indianapolis: Hackett Publishing, 1992.
Political Thought in Early Fourteenth-Century England: Treatises by Walter of Milemete, William of Pagula and William of Ockham, ed. C.J. Nederman.

Tempe: Arizona Center for Medieval and Renaissance Studies/ Brepols, 2002.

The Politics of Fifteenth-Century England: John Vale's Book, ed. M.L. Kekewich et al.. Stroud: Alan Sutton for Richard III & Yorkist History Trust, 1995.

The Pricke of Conscience: A Northumbrian Poem, ed. R. Morris. Berlin: A. Asher for the Philological Society, 1863.

Ranulph Higden, *Speculum Curatorum: A Mirror for Curates: Book I: The Commandments*, ed. E.J. Crook and M. Jennings. Leuven: Peeters, 2012 .

Records of the City of Norwich, vol. 1, ed. W. Hudson. Norwich: Jarrold & Sons, 1906.

Reginald Pecock, *The Donet*, ed. E.V. Hitchcock. London: OUP for EETS, 1921.

____, *The Folewer to the Donet*, ed. E.V. Hitchcock. London: OUP for EETS, 1924.

Richard Lavynham, *A Litil Tretys on the Seven Deadly Sins*, ed. J.P.W. Zutphen. Rome: Institutum Carmelitanum, 1956.

The Riverside Chaucer, ed. L.D. Benson, 3rd edn. Oxford: OUP, 2008.

Robert Mannyng, *Handlyng Synne*, ed. I. Sullens. Binghamton: State University of New York, 1983.

Robert of Brunne's 'Handlyng Synne', A.D. 1303, ed. F.J. Furnivall. London: Kegan Paul, Trench, Trubner & Co. for EETS, 1901.

Robert of Flamborough, *Liber Poenitentialis: A Critical Edition with Introduction and Notes*, ed. J.J. Francis Firth. Toronto: Pontifical Institute of Mediaeval Studies, 1971.

The Rous Roll, ed. C. Ross. Gloucester: Sutton, 1980.

Select Cases before the King's Council 1243–1482, ed. I.S. Leadam. Cambridge, MA: Harvard University Press for the Selden Society, 1918.

Select Cases before the King's Council in the Star Chamber A.D. 1477–1509, ed. I.S. Leadam. London: Bernard Quaritch for the Selden Society, 1903.

Select Cases in Chancery A.D. 1364 to 1471, ed. W.P. Baildon. London: Bernard Quaritch for the Selden Society, 1896.

Select Cases in the Court of King's Bench under Richard II, Henry IV and Henry V, ed. G.O. Sayles. London: Selden Society, 1971.

Select Pleas in Manorial and Other Seignorial Courts, Reigns of Henry III and Edward I, ed. F. W. Maitland. London: Bernard Quaritich for the Selden Society, 1899.

The Sermons of Thomas Brinton, Bishop of Rochester (1373–1389), 2 vols, ed. M.A. Devlin. London: Royal Historical Society, 1954.

Songs, Carols and Other Miscellaneous Poems from Richard Hill's Commonplace Book, ed. R. Dyboski. London: Kegan Paul, Trench, Trubner for EETS, 1907.
Speculum Christiani, ed. G. Holmstedt. London: Humphrey Milford, OUP for EETS, 1933.
Le Speculum Laicorum: Edition D'une Collection D'exempla Composee en Angleterre a la Fin du XIII[e] Siecle, ed. J.T. Welter. Paris: Auguste Picard, 1914.
Speculum Sacerdotale, ed. E.H. Weatherly. London: OUP for EETS, 1936.
Speculum Vitae: A Reading Edition, ed. R. Hanna, 2 vols. Oxford: OUP for EETS, 2008.
Statutes of the Realm: Printed by Command of His Majesty King George the Third. London: Dawsons, 1963.
The Stonor Letters and Papers, 1290–1483, ed. C.L. Kingsford, 2 vols. London: Royal Historical Society, 1919.
Testamenta Eboracensia or Wills Registered at York: Part 1: Year MCCC Downwards, ed. J. Raine. London: J.B. Nichols for the Surtees Society, 1836.
Testamenta Eboracensia: A Selection of Wills from the Registry at York: Part II, ed. J.Raine. Durham: George Andrews for the Surtees Society, 1855.
Testamenta Eboracensia: A Selection of Wills from the Registry at York: Part III, ed. J. Raine. Durham: Andrews & Co for the Surtees Society, 1865.
Testamenta Eboracensia: A Selection of Wills from the Registry at York, Part IV, ed. J. Raine. Durham: Andrews & Co for the Surtees Society, 1869.
Thomas Aquinas, *Commentary on the Nicomachean Ethics*, trans. C.I. Litzinger, vol. 1. Chicago: Henry Regnery, 1964.
——, *On Evil by Thomas Aquinas*, ed. B. Davies. Oxford: OUP, 2003.
——, *Summa Contra Gentiles, Book III, Providence, Part II*, ed. Vernon J. Bourke. London: University of Notre Dame Press, 1975.
——, *Summa Theologiae: Latin Text with English Translation.* London: The Blackfriars with Eyre and Spottiswoode, 1963.
Thomae De Chobham: Summa Confessorum, ed. F. Broomfield. Louvain: Editions Nauwelaerts, 1968.
Thomas De Chobham: Summa De Arte Praedicandi, ed. F. Morenzoni. Turnhout: Brepols, 1988.
Thomas De Chobham: Sermones, ed. F. Morenzoni. Turnhout: Brepols, 1993.
Thomas Hoccleve, *The Regiment of Princes*, ed. Charles R. Blyth. Kalamazoo: TEAMS/Medieval Institute Publications, 1999.
Two Wycliffite Texts: The Sermon of William Taylor 1406; the Testimony of William Thorpe 1407, ed. A. Hudson. Oxford: OUP for EETS, 1993.
Walter of Henley's Husbandry together with an Anonymous Husbandry, Seneschaucie and Robert Grosseteste's Rules, ed. E. Lamond. London: Longmans Green, 1890.

Walter Hilton, *Mixed Life: Walter Hilton*, ed. R. Dorward. Oxford: SLG Press, 2001.

Walter Hilton, *'Mixed Life' Edited from Lambeth Palace Ms 472, 92, no. 15*, ed. S.J. Ogilvie-Thomson. Salzburg: Institut fur Anglistik und Americanstik, Universitat Salzburg, 1986.

William Langland, *The Vision of Piers Plowman: A Critical Edition of the B-Text Based on Trinity College Cambridge MS B.15.17*, ed. A.V.C. Schmidt. London, J.M. Dent, 1995.

William of Ockham: A Letter to the Friars Minor and Other Writings, ed. A.S. McGrade and J. Kilcullen. Cambridge: CUP, 1995.

William of Ockham: A Short Discourse on Tyrannical Government over Things Divine and Human, ed. A.S. McGrade. Cambridge: CUP, 1992.

Wills from Doctors' Commons: A Selection of the Wills of Eminent Persons Proved in the Prerogative Court of Canterbury, 1495–1695, ed. J.G. Nichols and J. Bruce. London: Camden Society, 1863.

Wills of the Archdeaconry of Sudbury 1439–1474: Wills from the Register 'Baldwyne': Part I: 1439–1461, ed. P. Northeast. Woodbridge: Boydell, 2001.

Wills of the Archdeaconry of Sudbury 1439–1474: Wills from the Register 'Baldwyne' Part II: 1461–1474, ed. P. Northeast and H. Falvey. Woodbridge: Boydell, 2010.

Wimbledon's Sermon: Redde Racionem Villicationis Tue: A Middle English Sermon of the Fourteenth Century, ed. I.K. Knight. Pittsburgh: Duquesne University Press, 1967.

The Works of a Lollard Preacher, ed. A. Hudson. Oxford: OUP for EETS, 2001.

Wynnere and Wastoure, ed. S. Trigg. London: OUP for EETS, 1990.

York Civic Records, vol. 1, ed. Angelo Raine. Yorkshire Archaeological Society, 1939.

York Memorandum Book, Part I, ed. M. Sellers. Durham: Andrews & Co., for Surtees Society, 1912.

York Memorandum Book, Part II (1388–1493), ed. M. Sellers. Durham: Surtees Society, 1915.

Secondary Sources

Aers, David, "Piers Plowman and the Problems in the Perception of Poverty: A Culture in Transition", *Leeds Studies in English* 14(1983) 5–25.

——, "Justice and Wage-Labor after the Black Death: Some Perplexities for William Langland", in *The Work of Work: Servitude, Slavery and Labor in*

Medieval England, ed. Allen J. Frantzen and Douglas Moffat, 169–90. Glasgow: Cruithne Press, 1994.

——, *Faith, Ethics and Church: Writing in English, 1360–1409.* Cambridge: D.S. Brewer, 2000.

Akae, Y., "A Study of the Sermon Collection of John Waldeby, Austin Friar of York in the Fourteenth Century" (PhD thesis, University of Leeds, 2004).

——, "Between *Artes Praedicandi* and Actual Sermons: Robert of Basevorn's *Forma Praedicandi* and the Sermons of John Waldeby, Oesa", in *Constructing the Medieval Sermon*, ed. Roger Andersson, 9–32. Turnhout: Brepols, 2007.

Alexander, C., et al., *The Evolutionary Dynamics of the Credit Relationship between Henry III and Flemish Merchants, 1247–1270.* Reading: ICMA Centre, University of Reading, 2011 .

Amor, N.R., "Late Medieval Enclosure: A Study of Thorney, near Stowmarket, Suffolk", *Proceedings of the Suffolk Institute of Archaeology and History*, 41 (2006) 175–97.

Appleby, J.C., and P. Dalton (eds), *Government, Religion and Society in Northern England 1000–1700.* Stroud: Sutton, 1997.

Appleford, A. and N. Watson, "Merchant Religion in Fifteenth-Century London: The Writings of William Litchfield", *Chaucer Review* 46 (2011) 203–22.

Ashley, W.J., *An Introduction to English Economic History and Theory: Part 1: The Middle Ages: Book 1: From the Eleventh to the Fourteenth Century*, 4th edn. London: Longmans, Green & Co., 1925.

____, *An Introduction to English Economic History and Theory: Vol 1: Part 2: The End of the Middle Ages.* London: Longmans Green, 1925.

Bailey, M. "Villeinage in England: a Regional Case Study, c. 1250 –c.1349", *Economic History Review*, New Series, 62 (2009) 430–57.

Baker, J.H., "Famous English Canon Lawyers II: William Poul (or Paull) D.Cn. L. (+1332) Vicar of Winkfield, Berkshire", *Ecclesiastical Law Journal*, 1 (1989) 8–11.

____, *An Introduction to English Legal History.* London: Butterworths, 1990.

____, *Monuments of Endlesse Labours: English Canonists and Their Works, 1300–1900.* London: Hambledon Press with the Ecclesiastical Law Society, 1998.

Baldwin, J.F., "The King's Council and the Chancery, II", *American Historical Review* 15(1910).

____, *The King's Council in England during the Middle Ages.* Oxford: Clarendon Press, 1913.

Baldwin, J.W., "The Medieval Theories of the Just Price; Romanists, Canonists and Theologians in the Twelfth and Thirteenth Centuries", *Transactions of the American Philosophical Society* 49 (1959) 1–92.

____, *Masters, Princes and Merchants: The Social View of Peter the Chanter and His Circle*, 2 vols.. Princeton: Princeton University Press, 1970.

Barath, D., "The Just Price and the Costs of Production according to St Thomas Aquinas", *The New Scholasticism* 34 (1960) 413–30.

Barr, H., *Socioliterary Practice in Late Medieval England.* Oxford: OUP, 2001.

Barron, C.M., *London in the Later Middle Ages, Government and People, 1200–1500.* Oxford: OUP, 2004.

Beadle, R., "Sir John Fastolf's French Books", in *Medieval Texts in Context*, ed. Graham D. Caie and Denis Renevey, 96–112. Abingdon: Taylor & Francis, 2008.

Bean, J.M.W., *From Lord to Patron: Lordship in Late Medieval England.* Philadelphia: University of Pennsylvania Press, 1989.

Beer, M., *Early British Economics from the XIIIth to the Middle of the XVIIIth Century*. London: Allen & Unwin, 1938.

Beilby, M., "The Profits of Expertise: The Rise of the Civil Lawyers and Chancery Equity", in *Profit, Piety and the Professions in Later Medieval England*, ed. Michael Hicks, 72–90. Gloucester: Sutton, 1990.

Bejczy, I.P., "The Cardinal Virtues in Medieval Commentaries on the *Nicomachean Ethics*, 1250–1350", in *Virtue Ethics in the Middle Ages: Commentaries on Aristotle's Nicomachean Ethics, 1200–1500*, ed. Istvan P. Bejczy, 199–209. Leiden: Brill, 2008.

Bell, A.R., C. Brooks and T.K. Moore, "Interest in Medieval Accounts: Examples from England, 1272–1340", *History* 94 (2009) 411–33.

Benson, C.D., *Public Piers Plowman: Modern Scholarship and Late Medieval English Culture.* University Park: Pennsylvania State University Press, 2004.

Bestul, T., *Satire and Allegory in Wynnere and Wastoure.* Lincoln: University of Nebraska Press, 1974.

Biancalana, J., "Contractual Problems in the King's Court 1260–1360", *Cambridge Law Journal* 64 (2005) 212–42.

Biller, P. and A.J. Minnis (eds), *Handling Sin: Confession in the Middle Ages.* Woodbridge: York Medieval Press, 1998.

Birnie, A., *An Economic History of the British Isles*, 8th edn. London: Methuen, 1955.

Bisson, T.N., "Medieval Lordship", *Speculum* 70 (1995) 743–59.

Bitterling, K., "An Abstract of John Mirk's 'Instructions for Parish Priests'", *Notes and Queries* 24 (1977) 146–48.

Black, A., *Political Thought in Europe, 1250–1450*. Cambridge: CUP, 1992.
Bloomfield, F. et al., *Incipits of Latin Works on the Virtues and Vices, 1100–1500 A.D.* Cambridge, MA: Medieval Academy of America, 1979.
Bloomfield, M.W., *The Seven Deadly Sins: An Introduction to the History of a Religious Concept, with Special Reference to Medieval English Literature*. East Lansing: Michigan State University Press, 1952.
Bolton, J.L., *The Medieval English Economy 1150–1500*. London: J.M. Dent, 1980.
____, "London Merchants and the Borromei Bank in the 1430s: The Role of Local Credit Networks", in *The Fifteenth Century X: Parliament, Personalities and Power: Papers Presented to Linda S. Clark*, ed. Hannes Kleineke, 53–73. Woodbridge: Boydell, 2011.
____, *Money in the Medieval English Economy: 973–1489*. Manchester: Manchester University Press, 2012.
Borgstrom, E., "The Complaint of God to Sinful Man and the Answer of Man by William Litchfield", *Anglia* 34 (1911) 498–525.
Bossy, J., "A Social History of Confession", *Transactions of the Royal Historical Society* 25 (1975) 11–38.
Bowers, R.H., "A Middle English Mnemonic Poem on Usury", *Medieval Studies* 17 (1955) 226–32.
____, "From Rolls to Riches: King's Clerks and Moneylending in Thirteenth-Century England", *Speculum* 58 (1983) 60–71.
Boyle, L.E., "The *Oculis Sacerdotis* and Some Other Works of William of Pagula", *Transactions of the Royal Historical Society*, 5th Series, 5 (1955) 81–110.
____, "The *Summa Summarum* and Some Other English Works of Canon Law", in *Proceedings of the Second International Congress of Medieval Canon Law*, vol. 1, ed. S. Kuttner, 415–56. Rome: S. Congregatio de Seminariis et Studiorum Universitatibus e Civitate Vaticana, 1965.
____, "William of Pagula and the *Speculum Regis Edwardi III*", *Medieval Studies* 32 (1970) 329–36.
____, "The Summa for Confessors as a Genre, and Its Religious Intent", in *The Pursuit of Holiness in Late Medieval and Renaissance Religion: Papers from the University of Michigan Conference*, ed. Charles Trinkhaus and Heiko A. Oberman, 126–30. Leiden: Brill, 1974.
____, "The *Summa Confessorum* of John of Freiburg and the Popularization of the Moral Teaching of St. Thomas and Some of His Contemporaries", in *St. Thomas Aquinas, 1274–1974, Commemorative Studies*, ed. Armand A. Maurer, 245–68. Toronto: Pontifical Institute of Mediaeval Studies, 1974.

____, "The Fourth Lateran Council and Manuals of Popular Theology", in Thomas J. Heffernan (ed.), *The Popular Literature of Medieval England*, ed. Thomas J. Heffernan, 30–43. Knoxville: University of Tennessee Press, 1985.

Brand, P., "Inside the Courtroom: Lawyers, Litigants and Justices in England in the Later Middle Ages", in *The Moral World of the Law*, ed. Peter Coss, 91–112. Cambridge: CUP, 2000.

____, "Understanding Early Petitions: An Analysis of the Context of Petitions to Parliament in the Reign of Edward I", in *Medieval Petitions: Grace and Grievance*, ed. W. Mark Ormrod, Gwilym Dodd and Anthony Musson, 99–119. Woodbridge: York Medieval Press, 2009.

Breeze, A., "Sir John Paston, Lydgate, and the Libelle of Englyshe Polycye", *Notes and Queries* 48 (2001) 230–31.

Brewer, D., *Concordance to John Gower's Confessio Amantis.* Woodbridge: D.S. Brewer, 1987.

Brewer, T., *Memoir of the Life and Times of John Carpenter, Town Clerk of London.* London: Arthur Taylor, 1856.

Bridbury, A.R., *Historians and Open Society.* London: Routledge & Kegan Paul, 1972.

____, *The English Economy from Bede to the Reformation.* Woodbridge: Boydell, 1992.

____, *Medieval England: A Survey of Social and Economic Origins and Development.* Leicester: Matador, 2008.

Briggs, C., "Seignorial Control of Villagers' Litigation Beyond the Manor in Later Medieval England", *Historical Research* 81 (2008) 399–422.

____, *Credit and Village Society in Fourteenth-Century England.* Oxford: OUP, 2009.

Briggs, C. and Mark Koyoma, *Pledging and Credit Markets in Medieval England*, Cambridge: University of Cambridge, 2012 (CWPESH no. 5).

Britnell, R.H., "*Advantagium Mercartoris*: a Custom in Medieval English Trade", *Nottingham Medieval Studies* 24 (1980) 37–50.

____, "Minor Landlords in England and Medieval Agrarian Capitalism", *Past & Present* 89 (1980) 3–22.

____, "Agriculture in a Region of Ancient Enclosure, 1185–1500", *Nottingham Medieval Studies* 27 (1983) 37–55.

____, "Forstall, Forestalling and the Statute of Forestallers", *English Historical Review*102 (1987) 89–102.

____, "The Pastons and Their Norfolk", *Agricultural History Review* 36(1988) 132–44.

____, *The Commercialisation of English Society 1000–1500.* Cambridge: CUP, 1993.

____, "Morals, Law and Ale in Medieval England", in *Le Droit et sa Perception dans la Litterature et les Mentalites Medievales*, ed. U. Mueller, F. Hundsnurcher and C. Sommer, 21–29. Goppingen, 1993.

____, "Price-Setting in English Borough Markets, 1349–1500", *Canadian Journal of History* 31 (1996) 1–15.

____, "Local Trade, Remote Trade: Institutions, Information and Market Integration, 1050–1330", in *Fiere e Mercati nella Integrazione delle Economie Europee Secc. XIII–XVIII*, ed. Simonetta Cavaciocchi, 185–203. Florence: Istituto Internazionale di Storia Economica, 2001.

____, "Markets, Shops, Inns, Taverns and Private Houses in Medieval English Trade", in *Buyers and Sellers: Retail Circuits and Practices in Medieval and Early Modern Europe*, ed. Bruno Blonde, et al, 109–23. Turnhout: Brepols, 2006.

____, *Markets, Trade and Economic Development in England and Europe, 1050–1550.* Farnham: Ashgate Variorum, 2009.

Bruce, I., "A Study of the Medieval Handbook for the Parish Priest, with Particular Reference to the Regimen Animarum Found in Ms Hatton 11 in the Bodleian Library at Oxford". MA Thesis, Dalhousie University, 1973.

Brundage, J.A., "The Ethics of the Legal Profession: Medieval Canonists and Their Clients", *Jurist* 33 (1973) 237–48.

____, "Legal Aid for the Poor and the Professionalization of Law in the Middle Ages", *Journal of Legal History* 9 (1988) 169–79.

____, *Medieval Canon Law.* London: Longman, 1995.

Burgess, C., "'By Quick and by Dead': Wills and Pious Provision in Late Medieval England", *English Historical Review* 102 (1987) 837–58.

Burns, J.H., *Lordship, Kingship and Empire: The Idea of Monarchy, 1400–1525.* Oxford: Clarendon Press, 1992.

Butt, R., *A History of Parliament in the Middle Ages.* London: Constable, 1989.

Campbell, B.M.S., "The Agrarian Problem in the Early Fourteenth Century", *Past and Present,* 188 (2005), 3–70.

Campbell, B.M.S., James A. Galloway and Margaret Murphy. "Rural Land-use in the Metropolitan Hinterland: the Evidence of *Inquisitiones Post Mortem*", *Agricultural History Review,* 40 (1992) 1–22.

Caplan, H., *Mediaeval Artes Predicandi: A Hand-List*, Ithaca, NY: Cornell University Press, 1934 .

Carlin, M., "Cheating the Boss: Robert Carpenter's Embezzlement Instructions (1261 X 1268) and Employee Fraud in Medieval England", in , *Commercial*

Activity, Markets and Entrepreneurs in the Middle Ages: Essays in Honour of Richard Britnell, ed. Ben Dodds and Christian D. Liddy, 183–97. Woodbridge: Boydell, 2011.

Carpenter, C., "Law, Justice and Landowners in Late Medieval England", *Law and History Review* 1 (1983) 205–37.

____, "The Stonor Circle in the Fifteenth Century", in *Rulers and Ruled in Late Medieval England: Essays Presented to Gerald Harriss*, ed. Rowena E. Archer and Simon Walker, 175–200. London: Hambledon Press, 1995.

Carruthers, L.M., "The Liturgical Setting of Jacob's Well", *English Language Notes* 24 (1987) 11–24.

____, "Lorens of Orleans and the *Somme Le Roi* or the *Book of Vices and Virtues*", *Vox Benedictina: A Journal of Translations from Monastic Sources* 5 (1988) 190–200.

____, "Two Emendations to *Jacob's Well*", *Notes and Queries* 35 (1988) 437–39.

____, "Richard Lavynham and the Seven Deadly Sins in *Jacob's Well*", *Fifteenth Century Studies* 18 (1991) 17–32.

____, "'And What Schal Be [Th]Ende': An Edition of the Final Chapter of *Jacob's Well*", *Medium Aevum* 61 (1992) 289–97.

____, "'Know Thyself': Criticism, Reform and the Audience of *Jacob's Well*", in *Medieval Sermons and Society: Cloister, City, University*, ed. Jaqueline Hamesse, et al., 219–40. Louvain-La-Neuve: College Cardinal Mercier, 1998.

Carus-Wilson, E.M., "Evidence of Industrial Growth on Some Fifteenth-Century Manors", *Economic History Review*, New Series 12 (1959) 190–205.

Catto, J., "New Light on Thomas Docking, O.F.M.", *Medieval and Renaissance Studies* 6 (1968) 135–49.

Catto, J., and R. Evans (eds), *The History of the University of Oxford; Vol.1: The Early Oxford Schools*. Oxford: Clarendon Press, 1984.

____, *The History of the University of Oxford: Vol. 2: Late Medieval Oxford*. Oxford: OUP, 1992.

Charland, T.-M., *Artes Praedicandi: Contribution a l'histoire de la Rhetorique au Moyen Age*. Paris: J. Vrin, Libr. Philosophique, 1936.

Clark, E., "Debt Litigation in a Late Medieval English Vill", in *Pathways to Medieval Peasants*, ed. J.A. Raftis, 247–82. Toronto: 1981.

____, "Medieval Labor Law and the English Courts", *American Journal of Legal History*, 27 (1983) 330–53.

Clough, S.B., and C.W. Cole, *Economic History of Europe*, 3rd edn. Boston, MA: D.C. Heath, 1952.

Cobban, A.B., "Theology and Law in the Medieval Colleges of Oxford and Cambridge", *Bulletin of the John Rylands Library* 65 (1982) 57–77.

____, *English University Life in the Middle Ages.* Columbus: Ohio State University Press, 1999.
Coleman, D.C., and A.H. John (eds), *Trade, Government and Economy in Pre-Industrial England.* London: Weidenfeld & Nicolson, 1976.
Coleman, J., "Property and Poverty", in *The Cambridge History of Medieval Political Thought*, ed. J.H. Burns, 607–48. Cambridge: CUP, 1988.
____, "Lay Readers and Hard Latin: How Gower May Have Intended the *Confessio Amantis* to be Read", *Studies in the Age of Chaucer* 24 (2002) 209–35.
Coss, P. (ed.), *The Moral World of the Law.* Cambridge: CUP, 2000.
Courtenay, W.J., "The Effect of the Black Death on English Higher Education", *Speculum* 55 (1980) 696–714.
____, *Schools and Scholars in Fourteenth-Century England.* Princeton: Princeton University Press, 1987.
____, "Theology and Theologians from Ockham to Wyclif", in *Late Medieval Oxford*, ed. Jeremy Catto and Ralph Evans, 1–34. Oxford: OUP, 1992.
____, "Foreign Study in Time of War: English Scholars at Paris 1325–1345", *History of Universities* 14 (1998) 31–62.
Craun, E.D., *Ethics and Power in Medieval English Reformist Writing.* Cambridge: CUP, 2010.
Crofts, R.A., "The Common Good in the Political Theory of Thomas Aquinas", *The Thomist* 37 (1973) 155–73.
Crook, E.J., "A New Version of Ranulph Higden's *Speculum Curatorum*", *Manuscripta* 21 (1977) 41–49.
Crook, E.J. and M. Jennings, "Grading Sin: A Medieval English Benedictine in the *Cura Animarum*", *American Benedictine Review* 31 (1980) 335–45.
Crosby, R., "Oral Delivery in the Middle Ages", *Speculum* 11 (1936) 88–110.
Crosland, J., *Sir John Fastolfe: A Medieval 'Man of Property'.* London: Peter Owen, 1970.
Cullum, P.H., and P.J.P. Goldberg, "Charitable Provision in Late Medieval York: 'To the Praise of God and the Use of the Poor'", *Northern History* 29 (1993) 24–39.
Cunningham, W., *Christian Opinion on Usury with Special Reference to England.* London: Macmillan & Co., 1884.
____, "City Opinion on Banking in the Fourteenth, Fifteenth, Sixteenth and Seventeenth Centuries", *Journal of the Institute of Bankers* 8, Part 2, (1887) 55–72.

____, *The Growth of English Industry and Commerce during the Early and Middle Ages*, 5th edn, 1910. Reprinted New York: Augustus M. Kelley, 1968.

____, *The Progress of Capitalism in England.* Cambridge: CUP, 1916.

Das Neves, J.C., "Aquinas and Aristotle's Distinction on Wealth", *History of Political Economy* 32 (2000) 649–57.

Davies, R.G. and J.H. Denton (eds), *The English Parliament in the Middle Ages.* Manchester: Manchester University Press, 1981.

Davies, R.R., "Baronial Accounts, Incomes and Arrears in the Late Middle Ages", *Economic History Review* 21 (1968) 211–29.

____, *Lords and Lordship in the British Isles in the Late Middle Ages.* Oxford: OUP, 2009.

Davis, J., "Baking for the Common Good", *Economic History Review* 57 (2004) 465–502.

____, "Market Regulation in Fifteenth-Century England", in *Commercial Activity, Markets and Entrepreneurs in the Middle Ages: Essays in Honour of Richard Britnell*, ed. Ben Dodds and Christian D. Liddy, 81–105. Woodbridge: Boydell, 2011.

____, *Medieval Market Morality: Life, Law and Ethics in the English Marketplace, 1200–1500.* Cambridge: CUP, 2012.

Day, J., *The Medieval Market Economy.* Oxford: Basil Blackwell, 1987.

Dempsey, B.W., "Just Price in a Functional Economy", *American Economic Review* 25 (1935) 471–86.

Denholm-Young, N., *Seignorial Administration in England.* London: OUP, 1937.

De Roover, R., "The Concept of the Just Price Theory and Economic Policy", *Journal of Economic History* 18 (1958) 418–34.

____, *San Bernardino of Siena and Sant' Antonino of Florence: The Two Great Economic Thinkers of the Middle Ages.* Boston, MA: Baker Library, Harvard Graduate School of Business Administration, 1967.

____, *Business, Banking and Economic Thought in Late Medieval and Early Modern Europe.* Chicago: University of Chicago Press, 1974.

De Windt, A.A., "Peasant Power Structures in Fourteenth-Century King's Ripton", *Fordham Series in Medieval Studies* 38 (1976) 236–67.

Dijk, V., "Giving Each His Due: Langland, Gower and the Question of Equity", *Journal of English and Germanic Philology* 108 (2009) 310–35.

Dodd, G. "Conflict or Consensus: Henry IV and Parliament, 1399–1406", in *Social Attitudes and Political Structures in the Fifteenth Century*, ed. Tim Thornton, 118–49. Stroud: Sutton, 2000.

____, "The Hidden Presence: Parliament and Private Petition in the Fourteenth Century", in *Expectations of the Law in the Middle Ages*, ed. Anthony Musson, 135–50. Woodbridge: Boydell, 2001.

____, *Justice and Grace: Private Petitioning and the English Parliament in the Late Middle Ages.* Oxford: OUP, 2007.

____, "Thomas Paunfield, the 'heye Court of rightwisnesse' and the Language of Petitioning in the Fifteenth Century", in *Medieval Petitions: Grace and Grievance*, ed. W. Mark Ormrod, Gwilym Dodd and Anthony Musson, 222–41. Woodbridge: York Medieval Press, 2009.

____, "Writing Wrongs: The Drafting of Supplications to the Crown in Later Fourteenth-Century England", *Medieum Aevum* 80 (2011) 217–46.

Dodds, B., and C.D. Liddy (eds), *Commercial Activity, Markets and Entrepreneurs in the Middle Ages: Essays in Honour of Richard Britnell.* Woodbridge: Boydell, 2011.

Doe, N., *Fundamental Authority in Late Medieval English Law.* Cambridge: CUP, 1990.

Donahue, C., "*Ius Commune*, Canon Law and Common Law in England", *Tulane Law Review* 66 (1992).

Drew, K.F., *Magna Carta.* Westport, CT: Greenwood Press, 2004.

Duthie, D.W., *The Case of Sir John Fastolf and Other Historical Studies.* London: Smith, Elder, 1907.

Dyer, C., *Lords and Peasants in a Changing Society: the Estates of the Bishopric of Worcester, 680 – 1540* Cambridge: CUP, 1980.

____,"Memories of Freedom: Attitudes towards Serfdom in England, 1200–1350", in *Serfdom and Slavery: Studies in Legal Bondage*, ed. M.L. Bush, 277–95. London: Longman, 1996.

____, *Standards of Living in the Later Middle Ages: Social Change in England c. 1200–1520*, rev. edn. Cambridge: CUP, 1998.

____, *Everyday Life in Medieval England.* London: Hambledon & London, 2000.

____, *Making a Living in the Middle Ages: The People of Britain, 850–1520.* New Haven, CT: Yale University Press, 2002.

____, "Villeins, Bondsmen, Neifs and Serfs: New Serfdom in England, *c.* 1200–1600", in *Forms of Servitude in Northern and Central Europe: Decline, Resistance and Expansion*, ed. Paul Freedman and Monique Bourin, 419–35. Turnhout: Brepols, 2005.

____, "The Ineffectiveness of Lordship in England, 1200–1400", *Past & Present, Supplement* 2 (2007) 69–86.

____, "Did the Rich Really Help the Poor in Medieval England?", in *Ricos y Pobres: Opulencia y Desarraigo en el Occidente Medieval*, ed. Nicasio Salvador, 307–22. Pamplona: Gobierno de Navarra, 2010.

____, *A Country Merchant, 1495–1520: Trading and Farming at the End of the Middle Ages*. Oxford: OUP, 2012.

Dyson, P.W., *Normative Theories of Society and Government in Five Medieval Thinkers: St Augustine, John of Salisbury, Giles of Rome, St Thomas Aquinas and Marsilius of Padua*. Lewiston, NY: Edwin Mellen, 2003.

Echard, S. (ed.), *A Companion to Gower*. Woodbridge: D.S. Brewer, 2004.

Eiden, H., "Joint Action against 'Bad' Lordship: the Peasants' Revolt in Essex and Norfolk", *History* 83 (1998) 5–30.

Evans, G.R., *Fifty Key Medieval Thinkers*. London: Routledge, 2002.

Evans, G.R. (ed.), *The Medieval Theologians*. Oxford: Blackwell, 2001.

Faith, R., *The English Peasantry and the Growth of Lordship*. London: Leicester University Press, 1997.

Ferster, J., *Fictions of Advice: The Literature and Politics of Counsel in Late Medieval England*. Philadelphia: University of Pennsylvania Press, 1996.

Firth, J.J., "The 'Poenitentiale of Robert of Flamborough'", *Traditio* 16 (1960) 541–56.

Fitzgibbons, M., "*Jacob's Well* and Penitential Pedagogy", *Studies in the Age of Chaucer* 27 (2005) 213–37.

Fleming, P.W., "Charity, Faith and the Gentry of Kent 1422–1529", in *Property and Politics: Essays in Later Medieval English History*, ed. Tony Pollard, 36–58. Gloucester: Sutton, 1984 36–58.

Fletcher, A.J., "The Manuscripts of John Mirk's *Manuale Sacerdotis*", *Leeds Studies in English* 19 (1988) 105–39.

____, "'The Unity of the State Exists in the Agreement of Its Minds': A Fifteenth-Century Sermon on the Three Estates", *Leeds Studies in English* 22 (1991) 103–37.

____, "The Social Trinity of Piers Plowman", *Review of English Studies*, New Series 44 (1993) 343–61.

____, *Preaching, Politics and Piety in Late Medieval England*. Dublin: Four Courts Press, 1998.

Foot, R., "The Poverty of Francis of Assisi: Historical Actions and Mythologised Meanings", in *No Gods except Me: Orthodoxy and Religious Practice in Europe 1200–1600*, ed. Charles Zika, 37–58. Melbourne: History Dept., University of Melbourne, 1991.

Forde, S., "Nicholas Hereford's Ascension Day Sermon, 1382', *Medieval Studies* 51 (1989) 205–41.

Foss, D.B., "John Mirk's *Instructions for Parish Priests*", in *The Ministry: Clerical and Lay*, W.J. Sheils and Diana Wood, 131–40. Oxford: Blackwell for the Ecclesiastical History Society,1989.

Fox, H., "The Chronology of Enclosure and Economic Development in Medieval Devon", *Economic History Review* 28 (1975) 181–202.

Fox, H.S.A., "Exploitation of the Landless by Lords and Tenants in Early Medieval England", in *Medieval Society and the Manor Court*, ed. Z. Razi and R.M. Smith, 518–68. Oxford: Clarendon Press, 1996.

Friedman, D., "In Defence of Thomas Aquinas and the Just Price", *History of Political Economy* 12 (1980) 234–42.

Fryde, E.B., "The Deposits of Hugh Despenser the Younger with Italian Bankers", *Economic History Review* 3 (1951) 344–59.

____, "Loans to the English Crown, 1328–31", *English Historical Review* 70, (1955) 198–211.

____, *Some Business Transactions of York Merchants: John Goldbeter, William Acastre and Partners, 1336–1349.* York: St Anthony's Press, 1966.

____, *Studies in Medieval Trade and Finance.* London: Hambledon, 1983.

____, *Peasants and Landlords in Later Medieval England.* Stroud: Sutton, 1996.

____, "Economic Depression in England in the Second and Third Quarters of the Fifteenth Century: Effective Resistances of Tenants to Landlords as One of Its Consequences, Defiances and Rent Strikes", in *Violence in Medieval Society*, ed. Richard W. Kaeuper, 215–26. Woodbridge: Boydell, 2000.

Galloway, A., "The Economy of Need in Late Medieval English Literature", *Viator* 40 (2009) 309–31.

____, "Gower's 'Confessio Amantis', the 'Prick of Conscience' and the History of the Latin Gloss in Early English Literature", in *John Gower: Manuscripts, Readers, Contexts*, ed. Malte Urban, 39–70. Turnhout: Brepols, 2009.

Gay, E.S. and I.S. Leadam, "The Inquisitions of Depopulation in 1517 and the 'Domesday of Inclosures'", *Transactions of the Royal Historical Society*, New Series 14 (1900) 231–303.

Gibbins, H.D.B., *Industry in England: Historical Outlines*, 7th edn. London: Methuen & Co., 1912.

Gilchrist, J.T., *The Church and Economic Activity in the Middle Ages.* London: Macmillan, 1969.

Gillingham, J., "From *Civilitas* to Civility: Codes of Manners in Medieval and Early Modern England", *Transactions of the Royal Historical Society* 12, (2002) 267–89.

Given-Wilson, C., "Purveyance for the Royal Household, 1362–1413", *Bulletin of the Institute of Historical Research* 56 (1983) 145–63.

____, "Wealth and Credit, Public and Private: The Earls of Arundel 1306–1397", *English Historical Review* 106 (1991) 1–26.

____, "The Rolls of Parliament, 1399–1421", *Parliamentary History* 23 (2004) 57–72.

____, "The House of Lords, 1307–1529", in *A Short History of Parliament*, ed. Clyve Jones, 16–28. Woodbridge: Boydell, 2009.

Goddard, R., "Church Lords and English Urban Investment in the Later Middle Ages", *Past & Present Supplement*, 2 (2007) 148–65.

Goering, J., and F.A.C. Mantello, "*Notus in Iudea Deus*: Robert Grossteste's Confessional Formula in Lambeth Palace MS 499", *Viator* 18 (1987) 253–73.

Goering, J., and P.J. Payer, "The *Summa Penintente Fratrum Predicatorum*: A Thirteenth-Century Confessional Formulary", *Medieval Studies* 55 (1993) 1–50.

Goldberg, P.J.P., *Medieval England: A Social History 1250–1550*. London: Hodder Arnold, 2004.

Gorski, R., "Lordship, Gentility and Local Administration in Berkshire, 1350–1400", *Southern History* 22 (2000) 21–44.

____, *The Fourteenth-Century Sheriff: English Local Administration in the Late Middle Ages*. Woodbridge: Boydell, 2003.

Graus, F., "Social Utopias in the Middle Ages", *Past & Present* 38 (1967) 3–19.

Gregg, J. Y., "The Exempla of 'Jacob's Well': A Study in the Transmission of Medieval Sermon Stories", *Traditio* 33 (1977) 359–80.

Gwynn, A., *The English Austin Friars in the Time of Wyclif*. London: OUP, 1940.

Hamouda, O.F. and B.B. Price, "The Justice of the Just Price", *European Journal of the History of Economic Thought* 4 (1997) 191–216.

Hanham, A., *The Celys and Their World: An English Merchant Family in the Fifteenth Century*. Cambridge: CUP, 1985.

Harding, A., *The Law Courts of Medieval England*. London: Allen & Unwin, 1973.

Haren, M.J., "Social Ideas in the Pastoral Literature of Fourteenth-Century England", in *Religious Belief and Ecclesiastical Careers in Late Medieval England*, ed. Christopher Harper-Bill, 43–57. Woodbridge: Boydell, 1991.

____, "Confession, Social Ethics and Social Discipline in the *Memoriale Presbiterorum*", in *Handling Sin: Confession in the Middle Ages*, ed. Peter Biller and A.J. Minnis, 109–22. Woodbridge: York Medieval Press, 1998.

____, "The Interrogatories for Officials, Lawyers and Secular Estates of the *Memoriale Presbiterorum*", in *Handling Sin: Confession in the Middle Ages*, ed. Peter Biller and A.J. Minnis, 123–63. Woodbridge: York Medieval Press, 1998.

____, *Sin and Society in Fourteenth-Century England: A Study of the Memoriale Presbiterorum.* Oxford: Clarendon Press, 2000.

Harjunpaa, T., "Preaching in England During the Later Middle Ages", *Acta Academiae Aboensis, Series A: Humaniora* 29 (1965) 1–38.

Harper-Bill, C. (ed.), *Religious Belief and Ecclesiastical Careers in Late Medieval England.* Woodbridge: Boydell, 1991.

Harriss, G., "Cardinal Beaufort: Patriot or Usurer?", *Transactions of the Royal Historical Society*, 5th Series, 20 (1970) 129–48.

____, *King, Parliament, and Public Finance in Medieval England to 1369.* Oxford: Clarendon Press, 1975.

Hartung, A.E., "'The Parson's Tale' and Chaucer's Penance", in *Literature and Religion in the Later Middle Ages: Philological Studies in Honor of Siegfried Wenzel*, ed. Richard G. Newhauser and John A. Alford, 61–80. Binghamton, NY: 1995.

Haskett, T.S., "Country Lawyers? The Composers of English Chancery Bills", in *The Life of the Law: Proceedings of the Tenth British Legal History Conference, Oxford, 1991*, ed. P. Birks, 9–23. London: Hambledon Press, 1993.

____, "The Medieval Court of Chancery", *Law and History Review* 14 (1996) 245–313.

____, "Conscience, Justice and Authority in the Late-Medieval English Court of Chancery", in *Expectations of the Law in the Middle Ages*, ed. Anthony Musson, 151–63. Woodbridge: Boydell, 2001.

____, "Access to Grace: Bills, Justice and Governance in England, 1300–1500", in *Suppliques et Requetes: le Gouvernement par la Grace en Occident (XIIe–XVe Siecle)*, ed. Helene Millet, 297–317. Rome: Ecole Française de Rome, 2003.

Hatcher, J., "Non-Manorialism in Medieval Cornwall", *Agricultural History Review* 18 (1970) 1–16.

____,*Plague, Population and the English Economy 1348–1530.* London: Macmillan, 1977.

____, "English Serfdom and Villeinage: Towards a Reassessment", *Past & Present* 90 (1981) 3–39.

____, "Lordship and Villeinage before the Black Death: From Karl Marx to the Marxists and Back Again" in *Peasants and Lords in the Medieval English Economy; Essays in Honour of Bruce M.S. Campbell*, ed. Maryanne Kowaleski, John Langdon and Philipp R. Schofield, 113–45. Turnhout: Brepols, 2015.

Hatcher, J., and M. Bailey, *Modelling the Middle Ages: The History and Theory of England's Economic Development.* Oxford: OUP, 2001.

Heath, P., "Urban Piety in the Later Middle Ages: The Evidence of Hull Wills", in *The Church, Politics and Patronage in the Fifteenth Century*, ed. R.B. Dobson, 209–34. Gloucester: Sutton, 1984.

Heaton, H., *Economic History of Europe*, rev. edn. New York: Harper & Brothers, 1948.

Helmholz, R.H., "Usury and the Medieval English Church Courts", *Speculum* 61 (1986) 364–80.

____, *The Spirit of Classical Canon Law.* Athens: University of Georgia Press, 1996.

____, "Magna Carta and the *Ius Commune*", *University of Chicago Law Review*, 66 (1999) 297–371.

____, *The Ius Commune in England: Four Studies.* Oxford: OUP, 2001.

____, "The Law of Charity in the English Ecclesiastical Courts", in *The Foundations of Medieval English Ecclesiastical History*, ed. Philippa Hoskin, Christopher Brooke and Barrie Dobson, 111–23. Woodbridge: Boydell, 2005.

Hicks, M., "Restraint, Mediation and Private Justice: George, Duke of Clarence, as 'Good Lord'", *Journal of Legal History* 4 (1983) 56–71.

____, *Bastard Feudalism.* London: Longmans, 1995.

Hicks, M. (ed.), *Profit, Piety and the Professions in Later Medieval England.* Gloucester: Sutton, 1990.

Hilton, R.H., "Peasant Movements in England before 1381", *Economic History Review,* New Series 2 (1949) 117–136.

____, "A Study in the Pre-history of English Enclosure in the Fifteenth Century" in his *The English Peasantry in the Later Middle Ages the Ford Lectures for 1973 and Related Studies,* 161–73. Oxford: Clarendon Press, 1975.

Hodgson, P., "Ignorancia Sacerdotum: A Fifteenth-Century Discourse on the Lambeth Constitutions", *Review of English Studies* 24 (1948) 1–11.

Horner, P., "Preachers at Paul's Cross: Religion, Society and Politics in Late Medieval England", in *Medieval Sermons and Society: Cloister, City, University*, ed. Jaqueline Hamesse, et al., 261–82. Louvain-La-Neuve: College Cardinal Mercier, 1998.

Hughes, J., *Pastors and Visionaries: Religion and Secular Life in Late Medieval Yorkshire.* Woodbridge: Boydell, 1988.

____, "The Administration of Confession in the Diocese of York in the Fourteenth Century", in *Studies in Clergy and Ministry in Medieval England: Purvis Seminar Studies,* ed. David M. Smith, 87–163. York: University of York, Borthwick Institute of Historical Research, 1991.

____, "Stephen Scrope and the Circle of Sir John Fastolf: Moral and Intellectual Outlooks", in *Medieval Knighthood IV: Papers from the Strawberry Hill Conference 1990*, ed. Christopher Harper-Bill and Ruth Harvey, 109–47. Woodbridge: Boydell, 1992.

____, "The Moral and Spiritual Life of William of Nassington, a Fourteenth-Century Ecclesiastical Lawyer", *Medieval Yorkshire* 26 (1997) 11– 35.

____, "Educating the Aristocracy in Late Medieval England", *History Today* 49 (1999) 26–34.

Hyams, P.R., *Kings, Lords and Peasants in Medieval England: The Common Law of Villeinage in the Twelfth and Thirteenth Centuries.* Oxford: Clarendon Press, 1980.

Imray, J., *The Charity of Richard Whittington: A History of the Trust Administered by the Mercers' Company, 1424–1966.* London: University of London/Athlone Press, 1968.

Jacob, E.F., "Reginald Pecock, Bishop of Chichester", in *Essays in Later Medieval History*, ed. E.F. Jacob, 1–34. Manchester: Manchester University Press, 1968.

James, M.K., "A London Merchant of the Fourteenth Century", *Economic History Review* 8 (1956) 356–76.

Jarrett, B., *Social Theories of the Middle Ages, 1200–1500.* London: Frank Cass, 1968.

Jefferies, P.J., "Profitable Fourteenth-Century Legal Practice and Landed Investment: the Case of Judge Stonor *c.* 1281–1354", *Southern History* 15 (1993) 18–35.

Jennings, M., "Monks and the *Artes Praedicandi* in the Time of Ranulph Higden", *Revue Benedictine* 86 (1976) 119–28.

____, "Higden's Minor Writings and the Fourteenth Century Church", *Proceedings of the Leeds Philosophical and Literary Society, Historical Section*, 16 (1977) 149–58.

Jewell, H.M., "The Cultural Interests and Achievements of the Secular Personnel of the Local Administration", in *Profession, Vocation and Culture in Later Medieval England: Essays Dedicated to the Memory of A.R. Myers*, ed. Cecil H. Clough, 130–54. Liverpool: Liverpool University Press, 1982.

____, "Women at the Courts of the Manor of Wakefield", *Northern History* 26 (1990) 59–81.

Johnson, H.J., "Just Price; Aquinas and the Labor Theory of Value", in *The Medieval Tradition of Natural Law*, ed. Harold J. Johnson, 75–86. Kalamazoo: Western Michigan University, 1987.

Jussi, H., *'And the Rich Man Also Died; and He Was Buried in Hell': The Social Ethos in Mendicant Sermons.* Helsinki: Suomen Historica Seura, 1997.

Kadish, A., *Historians, Economists and Economic History.* London: Routledge, 1989.

Kaeuper, R.W., "Law and Order in Fourteenth-Century England: the Evidence of Special Commissions of Oyer and Terminer", *Speculum* 54 (1979) 734–84.

Kaye, J., *Economy and Nature in the Fourteenth Century: Money, Market Exchange and the Emergence of Scientific Thought.* Cambridge: CUP, 1998.

____, 'Monetary and Market Consciousness in Thirteenth and Fourteenth Century Europe', in *Ancient and Medieval Economic Ideas and Concepts of Social Justice*, ed. S. Todd Lowry and Barry Gordon, 371–403. Leiden: Brill, 1998.

____, *A History of Balance, 1250–1375: The Emergence of a New Model of Equilibrium and its Impact on Thought.* Cambridge: CUP, 2014.

Keen, M., *England in the Later Middle Ages: A Political History*, 2nd edn. London: Routledge, 2003.

Kehnel, A., "The Narrative Tradition of the Medieval Franciscan Friars of the British Isles", *Franciscan Studies* 63 (2005) 461–531.

Keller, J.R., "The Triumph of Vice: A Formal Approach to the Medieval Complaint against the Times", *Annuale Mediaevale* 10 (1969) 120– 37.

Kemmler, F., *'Exempla' in Context: A Historical and Critical Study of Robert Mannyng of Brunne's 'Handlyng Synne'.* Tubingen: Gunter Narr Verlag, 1984.

Kempshall, M.S., *The Common Good in Late Medieval Political Thought: Moral Goodness and Material Benefit.* Oxford: Clarendon Press, 1999.

Kendall, E., *Lordship and Literature: John Gower and the Politics of the Great Household.* Oxford: OUP, 2008.

Ker, N., "Liber Custumarum and Other Manuscripts Formerly at the Guildhall", *The Guildhall Miscellany* 3 (1954) 37–45.

Kermode, J., "The Merchants of Three Northern English Towns", in *Profession, Vocation and Culture in Later Medieval England: Essays Dedicated to the Memory of A.R. Myers*, ed. Cecil H. Clough, 7–50. Liverpool: Liverpool University Press, 1982.

____, "Money and Credit in the Fifteenth Century: Some Lessons from Yorkshire", *Business History Review* 65 (1991) 475–501.

____, "Medieval Indebtedness: The Regions Versus London", in *England in the Fifteenth Century: Proceedings of the 1992 Harlaxton Symposium*, ed. Nicholas Rogers, 72–88. Stamford: Paul Watkins, 1994.

____, *Medieval Merchants: York, Beverley and Hull in the Later Middle Ages.* Cambridge: CUP, 1998.

Kerridge, E., "The Returns of the Inquisitions of Depopulation", *English Historical Review* 70 (1955) 212–28.

Keys, M., *Aquinas, Aristotle and the Promise of the Common Good.* Cambridge: CUP, 2006.

Klinck, D.R., *Conscience, Equity and the Court of Chancery in Early Modern England*. Farnham: Ashgate, 2010.

Kuttner, S., "Pierre De Roissy and Robert of Flamborough", *Traditio* 2 (1944) 492–99.

Ladd, R.A., "The Mercantile (Mis) Reader in the Canterbury Tales", *Studies in Philology* 99 (2002) 17–32.

Langholm, O., *Price and Value in the Aristotelian Tradition: A Study in Scholastic Economic Sources*. Bergen: Universitetsforlaget, 1979.

____, *Wealth and Money in the Aristotelian Tradition: A Study in Scholastic Economic Source*. Bergen: Universitetsforlaget, 1983.

____, *Economics in the Medieval Schools: Wealth, Exchange, Value, Money and Usury According to the Paris Theological Tradition 1200–1350*. Leiden: Brill, 1992.

____, "The Medieval Schoolmen (1200–1400)", in *Ancient and Medieval Economic Ideas and Concepts of Social Justice*, ed. S. Todd Lowry and Barry Gordon, 439–501. Leiden: Brill, 1998.

____, *The Merchant in the Confessional: Trade and Price in the Pre-Reformation Penitential Handbooks*. Leiden: Brill, 2003.

____, "Monopoly and Market Irregularities in Medieval Economic Thought: Traditions and Texts to A.D. 1500", *Journal of the History of Economic Thought* 28 (2006) 395–411.

____, "The German Tradition in Late Medieval Value Theory", *The European Journal of the History of Economic Thought* 15 (2008) 555–70.

Larson, P.L., *Conflict and Compromise in the Late Medieval Countryside: Lords and Peasants in Durham, 1349–1400*. New York: Routledge, 2006.

Le Bras, G., "Conceptions of Economy and Society", in *The Cambridge Economic History of Europe Vol. 3: Economic Organizations and Policies in the Middle Ages*, ed. M.M. Postan, E.E. Rich and Edward Miller, 554–75. Cambridge: CUP, 1963.

Le Goff, J., "The Usurer and Purgatory", in *The Dawn of Modern Banking*, ed. Center for Medieval and Renaissance Studies, University of California, 25–52. New Haven: Yale University Press, 1979.

____, *Your Money or Your Life: Economy and Religion in the Middle Ages*. New York: Zone Books, 1988.

____, *Money and the Middle Ages*. Cambridge: Polity, 2012.

Leader, D.R., "Philosophy at Oxford and Cambridge in the Fifteenth Century", *History of Universities* 4 (1984/5) 25–46.

Leech, D., "'By the Evidence of This City': Enclosing Land and Memory in Fifteenth-Century Coventry", *Medieval History Journal* 15 (2012) 171–96.

Lio, H., *Determinatio 'Superflui' in Doctrina Alexandri Halensis eiusque Scholae*. Rome: Pontificium Athenaeum Antonianum, 1953.
Lipson, E., *The Economic History of England: I: The Middle Ages*, 5th edn. London: A. & C. Black, 1929.
Little, A.G., "The Franciscan School at Oxford in the Thirteenth Century", *Archivum Fransicanum Historicum* 19 (1926) 803–74.
____, *Franciscan Papers, Lists and Documents*. Manchester: Manchester University Press, 1943.
Little, L.K., "Pride Goes before Avarice: Social Change and the Vices in Latin Christendom", *American Historical Review* 76 (1971) 16–49.
____, *Religious Poverty and the Profit Economy in Medieval Europe*. London: Paul Elek, 1978.
Maddern, P., "Honour among the Pastons: Gender and Integrity in Fifteenth-Century English Provincial Society", *Journal of Medieval History* 14 (1988) 357–71.
____, "Social Mobility", in *A Social History of England, 1200–1500*, ed. Rosemary Horrox and W. Mark Ormrod, 113–33. Cambridge: CUP, 2006.
Maddicott, J.R., *Law and Lordship: Royal Justices as Retainers in Thirteenth- and Fourteenth-Century England*. Oxford: Past and Present Society, 1978.
____, "Magna Carta and the Local Community 1215–1259", *Past & Present*, no. 102 (1984) 25–65.
____, "Poems of Social Protest in Early Fourteenth-Century England", in *England in the Fourteenth Century: Proceedings of the 1985 Harlaxton Symposium*, ed. W. Mark Ormrod, 130–44. Woodbridge: Boydell, 1986.
____, "The English Peasantry and the Demands of the Crown, 1294–1341", in *Landlords, Peasants and Politics in Medieval England*, ed. T.H. Ashton, 285–359. Cambridge: CUP, 1987.
____, *The Origins of the English Parliament 924–1327*. Oxford: OUP, 2010.
Mair, O., "Merchants and Mercantile Culture in Later Medieval Italian and English Literature" PhD thesis, University of Western Australia, 2005.
Maitland, F.W., "Canon Law in England", *English Historical Review* 11 (1896) 241–65.
Maloney, R.P., "The Teaching of the Fathers on Usury: an Historical Study on the Development of Christian Thinking", *Vigiliae Christianae* 27(1973) 241–65.
Marrone, S.P., "Medieval Philosophy in Context", in *The Cambridge Companion to Medieval Philosophy*, ed. A.S.McGrade, 10–50. Cambridge: CUP, 2003.
Martin, C., "Walter Burley", in *Oxford Studies Presented to Daniel Callus*, ed. Oxford Historical Society, 194–230. Oxford: Clarendon Press, 1964.

Masschaele, J., "The Renaissance Depression Debate: The View from England", *History Teacher* 27 (1994) 405–16.

____, *Peasants, Merchants and Markets: Inland Trade in Medieval England 1150–1350*. New York: St Martin's Press, 1997.

____, "The Public Space of the Marketplace", *Speculum* 77 (2002) 383–421.

____, 'Tolls and Trade in Medieval England', in *Money, Markets and Trade in Late Medieval Europe: Essays in Honour of John H.A. Munro*, ed. Lawrin Armstrong, Ivana Elbl and Martin Elbl, 147–83. Leiden: Brill, 2007.

Mate, M., "High Prices in Early Fourteenth-Century England", *Economic History Review*, New Series 28 (1975) 1–16.

Matthews, G.B., "Augustinianism", in *Cambridge History of Medieval Philosophy*, ed. Robert Posnau, 86–98. Cambridge: CUP, 2010.

McFarlane, K.B., "Loans to the Lancastrian Kings: The Problem of Inducement", *Cambridge Historical Journal* 9 (1947) 51–68.

____, "The Investment of Sir John Fastolf's Profits of War", *Transactions of the Royal Historical Society*, 5th Series (1957) 91–116.

____, "A Business Partnership in War and Administration, 1421–1445", *English Historical Review* 78 (1963) 290–310.

____, *The Nobility of Later Medieval England*. Oxford: Clarendon Press, 1973.

____, *England in the Fifteenth Century: Collected Essays*, ed. G.L. Harriss. London: Continuum, 1981.

McIntosh, M. K., "The Privileged Villeins of the English Ancient Demesne", *Viator* 7 (1976) 295–328.

____, *Controlling Misbehaviour in England, 1370–1600*, Cambridge: CUP, 1998.

McLaughlin, T.P., "The Teachings of the Canonists on Usury [Part I]", *Medieval Studies* 1 (1939) 81–147.

Meredith, H.O., *Outlines of the Economic History of England: A Study in Social Development*. London: Pitman, 1933.

Mertes, K., "Aristocracy", in *Fifteenth-Century Attitudes: Perceptions of Society in Late Medieval England*, ed. Rosemary Horrox, 42–60. Cambridge: CUP, 1994.

Mews, C.J. and I. Abraham, "Usury and Just Compensation: Religious and Financial Ethics in Historical Perspective", *Journal of Business Ethics* 72 (2007) 1–15.

Milgate, M., "Paris, Robert, Thomas and the 'Heinous Sin' of Usury", *Australian Journal of Legal History* 5 (1999) 243–74.

____, *Canon Law, Civil Law and Usury – Complimentary, Competing or Just Oxymoron Terms*. Sydney: Macquarie University Dept of Business, 2000.

Miller, E., "The Economic Policies of Governments", in *The Cambridge Economic History of Europe, Vol. 3: Economic Organizations and Policies in the Middle Ages*, ed. M.M. Postan, E.E. Rich and Edward Miller, 281–339. Cambridge: CUP, 1963.

Miller, E., and J. Hatcher, *Medieval England: Rural Society and Economic Change 1086–1348*. London: Longman, 1978.

____, *Medieval England: Towns, Commerce and Crafts 1086–1348*. London: Longman, 1995.

Milner, F., *Economic Evolution in England*. London: Macmillan, 1931.

Minnis, A. and I. Johnson (eds), *The Cambridge History of Literary Criticism, Vol. 2: The Middle Ages*. Cambridge: CUP, 2005.

Mitchell, J.A., "Gower's *Confessio Amantis*, Natural Morality, and Vernacular Ethics", in *John Gower: Manuscripts, Readers, Contexts*, ed. Malte Urban, 135–53. Turnhout: Brepols, 2009.

Mohl, R., *The Three Estates in Medieval and Renaissance Literature*. New York: Frederick Ungar, 1933.

Moore, Tony K., "Credit Finance in the Middle Ages", Economic History Society Conference Paper, 2009.

Morrin, M.J., *John Waldeby, O.S.A. c. 1315–c. 1372: English Augustinian Preacher and Writer with a Critical Edition of his Tract on the 'Ave Maria'*. Rome: Analecta Augustiniana, 1975.

Muessig, C., "Audience and Preacher: *Ad Status* Sermons and Social Classification", in *Preacher, Sermon and Audience in the Middle Ages*, ed. C. Muessig, 225–76. Leiden: Brill, 2002.

Muldrew, C., *The Economy of Obligation: The Culture of Credit and Social Relations in Early Modern England*. Basingstoke: Macmillan, 1998.

Muller, M., "A Divided Class? Peasants and Peasant Communities in Later Medieval England", *Past & Present Supplement* 2 (2007) 115–31.

Myers, A.R., "Parliamentary Petitions in the Fifteenth Century", *English Historical Review* 52 (1937) 385–404; 590–613.

____, *Crown, Household and Parliament in Fifteenth-Century England*, ed. Cecil H. Clough. London: Hambledon, 1985.

Nederman, C.J., "Property and Protest: Political Theory and Subjective Rights in Fourteenth-Century England", *Review of Politics* 58 (1996) 323–44.

____, "The Monarch and the Marketplace: Economic Policy and Royal Finance in William of Pagula's *Speculum Regis Edward III*", *History of Political Economy* 33 (2001) 51–69.

Nelson, B.N., "Religion: The Usurer and the Merchant Prince: Italian Businessmen and the Ecclesiastical Law of Restitution, 1100–1550", *Journal of Economic History* 7 (1947) 104–22.

Nelson, V., "Cot. Tiberius E.VII: A Manuscript of the *Speculum Vitae*", *English Studies* 59 (1978) 97–113.

Newhauser, R. (ed.), "The Love of Money as Deadly Sin and Deadly Disease", in *Zusammenhange, Einflusse, Wirkungen: Kongressakten Zum Ersten Symposium Des Medievistenverbandes, 1984.* Tubingen: Walter de Gruyter, 1986.

Newhauser, R., *The Early History of Greed: The Sin of Avarice in Early Medieval Thought and Literature.* Cambridge: CUP, 2000.

____, "The Parson's Tale and Its Generic Affiliations", in *Closure in the Canterbury Tales: The Role of the Parson's Tale*, ed. David Raybin and Linda Tarte Holley, 45–76. Kalamazoo: Medieval Institute Publications, 2000.

____, "Historicity and Complaint in *Song of the Husbandman*", in *Studies in the Harley Manuscript: The Scribes, Contexts and Social Contexts of British Library Ms Harley 2253*, ed. Susanna Fein, 203–17. Kalamazoo: Medieval Institute Publications, 2000.

____, "A Middle English Poem on the Fleeting Nature of Material Wealth", *Medium Aevum* 71 (2002) 74–81.

____, "Justice and Liberality: Opposition to Avarice in the Twelfth Century", in *Virtue and Ethics in the Twelfth Century*, ed. Istvan P. Bejczy and Richard G. Newhauser, 295–315. Leiden: Brill, 2005.

____, "Preaching the 'Contrary Virtues' ", *Medieval Studies* 70 (2008) 135–62.

Newhauser, R., and S.J. Ridyard (eds), *Sin in Medieval and Early Modern Literature.* Woodbridge: York Medieval Press, 2012.

Nichols, J.G., "Two Sermons Preached by the Boy Bishop", *Camden Miscellany*, 7 1875, 1–13.

Nicholson, P., *Love & Ethics in Gower's Confessio Amantis.* Ann Arbor: University of Michigan Press, 2005.

Nightingale, P., "Monetary Contraction and Mercantile Credit in Later Medieval England", *Economic History Review*, 2nd series, 63 (1990) 560– 75.

____, "Knights and Merchants: Trade, Politics and the Gentry in Late Medieval England", *Past & Present* 169 (2000) 36–62.

____, "The English Parochial Clergy as Investors and Creditors in the First Half of the Fourteenth Century", in *Credit and Debt in Medieval England c. 1180–c. 1350*, ed. P.R. Schofield and N.J. Mayhew, 89–105. Oxford: Oxbow Books, 2002.

____, "Money and Credit in the Economy of Late Medieval England", in *Medieval Money Matters*, ed. Diana Wood, 51–71. Oxford: Oxbow Books, 2004.

____, "The Intervention of the Crown and the Effectiveness of the Sheriff in the Execution of Judicial Writs *c.* 1355–1530", *English Historical Review* 123 (2008) 1–34.

Noble, E., *The World of the Stonors.* Woodbridge: Boydell, 2009.

Nolan, M., *John Lydgate and the Making of Public Culture.* Cambridge: CUP, 2005.

Noonan, J.T., *The Scholastic Analysis of Usury.* Cambridge, MA: Harvard University Press, 1957.

O'Brien, G.A.T., *An Essay on Medieval Economic Teaching.* New York: Burt Franklin, 1920.

Ormrod, W.M., "The Crown and the English Economy, 1290–1348", in *Before the Black Death: Studies in the 'Crisis' of the Early Fourteenth Century*, ed. Bruce M.S. Campbell, 149–83. Manchester: Manchester University Press, 1991.

Ormrod, W.M., G. Dodd, and A. Musson (eds), *Medieval Petitions: Grace and Grievance.* Woodbridge: York Medieval Press, 2009.

Oross, D.E., "John Bromyard, Medieval Sermon Encyclopedist" PhD Thesis, St Louis, 1971.

Oschinsky, D., *Walter of Henley and Other Treatises on Estate Management and Accounting.* Oxford: Clarendon Press, 1971.

Owen, D.M., "Ecclesiastical Jurisdiction in England 1300–1500: The Records and Their Interpretation", *Studies in Church History* 11 (1975) 199–221.

____, *The Medieval Canon Law: Teaching, Literature and Transmission.* Cambridge: CUP, 1990.

Owen, J.R., "The Moral Economy of Saint Thomas Aquinas: Agent, Sovereignty, Customary Law and Market Convention", *The European Legacy* 12 (2007) 39–54.

Owen, Nancy H., "Thomas Wimbledon's Sermon: *Redde Racionem Villicacionis Tue*", *Medieval Studies* 28 (1966) 176–97.

Owst, G.R., *Preaching in Medieval England.* Cambridge: CUP, 1926.

____, *Literature and Pulpit in Medieval England: A Neglected Chapter in the History of English Letters & of the English People.* Cambridge: CUP, 1933.

____, *The 'Destructorium Viciorum' of Alexander Carpenter: A Fifteenth-Century Sequel to Literature and Pulpit in Medieval England.* London: S.P.C.K., 1952.

Palmer, R.C., *English Law in the Age of the Black Death, 1348–1381: A Transformation of Governance and Law.* Chapel Hill: University of North Carolina Press, 1993.

Pantin, W.A., *The English Church in the Fourteenth Century.* Cambridge: CUP, 1955.

Parker, D., "The Importance of the Commonplace Book, London, 1450–1550", *Manuscripta* 40 (1996) 29–48.

Payer, P.J., "The Origins and Development of the Later *Canones Penitentiales*", *Medieval Studies* 61 (1999) 81–105.

Payling, S.J., "Inheritance and Local Politics in the Later Middle Ages: The Case of Ralph, Lord Cromwell, and the Heriz Inheritance", *Nottingham Medieval Studies*, 1986, 67–95.

____, "A Disputed Mortgage: Ralph, Lord Cromwell, Sir John Gra and the Manor of Multom Hall", in *Rulers and Ruled in Late Medieval England: Essays Presented to Gerald Harriss*, ed. Rowena E. Archer and Simon Walker. London: Hambledon, 1995, 117–36.

Pearsall, D., *John Lydgate.* London: Routledge & Kegan Paul, 1970.

Peck, R.A., *Kingship and Common Profit in Gower's 'Confessio Amantis'.* Carbondale and Edwardsville: Southern Illinois University Press, 1978.

Peterson, I.J., *William of Nassington: Canon, Mystic, and Poet of the Speculum Vitae.* New York: Peter Lang, 1986.

Plucknett, T.F.T., *The Medieval Bailiff.* London: Athlone Press, 1954.

Pollard, A.J., "Estate Management in the Later Middle Ages: The Talbots and Whitchurch, 1383–1525", *Economic History Review*, New Series 25 (1972) 553–66.

Pollock, F., and F.W. Maitland, *The History of English Law before the Time of Edward I*, 2 vols, 2nd edn. London: CUP, 1898.

Postan, M., "Credit in Medieval Trade", *Economic History Review* 1 (1928) 234–61.

____, "Private Financial Instruments in Medieval England", *Vierteljahrschrift fur Sozial-Und Wirtschaftgeschichte* 23 (1930) 26–75.

____, *The Medieval Economy and Society: An Economic History of Britain in the Middle Ages.* London: Weidenfeld and Nicolson, 1972.

Potts, T.C., *Conscience in Medieval Philosophy.* Cambridge: CUP, 1980.

Prestwich, M., *War, Politics and Finance under Edward I.* Totowa, NJ: Rowan & Littlefield, 1972.

____, "Italian Merchants in Late Thirteenth and Early Fourteenth Century England", in *The Dawn of Modern Banking*, ed. University of California Center for Medieval and Renaissance Studies, Los Angeles, 77–104. New Haven: Yale University Press, 1979.

Price, L.L., *A Short History of English Commerce and Industry*, 2nd edn. London: Edward Arnold, 1904.

Raftis, J.A. *Warboys: Two Hundred Years in the Life of a Medieval English Village.* Toronto: Pontifical Institute of Medieval Studies, 1974.

____, "Social Structures in Five East Midlands Villages: a Study of the Possibilities in the Use of Court Roll Data", *Economic History Review*, 2nd series (18) 1965 83–100.

Rawcliffe, C., "The Great Lord as Peacekeeper: Arbitration by English Noblemen and Their Councils in the Later Middle Ages", in *Law and Social Change in British History*, ed. J.A. Guy and H.G. Beale, 34–54. London: Royal Historical Society, 1984.

Razi, Z., *Life, Marriage and Death in a Medieval Parish: Economy, Society and Demography in Halesowen 1270–1400*. Cambridge: CUP, 1980.

____, "The Struggles between the Abbots of Halesowen and their Tenants in the Thirteenth and Fourteenth Centuries" in Social Relations and Ideas: Essays in Honour of R.H. Hilton, ed. T.H. Aston et al, 151–67. Cambridge: CUP, 1983.

Renshaw, A., "The Authoritative Conscience: The Function and Significance of the Conscience in Three Religious Manuals for the Layman", in *Authority and Community in the Middle Ages*, ed. Ian P. Wei, Donald Mowbray and Rhiannon Purdie, 139–52. Stroud: Sutton, 1999.

Richmond, C., *John Hopton: A Fifteenth Century Suffolk Gentleman.* Cambridge: CUP, 1981.

____, *The Paston Family in the 15th Century: The First Phase.* Cambridge: CUP, 1990.

____, "Landlord and Tenant: The Paston Evidence", in *Enterprise and Individuals in Fifteenth-Century England*, ed. Jennifer Kermode, 25–42. Stroud: Sutton, 1991.

____, "Religion", in *Fifteenth-Century Attitudes: Perceptions of Society in Late Medieval England*, ed. Rosemary Horrox, 183–201. Cambridge: CUP, 1994.

____, *The Paston Family in the 15th Century: Fastolf's Will.* Cambridge: CUP, 1996.

____, *The Paston Family in the 15th Century: Endings.* Cambridge: CUP, 2000.

____, "The Pastons and London", in *Courts and Regions in Medieval Europe*, ed. Alastair J. Minnis, Richard Marks and Sarah Rees Jones, 211–26. Woodbridge: York Medieval Press, 2000.

____, "Sir John Fastolf and the Land Market: An Enquiry of the Early 1430s Regarding Purchasable Property", in *East Anglia's History: Studies in Honour of Norman Scarfe*, ed. Christopher Harper-Bill, Carole Rawcliffe and Richard G. Wilson, 107–21. Woodbridge: Boydell, 2002.

____, "Once Again: Fastolf's Will", in *Essays in Later Medieval and Early Tudor England in Honour of Ralph A. Griffiths*, ed. Keith Dockray and Peter Fleming, 115–130. Stroud: Nonsuch, 2005.

____, "Sir John Fastolf, The Duke of Suffolk and the Pastons" in *Rule, Redemption and Representations in Late Medieval England*, ed. Linda Clark, 73–103. Woodbridge: Boydell, 2008.

Rider, C., "Lay Religion and Pastoral Care in Thirteenth Century England: The Evidence of a Group of Short Confession Manuals", *Journal of Medieval History* 36 (2010) 327–40.

Rigby, S.H., "Urban 'Oligarchy' in Late Medieval England", in *Towns and Townspeople in the Fifteenth Century*, ed. J.A.F. Thomson, 62–86. Gloucester: Sutton, 1988.

____, *English Society in the Later Middle Ages: Class, Status and Gender.* Basingstoke: Macmillan, 1995.

____, "Introduction: Social Structure and Economic Change in Late Medieval England", in *A Social History of England, 1200–1500*, ed. Rosemary Horrox and W. Mark Ormrod, 1–30. Cambridge: CUP, 2006.

Rigby, S.H., and E. Ewan, "Government, Power and Authority 1300–1540", in *The Cambridge Urban History of Britain: Volume 1: 600– 1540*, ed. D.M. Palliser, 291–312. Cambridge: CUP, 2000.

Robertson, D.W., "The Cultural Tradition of *Handlyng Synne*", *Speculum* 22 (1947) 162–85.

____, "Certain Theological Conventions in Mannyng's Treatment of the Commandments", in *Essays in Medieval Culture*, ed. D.W. Robertson, 105–113. Princeton: Princeton University Press, 1980.

Roest, B., *Franciscan Literature of Religious Instruction before the Council of Trent.* Leiden: Brill, 2004.

Roney, L., "Winner and Waster's 'Wyse Wordes': Teaching Economics and Nationalism in Fourteenth-Century England", *Speculum* 69 (1994) 1070–1100.

Rose, J., "Litigation and Political Conflict in Fifteenth-Century East Anglia; Conspiracy and Attaint Actions and Sir John Fastolf", *Journal of Legal History* 27 (2006) 53–80.

Rosenthal, J.T., "The Assizes of Weights and Measures in Medieval England", *Western Political Quarterly* 17 (1964) 409–22.

____, *The Purchase of Paradise: Gift-Giving and the Aristocracy 1307–1495.* London: Routledge & Kegan Paul, 1972.

Ross, A.S.C., "The Assize of Bread', *Economic History Review,* 2nd series 9, (1956) 332–42.

Ross, G.M., "Seneca's Philosophical Influence", in *Seneca,* ed. C.D.N. Costa, 116–65. London: Routledge & Kegan Paul, 1974.

Royster, J.F., "A Middle English Treatise on the Ten Commandments: Part 1: Text and Notes", *Studies in Philology* 6 (1910) 1–39.

Rubin, M., *Charity and Community in Medieval Cambridge.* Cambridge: CUP, 1987.

Russell, G.H., "Vernacular Instruction of the Laity in the Later Middle Ages in England: Some Texts and Notes", *Journal of Religious History* 2 (1962) 98–119.

Ryan, J.K., and B.M. Bonansea (eds), *John Duns Scotus 1265–1965.* Washington, DC: Catholic University of America, 1965.

Sacks, D.H., "The Greed of Judas: Avarice, Monopoly and the Moral Economy in England *c.* 1350–*c.* 1600", *Journal of Medieval and Early Modern Studies* 28 (1998) 263–307.

Salzman, L.F., *English Trade in the Middle Ages.* London: H. Pordes, 1964.

____, *English Industries of the Middle Ages.* London: H. Pordes, 1970.

Saul, N., "The Commons and the Abolition of Badges", *Parliamentary History* 9 (1990) 302–15.

____, *Richard II.* New Haven: Yale University Press, 1997.

Scase, W., "Reginald Pecock, John Carpenter and John Colop's "Common Profit" Books: Aspects of Book Ownership and Circulation in Fifteenth-Century London", *Medium Aevum* 61 (1992) 261–74.

____, "Satire On the Retinues of the Great (Ms Harley 2253): Unpaid Bills and the Politics of Purveyance", in *Studies in Late Medieval and Early Renaissance Texts in Honour of John Scattergood,* ed. Anne Marie D'Arcy, Alan J. Fletcher and V.J. Scattergood, 305–20. Dublin: Four Courts Press, 2005.

____, *Literature and Complaint in England, 1272–1553.* Oxford: OUP, 2007.

Schaaf, B.M.V.D., "The Manuscript Tradition of 'Handlyng Synne' ", *Manuscripta* 24 (1980) 119–26.

Schmidt, A.V.C., "Chaucer and the Golden Age", *Essays in Criticism* 26 (1976) 99–115.

Schofield, P.R., "Lordship and the Peasant Economy *c.* 1250–*c.* 1400: Robert Kyng and the Abbot of Bury St Edmunds", *Past & Present Supplement* 2 (2007) 53–68.

____, "The Social Economy of the Medieval Village in the Early Fourteenth Century", *Economic History Review* 61 (2008) 38–63.

Scott, A.M., '*Piers Plowman' and the Poor.* Dublin: Four Courts Press, 2004.

____, "'For Lewed Men Y Vndyr Toke on Englyssh Tonge to Make This Boke': *Handlyng Synne* and English Didactic Writing for the Laity", in *What Nature Does Not Teach: Didactic Literature in the Medieval and Early-Modern Periods.* ed. Juanita Feros Ruys, 377–400. Turnhout: Brepols, 2008.

Seabourne, G., "Controlling Commercial Morality in Late Medieval London: The Usury Trials of 1421", *Journal of Legal History* 19 (1998) 116–42.

____, "Law, Morals and Money: Royal Regulation of the Substance of Subjects' Sales and Loans in England, 1272–1399", in *Expectations of the Law in the Middle Ages*, ed. Anthony Musson, 117–34. Woodbridge: Boydell, 2001.

____, *Royal Regulation of Loans and Sales in Medieval England.* Woodbridge: Boydell, 2003.

____, "Assize Matters: Regulation of the Price of Bread in Medieval London", *Journal of Legal History* 27 (2006) 29–52.

Shaw, J., "The Influence of Canonical and Episcopal Reform on Popular Books of Instruction", in *The Popular Literature of Medieval England*, ed. Thomas J. Heffernan, 44–60. Knoxville: University of Tennessee Press, 1985.

Shepherd, G., "Poverty in *Piers Plowman*", in *Social Relations and Ideas: Essays in Honour of R.H. Hilton*, ed. T.H. Ashton, et al., 169–89. Cambridge: CUP, 1983.

Shinners, J., and W.J. Dohar, *Pastors and the Care of Souls in Medieval England.* Notre Dame, IN: University of Notre Dame Press, 1998.

Shogimen, T., *Ockham and Political Discourse in the Late Middle Ages.* Cambridge: CUP, 2007.

Smith, A., "Litigation and Politics: Sir John Fastolf's Defence of His English Property", in *Property and Politics: Essays in Later Medieval English History*, ed. Tony Pollard, 59–75. Gloucester: Sutton, 1984.

____, "'The Greatest Man of That Age': The Acquisition of Sir John Fastolf's East Anglian Estates", in *Rulers and Ruled in Late Medieval England: Essays Presented to Gerald Harriss*, ed. Rowena E. Archer and Simon Walker, 137–53. London: Hambledon, 1995.

____, "'My confessors exorted me gretely therto …': Sir John Fastolf's Dispute with Hickling Priory", in *St George's Chapel, Windsor in the Late Middle Ages*, ed. Colin Richmond and Eileen Scarff, 57–70. Leeds: Maney Publishing, 2001.

Somerset, F., *Clerical Discourse and Lay Audience in Late Medieval England.* Cambridge: CUP, 1998.

Spencer, H.L., *English Preaching in the Late Middle Ages.* Oxford: Clarendon Press, 1993.

____, "Sermon Literature", in *A Companion to Middle English Prose,* ed. A.S.G. Edwards, 151–74. Cambridge: D.S. Brewer, 2004.

Stark, W., *The Contained Economy: An Interpretation of Medieval Economic Thought.* London: Blackfriars Publications, 1956.

Steel, A., "English Government Finance, 1377–1413", *English Historical Review* 51 (1936) 29–51.

Stockton, E.W., *The Major Latin Works of John Gower: The Voice of One Crying and the Tripartite Chronicle.* Seattle: University of Washington Press, 1962.

Storey, R. L., *The Reign of Henry VII.* London: Blandford, 1968.

Suk, O., "The Connection of the Virtues According to William of Ockham", *Franciscan Studies* 10 (Supplement) (1950) 9–32; 91–113.

Swanson, J., *John of Wales: A Study of the Works and Ideas of a Thirteenth-Century Friar.* Cambridge: CUP, 1989.

Takamiya, T., "'On the Evils of Covetousness': An Unrecorded Middle English Poem", in *New Science out of Old Books: Studies in Manuscripts and Early Printed Books in Honour of A.J. Doyle,* ed. Richard Beadle and A.J. Piper, 189–206. Aldershot: Ashgate, 1995.

Taylor, A., 'Translation, Censorship, Authorship and the Lost Work of Reginald Pecock', in *The Politics of Translation in the Middle Ages and Renaissance,* ed. Renate Blumenfled-Kosinski, Luise Von Flotow and Daniel Russell, 143–60. Ottawa: University of Ottawa Press, 2001.

Tentler, T. N., "The Summa for Confessors as an Instrument of Social Control", in *The Pursuit of Holiness in Late Medieval and Renaissance Religion: Papers from the University of Michigan Conference,* ed. Charles Trinkhaus and Heiko A. Oberman, 103–26. Leiden: Brill, 1974.

____, *Sin and Confession on the Eve of the Reformation.* Princeton: Princeton University Press, 1977.

Thomson, J.A.F., "Piety and Charity in Late Medieval London", *Journal of Ecclesiastical History* 16 (1965) 178–95.

____, "Wealth, Poverty and Mercantile Ethics in Late Medieval London", in *La Ville, la Bourgeoisie et la Genese de L'etat Moderne (XIIe–XVIIIe siecles)* ed. Neil Bulst and Jean-Philippe Genet, 265–78. Paris: CNRS, 1988.

Thrupp, S.L., *The Merchant Class of Medieval London (1300–1500).* Chicago: University of Chicago Press, 1948.

____, "The Grocers of London, a Study of Distributive Trade", in *Studies in English Trade in the Fifteenth Century*, ed. Eileen Power and M.M. Postan. London: Routledge, 1933 repr. New York, Barnes & Noble, 1966.

Tierney, B., *Medieval Poor Law: a Sketch of Canonical Theory and its Application in England.* Berkeley: University of California Press, 1959.

Tout, T.F., *The Place of Edward II in English History*, 2nd edn. Manchester: Manchester University Press, 1936.

Trigg, S., "The Rhetoric of Excess in Wynnere and Wastoure", *Yearbook of Langland Studies* (1989) 91–108.

Turner, H.L., "Reputational Damage: William Wilmington and the Supposed Enclosure of Barcheston", *Midland History* 37 (2012) 222–29.

Turville-Petre, T., "The Prologue of Wynnere and Wastoure", *Leeds Studies in English* 18 (1987) 19–29.

Vale, M.G.A., *Piety, Charity and Literacy among the Yorkshire Gentry, 1370–1480.* York: University of York, 1976 (Borthwick Papers No. 50).

Viner, J., "Religious Thought, Economy and Society", *History of Political Economy* 10 (1978) 1–192.

Vitullo, J. and D. Wolfthal (eds), *Money, Morality and Culture in Late Medieval and Early Modern Europe.* Farnham: Ashgate, 2010.

Walker, S., "Profit and Loss in the Hundred Years' War: The Subcontracts of Sir John Strother", *Historical Research* 58 (1985) 100–06.

____, "Order and Law", in *A Social History of England, 1200–1500,* ed. Rosemary Horrox and W. Mark Ormrod, 91–112. Cambridge: CUP, 2006.

Walls, K., *John Bromyard on Church and State: The Summa Predicantium and Early Fourteenth-Century England: a Dominican's Books and Guide for Preachers.* Market Weighton: Clayton-Thorpe Publications, 2007.

Walsh, A., "The Morality of the Market and Medieval Schoolmen", *Politics, Philosophy and Economics* 3 (2004) 241–59.

Walsh, A. and T. Lynch, *The Morality of Money: An Exploration in Analytic Philosophy.* Basingstoke: Palgrave Macmillan, 2008.

Watkins, A., "Peasants in Arden", in *Daily Life in the Late Middle Ages,* ed. Richard Britnell, 83–102. Stroud: Sutton, 1998.

Weaver, C., "From Private Pursuit to Public Playground: The Enclosure of Malvern Chase", *Transactions of the Worcestershire Archaeological Society*, Series 3, no. 16 (1998) 207–19.

Wenzel, S., "Notes on the 'Parson's Tale'", *Chaucer Review* 16 (1982) 237–56.

____, "A Sermon in Praise of Philosophy", *Traditio* 50 (1995) 249–59.

____, *Latin Sermon Collections from Later Medieval England: Orthodox Preaching in the Age of Wyclif.* Cambridge: CUP, 2005.

____, "Bromyard's Other Handbook: Canon and Civil Law for Preachers", in *Studies in Medieval and Renaissance History,* ed. Roger Dahood and Peter Medine, 93–123. New York: AMS Press, 2009.

Wilson, E., *A Descriptive Index of the English Lyrics in John of Grimestone's Preaching Book.* Oxford: Blackwell, 1973.

Wood, D., "'Lesyng of Tyme': Perceptions of Idleness and Usury in Late Medieval England" in *The Use and Abuse of Time in Christian History,* ed. R.N. Swanson, 107–16. Woodbridge: Boydell for the Ecclesiastical History Society, 2002.

_____, *Medieval Economic Thought.* Cambridge: CUP, 2002.

Wood, R., *Ockham on the Virtues.* West Lafayette: Purdue University Press, 1997.

Wren, D.A., "Medieval or Modern? A Scholastic's View of Business Ethics, Circa 1430", *Journal of Business Ethics* 28 (2000) 109–19.

Yunck, J.A., *The Lineage of Lady Meed: The Development of Medieval Venality Satire.* Notre Dame, IN: University of Notre Dame Press, 1963.

Online Sources

Calendar of Close Rolls, Edward I–Henry VII: www.british-history.ac.uk

Calendar of Patent Rolls, Henry III – Henry VI: www.uiowa.edu

Court of Common Pleas: The National Archives CP40 1399–1500: www.british-history.ac.uk

The Parliament Rolls of Medieval England, 1275–1504, ed. C. Given-Wilson: www.british-history.ac.uk

Petrus Cantor, *Verbum abbreviatum,* ed. J.P. Migne, *Patrologia Latina,* vol. 205: http://.www.documentacatholicaomnia.com

Index

J. Hole, *Economic Ethics in Late Medieval England, 1300–1500*,
Archival Insights into the Evolution of Economics,
DOI 10.1007/978-3-319-38860-1

W

Y

The manufacturer's authorised representative in the EU is Springer Nature Customer Service Centre GmbH, Europaplatz 3, 69115 Heidelberg, Germany. If you have any concerns regarding our products, please contact ProductSafety@springernature.com

Printed and bound by CPI Group (UK) Ltd, Croydon, CR0 4YY

30/09/2026

02225649-0011